THE STORY OF *600* CONFEDERATE OFFICERS
AND THE
UNITED STATES PRISONER OF WAR POLICY

by Mauriel P. Joslyn

 White Mane Publishing Company, Inc.

This White Mane Publishing Co., Inc. publication was printed by:
 Beidel Printing House, Inc.
 63 West Burd Street
 Shippensburg, PA 17257 USA

In respect for the scholarship contained herein, the acid-free paper used in this book meets the guidelines for permanence and durability of the Committee on Production Guidelines for Book Longevity of the Council on Library Resources.

For a complete list of available publications please write:
 White Mane Publishing Co., Inc.
 P.O. Box 152
 Shippensburg, PA 17257-0152

Library of Congress Cataloging-in-Publication Data

Joslyn, Mauriel, 1955-
  Immortal captives : the story of 600 Confederate officers and the United States prisoner of war policy / by Mauriel P. Joslyn.
    p.   cm.
  Includes bibliographical references and index.
  ISBN 0-942597-96-6 (alk. paper)
  1. United States--History--Civil War, 1861-1865--Prisoners and prisons. 2. Prisoners of war--United States--History--19th century. 3. Confederate States of America. Army--Officers--Registers. I. Title.
E615.J684 1996
973.7'72--dc20   95-45256
                                                               CIP

This Book is Dedicated to
the Officers of The Immortal Six Hundred

May their story remain an inspiration
to future generations and
their sacrifices never
be forgotten

CONTENTS

LIST OF ILLUSTRATIONS

PREFACE

Roget describes "immortal" as "lasting and undying fame; a secure place in history." Certainly the story of the 600 men told here fits those definitions.

It is never too late to recount actions of individual heroism and courage. As we read history, we remember unusual things on a large scale which changed the world. Battles and wars are pointed out, and time is measured by their dates. Yet we frequently overlook highly dramatic and compelling events, which took place on a smaller stage with few players. It is these human dramas of courage which affect us as individuals, because they are personal.

I had always carefully avoided prisoner of war stories. Libby, Elmira, Fort Delaware, Johnson's Island—they were all familiar names synonymous with suffering, abuse, misery and sadness. These places represented the last earthly days where a loved one died in agony, never to return home, never given a proper burial. I would occasionally read some soldier's experience in a diary or memoir. As a Southerner, I grew up with history's condemnation for Andersonville, the many misconceptions and reminders flaunted concerning that prison. *All* prisons during the Civil War were horrible, and blame should be placed equally where earned.

The horrors of those prisons cannot be denied. They can be explained, and forgiven, to a certain extent, by the fact that under the conditions of the nineteenth century, it was tremendously difficult to care for thousands and thousands of men confined in small areas, given the sanitary and medical resources known at that time. It would be difficult today. But what makes the Civil War prison conditions unforgivable, is when the conditions were allowed and even caused on purpose. That is what this story is about—The United States Policy of Retaliation. It is a dark side of American history, one rarely acknowledged, let alone included in history books. It comprises a shameful chapter in this country's past, which we condemn other nations for under the cause of human rights. Today, the Laws of the Geneva Convention and organizations such as Amnesty International exist to prevent such an act. But it happened in the United States, ironically, the very year that the

Geneva Convention met for the first time. We must not ignore those less appealing acts of our government, but keep them in the light, so that hypocrisy cannot thrive—and that it may not happen again.

This book is not intended to be a study of Civil War prisons. Nor does it profess to be a detailed explanation of the political acts of desperation by Northern authorities to fight an unpopular war. I leave those topics for a book in themselves. A certain amount does have to be understood, however, to appreciate what happened as a consequence. Therefore it is explained briefly. The prisoner exchange system was straightforward diplomacy which the exchange agents of both sides efficiently and conscientiously carried out. It was not their fault that it failed. The failure of that system was a purposeful, politically motivated war measure on the part of Northern Secretary of War Edwin M. Stanton, Major General Henry W. Halleck, and later, Lieutenant General Ulysses S. Grant. Fabricated stories of intentional abuse of Union prisoners of war by Confederate authorities were the fuel to stoke the fires of half-hearted citizens, and entice them to support a war they were beginning to see as unnecessary. The basic subject of this book is the day-to-day hopes, dreams, fears, and endurance of 600 ordinary soldiers who became scapegoats, and exhibited rare qualities under pressure which the human spirit is only occasionally called on to display.

My decision to write this book came about slowly, and was actually the result of my "acquaintance" with a few of its subjects. On reading a collection of personal accounts on various topics of the Civil War, I came across the pictures of four Confederate officers, exceedingly handsome men in their prime. Their faces reflected genteel pride, not defiant hatred. I was sickened to learn of their fate. One died of government-sanctioned cruelty. Another, severely wounded, was subjected to conditions which broke down the healthiest men. Of the last two, one was in prison over two years, enduring every conceivable horror as a prisoner of war. They were part of a unique and fascinating group whom the misfortunes of war brought together as the **Immortal Six Hundred**. It is a story which the best writers of fiction could scarcely dream up, and it is a story worthy of telling.

The men and boys who left home in 1861 to join the Confederate army mostly fall into one of three categories: young men 20-22 years of age, single, asserting their independence and stepping into the world for the first time; boys on the verge of manhood, living with parents; and young husbands and fathers with new families, leaving wives with little ones. The Six Hundred reflect those categories, with the addition of a sprinkling of men whose careers and families were firmly established. Yet they left even that behind. Only because they felt they had to protect their loved ones from an invading force would they leave so much, at the risk of losing their lives. This is why they fought. This is what they recorded in their diaries and letters from battlefield and prison camp.

In order to make the diaries easier to understand I have made a few typographical corrections. Not many were necessary, as the writers used good spelling and grammar. Only Captain Junius Hempstead wrote without punctuation, so that has been added. Most corrections have not been to the original material, but to the transcripts found in collections, such as misspelled names due to handwriting interpretations. I have corrected the spelling of names mentioned so they can be easily found in the service records. Any deletion of words in a direct quote is signified by ... and any insertion of a word for correction or clarification is enclosed in brackets. Nothing has been deleted which in any way changes the original meaning.

One of the greatest thrills of my searches was finding the original list made by Captain John L. Cantwell. I also compared his with other prisoners' lists to come up with an accurate total. By using the Union prison lists, I was able to reconstruct—for the first time—an accurately spelled list of the original Six Hundred. I found the Fort Delaware list originally used on August 12, 1864, the first day the prisoners knew of their selection, and was able to pinpoint the men who exchanged places that day by using comparisons to the diaries and Cantwell's list. I discovered an incredible consistency in the diaries, over twenty were used, and I believe everything recorded to be highly accurate. Recognizing the fact that memory is flawed, rather than depend on memoirs and post-war accounts, I chose to use as many diaries as I could find. Writing in the damp dungeons of prison, a man was most likely to record exactly how he felt at the time, and accurately describe events as he perceived them. However, the diary entries for the months of January and February 1865 are not as frequent nor as long. Presumably the condition of their health at that time is the cause. Though the officers wrote many letters from prison, most were never allowed by prison officials to go through, but were instead destroyed. So letters are rare. I was fortunate to find a few.

I only used post-war accounts if they were confirmed by war-time diaries or letters. I find most post-war accounts date from the 1890s, the usual length of time following events to be thirty years. This trend seems to apply to veterans of all wars. As they reach middle age, they tend to reminisce, and look back on their experiences.

The Union sources are sketchy, as I found no diaries or papers pertaining to the treatment of the prisoners. Major General John G. Foster died in 1871, and although I found a collection of his letters, the correspondence for the year 1864 was missing. Colonel Philip P. Brown died in 1881, and I was unable to locate any post-war accounts by either of them.

I have tried to avoid bias in this book, by using both Union and Confederate personal accounts. If it reads otherwise, it is no one's fault. It is a true story, told by the participants, in their own words about their own experience. It is a story of men who never succumbed to the inhumanity around them; who came home broken in body, but not in spirit, returning to a devastated land where most had lost everything. They renewed their lives with no financial aid or pensions from a victorious government. In some cases their antebellum careers as lawyers or public servants were denied them under a military occupation.

I came to "know" these Six Hundred, some better than others, because some left more recorded history. I followed them from boyhood to old age, attempting to find out as much about their lives as possible. Reading their diaries, I sometimes laughed and often cried, and was constantly amazed at their faith and acceptance, and the ability to keep their humanity in the face of inhumanity.

Although it was a tedious project, due to the amount of original research, I am thankful for all the wonderful people I have met because of it. Not only the soldiers themselves, but all those who helped make this book possible.

I hope this story will encourage others to read about the Civil War prisoners of war, a largely neglected subject in the field. It has also been a misinterpreted and distorted one, probably because of the emotions it raises. The rewards are there to be reaped. Those men served their country in a less glamorous but far more painful way than their comrades who remained free on the battlefield. It is important that we do not ignore their contributions to this aspect of our history.

So often the words "courage," "valor" and "heroic" are applied in describing Civil War deeds that their meaning becomes lost and diminished through repetition. This is unfortunate, because they are still fitting adjectives to choose to describe the steadfast endurance those men exhibited as prisoners of war. But there is a term among those who breed Thoroughbred horses that signifies having in the blood a determination to finish a race at all costs, even enduring physical pain and shattered legs. It is "heart". The Six Hundred had "heart." Their story has many positive attributes about which we need to be reminded in the late twentieth century. That is: unselfishness, faith, loyalty, principled behavior, and compassion for our fellow man. This was their contribution to the legacy that was the Confederate soldier.

ACKNOWLEDGMENTS

I am deeply and immeasurably indebted to many people for the cooperation and time spent in making this book possible. The fact that there has been nothing written on the Immortal Six Hundred since their own accounts has made the research difficult on many individual lives. Through various university manuscript collections, other researchers' findings, and the archives of the Fort Delaware Society and Fort Pulaski National Monument, I have solved mysteries and pieced together a puzzle to recreate the detailed experience of the Immortal Six Hundred. I am also indebted to the descendants of those men, who have been so supportive in recording an event of which their family history was so much a part.

Librarians and archivists across the South have made the experience of research on a limited time schedule a possibility, and the U.S. Mail has played its part in this project also.

Some have gone beyond the call of duty. They start with my County librarians, Karen Meeks, Annie Lundy and the excellent inter-library loan department of the Uncle Remus Regional Library System, particularly Tamela Thomas and Gloria Ward.

Tally Kirkland, the park historian at Fort Pulaski, was the first official I contacted for this project, and the patience of the staff there gave me a positive start. Fort Delaware State Park and the Fort Delaware Society staff were a tremendous help, and I salute the dedication of these volunteers for their work at preserving the place where this story started.

The National Archives and Library of Congress staff members were always pleasant and patient, a fact that left me dumbfounded when I saw the harried state they were in most of the time. In particular, I want to thank Mr. Michael Meier, and Mr. Michael Musick, both of the Military History Branch, for their patience and the time they took on scavenger hunts for obscure records.

All the staff at the State Archives of Georgia, Alabama, Virginia, Louisiana, South Carolina, Mississippi, and North Carolina were efficient and knowledgeable. Mr. Weymouth T. Jordan at the Department of Historical Publications at the North Carolina Archives and History was especially helpful on the one hundred and eleven North Carolinians included in this study.

The universities with collections containing a gold mine of information include the University of North Carolina, the Southern Historical Collection, and I thank Mr. Richard Shrader for his time there. The University of South Carolina, the University of Georgia, Louisiana State University, Tulane and Auburn were all patient with a stranger on campus. Virginia Military Institute, my husband's alma mater, has wonderful personal files on each of its sons who were members of the Six Hundred, and Colonel Keith Gibson earned a special thank you as a friend and museum director who was interested in this project. Randall Gooden and the library staff at West Virginia University were kind and patient with much that had to be done over the phone, and I thank them for their help. Randy Roberts at the University of Missouri at Columbia was extremely helpful and gracious with requests.

Museums which yielded up artifacts, and pieces of the puzzle, include the Port Hudson State Commemorative Area, Confederate Memorial Hall in New Orleans, and the Museum of the Confederacy in Richmond. Mr. Robert Krick's wealth of information at Fredericksburg National Military Park in Fredericksburg, Virginia provided many details. Every small library and historical society from each county one of the Six Hundred called home contributed their time and resources in searching for clues.

I cannot forget my friends who kept up the enthusiasm and gave their time to the research efforts. Those who deserve a special mention include Cari Schwarz and Johnny Gosselin for researching service records and archives on their own time, as well as the financial investment in xerox copies they made. I thank Sheila Kahn for providing a taxi and bed-and-breakfast for me during a week's stay in Richmond. Gary Ford of the *Southern Living Magazine* staff, who offered to edit the manuscript, and was particularly encouraging receives a special thank you.

For packing lunches and car snacks for a hungry husband and two small children, on the Louisiana excursions, my mother also receives a special mention.

Probably the most taken for granted, last of all I want to thank my husband, Rick. Without his assistance and criticism, which a stubborn wife did not always agree with, the book may never have been completed. He rivaled Captain John Cantwell in his meticulous preparation of the list of the Six Hundred, and the checking and rechecking of spelling, regimental numbers, and statistics. Without his computer skills, I would still be shuffling papers.

There are many others, only some of whom are listed below, who helped provide a simple date or name which made a life that much more complete. I hope the publication of this book will uncover more information, so that the personal statistics on each officer may paint a more complete picture of his experience and how he was affected.

Virginia Historical Society, Richmond, Va.

The Museum of The Confederacy, Richmond, Va.

Save Our Cemeteries, New Orleans, La.

The Historic New Orleans Collection

Mr. Mark Lemon, Richlands, N.C.

Mr. John Segrest, Tuskegee, Ala.

Mr. T. C. Greever, Alexandria, Va.

Mr. Mike James, Rumford, R.I. (a displaced Tennessean)

South Carolina Historical Society, Charleston, S.C.

Fort Sumter National Monument, Charleston, S.C. Mr. Rick Hatcher and the staff

Mr. Willis Keith, Fort Johnson; Charleston, S.C.

Mr. Bill Haynes, McKinney, Tx.

Mr. Roger Hanson, Pascagoula, Miss.

Mr. Richard Smith, Byron, Ga.

Mr. Bob Betterton, Sons of Confederate Veterans HQ., Columbia, Tenn.

Mr. Randy Roberts, University of Missouri-Columbia, Columbia, Mo.

The Cortland County Historical Society, Cortland, N.Y.

Colgate University, Madison, N.Y.

Mrs. Frances Fox, Thomas and Carol Pinckney, Mrs. Dolores Smith, Mrs. Guida Jackson-Laufer, and countless others.

CHAPTER ONE

"Where Every Man in Uniform Carried His Leave in His Pocket and His Heart on His Sleeve"

CHARLESTON, the City by the Sea. In the summer of 1864 it was a city under siege, a victim of slow strangulation. Its inhabitants were almost nonchalant about the continuous Federal bombardment, and made a brave show of their carefree social life almost to the bitter end.

When Fort Sumter fell in April 1861, the Confederates inherited with it Castle Pinckney, Fort Johnson and Fort Moultrie—the only defenses in Charleston Harbor. These had been neglected until a few months prior to the crisis, when Major Robert Anderson had begun to strengthen them in the face of mounting hostilities. Castle Pinckney was too small and close to Charleston to be of any use in harbor defenses.

Fort Sumter was incomplete, with few guns mounted. Upon evacuating Sumter, the Federals had spiked what guns were there and burned the carriages. The first commander, Brig. General Pierre Gustave Toutant Beauregard, instigated a system of defense early in the spring of 1861, before he was sent to the warfront in Virginia. For miles up and down the coastal islands, from Hilton Head to Winyah Bay, small defenses were erected, named in honor of Confederate officers killed in action. With the channel over two and one half miles wide, all the guns of smoothbore, and little to no assistance possible from anything the Confederate navy had afloat, the best defense Charleston had was Southern pluck and ingenuity. Fortunately, this proved sufficient for the short time necessary.[1]

Upon returning as commander to the Department of South Carolina, Georgia and Florida in 1862, General Beauregard began to acquire rifled siege guns, both Blakleys and Whitworth rifles. The timing could not have been more critical.

In April 1863, Union Rear Admiral Samuel Francis Du Pont attacked Fort Sumter with his fleet of ironclads, and was repulsed after a hot action of

1

over two hours' duration. In addition to Fort Sumter, the forts engaged were Moultrie and Battery Bee on Sullivan's Island, and Batteries Gregg and Wagner on Morris Island. That action ended Northern hopes for a quick victory, and both sides settled into a stalemate. Du Pont was replaced on July 6, 1863.

The next commander of the Federal forces, Major General Quincy A. Gillmore, grew more and more frustrated with the stubborn resistance of Beauregard's troops. In an effort to force the Confederates to capitulate on Morris Island and at Fort Sumter, on August 21, 1863 he issued an ultimatum. In effect, he demanded "the immediate evacuation of Morris Island and Fort Sumter." Should Beauregard refuse to comply, Gillmore would "open fire on the city of Charleston from batteries already established within easy and effective [range] of the heart of the city." Four hours were given to comply, or else the bombardment would begin. The time elapsed, Beauregard refused, and the bombardment continued.[2]

With the Federal gunboats repulsed, Confederate attention was once more turned toward the mainland, and the works at the south end of Morris Island were neglected. It was due to that open back door, that Federal troops occupied the abandoned Confederate defenses on the Stono River and gained a foothold on Morris Island, five miles across the harbor from Charleston. Simultaneously, the Confederates worked to strengthen the batteries commanding the harbor.[3] Fort Sumter also claimed attention. Under the command of Captain John C. Mitchel, its works were capably fortified against the long range rifle batteries of the Federal forces. Though pounded almost into rubble by Union guns, the work was continually repaired—nightly, and often under fire. The casemates were filled with sand and cotton, and the armament removed to the inner harbor forts.[4]

The decision to evacuate Battery Wagner at the harbor end of Morris Island came in September 1863, after it had repulsed an attack the previous July, led by the 54th Massachusetts Colored Infantry. The Charleston defenses were contracted due to a lack of troops to defend the outer works on Morris and James Islands, forming a tight ring around the city and the harbor.

On September 9, 1863, under cover of night, Confederate forces withdrew from Battery Wagner, and the fort was occupied by the Federals a short time later, principally the 54th Massachusetts Infantry and the 3rd Rhode Island Heavy Artillery. New Yorkers and Pennsylvanians made up a large number of the troops who hammered away unsuccessfully at Forts Sumter and Moultrie. The Union forces also occupied Battery Gregg on the northern tip of Morris Island, and directed from there most of the artillery fire aimed at Fort Sumter.

That tenuous toehold on the island enabled attack by a big gun known as the Swamp Angel. The long range gun began its bombardment in August 1863, and lobbed 150-pound shells a range of 8,000 yards into Charleston, an incredible distance at that time. But even that did not cause the inhabitants to lose heart or courage. On its thirty-sixth round, the barrel burst, putting the gun out of commission for the rest of the war. It was then replaced by another 200-pounder.[5]

One of the civilians staying in the safe area of Charleston was Emma Holmes, who recorded her observations in her diary, after a walk through the frequently fired-on area.

Dear old Charleston still receives daily her allotted portion of battering, and "The Gillmore District" is showing ghastly rents in many a once fair and goodly mansion. Portions of two shells have entered uncle James' without, however, doing much damage. I came down yesterday and went directly to shop; while in Mrs. Maule's above George St., a fragment of a time fuse shell whizzed overhead with a loud report and fell into the next yard. The Yankees have only been firing this kind during the last fortnight, and the casualties are becoming serious. The shells will burst in the lower part of town, but the fragments fly over a mile up town, killing or injuring passerby and animals; they do not penetrate houses, but cause loss of life, and it is really dangerous walking out below John St. for the fragments fall in Vanderhorst St. and that portion of the city where I am going to stay and so many of our friends live. Last night one of them set a house on fire and as soon as our demon foes saw the blaze and knew our firemen were at work, the shells were fired thick and fast, sometimes two or three at one time. I shuddered to hear the dull distant boom of the discharge, then watch their flight through the air like meteors; when near, the scream, followed by the sudden deafening report, was terrible. It was kept up all night, and they made my dreams hideous.[6]

The New Year of 1864 saw Charleston as virtually the only accessible Southern port outside of Wilmington, North Carolina. Major General John G. Foster replaced Union General Quincy Adams Gillmore as commander of the Department of the South in May, and heavily reinforced the gunboats already in Charleston Harbor with others from the Federal fleet at Cape Fear, North Carolina. By being in possession of Fort Wagner, the Union forces could shell the city from land as well as sea.

Since the bombardment of 1863, Charlestonians had persevered. They simply moved out into the country, or across town out of the range of the Swamp Angel and batteries at Fort Wagner, which was still under fire from Fort Moultrie in Confederate hands. However, there was much indignation when ten Union shells penetrated St. Philips Church on Church Street, wrecking the chancel and destroying the organ.[7]

That summer of 1864, Major Edward Manigault of the 1st South Carolina Artillery was in charge of Fort Johnson, part of the thin line of defenders stretched around the mouth of the harbor. He surveyed the damage of the Union shells along the waterfront.

MAJ. EDWARD
MANIGAULT, 1ST
S.C. ARTY.

After getting through my more immediate business, I walked through the lower part of the City. From the "Bend" of King Street, fennel, weeds & grass growing in gutters. Broad Street has the pavement Clear for the breadth of a single Carriage way; all the rest grown up in Grass with Weeds & Fennel in the Gutters, some of the fennel more than 6 feet high. The Cows are actually grazing in the lower part of Meeting & Church Streets.[8]

The pounding began to take its toll. Three years into the war, the whole life and business of Charleston had retreated into a few squares above Calhoun Street and along the Ashley River. The area was safely out of the range of enemy shells and in this haven of refuge was located the prisons and hospitals, marked by yellow flags. The lower part of town resembled a ghost town, haunted by shattered houses, their broken windows staring out at the harbor. Grass and bushes grew in the neglected streets and the city became a shadow of its former self.

MAJ. EDWARD
MANIGAULT

Col. Ashe's House on South Bay (modern 32 South Battery Street) has been struck by two Shells (I only saw one however). I saw no marks of Shells on the neighboring houses. Mr. John Ravenal's (modern 5 E. Battery) Stable has been struck by a shell. The Roper house (9 E. Battery) has had the architectural projection of the porch blown away by a shell. Mr. William Ravenel's house (13 E. Battery) has been struck by one Shell. A small portion of the parapet of Mr. Charles Alston's house (21 E. Battery) has been demolished by a shell which also apparently penetrated Mr. Dan Heyward's Stable (25 E. Battery) in rear. The front Steps & Entrance of Mr. D. Heyward's house have been demolished by a Shell.

Along East Bay I noticed but little damage in addition to what I noticed in December or Jany. last (8 March 1864). The old (Colonial) post Office & Custom House (Old Exchange Building, East Bay at Broad) appears to have been struck by two shells.

In passing along Broad Street I noticed that just where I used to sit making out Estimates, Returns, Monthly do, Requisitions, &c in the then office of C&S (Charleston and Savannah R.R., 34 Broad St.) a shell had knocked away the wall. If I had been sitting there at the time I would have had no further trouble in this life. This was in 3rd Story over Edgerton & Richard's Store (merchant tailors, 32-34 Broad St.).

St. Philip's Church has been struck by three Shells, one of which has done Considerable damage. On way back passed the scene of fire at Force & Mitchell's. The fire subdued and Engines returning. Interior of Store Completely ruined.[9]

Charleston had almost ceased to exist as a blockade running port by 1864 and the few shops left open sold inferior goods at exorbitant prices.

Endless experiments searched for a way to loosen the Union grip. Torpedoes were made of the copper from roof gutters, river boats were converted to rams, and even the bells of St. Philips were melted down and molded into cannon, all to no avail. General William T. Sherman was inching toward Atlanta by July, but hopes were still high that he would be stopped, if the citizens could just hold out. Meanwhile, Charleston had become a trophy of importance to the North as the symbol of secession, while its defense had become a source of pride to the defenders.[10]

Major General Samuel Jones, a Virginian by birth and West Point graduate, succeeded Beauregard in command of the Department of South Carolina. His military career began on the Maine frontier from 1841 to 1843 and in Florida from 1845 to 1846, when he returned to West Point as an instructor of mathematics, and infantry and artillery tactics. Promoted to captain in 1853, in 1858 he was named assistant judge advocate for the army in Washington, D.C. When the war started, he resigned his commission in April 1861 and volunteered for service in the Confederate army. Beauregard's chief of artillery at First Manassas, Jones was promoted to brigadier general on July 21, 1861 and in January 1862 relieved Braxton Bragg at Pensacola, where he received his commission as major general in command of the Department of Alabama and West Florida, formed in March 1863. Jones refused to send reinforcements to Bragg in Kentucky because he believed the request unnecessary, and as a consequence was transferred to West Virginia, which he defended until March 1864. He was relieved of his command after losing the confidence of General Robert E. Lee and the Virginia government, and succeeded Beauregard as head of the Department of South Carolina, Georgia and Florida. At age forty-five he found himself in a beleaguered city, surrounded by a ring of fortifications and with few troops to man them. The estimated forces for all of Charleston only totaled 5,841 effective troops spread from the city across James' Island and Sullivan's Island.[11]

His counterpart, four miles away on Morris Island, Major General John G. Foster, had begun his career in the theater of war of which he was now in command. Born in Whitefield, New Hampshire in 1823, he entered West Point at age eighteen and graduated fourth in the class of 1846, probably having Jones as a math instructor. He also had participated in the Mexican War, following which he engaged in various engineer and coast-survey duties. In 1861, he had been on the inside of Fort Sumter with Major Robert Anderson, as an officer of engineers.[12] On May 26, 1864 he found himself on the outside trying to get in. He had a personal stake in his mission against Charleston. Foster had perfected these fortifications on the eve of the war, and had argued against Anderson's surrendering.

Succeeding Gillmore as the fourth commander in less than four years, the pressure was on Foster to take Charleston. He was confident, and four days after taking command, aimed a heavy bombardment on Fort Sumter. It was a complete failure. By the end of the day on June 5, it was apparent that more would be needed than simply land batteries and gunboats. Foster prepared an assault on Charleston, a five-pronged attack led by land troops. Preparations were carefully laid, calculations perfected, and by June 27 all was ready.[13]

Phase one of his plan was to send a force to cut the Charleston and Savannah Railroad at White Point on the North Edisto River. Simultaneously, Brigadier General Alexander Schimmelfenning would land a column on James' Island. Secondly, a thousand-man force, would be sent on barges from Morris Island, to assault Fort Johnson, and Battery Simkins on the northeast point of James' Island at daylight on July 3.

The third phase of the plan would land an invading force of 5,000 U.S. troops on John's Island, to march northeast and attack Confederate forces on the Upper Stono River. In addition a naval bombardment by monitors and wooden vessels against the Confederate forces at the Stono river batteries would support the Federal landing party from the river on the southwest end of James' Island. Simultaneous to all this activity was the concentrated shelling of Fort Sumter.

Foster's extensive and carefully laid plans were launched with unexpected results. On July 2, the Confederates counterattacked on James' Island, and the Union troops fell back to the Stono where their gunboats covered them successfully enough to prevent annihilation. The attack on Fort Johnson and Battery Simkins, too feebly supported, failed, and 140 prisoners, including the commander of the 52nd Pennsylvania Infantry, Colonel Henry M. Hoyt, fell into Confederate hands. After two days of skirmishing, Union forces on John's Island withdrew. By July 11 the operation was over, an astounding defeat. Union losses for these nine days were 330, to a Confederate loss of only 17 killed. During the whole of this operation, Fort Sumter was constantly bombarded as well, making it pretty hot for the 300 troops of the 1st South Carolina Artillery holding it. The flag was shot away four times on July 7, and a total of 784 rounds were expended on the fort over a two-day period. Huge 300-pounder rifled guns on Morris Island kept up the firing by daylight, while mortars did their duty at night, keeping a continual, twenty-four-hour bombardment. Each night the Southerners worked under fire to repair the damage done daily. U.S. Rear Admiral John A. Dahlgren, in command of the Union fleet under Foster's orders, recorded his opinion in his diary as "utterly disgusted."[14] Thus ended a three-week campaign.

Foster recoiled in shock at the failure to take Sumter, and Rear Admiral Dahlgren accompanied him on an observation of the fort on July 21. In his diary, Dahlgren recorded: "I went up in the *LeHigh* with General Foster to look at Sumter. He said he had not before had such a good view of it. The north-east front still stands erect, and the work is nearly impregnable."[15]

Foster refused to admit defeat, and literally became obsessed at taking the prize so long coveted by the Union. He was determined to crack Charleston, and Fort Sumter was the jewel in that crown of secession. Desperate measures were beginning to look logical, and a rather unorthodox scheme was devised.

Having become convinced that the enemy was strengthening themselves in Fort Sumter and making arrangements for defense, I have concluded that it is necessary to more effectually demolish the walls of that fort. For this purpose I have ordered the bombardment to be renewed tomorrow morning, and all the guns to be so aimed as to breach the wall in a horizontal line on that part of the wall which is now standing vertical. As soon as a good cut is made through the wall, I shall float down against it and explode large torpedoes, until the wall is shaken down and the surrounding obstructions are entirely blown away. I shall continue this until the walls are demolished as far as possible. I am convinced that the fort can, after such a bombardment, be assaulted and taken by boats, and that it can be held without any great loss of life. The only reasons in favor of taking it beyond its occupation by our troops are that it would afford a shelter or starting-point by which boat-expeditions can again attack Fort Johnson or Mount Pleasant. It now serves as a watchtower to the enemy.[16]

MAJ. GEN. JOHN G. FOSTER, U.S. COMMANDER

His plan showed imagination, but not rationality. The walls were merely crumbling debris, ranging from one foot to at the most only five feet high.[17] Foster was so obsessed with what he perceived as the objective, that he really did very little to change the balance of power in Charleston.

However, the violence of the bombardment in the first week of July had alarmed Captain John C. Mitchel. The young Irish commander of Fort Sumter was concerned, and, consequently, worked the garrison diligently to strengthen the bombproofs and gun emplacements. Foster's floating torpedo rafts were prepared to launch on July 21 but were delayed by a storm, and the exchange of fifty Union officers for fifty Confederates, prisoners of war, in Charleston Harbor off Fort Sumter. Finally on August 4, Foster's plan materialized. Guns requested from Dahlgren to strengthen the Morris Island batteries were placed, and a continual firing on Fort Sumter began. The torpedo rafts floated toward the fort and, spotted by the garrison, the alarm went out to be prepared. But it was soon apparent there would be no danger. The rafts exploded prematurely 300 yards from the fort walls. Foster tried unsuccessfully twice more to float the torpedo rafts toward the fort, on August 30 and September 1. The fort was untouched, and for all his elaborate plans, Foster was no nearer to a breakthrough than he had been in May. By the end of this sixty-day bombardment, ending September 8, an estimated 14,666 rounds of ammunition had been expended against Fort Sumter, averaging 392 shot and shell a day for the first week alone. The U.S. government apparently said enough, and Foster's illusions of grandeur as being the conqueror of Sumter were unrealized.[18]

Perhaps these events, combined with his compulsion to take the fort have a bearing on subsequent actions involving prisoners of war. He left little official correspondence, and as Dahlgren was attending to fleet business at Port Royal, history was deprived of his observations on Charleston for the rest of the summer.

CHAPTER TWO

"In No Circumstances Will He Be Allowed to Make Exchanges of Prisoners of War."[1]

FOR those unfortunates who were to become prisoners of war, the Dix-Hill cartel agreed upon in 1862 was a salvation. Though the carnage and bloodshed of battle seem far removed from any resemblance to order, there were certain laws of war which were honored to impend a civilizing influence and limit the brutality. These rules were rooted in the chivalric code adhered to in medieval France and England during the 1300s, reaching perfection during the Hundred Years' War, and indeed were the basis for the prisoner exchange system of the nineteenth century.[2]

Originally a captured knight gave his ransom, which stipulated he be held until someone representing his army paid a sum of money for his release, or until a substitute prisoner was furnished in his place. A form of this system evolved through the centuries, becoming by the nineteenth century what was termed "parole on honor" on which both Union and Confederate armies agreed. In that arrangement, soldiers were paroled when captured and sent to a neutral place, or sent home. The parole served as a waiting period which could be spent outside prison. When an official exchange was made, the paroled soldier was free. Obviously he, and the man he was exchanged for, returned to their own sides, and this was accepted. Under the cartel of 1862 an exchange system was worked out, officer for officer, private for private or a certain number of privates for commissioned officers depending on rank (see appendix). According to the laws of war, any prisoner captured in an armed contest between two belligerent armies must be protected, entitled to proper quarters, clothing, bedding and camp equipage. He was also due the same rations as that of his captors, and not required to labor on military works or menial jobs. If an escape attempt was made it was not considered a crime. On the contrary, it was accepted as a duty to try to escape and was not punishable.[3]

9

These were ordinary dictates of humanity, and western nations had prided themselves for centuries on their Christian restraint of barbarism under circumstances of war. Of course violations have been recorded, excused when unintentional, or condemned when sanctioned. In 1861 these rules were still the accepted norm. However they were complicated by one main factor—the United States government chose the policy of not recognizing the Confederacy as an independent belligerent.

President Abraham Lincoln's administration announced early in the war that the Southern states were "in rebellion," and therefore any prisoners taken were to be treated as traitors. An agreement to exchange them as prisoners of war signified recognition of the South's status as a nation.[4] Condoning secession also implied legitimate nationhood. Thus neither could be allowed. That attitude was to have far-reaching and unpleasant consequences for soldiers taken prisoner, as they became pawns in a game of politics.

The first incident to test the strength of the Federal position was the arrest of Confederate naval personnel June 3, 1861. Lincoln issued a proclamation stating they would be tried as pirates. However, the denouncement of that action by Great Britain, combined with the promise on the part of President Jefferson Davis to do likewise with captured Northern officers, forced the Union to back down, and the threat to hang the officers was dropped.[5]

Still Lincoln was determined at all costs to refrain from recognition of the South, and only supported special exchanges of those who had influential connections or status. But the public pressure would not tolerate such preferential treatment, which released only a few captives. Finally, Congress forced the president to yield in a resolution passed in December 1861 which declared negotiations for a prisoner of war exchange cartel be agreed upon.

Lincoln designated Brigadier General John E. Wool to represent the U.S. position at the negotiations, but stressed that the terms of any agreement should not result in any way favorable to the recognition of the Confederacy. Wool met with Confederate Major General Benjamin Huger, and on February 23, 1862, they decided on what was known as the Winder cartel of 1814 as a basis for a new document.[6]

However, Confederate defeats in the West burdened the North with more prisoners. Lincoln immediately reversed his already reluctant position on exchanges, and urged a return to special exchanges. The South remained adamant for a cartel. Negotiations broke off without any resolution, and a stalemate resulted.

Battlefield victories for the South during Jackson's Valley Campaign the spring of 1862 resulted in thousands of Federal prisoners of war taken, and authorities stressed that these prisoners would be treated exactly as Southerners were treated by the Union. Lincoln was once again forced to reconsider his official policy for prisoner exchange. This time he named Major General John Dix to represent his position, and negotiations were resumed, with Confederate Major General Daniel Harvey Hill.

At their meeting on July 22, 1862 the Dix-Hill exchange cartel was adopted, with a special provision pledging both sides to continue exchanges even if disputes over the exact terms occurred in the future. Their decision was a foreshadowing of things to come. After adopting the cartel, an unofficial acceptance of the South as a recognized belligerent was inescapable. However, the lack of a definite official position continually caused inconsistencies and contradictions in Union actions pertaining to exchange, depending on whether, under certain circumstances, the recognition of the Confederacy benefited Northern interests.[7]

As the war escalated, exchanges helped prevent overcrowding in both Northern and Southern prisons. Most prisoners were housed in old forts, or existing prisons which had previously held convicts. As more and more men were captured in larger numbers, makeshift prisons became necessary. Since exchange was expected, these temporary arrangements were only crowded for days or a few weeks. They were as simple as tent cities surrounded by wooden stockades with guards, or often converted warehouses in cities, or barracks at what were previously military drill camps.[8]

Under the exchange policy, each government appointed neutral agents to represent the prisoners of their armies. The actual exchange, which was negotiated on truce ships under a white flag, occurred at specified areas designated in the cartel. The main locality for exchange in 1862 was City Point on the James River outside Richmond, and the mouth of the Mississippi at New Orleans for men from prisons located in the western theater of the war.

Colonel Robert Ould was the Confederate agent for exchange. A Virginian by birth and graduate of William and Mary College he had been a lawyer for nineteen years before the war, and had first held the position of assistant secretary of war under Jefferson Davis. He was assigned agent of exchange in 1862, and given a free rein by his government in the position. Careful of details, and always with the men's best interest at heart, he also headed the Confederate Secret Service.[9]

The Federal government assigned several agents of exchange, according to different geographical departments, two of the principle men in Charleston being Colonel John Elmer Mulford and Colonel Stewart L. Woodford in 1864.

Problems with the cartel began immediately after its acceptance, mostly due to changing Federal interpretations, and indecisive recognition of the Confederacy. The first was an order by Secretary Edwin Stanton on July 22, the very day the cartel was adopted. It implied that private citizens of the Confederacy were to be arrested by any invading force, their private property seized without compensation and no accord under the proper laws of war due them.[10]

President Jefferson Davis countered, suggesting that Union soldiers would thus be considered robbers and murderers and not entitled to the

treatment as prisoners of war under the cartel. The Union rejected that interpretation, and threatened that in that case, blockade runners, guerrillas,
and bushwhackers would not be considered for exchange. The list of
ineligibles would also be extended to include men who were engaged in
raising companies, but not formally mustered into service. The threats and
counter-threats mounted in a crescendo of political rhetoric on both sides,
despite which the agents of exchange continued their merciful missions,
and many elated prisoners of both armies returned home to such an extent
that by September 1862 the prisons were practically empty.[11]

Such an efficient system of exchange kept the burden of feeding and
housing thousands of enemy soldiers from falling on the government of
either side. It was a tremendous task to provide food, shelter, and guards,
especially for the strapped resources of the South. There would appear to be
no reason for interfering with this agreement, except for the fact that the
North found a way to use it as a measure against the South.

Brigadier General William Hoffman was appointed commissary of prisoners in October 1861. By 1862, he was made entirely responsible for the
supervision of prisoners. There was a communication problem between
Hoffman and his government. Though given entire supervision, he was under the orders of Secretary of War Edwin M. Stanton, which curtailed his
authority. Hoffman complained that the generals in the field bypassed notifying him of the dispositions of prisoners taken. He had to learn the details
from the newspapers. Adding to this problem was the Union policy of changing commanders in the role of commissary general of prisoners, about once
a year. Not only did this cause inconsistency, but the already inefficient
system was hampered when on November 11, 1864 the office was divided,
placing Hoffman in charge west of the Mississippi, and appointing Brigadier
General Henry W. Wessells in charge east of the Mississippi.

The Union army had one problem in particular that was rare to the Confederates, and became a key factor in the eventual suspension of exchange.
Northern prisoners once released rarely went back to their regiments, because in many cases their one year enlistments were up, while Southern
soldiers almost immediately returned to the ranks. That difference in patri-
otic duty led to doubts on the wisdom of any further exchanges on the part
of the Union. The army was not receiving the full benefit of the returned
men, as few reenlisted. Those parolees were actually becoming more of a
burden to the North than the Confederate prisoners. Stanton admitted of
the shirkers, "There is reason to fear, that many voluntarily surrender for
the sake of getting home."[12] Lincoln, who had been forced into the idea of an
exchange cartel in the first place, was receptive to any arguments against
honoring it. Stanton convinced him that the evils outweighed the benefits.
Therefore, the president was determined to cancel exchanges, and the first
step was in December 1862 when Stanton refused to exchange any more
commissioned officers. Special exchanges of enlisted men continued under

the reluctance of Colonel Ould, who considered Stanton's position a violation of the 1862 cartel. The order made the cartel equivalents impossible to fill, and Ould demanded an even man-for-man exchange under the circumstances. The value of a Southern fighting man was increasing to the South as its ranks were being stretched thinner and thinner.

On November 15, 1862, the Union appointed Major General Ethan Allen Hitchcock as commissioner for the exchange of prisoners. Hitchcock was chosen because he would uphold Stanton's position to stop exchanges. That inflexible and uncompromising stand would cause a severe break in the negotiations for reinstating the cartel. After every inquiry from Hoffman and other agents of exchange to reinstate the cartel, Hitchcock's stern suggestion was that the best way to alleviate the suffering was to defeat the Confederate army.

After the Antietam Campaign, Lincoln decided to issue the Emancipation Proclamation. That document, announcing that slaves in those states which had seceded were freed, complicated the prisoner exchange cartel to a considerable degree. The North now forced the question on the status of black troops. Previously, the South had declared any former slave captured in uniform was to be returned to his master, as property recovered. The North, having adopted the goal of freeing the slaves, declared any former slave who had joined the Union army free from any previous designation as property, and entitled to be treated as a regular prisoner of war. The Confederate Congress declared free blacks in uniform to be treated equally with white soldiers, but the issue on the status of former slaves as being entitled to equal treatment as white soldiers was not to be compromised. The new question became the pivot on which the whole exchange question turned. It was not a popular decision in the North, where the demands for exchange were a growing concern.[13]

Lincoln was walking a fine line to justify his stance, and he knew it. It took skillful manipulation of the international laws of war to support his policy, and he needed an architect to redesign the laws of war to conform with his determination to force the prisoner cartel in his favor without recognizing the Confederacy. He found his expert in Francis Lieber, a professor of law, who had come to America from Prussia in the 1840s. Settling in South Carolina, Lieber taught at South Carolina College in Charleston until 1856. Leaving that school he taught at Columbia University. In 1861, he was chosen to confer an honorary Doctor of Letters on Lincoln. Lieber was known for his lectures on the United States Constitution and strong principles upholding individual rights.[14]

When the war began, the United States attorney general, Edward Bates, consulted Lieber as an unofficial advisor, drawing him into discussions on the points of law in a search for precedents to justify Lincoln's war measures.[15] Suddenly America's most widely quoted defender of civil liberties was appointed to search for legal justification for the administration's po litical arrests and the suspension of the writ of habeas corpus. Reluctantly he agreed to the task, and despite his true doubts of their legality, he came up with a defense.[16]

In May 1863, Lieber was again called on, this time to codify the rules of war. His skill and knowledge of international law led to the creation of General Orders No. 100, or what became known as the Lieber Code, a humanitarian document defining the rules for prisoners of war, but based on precedents which involved neither the recognition of the rebels nor foregoing the right to try them for treason after the war was over. The Lieber Code became the official U.S. policy. It was vague enough to accomplish Lincoln's goal, yet humane enough to appease the populace. It has been criticized as too reflective of the nature of a fratricidal conflict, and contains contradictions. However, it is recognized as the first concept of an international policy pertaining to the disposition of prisoners of war.[17]

Lieber favored exchange, and had every right to hope for it—he had sons fighting on both sides. Yet he worked diligently for the suppression of the rebellion at all costs. He became an advocate for the preservation of the Union, abandoning one of his firmest positions—his thirty-year contention that slavery was a state institution which the Federal government had no right to touch.[18] That attitude added weight to the demand that captured black troops not be retained as former slaves.

Two more dramatic events impacting the lives of many Confederate officers occurred in July 1863—Gettysburg and the surrender of the Vicksburg and Port Hudson garrisons on the Mississippi River. Those Federal victories threw the numbers in favor of the Union, making more Confederate prisoners in Union hands than vice versa. Major General Ulysses S. Grant paroled the 30,000 Vicksburg prisoners. Major General Nathaniel Banks paroled the Port Hudson men, saying it was necessary because he did not have sufficient troops to guard the prisoners.

Neither knew that on July 3, 1863 Stanton issued General Orders No. 207, which declared all paroles after this date worthless. Exchange was cancelled. The Port Hudson paroles illustrate a perfect example of the vacillation of the North concerning the exchange question. When Banks accepted the paroles, he was under the impression that he had strictly adhered to the terms of the cartel, which stipulated that exchanges were allowed by two opposing commanders who were authorized to exchange, as long as the prisoners were delivered to designated places of exchange. He wrote to Halleck on August 7, 1863, ". . . The parole of the prisoners captured at Port Hudson was strictly in accordance with the cartel. . . . It was almost a matter of necessity that we should parole them. . . . we had neither men to guard nor transports to move them to a place of safety." After he and Confederate Major General Franklin Gardner, who commanded the Port Hudson garrison, signed the paroles, Banks notified Halleck. But Halleck declared the paroles were invalid on account of not adhering to the cartel. Halleck's interpretation was that, first of all, Gardner was a prisoner and was not authorized to represent his government by accepting the parole. Second, Port Hudson was not a place recognized by the cartel for exchange. Technically the act of declaring the paroles illegal at once set the Confederate prisoners free. Halleck admitted to Banks on July 25, 1863, "Should these prisoners be returned to the ranks without exchange, would we be justified in punishing them for violation of parole? I fear not, for an illegal parole is null and void. All prisoners captured from Lee's army and improperly paroled were immediately returned to duty and we could make no complaint."[19]

Under the circumstances, Ould legally declared the men exchanged and free to return to their regiments. Then Halleck changed his stance on the issue. Dismissing the fact that it was his own interpretation, he about-faced and said the paroles were legal, and the Confederacy owed him men in exchange. He also refused to release the 405 officers of the Port Hudson garrison. They would be held as hostages in New Orleans until he received Union prisoners in return. But Ould would not bend, and those men, so close to freedom yet caught by a technicality, would spend the last two years of the war in prison, the worst for overcrowding, suffering and privation due to the cancellation of exchanges. Grant's action was declared legal while Banks' same action was declared in violation. The North continued to be inconsistent on the issue of exchange.[20]

The appointment of Major General Benjamin F. Butler in April 1864 as the Federal agent for exchange was an outrage to the Confederate government. Because of Butler's tyrannical rule over New Orleans, and the execution of William Mumford for taking down a United States flag, Butler had been declared an outlaw, and President Jefferson Davis refused to treat with the Union as long as Butler was in charge. Butler, however, realized the North had the upper hand in the number of men held, and that caring for the many prisoners of war was not only a burden to the government, but hard on the captives as well. According to the numbers, he could free all Union prisoners in Southern prisons by exchange, and still have 13,000 Confederate prisoners to bargain with.[21] Therefore he pushed for the reinstatement of exchange. He corresponded favorably with Colonel Ould, both shrewd lawyers who enjoyed the parrying back and forth. Ould convinced the Confederate Congress and Davis that Butler was their best hope, and the previous feelings were kept in check. But fate once again interceded, when Grant easily convinced Stanton that exchanges must be forbidden under any circumstances. It was preferable to feed prisoners than to fight soldiers, and although conditions were rapidly deteriorating in both Northern and Southern prisons, lives were becoming tokens in a high stakes game of attrition. Northern soldiers were sacrificed by their government for the sake of finding a way to quell the rebellion.[22]

Union First Lieutenant James Madison Page had been captured in September 1863 by Colonel John S. Mosby's cavalrymen outside Culpeper, Vir-

ginia. The first stop in his many transfers to prisons in the South was Belle
Isle, near Richmond, where he remained until the early part of 1864, when
he was transferred to the new facility at Anderson's Depot in Georgia.

1LT. JAMES M. PAGE, 6TH MICH. CAV.	*The report was brought to us by the incoming prisoners that the authorities had about shut down on exchanging prisoners. "Who enter here leave hope behind" was now fully exemplified. As yet it was only a surmise, but a few weeks later, or about the first of August (1864), we heard the ukase from Edward M. Stanton, that exchange of prisoners was at an end....It had become evident beyond any doubt that our Government had decided it to be a fit and necessary "war measure for repressing the rebellion" that we should be sacrificed. As this became more apparent it was so understood. The Government had passed that verdict upon us. We know it now, and it was pathetic to note the effect it had upon different dispositions, some praying, some cursing, some gambling, and others dying with curses on their lips against the Government.[23]*

The Confederate government pleaded on humanitarian grounds, it was
even willing to send Union soldiers home without exchanging Confederates,
sending 13,000 to Savannah to be transported north in the fall, the Confederacy receiving no prisoners back. The South hoped those men would be
available to vote in the United States presidential election in November 1864.
Lincoln was unpopular and presidential candidate Major General George B.
McClellan's peace platform could win the Confederacy independence without further bloodshed.[24]

For those in prison, in the midst of the negotiations, and the suspend-
ing and reinstating of the cartel, daily life was spent in anticipation of hearing their name called for exchange. Fifty high-ranking Union officers held
that hope in a Charleston prison that was actually a home in a residential
section of the city. Owned by Colonel James O'Connor, the house stood at
what is now 180 Broad Street, near the location of Roper Hospital.[25] Five
generals and forty-five colonels, lieutenant-colonels, and majors arrived there
in early June, and were there at the time Foster launched his desperate at-
tacks on Fort Johnson and Fort Sumter in July 1864. During the months of
July through September, her defenders saw a dramatic increase in the shelling of Charleston.

CAPT. LUIS F. EMILIO, 54TH MASS. INF.	*For some weeks Sumter had been bombarded with unusual vigor, as during our season of quietness the enemy had constructed two large bombproofs there, and mounted five guns on the channel face. It was estimated that one hundred of the garrison were killed or wounded during this latest bombardment. Captain Mitchel, its commander was killed, July 19, by a mortar-shell, and was succeeded by Capt. T.A. Huguenin, First South Carolina (regulars), who continued in charge until its final abandonment.[26]*

Major Edward Manigault noted in his diary for July 20, "Heavy firing on Sumter. 425 Shots in all." This was an average day's bombardment during Foster's stepped-up shelling.[27]

The bombardment was beginning to threaten those areas previously considered safe, and many of the inhabitants were becoming nervous. Major General Sam Jones, hoping to appeal to Foster's sense of honor and humanity, notified him that no military targets were located in that part of town, and that it should be spared. Foster refused to comply, stating, "Charleston must be considered a place of arms. . . . In reference to the women and children of the bombarded city, I therefore can only say the same situation occurs wherever a weak and strong party are at war."[28] Jones concluded that it would be more of an incentive for Foster to reconsider if the prisoners were also located in these non-combatant sections of the city. Jones notified Bragg on June 1, "The enemy continue their bombardment of the city with increased might, damaging private property and endangering the lives of women and children. . . . I can take care of a party, say fifty Yankee prisoners . . . to be confined in parts of the city still occupied by citizens, but under enemy fire."[29] Therefore on June 13, 1864, Jones notified Foster of the presence of Union officers in Charleston, stating, "They are provided with commodious quarters in a part of the city occupied by non-combatants, the majority of whom are women and children. It is proper, however, that I should inform you that it is a part of the city which has been for many months exposed day and night to the fire of your guns."[30]

Unfortunately his decision was to set off a chain of events which shook prison life across the North for those Confederates no longer eligible for exchange. It also set a precedent for the Federal government to use over and over as an excuse for "retaliatory measures," at an opportune time when the frustration at the Charleston defenders surpassed logical reason.

Foster immediately notified Jones on June 16, that he had been clearly warned that Charleston would be bombarded, and referred to the previous correspondence between Gillmore and Beauregard. But Foster mistakenly alluded to Gillmore's previous letter as being notification that "non-combatants might be removed, and thus women and children be spared from harm."[31] Foster went on to describe Charleston as a depot for military supplies, munitions factories and foundries for war materiel. "To destroy these means of continuing the war is, therefore, our object and duty."[32] He then stated he would place "an equal number of prisoners of the like grades...in positions exposed to the fire of your guns so long as you continue the course you stated in your communication."[33]

Jones was outraged. He interpreted Gillmore's letter of August 1863 as a threat to destroy a civilian city in a dishonorable attempt to force a surrender. He challenged Foster's allegations that Charleston was a legitimate target. "The manner in which the fire has been directed from the commencement shows beyond doubt that its object was the destruction of the city

USMHI Carlisle Barracks

Maj. Gen. Samuel Jones
Confederate commander in Charleston
when the Six Hundred were held under
fire.

USMHI Carlisle Barracks

Maj. Gen. John G. Foster
Union commander of the Department of
the South.

National Archives, Brady Collection

Roper Hospital in Charleston,
where Union prisoners were confined during August and September in 1864.

Museum of the Confederacy
Col. Robert Ould,
the Confederate agent of exchange.

National Archives
Col. Edward N. Hallowell,
the commander of the 54th Massachusetts Infantry. The regiment were the guard troops for the Six Hundred while confined on Morris Island.

National Archives
Maj. John E. Mulford,
the Union agent of exchange.

itself . . . and not, as you assume, to destroy certain military and naval works. . . . The shells have been thrown at random, at any and all hours, day and night, falling promiscuously . . . when it was impossible to see the object fired at."[34] Jones went on to describe how only civilians had been killed, while soldiers and laborers went about their duties at the batteries unharmed. "We direct our fire only on your batteries, shipping and troops. If you will direct your guns only on the works that you distinctly specify as the objects of your fire . . . the prisoners of war and their neighbors, non-combatants, women and children among whom they live, will be in no danger whatever from the effects of your shot."[35]

Foster, however, proceeded with retaliation and immediately asked that fifty Confederate officers of the same rank be sent to him. They were to be placed under fire by splitting them up, placing twelve to fifteen officers in barracks to be constructed in each of the Union forts, thus protecting the whole Union force on Morris Island.[36]

The Union prisoners of war quartered in the comfortable O'Connor house were evidently oblivious to the political bustle generated by their location. Major Orlando Smith bore testimony that the officers confined in the same area with him received fair treatment, as did other Union prisoners in the vicinity.

MAJ. ORLANDO J. SMITH, 6TH IND. CAV.

We were treated exactly as well as the Confederates. We were hungry sometimes and so were they.[37]

LT. LOUIS R. FORTESCUE, U.S. SIGNAL CORPS

Aug. 1.- Very warm today. Nothing of interest transpired with the exception of the shelling which was very brisk in the direction of Fort Sumter.[38]

1LT. ASA B. ISHAM, 7TH MICH. CAV.

We were under the fire of our guns on Morris Island, in order to protect the city, it was said. At night, by the lighted fuse, we could trace the winged messengers of destruction, as they sped high over us to create consternation further on. Day and night we could hear their explosions all around, and whenever there was an indication that considerable damage had been wrought we would "make the welkin ring." We rather enjoyed being under fire, for every "boom" and every shrieking shot were hailed as messages of joy, bidding us wait but a little longer. We were only in danger when shots fell short, as only happened on two occasions, inflicting but slight injuries upon two or three prisoners. Our gunner, from long practice, had the range of every portion of the city, and knowing where we were stationed, they threw the shots beyond us.[39]

Jones sincerely saw nothing wrong in his decision to place the officers in the non-combatant areas of Charleston and reinforced his actions with candid honesty, stating to superiors, "The right and expediency of confining prisoners of war in this city is eliciting some discussion in and out of the public prints, and the actual facts of the matter do not seem to be correctly understood by the public. . . . It may be well to publish the correspondence between Foster and myself."[40]

Upon hearing of Foster's excited reply to Jones, the five generals in the O'Connor house sent a letter to Foster, hoping to head off any heedless and unnecessary action. To reassure their commander, they wrote the following:

> *The journals of this morning inform us, for the first time, that five general officers of the Confederate service have arrived at Hilton Head, with a view to their being subjected to the same treatment that we are receiving here. We think it just to ask for these officers every kindness and courtesy that you can extend to them in acknowledgment of the fact that we, at this time, are as pleasantly and comfortably situated as is possible for prisoners of war, receiving from the Confederate authorities every privilege that we could desire or expect, nor are we unnecessarily exposed to fire.*[41]

The Confederate officers referred to were not simply five generals, but fifty high ranking officers, picked as "an eye for an eye" measure to use as bargaining chips for the Union prisoners. Foster had immediately asked Fort Delaware prison to send the officers to be placed under fire in retaliation for the O'Connor house officers. This overreaction astounded all involved, one of whom was Confederate Brigadier General Basil Duke, brother-in-law and second in command to Brigadier General John Hunt Morgan.

In the summer of 1864, a rumor reached Washington to the effect that fifty Federal officers of various grades, prisoners in the Confederate hands, had been placed at Charleston—then closely besieged and fiercely bombarded—in a situation which exposed them **BRIG. GEN. BASIL DUKE, CSA** *to the fire of the Federal fleet. Crediting this report, the Federal authorities at once issued orders that fifty Confederate prisoners of corresponding rank, should be taken to Charleston—or rather as near thereto as possible—and exposed, in retaliation, to the fire of the Confederate batteries.*

Thus, by a novel turn of fortune, these soldiers of the South were selected—although, happily, not destined—to serve their flag, under the fire of their own comrades.

. . . The list of fifty was completed by the addition of a number of colonels, majors, and captains. It was made almost entirely from prisoners confined at Fort Delaware, and I was so lucky as matters turned out, to be on it.

But our chief reason for regarding the matter with little or no apprehension was the fact that none of us believed the truth of

the report that the Federal prisoners had been placed under fire.
We, therefore, had no fear that we ourselves would be subjected
to any such ordeal, but, on the contrary, hoped that, when the
true state of affairs became known, an exchange of the members
of the respective details would be arranged; and for the sake of
such a result we would very gladly have encountered a much
more serious risk. We, therefore, started upon this excursion in
high spirits, and with most pleasant anticipations which were, for
once, destined to be realized.[42]

Also among the Confederate hostages were Brigadier General Franklin
Gardner and Lieutenant Colonel Marshall J. Smith from the Port Hudson
garrison. The situation was deemed so uncivilized by both parties, that
negotiations were started between Ould and Mulford, hoping to reach a
conclusion to such an embarrassing position of intentional harm to prisoners. Finally after three weeks, an exchange agreement was reached and
all ended amiably.

BRIG. GEN.
BASIL DUKE,
CSA

After the customary formalities had been gone through with and
the exchange completed, a banquet was given the prisoners on
both sides, in which the officers conducting the exchange and some
of the officers of the fleet participated. To the Confederates and
doubtless to the others so long accustomed to prison fare, this
feast seemed ambrosial, almost incredible, and was done ample
justice. . . . It had been agreed that all real firing should be sus-
pended for the day, both by the fleet and the Confederate batter-
ies, but, in honor of the occasion, the big guns on both sides boomed
out thunderous salutes when the exchange was concluded.[43]

No doubt many involved in this incident breathed a sigh of relief at the
narrow escape from a very sticky situation. No more prisoners of war were
immediately in Charleston, and Jones hoped to keep it that way. However,
events out of his control elsewhere would complicate matters.

CHAPTER THREE

"For Retaliation"

ANDERSON, Georgia was merely a railroad station when the war started, down in the sleepy, flat, South Georgia county of Sumter, twelve miles north of Americus. Captain William Sidney Winder was sent there on November 27, 1863 from Richmond, by his father Brigadier General John Henry Winder, Confederate commissary general of prisoners. His mission was to find a suitable locality for a prisoner of war camp, far removed from the battle front of Virginia. Libby and Belle Isle, the Richmond prisons, were being threatened by Major General Ulysses S. Grant's forces.[1]

Captain Winder decided on the location of Anderson, for its rail connections, and excellent terrain. The official name of the facility was Camp Sumter, and the prison itself of the stockade type, an enclosure built of logs with a parapet for sentries. Tents were used by the prisoners as temporary shelter. A barracks would be added later, large enough to house 8,000 to 10,000 men.

The initial stockade enclosed seventeen acres. The facilities were started in January, and completed just in time for the first inmates, who arrived in February 1864.

Visions of exchange were dispelled when we left the cars and stood in line before the south gate of Andersonville Prison. This was on the 27th day of February, 1864. It was between 10 and 11 a.m. when I was ushered in. I spent the remainder of the day exploring the camp to find a favorable place for our habitation.

2Lt. James M. Page, 6th Mich. Cav.

The camp was situated in what had been heavy pine timber, but the trees had been cut down. There was a stream of clear water running east through the prison grounds. The stockade was built of pine logs cut twenty feet long and hewed to the thickness of one foot and set in a trench five feet deep, making a wall fifteen feet

*high, on top of which were sentry boxes about thirty-five feet apart.
The stockade was not quite completed when we arrived, but a strong
force of men was at work at it. When completed it would comprise
about eleven acres. There were only about 2,000 prisoners confined there upon our arrival.*

*My occupation before I enlisted was that of surveyor, and by scien-
tific friends and those seeking favors I was often referred to as a
"civil engineer." The Confederate officer who selected Andersonville
gave evidence of his being an engineer of no mean caliber. It was
testimony that in his profession he was above mediocrity. I don't
believe that in the whole State of Georgia a better choice could
have been made. The place was healthful and salubrious and the
water was good.*[2]

Initially, conditions at Andersonville were not unpleasant under the circumstances. The winter weather was mild, as the prison was located so far
South, and food and treatment was tolerable. With the clay-based soil the
prisoners actually made bricks and built chimneys onto their tents. Rations
were those accorded under the rules of war, identical to that which the guards
received.

**2LT. JAMES M.
PAGE,
6TH MICH. CAV.**
*We were guarded by the Twenty-fifth Alabama Infantry, veteran
troops, who knew how to treat prisoners. And I said then, and have
ever since said, in speaking of our guards, the Twenty-fifth Alabama Infantry, I have never met the same number of men together
who came much nearer to my standard of what I call gentlemen.
They were respectful, humane and soldierly. We were organized
into squads of ninety, and I soon discovered that the young rebel
sergeant in charge of our squad was a fine young fellow.*[3]

**"M.H.S.",
FEDERAL
PRISONER OF WAR**
*The cooks were our own men liberated from the stockade for this
special duty on parole, and receiving therefore an extra ration
and the liberty of the entire post, with other privileges. As for the
quantity of food, I know that until Generals Sherman and Kilpatrick
destroyed the railroad communications of the South, the rations
as issued by post commissary was nearly if not equal to that of our
guards.*[4]

**T. H. MANN,
FEDERAL
PRISONER OF WAR**
*Our guard used us well, and I would say here that during our whole
captivity we always experienced good usage from an old soldier.
Corn bread and bacon were issued to us in fair quantities.*[5]

Ambrose Spencer, a local citizen and Union sympathizer, would later
be a critic of the situation of Andersonville in the post-war hysteria to
find scapegoats. Yet even he admits the kindness of Colonel Alexander

W. Persons and the 25th Alabama. He wrote of Persons that "he used all the facilities in his power to mitigate the condition in which his prisoners were placed" and "permitted squads to go out daily for the purpose of obtaining fuel."[6]

Early in April 1864, Persons and his infantry left for the front, and a new commander arrived. Captain Henry Wirz was of Swiss nationality, a physician by training who lived in Louisiana when the war began. He enlisted as a private in the 4th Louisiana Infantry, and was severely wounded at Seven Pines in 1862. His right arm was so disabled that he learned to write with his left hand. Unfit for duty in the field, he was assigned to General Winder for service in the prisons around Richmond. When construction began on Camp Sumter, Winder chose Wirz as commander at the sight, which assignment he reached simultaneously with large shipments of prisoners.[7]

The descriptions given by others of Captain Wirz are so erroneous, misleading, and untrue that I will describe him as well as I can at this late day [1908]. He was of good height, perhaps five feet eight inches; slim in build, with a handsome face, aquiline nose, even features and a high forehead. His eyes were gray in color. At this time he wore a short, partially full beard. There was a quiet, subdued expression of sadness in his countenance, particularly in his eyes.[8]

2LT. JAMES M. PAGE, 6TH MICH. CAV.

Between the jailer and the jailed, there could not and never can be any peculiar love; but, under a rough exterior, more often assumed than felt, this Captain Wirz was as kind-hearted a man as I ever met. Being myself at headquarters I learned his character, and the opinion I formed of him when in the stockade, which was one of a bitter kind enough, I had to change when I came really to know the man.[9]

EDWARD WELLINGTON BOATE, 42ND N.Y. INF.

At Andersonville, Wirz was only officially in charge of the interior of the stockade. Therefore, his duties were only to see that order was maintained, sanitary regulations enforced, and prisoner complaints heard. The official commander of the prison was General Winder, who was in charge of all the Southern prisons east of the Mississippi. This consolidation of command was a step long needed in the Confederate government's management of their military prisons. However, it came too late to save the Union soldiers who were innocent victims fated to die at Andersonville. It also came too late to prevent the backlash against Confederate captives.[10]

Wirz immediately set about to improve the conditions, which were becoming crowded, by enlarging the enclosure an additional ten acres. He requisitioned tools to enable the men to build shelter, and speed up the process of construction, but tools were among the many scarce items in the Confederacy in 1864. He did improve the hospital to better care for the sick.[11]

EDWARD
WELLINGTON
BOATE,
42ND N.Y. INF.

I can honestly say—and every man who was connected with the hospital department will bear me out—that the twenty-five or thirty Confederate surgeons who were in attendance at the hospital and in the stockade, acted with as much humanity toward the prisoners as the disheartening circumstances would permit. We were often a fortnight without being able to get medicine. They had no quinine for fever and ague; they had no opium for diarrhoea and dysentery. Our government made medicine a contraband of war, and wherever they found medicine on a blockade runner, it was confiscated, a policy which indicated, on the part of our rulers, both ignorance and barbaric cruelty.[12]

2LT. JAMES M.
PAGE,
6TH MICH. CAV.

They claim that the sick prisoners had not proper accommodations. That is true. They claim that the food was not sufficiently nourishing. That is true. And that there was not proper medicine or a sufficiency of it to be used in the care of the sick is correct. But we must remember that all the time during 1864 the Confederate Government was in an impoverished condition; the troops in the field were without proper supplies and that they were limited in the hospital supplies is undeniable. The Confederate Government itself was suffering for the want of food, clothing, and medicine.

Of course there were thousands in the hospitals at Andersonville, the suffering was awful, and there were thousands of deaths, but the surgeons in attendance were no more accountable or to blame for it than babes. Neither was Captain Wirz to blame for it. I think that he and the physicians did everything in their power with the means at their command to care for the sick and to alleviate the suffering. They did their duty like Christians and like men.[13]

In July, the new stockade enlargement was completed and "moving day" commenced. The thousands of cramped prisoners were able to spread out and build new residences, some using the bricks made inside the stockade itself. For a time conditions improved, but soon more prisoners arrived, relocated South from Major General William Tecumseh Sherman's advance north of Atlanta, and Grant's siege of Petersburg, as well as the humanitarian reasons of food shortages in Richmond. However, once again conditions deteriorated due to overcrowding and lack of supplies at the new location. Rations became hard to come by, first from want of dishes, and pots and pans, to serve and cook in. Later the inability to acquire the food itself led to much sickness and suffering.[14]

EDWARD
WELLINGTON
BOATE,
42ND N.Y. INF.

Vegetables could not be had for love or money, although for miles the country was scoured, and I knew Chief Surgeon White to pay from a hundred to two hundred dollars for a quantity of squashes, collards, onions and other garden stuff which could have been pur-

chased in Fulton or Washington market for five or six dollars. . . .
Fresh beef was supplied to the hospital two or three times a week,
and sometimes to the stockade, when it could be had, cattle hav-
ing for this purpose been sought for miles around the country. To
provide more room both inside the hospital itself, as well as the
stockade, the tents erected for the hospital were moved outside
the stockade. This facility itself consisted of groups of worn out
tents with straw pallets on the ground for the men to lay on. An-
other reason for moving the medical facilities was because the
well prisoners were continually stealing the medicine and annoy-
ing the sick.[15]

In the stockade, with the exception of the damp lowlands border-
ing the small streams, the surface was covered with huts and small
ragged tents, and parts of blankets and fragments of oilcloth, coats,
and blankets stretched upon sticks. The tents and huts were not
arranged according to any order, and there was in most parts of
the enclosure scarcely room for two men to walk abreast between
the tents and huts. . . . Masses of corn bread, bones, old rags, and
filth of every description were scattered around or accumulated
in large piles. If one might judge from the large pieces of corn
bread scattered about in every direction on the ground, the pris-
oners were either very lavishly supplied with this article of diet or
else this kind of food was not relished by them.[16]

DR. JOSEPH
JONES,
CONFEDERATE
SURGEON

With an average of 400 men arriving daily, something had to be done.
The meagre resources on hand were unable to provide for the numbers.
Disease was becoming prevalent due to poor sanitation. In August 1864
Andersonville reached its maximum of 32,899 prisoners in the stockade,
and scores were dying daily.[17] The Confederate government decided the only
recourse was another appeal to the Union to reinstate exchange. In a desperate act to convince Union Secretary of War Stanton, a delegation of paroled
Union soldiers from Andersonville was sent to Washington. Among the prisoners was Edward Wellington Boate.

The great paramount idea of the prisoners was exchange. They
accordingly called a great meeting, and after some preliminary
proceedings, resolutions, and a memorial to President Lincoln were
adopted, asking, in view of the suffering and mortality of our men,
that he should agree to an exchange of prisoners, as the Confed-
erates were willing to exchange man for man, and officer for of-
ficer, leaving the excess of prisoners at whichever side found. Six
prisoners, including myself as Chairman, were appointed a Com-
mission to proceed to Washington, and lay the whole question be-
fore the Executive. This was toward the close of August. After some
negotiations with General Winder, the balance of twenty-one men

EDWARD
WELLINGTON
BOATE,
42ND N.Y. INF.

due to our government, the six delegates being included, were per-
mitted to come North; and on our way through Macon we met
General Stoneman at Prison Oglethorpe, where the Federal offic-
ers were confined, and he gave us a letter to the President, strongly
urging the necessity of exchange, not for the officers he said, but
for the brave men who had fought so gallantly in the field, and
suffered so much in prison, and begging the President to forego
all idea of the exchange of negroes, if that were the point which
stood in the way.[18]

Arriving in New York, the four commissioners applied for the nec-
essary transportation at General Dix's office. It was refused, al-
though Colonel Hall, Deputy Provost Marshal at Hilton Head, had
given us letters to the headquarters of the department of the east,
stating our mission, etc. The Sanitary Commission however, sup-
plied the transportation and three of the commissioners proceeded
to Washington, I remaining, however, in this city through illness,
although I was not idle. They wrote to the President, and reported
the object of their visit on three consecutive days; but it distresses
me to state that the representatives of thirty-eight thousand Union
prisoners were treated with silent contempt, the President declin-
ing to see them or have any communication with them!!! For obvi-
ous reasons I shall be silent as to the motive of President Lincoln in
his treatment of the delegation. But I cannot help stating that the
lives of some ten or twelve thousand men might have been spared
had an exchange justly, I will not add generously, taken place at
this period.[19]

In July, 120 miles north of Andersonville, Atlanta was heavily under
siege by Sherman. Union troops had crossed the Chattahoochee River, and
Major General James B. MacPherson had moved toward Atlanta from Decatur
by July 21. Although the army was pushing for the fall of Atlanta, Major
General George Stoneman probed south of the main theater of conflict on
cavalry raids. These alarmed the authorities at Andersonville, which was far
from any prospects of attack when it was built five months earlier.[20] Now
panic ensued.

EDWARD
WELLINGTON
BOATE,
42ND N.Y. INF.

Toward the close of July, General Stoneman's raid at Macon took
place, and the Confederates immediately commenced, with their
available help of niggers, to fortify Andersonville, which they cer-
tainly believed was to be immediately attacked. At this very pe-
riod Dr. White, who had started for Macon to hurry up medicine,
was stopped at Fort Valley, half-way between Andersonville and
Macon; and instead of coming back with medicine, came to his
office armed to the teeth, announcing to the surgeons that they
must help to defend the place, according to the instructions of

General Winder, as the prison was to be immediately attacked. We, Federal paroled prisoners, it was announced, were to be sent down to the hospital. The cannon planted around headquarters, which dominated the prison, were charged and manned, and everything ready for defense. During the previous week of rumors of attack, huge breastworks were thrown up by niggers who labored at them night as well as day. Stoneman was, however, himself captured, and the excitement passed away. Thoughts of changing the location of the prison occupied the minds of the authorities, as they did not know what moment the prison would be attacked and the prisoners carried off.[21]

As soon as Sherman had come through, bodies of cavalry under the command of General Stoneman and others began to raid the rebel territory south of the line of Sherman's march across the country, with a view to reaching, if possible, the prisoners at Andersonville. While not able to reach Andersonville, or capture the prisoners, they made it so uncomfortable for the enemy that the prisoners were removed from there and run to other points in Georgia. The rebels were evidently feeling that they would have to get rid of the prisoners.[22]

MAJ. BENJAMIN W. THOMPSON, 32ND U.S. COLORED TROOPS

Toward the latter part of July it was rumored that we were to be removed to Charleston and Savannah, and soon a lot were started on the 29th inst., but brought back for fear he would recapture them. Great was the excitement among us about this time, which was brought to a climax on the first of August, when General Stoneman and his staff were added to our number. On the 11th of August, in company with about six hundred others, I was started for Charleston. Packed in box cars, fifty officers and five guards in each, we suffered intensely from heat and thirst.[23]

LT. BENJAMIN S. CALEF, 2ND REG. U.S. SHARPSHOOTERS, FEDERAL PRISONER OF WAR AT MACON, GA.

Winder was at a loss as how to alleviate the suffering. A new camp site was chosen at Millen, about seventy-five miles northwest of Savannah both to relieve the overcrowding at Andersonville, and also to remove the prisoners from any liberating troops of Sherman's army. This new camp became known as Camp Lawton.

Thus began a migration of Union prisoners to Savannah, and also to Charleston, with the reassurance that it was only a temporary measure to secure them, until Camp Lawton could be finished. Only 5,000 prisoners were left at Andersonville by September 1864. Over 10,000 would never leave, buried in marked graves outside the stockade.

Jones, commanding in Charleston, adamantly protested having more prisoners in that city, but his authority was overruled by sheer necessity.[24] Once again several hundred Union prisoners of war arrived in Charleston, in the vicinity of the Roper Hospital and the O'Connor house at 180 Broad Street. Others were located on the race course.

LT. BENJAMIN S.
CALEF, 2ND
REG. U.S.
SHARPSHOOTERS

We reached Charleston on the morning of August 13, and were kept waiting a long time in the street, when I procured some fresh figs, bread and milk, and, seated on the curb-stone, made an excellent breakfast.[25]

LT. LOUIS R.
FORTESCUE, U.S.
SIGNAL CORPS

Saturday, August 5, 1864.- Our quarters here are of the worst kind imagineable, 600 officers packed into a small prison yard not more than a hundred yards square with walls surrounding us at least 20 feet high and not a single shade tree. What would our kid gloved gentry of the North who are enjoying the seashore now say if they had to stand this sweltering heat.

Sunday, August 6, 1864.- The heat today is intolerable. Very brisk shelling this a.m. at intervals of about 15 minutes. Since our arrival here we have been expecting better quarters having been informed when we came that an empty building was being fitted up for us but owing as they say to their officers being placed between decks of a transport at Hilton Head they this morning countermanded the order to remove us and we must therefore content ourselves here and hope for better times.[26]

Fortescue was moved on August 14 to the vicinity of the jail, next to the Roper Hospital where Benjamin S. Calef was also imprisoned. According to both soldiers, their quarters in Charleston were comfortable and no complaints were made.

LT. LOUIS R.
FORTESCUE, U.S.
SIGNAL CORPS

Sunday, August 14, 1864.- Transferred this evening to the Marion Hospital a large building adjoining the Prison. It is quite commodious and are really the best quarters I have had the pleasure of enjoying since my advent into the Confederacy. My present location is room no. 6 second floor where all communications may be addressed.[27]

Other Union prisoners of war bypassed Charleston and went directly to Columbia, South Carolina, where a new prison was hastily prepared to remove the men from Sherman's path. It became the eventual destination for all.

The first stop on the way to Charleston for Lieutenant James Madison Page, however, was Savannah, where temporary stockades were constructed in the town squares, under the spreading shade of live oaks and palmettos. Colonel Edward Clifford Anderson was placed in charge of caring for these transient prisoners. He was formerly an officer in the Confederate States Foreign Service and Secret Service. Offered the position of assistant secretary of war in the Confederate government, he declined. He returned to Savannah and remained in command of the coastal defenses of Georgia. A native of

Savannah, Anderson had been wounded in June 1864, when serving as major of a Georgia battalion of artillery. When the prisoners had to be transferred to his city from Andersonville, he was in charge of their well-being.[28]

However, the first prisoners did not leave until August 5, and this date is of utmost importance in relation to the Union charges of retaliation and subsequent events.[29] Page left even later, during September after Atlanta fell, when the majority of prisoners were sent to Savannah.

In September there began a general movement of the prisoners from Andersonville. They went in detachments, many of them leaving during the first week of September, but 'our party' did not leave the prison until the middle of the month. Those prisoners were sent further south to Millen, Savannah, and other points. It was of course understood that our Government had changed its mind in regard to exchange and all were buoyed up with new hope.

At the end of the third day we reached Savannah, and were turned into a pen built of boards about fifteen feet high in one of the public squares of the city.

This ended our dream of home and friends, and nearly knocked the remaining life out of us; however, it was a change for the better, for there were only about 5,000 prisoners here, and the sanitary condition was a great improvement on Andersonville.[30]

2LT. JAMES M. PAGE, 6TH MICH. CAV.

Thursday 8th Sept. 64.- Nine hundred Yankee prisoners arrived at 10:30 a.m. and at 6 p.m. six hundred more arrived. They were marched out under charge of Col. Richard Wayne to the stockade in rear of the Jail. This enclosure, commenced yesterday afternoon was finished at sunset today. The Engineers have been working at it for six weeks and when I took charge of it yesterday, only the posts were put down. Ordered in Guerards Battery from the White Bluff station and Hugers Regulars from the Isle of Hope. Also called out 200 of the local troops. Rode out at sunset to the stockade and looked at the prisoners. They are a beggarly set of vagabonds. The 900 men first sent out make no showing. The space enclosed will accommodate 4500 men. I am told we are to have 5,000 or 10,000 of them. Directed Major Hersch to enlarge the enclosure to retain the labor impressed. The guard that came down with the first batch of prisoners will be retained. In the past week Atlanta has fallen and Hood's army fallen back towards Griffin. The removal of the prisoners from Andersonville is the consequence.[31]

COL. EDWARD C. ANDERSON, CSA, SAVANNAH

The construction on the stockade at Millen was hurried along, and by the first week of October, if completed, would boast of being the largest prisoner of war camp in the world. Designed to hold 40,000 men, this location had been originally chosen because of its apparent insignificance militarily. The food supply was much better and shelter was plentiful. However, that was before Sherman came. The surgeon in charge at Millen, Dr. Isaiah H. White, appealed to the government for money to alleviate the food and medical shortage. But there was no money in the Confederate treasury for any purpose, no matter how urgent.

COL. EDWARD C. ANDERSON, CSA
COMMANDER AT SAVANNAH

Wednesday, Oct. 5.- A despatch came down to night to say that 15 carloads of Yankee Prisoners were to be down in the morning (to-morrow). Major Williams sent up to Millen today to ascertain the progress of the stockade at that point, and to learn when it would be ready for the removal of the prisoners from this point. We now have confined here nearly 7,000 men in the stockade. I visited the hospital at sunset and found great negligence there. The guard was entirely insufficient and many of the boards along the enclosure have been loosened so as to afford easy egress to the prisoners. I have no doubt whatever but that they have been running at large over the city every night.

Thursday Oct. 6.- Nine hundred more Yankee prisoners came in this morning and were sent to the stockade. It is now full to its capacity. I have despatched to Gen. Winder that no more must be sent down. Major Williams returned this morning from Millen and reports that the stockade at that point will not be ready for the reception of prisoners before the end of the week, if then.[32]

2LT. JAMES M. PAGE, 6TH MICH. CAV.

(October 1864) We were soon after regularly 'booked,' and became inmates of Millen prison. There was a stream of good, pure water running through the camp, and our rations consisted of a pint of corn meal, about one-half cupful of cooked rice, and one-half pound of beef and a little salt every twenty-four hours.[33]

By autumn 1864, the Confederacy was fighting a four-front war. She had formed a hollow square with all brave backs together, determined to fight until the end. The Union prisoners of war were innocent victims in a situation unplanned by their captors. As Sherman cut a swath through Georgia and South Carolina, the care of enemy prisoners became secondary. There were too few troops to counter Sherman's army, and even fewer to spare for guarding prisoners. Therefore the concentration of prisoners to South Carolina was due to four events: the fighting at Petersburg; the closing in of Sherman's forces on Savannah; the stalemate in the question of prisoner of war exchange; and the increasing effectiveness of the blockade.[34]

With the Confederacy under pressure from all sides, the Union was finding yet another way to attack, with accusations of mistreatment of prisoners of war. Stanton and Grant were still putting the pressure on Butler to avoid at all costs any exchange of prisoners. The South had been agreeable under any circumstances; even the issue over black troops was settled.

Sir: You have several times proposed to me to exchange the prisoners respectively held by the two belligerents, officer for officer and man for man. The same offer has also been made by other officials having charge of matters connected with the exchange of prisoners. This proposal has heretofore been declined by the Confederate authorities, they insisting upon the terms of the cartel, which required the delivery of the excess on either side upon parole. In view, however, of the very large number of prisoners now held by each party, and the suffering consequent upon their continued confinement, I now consent to the above proposal, and agree to deliver to you the prisoners held in captivity by the Confederate authorities, provided you agree to deliver an equal number of Confederate officers and men. As equal numbers are delivered from time to time they will be declared exchanged.

LETTER, COL.
ROBERT OULD TO
MAJ. JOHN
MULFORD,
10 AUGUST 1864

This proposal is made with the understanding that the officers and men who have been longest in captivity will be the first delivered, where it is practicable. I shall be happy to hear from you as speedily as possible whether this arrangement can be carried out.[35]

But Butler was under strict orders to dodge all favorable negotiations. This involved using petty demands and outrageous ultimatums, intended because it was highly unlikely the South would agree.

To obtain the delivery of even sick and wounded prisoners without any in return would be a somewhat difficult operation, save that the enemy by giving us our wounded and sick in their hands, we retaining all the rebel sick and wounded in ours, burdened us with the care and cost of all the sick and wounded of both sides, an operation of which it is difficult to see the strategic value, and is only to be defended because of its humanity in rescuing our wounded from the destitution and suffering permitted to them by the Confederates. Nothing further was done with the exchange save to receive from Richmond such sick and wounded as they delivered to us, till the 15th of August, when I received a note from Major Mulford.[36]

MAJ. GEN.
BENJAMIN
BUTLER, USA

Mulford's note referred to the letter from Ould, and stated that the Confederate authorities were still willing to exchange man for man, totally in agreement with what the Federal government said its policy would be.[37] Hence, Butler was desperate to find an excuse for refusal.

In case the Confederate authorities should yield to the argument . . . and formally notify me that their slaves captured in our uniform would be exchanged as other soldiers were, and that they were ready to return to us all our prisoners at Andersonville and elsewhere in exchange for theirs, I had determined, with the con-

MAJ. GEN.
BENJAMIN
BUTLER, USA

sent of the lieutenant-general (Grant), as a last resort, in order to prevent exchange, to demand that the outlawry against me should be formally reversed and apologized for before I would further negotiate the exchange of prisoners.[38]

It may be remarked here that the rebels were ready enough to exchange prisoners at this time, man for man, where we would permit it to be done; because another exchange of a part of the prisoners captured from our navy, held by the Confederates, was arranged with the Secretary of the Navy.[39]

JEFFERSON DAVIS, PRESIDENT OF CONFEDERATE STATES

The Federal Government remaining deaf to all appeals for exchange of prisoners, it was manifest that the incarceration of their captured soldiers could no longer be of any possible advantage to us, since to relieve their sufferings that government would take no step, if it involved a similar release of our men in their hands. Indeed, it was manifest that they looked upon it as an advantage to them and an injury to us to have their prisoners in our hands to eat our little remaining substance. In view of all these factors and considerations, Generals Cobb and Pillow and I were of one mind, that the best thing that could be done was, without further efforts, to get instructions from Richmond, to make arrangements to send off all the prisoners we had at Eufaula and Andersonville to the nearest accessible Federal post, and having paroled them not to bear arms until regularly exchanged, to deliver them unconditionally, simply taking a receipt on descriptive rolls of the men thus turned over. . . . To my amazement the officer commanding the escort telegraphed back from Jacksonville that the Federal commandant at St. Augustine refused to receive and receipt for the prisoners till he could hear from General Grant, who was then in front of Petersburg, Va., and with whom he could only communicate by sea along the coast. . . . The real cause of all the protracted sufferings of prisoners, North and South, is directly due to the inhuman refusal of the Federal Government to exchange prisoners of war, a policy that we see, from the facts herein stated, was carried so far as to induce a commanding officer at St. Augustine to refuse even to receive and acknowledge that he had received over six thousand men of his own side, tendered to him unconditionally, from that prison in the South which, above all others, they charged to have been the scene of unusual suffering. . . . In our straitened circumstances there was no other practicable remedy than liberation by exchange or parole. The first had been discontinued by the United States officials; the last had been nullified by the United States War Department order of July 3, 1863.[40]

An outcry arose from citizens in the North demanding exchange be reinstated by the Lincoln administration. Walt Whitman, in a letter which appeared in the December 27, 1864 issue of the *New York Times*, wrote:[41]

In my opinion, the Secretary has taken and obstinately held a position of cold-blooded policy, (that is, he thinks it policy) in this matter, more cruel than anything done by the secessionists. Ostensibly and officially saying he will not exchange at all unless the secession leaders will give us, on average terms, all the blacks they capture in military action. The Secretary has also said (and this is the basis of his course and policy) that it is not for the benefit of the Government of the United States that the power of the secessionists should be repleted by some 50,000 men in good condition now in our hands, besides getting relieved of the support of nearly the same number of human wrecks and ruins, of no advantage to us, now in theirs.

Major General Butler, in my opinion, has also incorporated in the question of exchange a needless amount of personal pique and an unbecoming obstinacy. He too, has taken his stand on the exchange of all black soldiers, has persisted in it without regard to consequences, and has made the whole of the large and complicated question of general exchange turn upon that one item alone, while it is but a drop in the bucket. Then he makes it too much a personal contest and matter of vanity who shall conquer, and an occasion to revenge the bad temper, and insults of the South toward himself.

In my opinion, the anguish and death of these ten to fifteen thousand American young men, with all the added and incalculable sorrow, long drawn out, amid families at home, rests mainly upon the heads of members of our own Government; and if they persist, the death of the remainder of the Union prisoners, and often worse than death will be added.

It is worse than useless to disguise or ignore the fact that the condition of Union prisoners in rebel hands is exciting the profoundest feeling in the public mind, and that the action of the Government upon the subject is not regarded with satisfaction. This feeling is perfectly natural and not unreasonable. So far as the public has been informed of the action of the Government, that action does not seem adequate to the awful emergencies of the case. And while the whole subject is surrounded with difficulties, it is felt that nothing but absolute necessity—no question of ettiquette, no fear of embarrassing concessions, no question of policy and expediency merely, should lead the Government to permit forty thousand of our soldiers to perish by starvation and exposure at the hands of their Southern captors.

COL. EDWARD
C. ANDERSON,
CSA,
SAVANNAH

Saturday, Oct. 8, 1864- 26 Yankee prisoners died in the stockade last night—the cold weather has been fatal to all those cases of diarrhea which have been lingering for the past fortnight, thus accounting for the large increase in mortality among the prisoners.

Poor devils—it is pitiable to think that it is not in our power to succor them better, yet their government refuses to exchange them and by blockading our ports—prevents us from receiving those supplies from abroad which would enable us to cloth and care for our own men and their prisoners as well—Such is war. It was a sickening sight to see those wretched strangers—stretched out stark and stiff in the death line awaiting transportation to their place of burial. The flies were swarming over their faces and a crowd of prisoners had gathered nearby looking on in callous indifference and jesting among themselves as though there had never existed a feeling of pity in their hearts. I am told that a large number of the prisoners are affected with nostalgia, or homesickness—which is proving fatal in many cases among them.[42]

Soon Sherman's threat to Savannah made that city unfeasible for holding prisoners of war. Consequently, they were sent on to Charleston or Millen by the middle of October, and on to Columbia after that.

Many prisoners took advantage of the hasty move to make their escape. Blankets and clothing were lacking and the meat ration was often unobtainable by Confederate authorities. The Union soldiers who escaped, or those few who were exchanged, brought tales of suffering and bad conditions back to their homes and comrades. Undeniably they had suffered. Undeniably, too, the Confederate government and those in charge had never intentionally allowed the suffering to happen. All evidence points to the fact that all was done that could be, and the only solution was exchange, which Federal authorities forbade.

Stories of the horrible and shocking conditions at Andersonville, the extraordinarily high death rates, and conditions in general at all Confederate prisons led to outrage in the North. Union passions against the Confederacy ran so high that reason was blinded. Official correspondence is full of assumptions that Confederate authorities were intentionally mistreating prisoners, and retaliation was practiced for whatever United States authorities imagined. The result was that the exchange agents on either side became constantly swamped with investigating allegations of violations of the laws of war. That caused a further breakdown in efficiency, good relations, and communications, all delaying a solution to the exchange dilemma.[43]

The Union's military operations essentially set up a desperate situation for the Confederate government to deal with, then screamed "foul." The Federal government sought retribution for those wrongs, and adopted a policy of retaliation. Northern citizens and politicians far removed from the war, and unlikely to ever be any closer, took out their frustration on the Confederate soldiers confined in their midst. Although blankets, food, medicine, and supplies were plentiful and readily available to soldiers in Northern prisons, all necessities were withheld under the policy of "retaliation." The final act which carried out that policy on a mass scale occurred in August 1864.

There had been some isolated instances of retaliation reported previously. A returning soldier would testify that he knew of a Federal prisoner of war in close confinement, or on reduced rations as a punishment for misconduct. Similar incidents were reported at several Southern prisons. Subsequently, the authorities would pick a Confederate prisoner of war at random to be treated the same way, simply as a measure to make the Confederate authorities release the Federal prisoner from his punishment. Thus the prisoners in Northern camps were at the mercy of their keepers. Good behavior was no guarantee that they would escape bad treatment.

The practice of retaliation was suggested by Indiana Senator Henry Smith Lane, who proposed on January 16, 1865, what became known as the Lane Resolution to the 38th Congress. He had received a request from citizens in Fort Wayne, Indiana to retaliate "until the rebels exchange all of our men in their hands, or treat them with that degree of humanity that the rules of war require."[44] Of course the Confederacy was trying to comply. However, Lane wanted retaliation and retribution, not exchange. He wanted vengeance on the South, saying on the floor of Congress, "I would make the war still bloodier; I would make every rocky ravine in Southern Georgia and Alabama run red with the blood of traitors, and I would drive into the Gulf stream the last rebel there before I would recognize their independence."[45]

Lane proposed to especially single out officers for mistreatment, stating that the private soldiers had no choice but to serve the rebellion, while the officers were actual instigators in secession who should be severely punished for their treason.[46] He was joined vehemently in his enthusiasm for retaliation by Senators Benjamin F. Wade of Ohio and Morton Smith Wilkinson of Minnesota. The resolution, among other things, suggested that Confederate prisoners be at the mercy of jailors who had formerly been held in the South as prisoners of war, so they would tend to treat their captives as they had been treated.[47] The preamble to the resolution stated:

Rebel prisoners in our hands are to be subjected to a treatment finding its parallels only in the conduct of savage tribes and resulting in the death of multitudes by the slow but designed process of starvation and by mortal diseases occasioned by insufficient and unhealthy food and wanton exposure of their persons to the inclemency of the weather.[48]

Senator Lane was opposed in the argument for retaliation by Senators Charles Sumner of Massachusetts, Thomas Andrews Hendricks of Indiana, and Garrett Davis of Kentucky, among others. Senator Hendricks, from Lane's own state, protested on the grounds of breaking international law, saying the resolution blatantly stipulated:

> We should take the lives of prisoners, even by freezing and starvation, or turn them into living skeletons by act of Congress. The resolution declares that in the opinion of Congress 'such retaliation ought to be inflicted upon the insurgent officers now in our hands, or hereafter to fall into our hands, as prisoners; that such officers ought to be subjected to like treatment practiced toward our officers ... in respect to quantity and quality of food, clothing, fuel, medicine, medical attention, personal exposure, or other mode of dealing with them.' Do what? Assassinate a captive after he has surrendered? After he has laid down his arms at your feet, assassinate him in cold blood? Not only that, but we must expose them to the inclemency of the weather! Not only that, but we must give them unhealthy food, that disease may come upon them and they may die of horrible disease! Not only that, but we shall deny to them food, that they may die by starvation![49]

The more moderate senators were also concerned about how this fit with the Lieber Code, their own document which required them to treat prisoners of war humanely. Lieber was consulted. General Orders No. 100 did address retaliation as valid if used as a weapon to redress grievances. At the same time, the Code stipulated that prisoners were not to be endangered, food withheld as punishment, or subjected to intentional suffering or indignities.[50] Lieber's advice was to retaliate strictly by cutting off outside aid from friends and family. He was alarmed at the suggestions of the radical senators to interpret his code to legally murder prisoners. He urged Senator Charles Sumner of Massachusetts, who was by no means sympathetic to the South, to argue against retaliation. Sumner answered Lane's suggestion of mercilessness on the Senate floor, quoting from the Lieber Code, and pleading for a moderate stand.[51]

SENATOR
CHARLES SUMNER

> Retaliation is harsh always, even in the simplest cases, and is permissible only where, in the first place, it may reasonably be expected to effect its object, and where in the second place, it is consistent with the usages of civilized society; and that, in the absence of these essential conditions, it is a useless barbarism, having no other end than vengeance, which is forbidden alike to nations and to man.

> I believe that the best way in which we can retaliate upon the South for the cruel treatment of our prisoners, is for us to continue to treat their prisoners with entire humanity and all reasonable kindness; and not only so, but to seize every opportunity like the present to go beyond this.... Indeed, it is no more than our duty to treat the prisoner well. The law of nations requires it. The

Government that refuses or neglects it does not deserve the name of civilized.[52]

While it was hotly debated, and the South accused of "atrocities deliberately committed," those opposed to "retaliation in kind" pointed out that it too would be "atrocities deliberately committed," and that no such behavior should be enacted by law on testimony of "vague rumor" and "uncertain report." Retaliation could serve no purpose in alleviating the suffering of Northern prisoners. Senator Hendricks, who also had a brother in a Southern prison, pointed out that for every statement alleging cruelty on the part of Southern prison officials, one could be produced which showed kindness and no atrocities.[53]

I know how easy it is to exaggerate the report of these barbarities. I know how easy it is to impregnate the minds of the masses of the people with the idea that our soldiers are not as well treated as they should be.[54]

SENATOR EDGAR COWAN, OF PENNSYLVANIA

But the main curb was the law of nations, which stated emphatically that mistreatment of prisoners of war was a breach of the laws of war, and that retaliation was also a breach of those international laws.[55]

The more moderate senators preferred to reinstate the policy of exchange, not implement government-sanctioned murder. Senator Hendricks suggested an investigation of the secretary of war, on the grounds that it had been proven Stanton was directly involved in the curtailment of exchange.[56] Amendments were presented and voted on, and the debate raged through January 1865, when it passed the Senate. Within months it was outdated by the reinstatement of the 1862 cartel. Despite the fact that it was never widely adopted, retaliation became Union policy, left up to the discretion of field commanders. It was implemented with a vengeance by Major General John G. Foster, the commander in the Department of the South, with the support of Secretary of War Stanton, and Generals Henry W. Halleck and Ulysses S. Grant.

****

Immediately after the exchange of the fifty officers in Charleston Harbor on August 3, Jones was notified that he would have to accept a large number of the Andersonville prisoners temporarily. They would be confined on the race course on the edge of the city, as well as the old jail and in the vicinity of Roper Hospital. Jones pressured Richmond authorities not to send the men to Charleston. He wrote Secretary of War James A. Seddon, "Please have the order revoked or send me additional troops. It is with great difficulty that these now here can be guarded; no others can be at present."[57] Despite his objections, the prisoners were sent. There was no alternative. Jones continued to push for their removal, stating, "It is exceedingly embarrassing to me to have so many prisoners to provide for." On September 4, he wrote, "Please have U.S. officers, prisoners of war, now here under recent orders removed to some other place, taking them entirely from my control. It is very inconvenient and unsafe to keep them here." There is no evidence to suggest Jones had the officers there for exchange, or to be placed under fire.

However, when Foster was informed of the presence of more Union prisoners in Charleston by escaped officers, he surmised that Jones had more Federal officers in Charleston for the express purpose of placing them under fire from his batteries. Yet Foster contradicted himself. He had suggested on August 4 to Halleck, that, "I can easily have the matter arranged with the Confederate authorities so as to effect an exchange here. . . . I think the Confederate authorities are very desirous to have an exchange effected. . . . They have already been obliged to remove our officers from Macon, and 600 of them have already arrived in Charleston and others are to follow: this from its being the only secure place."[58] In another letter to Halleck dated August 18, Foster wrote, "He [Jones] stated that he did not place them there to be under fire, but that they were merely enroute. The truth is they are so short of men as guards they have no place to put their prisoners in except Charleston and Savannah. . . . As far as injury goes to them there can be none, for I know their exact position and direct the shells accordingly."[59]

Although he admitted there was no violation, Foster still demanded retaliation. He notified authorities of the situation and requested 600 Confederate officers be picked and sent to him. He then notified Jones on September 4, "I demanded the removal from under our fire of any prisoners of war who might be held by you in confinement at Charleston . . . you admit that you still retain prisoners of war at that point, where they are exposed to fire. . . . I have therefore to inform you that your officers, now in my hands, will be placed by me under your fire, as an act of retaliation."[60]

Upon receiving this, Jones shot back the reply that Federal prisoners were in the city only temporarily, denying any wrongdoing, and that he was arranging their removal. "You are mistaken if you suppose those prisoners have been sent here for the purpose of being placed in positions where they may be reached by your shot," he wrote. "When proper arrangements are made for their accommodation elsewhere they may be removed, but their removal will not be hurried or retarded by your threat to place an equal number of C.S. officers, prisoners of war, under our fire . . . the only treatment received by the prisoners of war now in our possession that is in disregard of the usages of civilized warfare they receive at the hands of their own government. They are certainly as prisoners of war justly entitled to fair and honorable exchange, and that their Government denies them."[61]

But it was too late for diplomacy. Even though Foster himself acknowledged that the prisoners in Charleston were not under fire, he immediately sought and received permission to transport the chosen 600 Confederate officers of all grades to use in retaliation: "As soon as the rebel officers arrive I shall place them immediately on Morris Island between Wagner and Gregg."[62]

They were to be taken from Fort Delaware, sent to Foster, and placed in a stockade exposed to Confederate batteries in the most frequently fired on area of Morris Island.

Those 600 became hostages, serving as a shield to Union troops as living breastworks. Foster hoped to check the fire on his own batteries with the lives of enemy officers. In addition, they were an experiment. Whatever was perceived as the treatment of Union soldiers, the same treatment would be carried out on these Confederate officers. The degree of severity in their case, however, was like repaying a bruised toe with a broken leg. The 600 would be crucified for every sin of which the South was blamed. The long history of the chivalric code, and the medieval laws of war governing captives bit the dust in that summer of 1864.

CHAPTER FOUR

"Joined the Post"

WHEN Captain Henry Clay Dickinson of the 2nd Virginia Cavalry arrived at Fort Delaware on June 25, 1864, he was relatively new to the role of prisoner of war. Captured at Yellow Tavern on May 11, the day Major General Jeb Stuart was mortally wounded, he had tried to escape numerous times, mostly through persuasion, which undoubtedly his work as a lawyer before the war had perfected.[1]

Dickinson spent his first weeks as a captive on various marches and boats, until confinement at Point Lookout, still recovering from a wound he received when captured. "The Point" as it was known, sat on the very tip of land of St. Marys County, Maryland, where the Potomac enters the Chesapeake Bay, and was simply a place of transfer for most of the officers brought there. Dickinson became friends with the first of many who would share the same fate, and was fortunate enough to receive good hospital care at Hammond Hospital where a case of food poisoning had put him. Point Lookout was extremely infamous for the cases of dysentery and diarrhea contracted there due to bad water.[2]

Point Lookout served as the first introduction of Captain Dickinson to Colonels Paul F. DeGournay and George Woolfolk, and four officers of the 4th South Carolina Cavalry, Captain Thomas Pinckney and Lieutenant David Gordon among them.

He only had to endure hardships there until about June 21, when he and approximately 600 other officers were shipped by boat to Fort Delaware, Delaware. Like many prisoners, Dickinson was constantly on the lookout for ways to freedom, and he immediately developed a plan to escape from the boat. The first few hours before going on board ship, he carefully picked thirteen accomplices for the purpose. Woolfolk and DeGournay would be in charge of operations, informing Dickinson and the others when to act.

All was set, they boarded the gunboat, but much to the captain's dismay one of the thirteen was missing. The plan was further complicated by their location below deck, with only two heavily guarded hatches to the upper deck. Whether the missing man had turned informant, or the guards' preparations routine, Dickinson did not know.

We who were of the thirteen did not even know all of the plan, but I knew that a special guard was detailed to seize the pilot and wheel, and another to take the engine; that five companies, of which mine was one, were to seize the guard on duty, whilst eight companies charged the guard off duty. One engineer, one pilot, all hands were nominated for their special duty. The signal of warning was, "These are hard times," when each captain was to get his squad well in hand; then at the word, "Liberty" the work was to be done . . . but when we were marched to the wharf, we found a gunboat with steam up, and, looking around, we missed our engineer, who at the last moment had been left behind. This looked still more suspicious, and then all hands of us, nearly six hundred officers, were ruthlessly thrust between decks . . . That our guards were apprised of our intended escape was now as certain as when they afterwards informed us that they knew all our plans . . . Escape was hopelessly impossible; we saw it, and submitted to our fate. In a few minutes the heat of our bodies generated a terrible atmosphere; men began to cry for water, water, air, air. We wrung the perspiration from our clothes, only to find it dripping off again in a few minutes. Some among so many suffering with diarrhoea asked to go to the water closet, but two only could go at once, and hence many relieved themselves in the hold of the vessel. Sleep was impossible, for the vessel did not contain room to lie down.

Thus we spent the slow hours from the evening of the twenty-first til mid-day of the twenty-fifth of June, when we disembarked at Fort Delaware. About fifty of us in all managed on the second day to get permission to stay on the top of the pilot house, but all of us, except Major Branch and one or two others, were either wounded or suffering with dysentery. My deliberate opinion is that no greater cruelty was ever practiced by any slaver. I shall never forget the horrors of the one night spent between those decks. Most fortunately the Atlantic was smooth as glass during the trip. If it had been even rough many of us must have died.[3]

CAPT. HENRY
DICKINSON,
2ND VA. CAV.

I never suffered any more in one night in my life. The heat was intense, and when we attempted to lie down, we had to lie across one another. Those at the bottom when their breath was almost mashed out of them would struggle to the top of this sweltering mass of humanity, to breathe, and thus catch a little sleep. No light was allowed, and any one trying to make their way to the open port had to walk across this living mass, and his progress was followed by a stream of imprecations and oaths.[4]

CAPT. THOMAS
PINCKNEY,
4TH S.C. CAV.

Another officer on the boat was Captain George Washington Nelson, known to friends and family as "Wash." Nelson was born into old aristocracy, and hailed from Clarke County, Virginia. He was captured at dinner with a friend, and confined at Old Capital Prison in Washington, D.C. before being sent to Point Lookout. There he divided his time between being a gymnastics instructor for the prisoners, and a lovesick youth writing letters to his girl Mollie Scollay in Shepherdstown, Virginia, trying to convince her to marry him.[5]

At the same time Captains Nelson, Dickinson and Pinckney were on their way to Fort Delaware, a twenty-one-year-old Louisianian, Captain Leon Jastremski, had already arrived—for the second time. Actually it was his third time as a prisoner of war.

He was first captured in the charge on Malvern Hill, a part of the Seven Days' Battles, on July 1, 1862. Sent to Fort Delaware, as a sergeant major he lived in the enlisted men's quarters, located within the fort. Soon he was exchanged, and captured a second time at Cedar Mountain a few weeks later. Exchanged within two weeks, he returned to his regiment, the 10th Louisiana, in time to take part in the Battle of Second Manassas, August 29, 1862, and was promoted to lieutenant of his company.[6]

His military career became sprinkled with famous places, such as Jackson's Valley Campaign, Antietam, Fredericksburg, Gettysburg, and Spotsylvania. At the latter place, the 10th held part of the crescent-shaped works known as the "Bloody Angle." It became a trap when Union forces attacked in a spearheaded charge on May 12, 1864. Once again, young Leon became a prisoner of war, and was sent to Fort Delaware. This time he was confined in the wooden officers' barracks outside the fort. Like Dickinson, whom he would meet shortly, Leon was constantly on the lookout for a way to escape.[7]

The new arrivals, or "fresh fish" as they were termed, probably received their first glimpse of Fort Delaware from the steamer *Salva*, one of the many ships pressed into service from a cargo steamer to a prison transport. Among them was a captain from Georgia, James Robert McMichael. He was twenty-six years old and living on his father's plantation in Buena Vista when Georgia left the Union. He had his photograph taken when he was elected second lieutenant of his company, and made a very military appearance at six feet, his auburn hair and blue eyes setting off his handsome features.

CAPT. JAMES ROBERT MCMICHAEL, 12TH GA. INF.

I was captured in battle near Spottsylvania Court House on the 10th of May, 1864. Under a strong and vigilant guard aboard the "Swan" and transferred from "Swan" to "Salva" at Fortress Monroe, and arrived at Fort Delaware, my present quarters, 17th of May, 1864. With me were brought about one hundred and fifty Confederate officers; among them are Lieutenant Col. Hardeman, Maj. Carson, Capt. Harris and six lieutenants of my regiment; also . . . about seventy distinguished officers of "Morgan's Crowd". I find them to be generous and kind.[8]

This fort is situated at the junction of the Brandywine with Dela-
ware River opposite Delaware City, and is built upon Pea Patch
Island, which contains about sixty acres and was formed, as I learn,
by the sinking of a Dutch ship loaded with peas. To us who had
seen neither grass or trees, the beautiful fields all the way up the
bay were most refreshing.

CAPT. HENRY
DICKINSON,
2ND VA. CAV.

The island was evidently much smaller when the fort was built on
its eastern or New Jersey edge, as there is considerable ground to
the north and west of it. A levee is constructed around the whole
island, but the spring tides sometimes carry the water over the
walls. The officers' gardens, I noticed, were in a high state of cul-
tivation; indeed, they ought to be, being of alluvial soil, and irri-
gated by the ditches which convey the water into the moat around
the fort. The fort walls were of granite or brown stone, quadran-
gular, and built for three tiers of guns. I expect if necessary two
hundred guns could be mounted. I counted once about seventy in
the western wall, besides twelve large guns on the parapet. The
officers' quarters, etc., were within the fort and made of brick. A
bridge with a draw led to the fort on the west side. When we
landed after much delay, we were marched on a lawn near the
hospitals, where we were counted, rolls were called and a full search
was made. I hid my money and valuables in the grass till the search
was over.[9]

Standing in line under the watchful eye of enemies, Dickinson was more
than likely thinking of his former life before the war, feeling his freedom
slipping away. Maybe his wife and four young daughters, back in Liberty,
Virginia were foremost in his thoughts. A fifth "little Miss Dickinson" was
born the very day he left Point Lookout. He would not learn of her birth for
several months. Now in enemy territory as a prisoner, he surely wondered
when he would see his family again.[10]

Dickinson settled into the routine of life at Fort Delaware. He was fortunate to find old friends from his native Bedford County; men he had known
before they all joined their respective arms of the service in 1861. Most
were foot soldiers. Dickinson was a cavalryman, and at age thirty-four, was
older than the average prisoner. Among the officers living in the barracks,
he became acquainted with men from all across the South. Little could he
know at that time, how their lives would become entwined, strengthening
each other morally and spiritually for a supreme test of endurance.

The commander of the garrison was Brigadier General Albin F. Schoepf.
He was given command on April 14, 1863 and was directly responsible for
all conditions or mishaps at Fort Delaware, which housed 10,000 men at
that time. Northern officials knew that the prison conditions there were
unhealthy and despicable. The prison barracks built outside the fort were
on marshy ground and the foundations sank while being constructed.[11]

It was in these barracks, referred to as divisions, that the line officers were quartered, the field and general officers being kept inside the fort. Known as the "Bull Pen," it comprised two acres, surrounded by a high wooden fence. This compound was divided by another fence, which was topped by a parapet, walked continually by sentries. On one side of this dividing fence, the privates lived. The other side contained the officers' barracks, a series of low buildings which measured about three hundred feet long. These were divided in sheds, forty-two feet long by twenty-three feet wide and twelve feet high. One stove provided the only heat for the drafty, plank-walled rooms.

Life was centered around a strict daily regimen. The divisions were each lit by a globe lamp, hung to a wire in the center of the room and kept burning all night. Private lights were allowed for reading until 9:00 p.m. bugle call. If not extinguished at once, the men were reprimanded, and some guards were insolent and punishing. Each division was broken into messes of from eight to ten officers each and numbered. Every man knew his place and went to it. There was also a chief appointed who superintended the dining room, appointed meetings, and kept an orderly way of life. There was a postmaster for each division, who attended roll call and brought back mail, and a money clerk who went to money call. Funds sent to prisoners were removed from their letters, recorded, and sutler's checks substituted for the cash. Boxes from home were allowed if permits were applied for in advance, and attached to the outside of the box, listing its contents. Anything not listed was confiscated by prison officials, who checked each box when received. Only one suit of clothes was allowed each man. Consequently there was much abuse by the officials, and many prisoners complained of not receiving what was sent to them.

An adjutant was also appointed to act as secretary at all meetings and to make sure the division was policed and swept twice a day, and the drinking water buckets kept full. Newspapers were limited to only one *Philadelphia Enquirer* in the pen at a time.[12]

While they could officially blame Schoepf for the bad conditions, the most despised officers were Lieutenant George Ahl, adjutant to General Schoepf, and Lieutenant George Wolff, who were directly responsible for all that occurred inside the prison. Known by such names as "Awful Ahl" and aided by a petty criminal and Federal deserter known as "Hackout," their reputations were recorded by the prisoners as abusive and unfair.

CAPT. HENRY DICKINSON, 2ND VA. CAV.

The presiding genius of this place was a fat old Dutchman speaking English badly, by rank a brigadier general and named A. Schoepf, pronounced Sheff. He was promoted for killing Gen. Zollicoffer, but I learned he did not like to be complimented for this act. So far as administrative ability went he was totally unfitted to command. He had neither tact, judgement or system. The veriest simpleton in Dixie would have reduced the plan of governing the prison to more order and simplicity.

His wife was said to be a strong sympathizer with the South, and
I have been told by high authority that Schoepf himself desired to
be kindly disposed toward the prisoners, but feared his adjutant
general, [G].W. Ahl, who was the real head of the establishment.
Ahl was a New England Abolitionist and had a company of artillery made up of deserters. Of course he had no friendship for a
"Reb", and receiving his appointment from Abraham the First, he
ruled Schoepf as he chose . . . I have many reasons to believe that
Schoepf was not as good as the most partial represent him, though
it is possible that the abuses existed because of a want of system,
added to the influence of Ahl. On one occasion, when the ration
was exhibited to him in person, he seemed surprised and professed
his determination to correct it at once. On the next day all the
knives, forks and plates were removed and for two subsequent
days we got no meat for breakfast. Those who aver that Schoepf
was disposed to treat us kindly say that Schoepf did order an improvement and hauled the commissary over the coals, who, knowing that his act would not be discovered, wreaked his spite on us.

Schoepf's right hand man was Lt. Wolfe, who had been promoted
from a sergeant for his fidelity and business qualities. This fellow
was a shuffling, hurrying, business-looking man, but in reality
had no idea of business, and was besides too fond of whiskey. The
obsequiousness of many officers gave Wolfe great consequence
and his daily entry into the pen was the signal for a rush for favors, news, etc. Wolfe was the eye and ear of our camp; he examined every letter, and consequently his power was supreme. Abuses
might exist, Wolfe or his tools might perpetrate any cruelty with
impunity, for no one knew anything except through him.[13]

General Schoepf, U.S.V., commandant of the post, was a German, *CAPT. J. OGDEN MURRAY, 11TH VA. CAV.*
in his way a very good sort of an old fellow who, no doubt, did all
he dare do, if report is correct, to alleviate the condition of Confederate prisoners of war. But he had about him some very mean,
low men and prison officials. It was the general report amongst
the prisoners of war that General Schoepf's wife was a Virginia
lady who was in sympathy with her State and people. For this
reason the General was not given a command in the field, but
assigned to command of Fort Delaware prison that he might be
kept under surveillance from Washington City. Report also said
Capt. A.A. Ahl, his Asst. Adjt. General, was forced upon him as a
spy, and was not at all agreeable to the General. Ahl was the moni-
tor placed over him by Secretary of War Stanton. If this report be
true or false I do not know; but this I do know, that Captain Ahl
did most intensely hate Confederate prisoners of war, and it is

*susceptible of proof that all the drastic orders issued for the gov-
ernment of Fort Delaware military prison were the conceptions
and work of this fellow Ahl, and their enforcement compelled by
his diction and domination over General Schoepf. While Fort Delaware prison was a hell upon earth for both officers and men . . . it
is said by prisoners of war confined in other Northern prisons to
be the best of the lot.*

*The assistant provost-marshal in charge of the officers' prison at
Fort Delaware was a Dutchman, Lt. Woolf, a graduate from the
slums of Philadelphia City, a coarse, brutal creature, with all the
mean, cowardly, and cruel instincts of the beast from which his
name was taken; . . . who took much delight in insulting the Confederate officers that the misfortunes of war had made prisoners. . . .
His assistants were as miserable fellows as himself. Aided by these
assistants . . . this fellow Woolf made the prison of the Confederate
enlisted men a veritable torture-house. After taps were sounded I
would often, with the aid of Lt. Bob Bowie and Capt. Tom Roche,
my bunk-mates, steal into the enlisted men's camp next to ours
separated by a high board fence, and hear from the men the story
of the atrocious treatment this fellow [Wolff], Hackout and the other
scoundrels would inflict upon the helpless sick and poor Confederate prisoners of war, who could not make complaint, for the reason their complaints never got further than Captain Ahl, who never
brought the matter to Gen. Schoepf's attention.*[14]

Prison life proved to be a blend of ingenuity, creativity, and a constant
battle against monotony and trigger-happy guards. Treated like criminals,
though their only crime was love of their country and dedication to a cause,
most prisoners suffered humiliation and mistreatment at the hands of their
captors. The only constant was the painful uncertainty of when release would
come. The daily drudgery never varied.

The roll was not called, supposedly because it was deemed unnecessary.[15] Two meals were served a day, breakfast at 8:00 a.m. and dinner at
2:00 p.m., but the times were not strictly adhered to. The food was too little
in quantity and nothing to brag of in quality. Twice a day, the men lined up
and marched into a common mess hall, where they were served and either
stood and ate there, or took it back to their bunks.

CAPT. HENRY
DICKINSON,
2ND VA. CAV.

*Breakfast consisted of a cup of water, about four ounces of light
bread, and say five ounces of pork. Several times the pork was
omitted. At dinner we were given a small amount of bread and
meat, and, in addition, we received a pint of bean soup. This soup
was generally burned, and always made of old beans; altogether, it
was the most nefarious stuff I ever tasted. The fresh beef was fat
and could have been made good, but it was killed the day previous*

and brought into the pen about 9:00 a.m. covered with a swarm of green flies, and often was so tainted that it could not be eaten. Many of the officers, of course, had friends in the North, who sent them various articles of food, so that not a few of us never saw the table.[16]

While at the Old Capital Prison we were well treated, and the rations were all we could wish. At Fort Delaware it was very different. The rations were badly cooked and scarcely sufficient in quantity to sustain life, besides being very inferior in quality. There were only two meals a day; breakfast at eight a.m., and dinner at four p.m. We got to Fort Delaware in the afternoon. I was not feeling very well and did not go to dinner. We had some rations brought from Washington. Captain Horton went, and the first thing he said when he came back was, "Take care of that meat, it is as scarce as hen's teeth here." In truth it was very, very scarce.[17]

Capt. William
Morgan,
11th Va. Inf.

As long as the men had money, they were allowed to buy from Union sutlers provided for the purpose. The prices were often outrageous, although they were supposed to sell to the prisoners at the same price they sold to Union soldiers. Those who did not have friends on the outside to send them money and goods, resorted to their wits to raise the necessary capital in various ways. The prison officials never seemed to mind these enterprises, possibly because it kept men from spending their time planning an escape.

The clothes were washed in the main ditch, within a few feet of the sink, which was so filthy that the clothes never could look clean, but our "washwomen" by ironing, improved the general appearance very much. These "washwomen" were brother officers who, being out of funds, did this work as a support, and the great number produced such competition that washing a garment only cost five cents and ironing five cents.[18]

Capt. Henry
Dickinson,
2nd Va. Cav.

One of these "washwomen" was Second Lieutenant Joseph W. Mauck of the 10th Virginia Infantry. Funds were hard to come by and the many notations in his diary speak for themselves. "Money out, hard times again." He noted on August 1, "Out of tobacco, out of money, out of humor." He had been at Fort Delaware for over a month, and was an old hand at life there. His talent as a jewelry maker was another way of earning money, and knowing new tenants meant a new shipment of items sought after in prison, he was eager to make acquaintances.[19]

A goodly number became jewelry-makers, the material in every case being gutta-percha. Many made rough, uncouth articles, which they never could improve; others having "form" highly developed, fashioned many little articles elegantly and thereby supported themselves handsomely. The Yankees had a mania for seal rings,

Capt. Henry
Dickinson,
2nd Va. Cav.

*breast-pins, etc., and gave good prices. . . . The rings were made of
common gutta-percha buttons, boiled to bring out the shape. The
watch seals and chains were made of tubes of gutta-percha, the
sets were brass, silver and gold tin-foil, copper, or more generally
the shell of the mussel found at Mussel Shoals, in the Tennessee
River. Any shell, however, polishes easily, and looks like the finest
pearl. The stock in trade of a ring-maker was a common knife, a
rat-tail and a few other small files, a small hammer, some awls
made of needles, a piece of sandpaper, and a piece of leather
greased and rubbed in the shell dust or emery. We had one cob-
bler and one tailor in the pen, each of whom was kept busy in his
line, generally mending and patching.*[20]

CAPT. THOMAS
PINCKNEY,
4TH S.C. CAV.

*The most popular industry was the making of finger rings, from
horn or tortoise shell combs, which was most ingeniously inlaid
with bits of pearl or ivory, such as could be obtained from knife
handles of the "fresh fish" before they became aware of the prison
value of these much desired articles.*[21]

Other enterprising individuals ran beer, lemonade or food stands selling ginger and lemon cakes. Some plied their talents as barbers and hair-
dressers, creating a self-supporting community within the prison sustained
by the funds received from the outside.

Their free time was spent in pursuits of any pleasure obtainable, and
mostly included reading, writing letters home, or playing games. All the
capital generated inside inevitably led to the opening of an establishment
where games of chance claimed much of the hard-earned cash.

CAPT. HENRY
DICKINSON,
2ND VA. CAV.

*The gambling saloons were a curious feature in prison, and were
not only numerous but well patronized. Captain Coffee, of Mississippi, was the prince of faro dealers, being always gentlemanly in
his manners and always attracting the greatest crowd. He never
played cards until he was captured, except for amusement, and I
am told that a Yankee guard was his first victim. The bettor wa-
gered in either Confederate or Yankee money. He always had a
large and anxious looking crowd around his booth. Some quarter-
masters having been captured, the amount of Confederate money
in prison was very large, and changed hands frequently. I heard
that Coffee once sent to Dixie from Point Lookout ten thousand
dollars. How much United States money he made I cannot say,
though at one time, when the Yanks were about searching quarters and persons, he hid in the grass one hundred and eleven dollars in gold, a gold watch, and several hundred dollars in notes,
which, of course, some Yank, who knew he was flush, had seen
him hide and took care to not let him find it again. Many men in
prison wrote letters for money of the most importune character,*

and when the money was received it was at once deposited in this bank. Some sent for clothing which they sold or raffled off, that they might invest with Coffee.[22]

After the war, Captain Holland Coffee found this experience helpful, and pursued a successful banking career in Tennessee. The prisoners played many other games still popular today, although known by different names. "Keno" is described exactly like "bingo" and was played the same. Officers who were opposed to gambling played whist (a kind of bridge), backgammon, or chess which became the rage. Marbles were played "almost every day" and "a game of base"—or baseball. Debating societies and dancing lessons improved many social graces.

Strong friendships were made, as the men lived so close, two sharing one bunk. The bunks were built in three tiers along the walls of each division, quartering around one hundred men. Henry Dickinson lived in Division 32, along with Lieutenant Colonel DeGournay, Captain Griffin, and others. Captains William Morgan and Thomas B. Horton shared a bunk. Major William Emanuel, Captain Pinckney, Lieutenants David Gordon and William Epps all shared adjoining bunks. Like many bunkmates, they were all of the same regiment, the 4th South Carolina Cavalry.

In Division 31 lived another South Carolinian, Second Lieutenant Samuel T. Anderson. He graduated from Medical School in 1860, with high honors. The young doctor joined the 1st South Carolina Cavalry as a private, serving with distinction in the ranks, and was promoted to lieutenant when he reenlisted after one year. In December 1862, he went home on furlough to return a comrade who had been killed. While there he took the opportunity to marry his fiancee and spend Christmas together. The next day he returned to his regiment in Virginia, and was captured six months later.[23]

It had been nearly eighteen months since he had seen his bride. With his medical training he did what he could for his brother officers, though he had no medicine to prescribe, and was denied official permission to practice in prison to aid the suffering men.

Being a prisoner of war was far more difficult than being on the battle line. Prison life was harsh and taxing, and it took more courage to uphold principles under the pressure of confinement than under fire. Disease made death in prison as likely as death in combat. As a consequence, religion flourished and most men attended prayer meetings, some becoming divinity students because of the introduction to it in prison.[24]

July 15, 1864.- Up to this time nothing of much interest deserves record. Our society is very good. We have religious services twice a day, and Masonic meetings of instruction once a week. I have written home one page—all that I was allowed to write. I also wrote to T.C. Brown of Kentucky hoping that he would be able and willing to assist me in this time of need, but unfortunate for me he was in

CAPT. JAMES
ROBERT
McMICHAEL,
12TH GA. INF.

Georgia, but his good wife received my letter and immediately sent me $5.00 with which I purchased vegetables to keep clear of scurvy.[25]

Living above the sally-port of the fort, were confined the political prisoners. One was a minister from Portsmouth, Virginia, Reverend Isaac W. Handy, who spent from June 1863 to October 1864, observing and writing about life at Fort Delaware. He was also available to all officers confined inside the fort for religious services, and came to know many of the men who lived there.[26]

The summer months dragged slowly by, the heat and sickness related to them depleting the ranks of the prisoners. A smallpox epidemic swept the camp and many died. On 6 July, a photographer from Philadelphia visited Fort Delaware, and many officers used the occasion to unpack their dress uniforms and have their pictures taken. Some men whose coats were not as presentable as they would like them to be were fortunate that the photographer happened to have several Confederate "prop" coats of generic design. Spirits received a lift from this little diversion, and many carte de visites were sent home to loved ones.

Aside from that, nothing occurred to vary the monotony except what little entertainment the men found for themselves, and the highly prized letters from home. Their letters were subject to inspection, and the men were so prolific in their correspondence that General Schoepf limited their messages to one page, as it took too many clerks to work as censors otherwise. Many of the letters were similar to that of Captain Leon Jastremski, who maintained a correspondence with his brother:

LETTER, CAPT. LEON JASTREMSKI, 10TH LA. INF., TO BROTHER, JOHN, JULY 19, 1864

Ere this you will have received my letters dated 29 June, the other July 6th, acknowledging the receipt of your remittance. Hereafter it will only be from time to time that I shall need call on you for money to purchase some necessaries. When you answer this, let me know whether you received the letters which I sent you last January and April.

It has been so long a time since you heard from me that you do not know anything of my career. I was wounded on the 3rd of May 1863 at Chancellorsville by a fragment of shell which struck me in the throat. It has altered my voice greatly and renders it very hoarse. I was also wounded slightly in the right hand at Gettysburg and lastly again slightly at Spotsylvania. I have participated in fifteen different engagements.

Enclosed you will find a small breast pin, the work of a fellow prisoner, which you will give to my little niece as a remembrance of her uncle. Give my love to my sister and to Mrs. Keays. Hoping to hear from you soon.

P.S. Let me hear from the family in your next and do not forget my niece. I will send you my daguerrotype as soon as I can.[27]

Yours of the 18th [sic] was received enclosing the breast pin which Ernestine appreciates a great deal. She asked me whether her uncle Leon was a little boy and if you were farther than New Orleans & when I told her that you were a Confederate officer she wanted to know if you were dressed in blue.

The letters which you sent me in January and April were received by me but not finding an opportunity to answer you I could not write nor send money you asked for.

The family are all well. In my last I wrote you that I could not for the present send you the money you asked for, but I think that in a short time I will be able to send you fifty dollars. Be assured that so soon as I will be able I will do so with the greatest of pleasure. For I am always pleased to accommodate you & whatever I can do for you will be done cheerfully.

In my last letter I send you a photograph of my little girl which you will have received before this reaches you. Hoping this war will soon be over & that you may come home, for my home will always be yours.

P.S. I send you my photograph. Send yours in your next, if possible.[28]

LETTER, JOHN JASTREMSKI, BATON ROUGE, TO CAPT. LEON JASTREMSKI, AUG. 6, 1864

For those men who could not correspond with family in Dixie, or whose family had no resources to send, sympathizers in the North alleviated the need. Most of these were women, from Baltimore, Philadelphia and New York. A regular pen-pal relationship grew between those women and the Confederate officers, many of whom received money, food, and clothing through the generosity of compassionate Northerners.

Melissa Baker was one example of this kindness. She met several of the officers captured at Gettysburg in 1863, visiting them in Letterman Hospital and nursing them there until they were transferred to Baltimore. A regular correspondence was kept up with some of the men as prisoners when they were moved to Fort Delaware. First Lieutenant Sanford Branch was one of her patients:

If I had known where to direct a letter I should certainly have written before this, and have been wishing so much to know how you were getting along. I was very much engaged at the time I received your last, and then waited to reply untill I had a box ready—and I was so disappointed when my boxes were returned to me from town, the order prohibiting them and also letters, having just been issued. I had a box for Major Goldsborough, and for Lieuts. Coon and Cowper. I regretted it the more as they were the first I had sent since they had been at Fort Delaware, but it is scarcely worth mentioning now. George [her brother] received a letter from Lieut. Cowper this week and I was very glad to know

LETTER, MELISSA BAKER TO LT. SANFORD BRANCH, 8TH GA. INF., 24 SEPT. 1864

where you were to be found and take the earliest opportunity of
writing . . . I have no fear but what you will again see your Mother
and hope to hear very soon of your exchange. . . . How very anxious
you must be to get home, do you hear from your Mother still? Will
you all forget to write to us after you reach home? I must hope
better things, though we have never received one yet from Dixie.
All your friends at "Athol" are well—Mrs. Baker goes still to see
after Lieuts. Ferguson and Campbell, they have been sick all sum-
mer, and very little hope for the recovery of the latter. Remember
me very kindly to all of our friends—tell Lieut. Breedlove he never
replied to my last. . . . Believe me your constant friend, M. Baker.[29]

Another correspondent was a young husband and father from Missouri,
Captain Moses J. Bradford. He joined the Confederate army in a state whose
sentiments were divided. Consequently, his family suffered when he was
declared a guerrilla by Union authorities and captured on July 4, 1863. He
wrote to the Federal provost marshal, requesting his family be safely escorted out of Union territory under Federal orders. From Fort Delaware, he
reassured his wife, and reflected on his situation:

CAPT. MOSES J.
BRADFORD, CO. G,
10TH MO. INF.,
TO MALISSA
BRADFORD,
JULY 3, 1864

Thank God I can say to you that I am well and hope these few lines
will find you all well. . . . I will write as often as I can while in
prison. Tomorrow will be one year that I have been in this horable
condition a prisoner. I cannot give you the least idea of such a life.
My heart has been gladened to know that I am not forgoten by
those that are most near to me. . . . Give my love to all for they are
not forgoten. I remain your husband truely, M.J. Bradford.[30]

Under such circumstances it was not surprising that when news
reached the officers that there would be a group selected for
exchange, spirits soared. Joy unsurpassed by anything except
news that the South had won the war, spread like wildfire among
the men. Hope and speculation filled the hours, and discussions
on who the lucky ones would be were more popular than the
debating society's topics.

REV. ISSAC
HANDY

Friday, Aug. 12th.- Great excitement has prevailed all day, in
consequence of a rumor, that six hundred officers are to embark,
to-morrow, for Hilton Head, South Carolina. Gen. Schoepf came
into "the pen" early this morning, attended by several assistants,
and remained during the calling of the roll. This is the first time
he has ever been present (since I have been in the barracks) on
such an occasion. Before he went out, he informed two officers
that they would be exchanged in a day or two, with many others.
This statement, with some conversations overheard among the
sentinels, and an order to a driver about his cart being needed to

carry bread to the boat, seems to settle the matter. Indeed, Lt. Andrews has assured me, that a Federal officer says the move will be made shortly, if not to-morrow. What hope! What buoyancy! How anxious are the thousands here imprisoned, to get back once more to friends and home! [31]

Through that incomprehensible means that cannot be defined nor explained, and is only known to prisoners of war, we, confined in the officers' camp . . . became possessed of the knowledge that there was to be an exchange of prisoners of war. We seldom saw a paper; they were not allowed us. If a letter was written a prisoner that contained the least particle of information about the outside world save that which pertained strictly to family affairs it never reached the prisoner to whom it was written. Yet news would get into our camp, and we called such news "grape." One day in August, 1864, news spread over the camp that the fifty general and field officers that had been sent in June to Charleston Harbor, S.C. had been exchanged, and that a general exchange of prisoners of war, which had been stopped, would now be resumed, and very soon we would all be back in Dixie. . . . The Yankee sergeant who called the prison roll confirmed this "grape", but gave no time as to when the exchange would begin or where it would take place. After this confirmation by the Yankee sergeant the only topic of conversation amongst the prisoners was exchange. The man who did not believe this "grape" of exchange was looked upon by his fellow-prisoners as a man to be watched—a skeptic beyond reformation. [32]

CAPT. J. OGDEN
MURRAY,
11TH VA. CAV.

Saturday, 13th.- A day of great excitement. At an early hour the Sergeant came in, and announced that the names of such persons as were to be sent off would soon be called, in the yard. All hands were up in a trice; and soon Gen. Schoepf, Capt. Ahl, and sundry clerks, with sergeants and guards, made their appearance. Orders were given to stand on the left of the long walk, running through the middle of the open area. Calls were made first for field officers; and then for captains and lieutenants, running down the rolls in an irregular manner, into the M's, and taking a few scattering names farther on in the alphabet. Upon what principle the elections were made, it is impossible to tell. Many were made glad; many were disappointed. One man said it made him think of the Day of Judgement. It was certainly very solemn, to see the crowds separating, some to the right, and others remaining on the left. Circumstances indicated the deep feeling, either of joy or regret, experienced by the mass. [33]

REV. ISSAC
HANDY

Engraving of Fort Delaware Prison.

Diary of Captain Henry C. Dickinson
Capt. Henry Clay Dickinson
Co. A, 2nd Virginia Cavalry.

Courtesy Mr. Thomas Pinckney II
Capt. Thomas Pinckney
Co. D, 4th South Carolina Cavalry.
Photograph taken 1870.

Courtesy Mrs. William Emanuel
Maj. William Pledger Emanuel
Co. D, 4th South Carolina Cavalry.

Special Collections L.S.U.
Capt. Leon Jastremski
Co. E & H, 10th Louisiana Infantry.
He escaped from the *Illinois* prison
ship March 13, 1865. Photo taken c.
1863.

Atlanta History Center
The Branch Brothers of Savannah, Ga.
John, killed at First Manassas. Hamilton,
and Sanford, all of the Oglethorpe Light
Infantry, later the 8th Georgia.

The Immortal Six-Hundred
Capt. John Ogden Murray
Co. A., 11th Virginia Cavalry.
Wrote *The Immortal Six-Hundred*
in 1905.

CAPT. J. OGDEN
MURRAY,
11TH VA. CAV.

We soon fell into line, the roll call began and went on, while the prisoners stood in death-like silence awaiting the call of their names, each man showing on his face the hope of his heart; each asking God, in silent, earnest prayer, that his name would be called. I have looked into the faces of men in line before a battle, when defeat seemed inevitable; I have seen the joy of victory take the place of doubt; but never in all my life did I witness joy so perfect as in the face of the man whose name was called, nor woe so abject as on the face of the men whose names were passed over.... When the M's were called on the roll I could hardly contain myself; when my name was called I could have shouted for joy; and I really felt sorry that all my comrades were not included in the list, as we thought, for exchange. And yet the sequel proved that those whose names were upon the list were the unfortunates, and not those whose names had been passed over.[34]

CAPT. THOMAS
PINCKNEY,
4TH S.C. CAV.

I had indulged in no hope of getting out as there were some of Morgan's and Forrest's Cavalrymen, whom I knew had been in prison for two and three years, but my heart began to bound when I recognized the names of men who had been captured with me, and skipping down our roll the last name called was "Pinckney, 4th South Carolina Cavalry". I jumped out of the window where I was sitting—not taking time to go round by the door, and hastened across the line.[35]

CAPT. JAMES
ROBERT
MCMICHAEL,
12TH GA. INF.

Saturday, August 13th.- Early roll call. Commence calling out the field officers that are to be sent off. Next captains, alphabetically. Some are left who have been in prison nearly two years. With great anxiety I listen to hear my name called, and when they got to the M's (to my great relief) but one was more fortunate than I. We were soon ready to start, but Sunday 14th finds us still in the barracks waiting.[36]

LETTER, FIRST
LT. SANFORD
BRANCH,
8TH GA. INF.,
TO HIS MOTHER
CHARLOTTE
BRANCH,
AUG. 1864

I wrote you a few days ago, but as there will probably be a flag of truce in a few days will write a few lines well knowing how welcome my careless letters are to you. I am in excellent health and spirits. I am one of the fortunate ones selected to be sent somewhere and as a change is always acceptable to a prisoner have concluded not to let anyone go in my place although have had several applications. Have just finished my evening repast. Fine ham and onions, sweet potatoes, and tomatoes prepared by myself. I am preparing myself to take charge of your culinary affairs. I can promise greater economy in fuel and materials than any artist you have ever had in your kitchen. I can bring satisfactory references. In writting be particular to address to Division 22, as there are several others of our illustrious name here. Your affectionate son.[37]

Days passed; the suspense heightened, then cooled. The 600 names on the list became a kind of celebrity group. At first it was simply called "the Six Hundred" to distinguish it and to fill conversations. Other terms were the "rumor roll" and the "que vive" list. The "grape" was that they were to be sent to Charleston like the fifty officers the previous month, to be placed under fire. Everyone knew that episode resulted in an exchange, and this was the accepted expectation of the Six Hundred. Nothing further happened, except that the roll was called twice more, as if to make certain of its members, on August 15 and 16. A few changed places with those whose names were on the list. Joseph Mauck was one, taking the number of Maurice Guiheen, 10th Virginia Infantry. Four others managed to bribe the lucky men of their opportunity. Many, anticipating leaving as the chosen ones, began saying their good-byes, and visits to Reverend Handy to give their lives to God, showed perhaps a sense of foreboding by some as one of those picked.

Tuesday, 16th.- ... I have been holding a sort of levee for several days, so many persons having been calling to see me, in anticipation of their expected exodus from the Fort. Many of these are persons with whom I have, heretofore, had little or no acquaintance; and in some instances I have regretted, exceedingly, that so little has been known of them before.[38]

REV. ISAAC HANDY

Finally, the morning of August 20, 1864, dawned hot and sunny. Something was afoot, and all had noticed the bustle and activity as provisions were carted to the boat, much of the work done by fellow prisoners from the privates' quarters.

The Six Hundred were ordered to be ready to go immediately. Each soldier carefully packed the few belongings he had managed to retain through all the moves from prison to prison. The most cherished items were cleverly hidden during searches, and always safely carried through the many changes of transports and prison barracks. The few remaining clothes and tattered blankets, which had been worn thin with much wash and wear, were the remnants of a former life of finery, and in many cases substantial wealth. Books, letters, a few pots and pans, toiletries, and the sabers they had been allowed to retain as officers, would complete all earthly possessions of comfort and pleasure.

I am one of a party of six hundred Confederate States officers who have this day been ordered to hold themselves in readiness to leave this place today. We are to be sent to Charleston, SC, for the purpose, I believe, of being placed under the fire of the Confederate batteries in retaliation for an equal number of Federal officers who have been placed in the city of Charleston, and are said to be exposed to the shelling of their own guns. I am glad of this move as it will be a diversion to the monotonous life led in prison. Little danger is to be apprehended from this movement. Indeed I am

LETTER, CAPT. LEON JASTREMSKI, 10TH LA. INF., TO BROTHER, JOHN, AUG. 20, 1864 *more inclined to think that it will lead to an exchange. Do not send me anything until you hear again from me. Present my love to my sister—also to Mrs. Keays, and kiss my niece from me, etc, etc. I shall write to you as soon as I reach my destination.*[39]

REV. ISSAC
HANDY

Saturday, 20th.- The roll was called, and every man took his place in the ranks, according to the number assigned him about a week ago. Much misunderstanding arose about the baggage. First, there seemed to be an order to take it into the ranks, and then to lay it down a few yards in front. Having repeatedly gone through the operation of being laid down and taken up, it was finally conveyed to the boat, in carts. After long delay—all being ready—the guards took their places, and the command was given to march through the sally-port, to the west end of the "bull-pen".[40]

CAPT. J. OGDEN
MURRAY,
11TH VA. CAV.

At 3 o'clock p.m., August 20th, the order came "Fall into line all you men whose names shall be called and be ready for exchange." The roll-call was made, five hundred and fifty sound, healthy men, and fifty wounded men fell into line and marched by fours out through the prison gate. While we stood in line in the prison yard awaiting the order to move there were some most pathetic as well as ridiculous scenes enacted between comrades who had stood in line of battle together, were captured together, and now one was going home, the other to remain a captive. We were saying good-bye, telling those we left behind to be of good heart, that it would be but a few days before they would join us in Dixie. We of that six hundred can now look back and laugh at the promises then made, some of them of the most impossible character. I recall one promise made . . . that was just as soon as we put foot in Richmond we were all to go in a body to President Davis and Congress and demand that our comrades in Fort Delaware should be sent for at once . . . I remember now Capt. George Kurtz, Company K, 5th Va. Inf., Stonewall Brigade. . . . As he reached me he said, "Ogden," and the great big tears began to run down his cheeks, "when you get back to the Valley I want you to get Harry Gilmore and a lot of the old brigade; get all you can, go down the Valley, capture Sheridan and hold him until you get me out of this place." Of course I promised to comply with his request, and we sealed the compact with a kiss. During this scene my eyes were not dry nor was my heart joyous in leaving behind me in prison grand old comrades I had learned to love.[41]

CAPT. THOMAS
PINCKNEY,
4TH S.C. CAV.

It did not take long to make our preparation, so as soon as the gates were opened on the 20th, with my frying pan on my shoulder, without which I never travelled, and with a biscuit box be-

tween Lt. Epps and myself, containing our few extra articles of clothing, some tin plates, cups, etc. we fell into the line.[42]

Saturday, 20th.- All were delighted with the prospect of "home again;" but there was not a heart there, that did not swell with emotion, in the prospect of immediate, and perhaps final separation, from friends and fellow-sufferers in that damp and murky "pen".

REV. ISSAC
HANDY

As the noble fellows marched out, I stood at the opening of the sally-port, as near by as the guards would allow, and until the very last man disappeared from the enclosure. "Good-bye! Goodbye!" was uttered, time and again, as the files moved on; and I could do nothing but return farewells, as some one or more in every rank would wave the parting salutation. . . . A number of them were zealous Christians; several of them young converts; most of them respecters of religion; and a majority, I think, men of unusually good morals. I felt sad, and more than once were my eyes in danger of betraying the deep welling within. Prayers went up to Heaven for the safety and happiness of the brave fellows, and we shall hope to hear soon of their arrival among friends at the South. . . . Several officers purchased their exchange. One—Lt. Mastin, of Alabama—gave a gold watch, which cost three hundred dollars in coin before the war. Two other gentlemen gave watches of less value. In some instances exchanges were made between the men themselves. . . . Some very strange and corrupt things will yet come to light, in regard to this exchange.[43]

Map No. 1

Richard S. Joslyn

Federal Prisons
where men of the Immortal Six Hundred were confined.

Chapter Five

"Rebel Officers"

THE *Crescent City* was an old sidewheel steamship, previously used as a cargo freighter in New Orleans. Before the war, she sailed a regular route between that city and Galveston, Texas, loaded with freight. Some of the same crew that worked her then were still on board in 1864. The ship had been pressed into service by the Union, and outfitted specifically as a prisoner transport. No doubt most of the Louisiana officers on board smiled fondly at the memories of their home in New Orleans which the old ship's name brought forth. The second deck, between the hold and top deck, consisted of a series of "shelves" built around the sides, four tiers high, to serve as berths for the prisoners to sleep. It was very crowded, four men to a bunk, with only two feet of space between the tiers.

The troops in charge as guards were the 110th and 157th Ohio militia, home guard regiments. Most prison guard units in the Union army were either inexperienced in battle, and used for less dangerous service, or were the newly organized black troops, which by 1864 were just beginning to see extensive use in the Federal army. Putting them in charge of Confederate prisoners was intended to be seen by the prisoners as an insult—former servants now in power over their "betters." It must be kept in context that the attitudes then were universal about the class system being directly tied to race, not peculiar only to the South. This attitude knew no geographical bounds. In many cases Union officers chose to put black troops in guard service because they thought them inferior for combat.[1]

A Captain Webster was in charge of the 110th Ohio, and Captain James H. Prentiss commanded the 157th. They were a nervous lot of 200 green troops, responsible for keeping in line 600 battle-toughened Confederate officers who had seen three to four years of service, having been in action at places famous even then—Antietam, Chancellorsville, Gettysburg, and Spotsylvania among them. There was an immediate resentment between captives and guards. The "100-day men" were looked down on as shirkers, having no nerve for battle.[2] They in turn scorned the prisoners as an inferior lot to be despised as the enemy.

The *Crescent City* itself was under separate civilian command, Captain Daniel D. Latham in charge. He had been in charge of the ship since the early days of the war. His First Mate John M. Brown had known Latham since 1861, but Second Mate William Baxter was new to the crew, only on board since July.[3]

After marching through the sally-port at Fort Delaware, the band of Six Hundred could not have felt happier. Visions of happiness filled every mind with thoughts of wives or sweethearts, friends and family. They were game for anything, knowing freedom and home were at the end of the journey. It was around 4:00 p.m. on the afternoon of August 20 when they marched aboard the *Crescent City*, taking their places in the hold. Many men kept diaries, and as they sailed recorded their experiences of the voyage.

CAPT. JAMES
ROBERT
McMICHAEL,
12TH GA. INF.

Saturday, August 20.- Bade farewell to friends in the barracks, and marched out to the wharf and then crowded with six hundred officers in the hold of the U.S. Steamer Crescent. *I felt proud to know that I was released from the guard and the walls of Delaware prison; yet, I was not free, no not free; glittering bayonets were still around me. About 5 p.m. the anchor weighed, we left the island so long to be remembered, and started to Charleston; then I bade farewell to Fort Delaware.*[4]

CAPT. GEORGE
W. NELSON, VA.
HANOVER ARTY.

Bunks had been fixed up for us. They were arranged in three tiers along the whole length of the ship, two rows of three tiers each on each side of the vessel, leaving a very narrow passageway, so narrow that two men could with difficulty squeeze by each other. In the centre of the rows the lower and centre tiers of bunks were shrouded in continual night, the little light through the port holes being cut off by the upper tier of bunks. My bunk, which was about five feet ten inches square, and occupied by four persons, was right against the boiler, occasioning an additional amount of heat, which made the sensation of suffocation almost unbearable. Here we lay in these bunks, packed away like sardines . . . in the hottest part of the summer. In two instances the guard placed in with us fainted. I heard one of them remark: "A dog couldn't stand this." Perspiration rolled off us in streams all the time. Clothes and blankets were saturated with it, and it constantly dripped from the upper to the lower bunks. Our sufferings were aggravated by a scarcity of water. The water furnished us was condensed, and so intense was the thirst for it, that it was taken from the condenser almost boiling hot and drunk in that state.[5]

The only water the prisoners had was sea water condensed in the ships, and issued out scalding hot in limited quantities. We would pour the hot water from one tin cup to another until cool enough to swallow without burning the throat.[6]

CAPT. WILLIAM
H. MORGAN,
11TH VA. INF.

Only one hatch was left open, so that the place was very close and dark. The August heat was intense even on deck. Imagine, then, the situation in this foul hold, near the steaming boilers and glowing furnaces, with six hundred seasick men, already enfeebled by close confinement, sweltering and gasping for water, which was doled out hot from the condensers![7]

CAPT. WALTER
G. MCRAE,
7TH N.C. INF.

It was a nasty trip on board this old freight ship, in the summer time. The prisoners were on the lower or freight deck, nearly on the water line. Two rows of temporary bunks had been built around the sides of the ship, two tiers high. These bunks were about six feet long and three feet wide, with two men in each bunk; a pretty close fit, especially if both occupants were good-sized men. The bunks did not afford sufficient room for all the prisoners, consequently a good many lay on the floor of the deck between the bunks. . . . I occupied a lower bunk on the inside row with Captain Horton, who was my messmate while a prisoner; a good fellow he was, too, and a good soldier. There was a guard of 150 soldiers on board, who occupied the upper deck.[8]

CAPT. WILLIAM
H. MORGAN,
11TH VA. INF.

The passage from Fort Delaware to Charleston was horrible. My bunk, a single one, was just under the shaft, and against the engine room of the steamer. I could not sit up in it nor lie down without almost squeezing myself under the shaft, while the partition between me and the boiler was so hot I could not bear my hand upon it. There in almost pitch darkness, without any clothing and drenched with perspiration, I had to remain for several days and nights. Our ration was a few crackers with a bit of salt beef or bacon, and the water that was condensed from the ocean as we steamed along.[9]

1LT. GEORGE
FINLEY,
56TH VA. INF.

I remained rather quiet, and only felt a little squeamish, but it was really amusing to see prisoners and sentinels holding on and straining as if they would burst a blood-vessel. After the fit of vomiting was over the poor fellows would lie as if they were almost dead with exhaustion.

CAPT. HENRY
DICKINSON,
2ND VA. CAV.

The suffering between decks was increased by the fact that the waves rendered it necessary to close the lower half of the four ports, thus excluding one-half of our modicum of air, and increasing the heat very much. Added to this the officers vomited in the

narrow passages from necessity, producing in a short while a terrible stench, and many of them, suffering for air, rushed to the
ports, thus crowding up the aisles and almost suffocating those who,
from seasickness, were compelled to remain in their bunks. On the
twenty-second, and indeed till our arrival at Hilton Head, this condition of things existed, the wind blowing less after the night of the
twenty-first, but the weather getting warmer each day.[10]

CAPT. JOHN J.
DUNKLE,
25TH VA. INF.

About three-fourths of us became very sick shortly after leaving
Fort Delaware. We contracted sea-sickness by not being familiar
with the sea and sea voyages. And as closely confined as we were,
the spectacle was horrid—the entire floor covered with sick men—
horribly sick, vomited to a fearful extent by the disease, and groan-
ing in a terrific manner—presented a sight too sickening to behold, and too repulsive to endure, and too wretched to describe.
Even those of us who were not infected by the sickening malady,
were made faint by the loathsome spectacle we were obliged to
witness.[11]

1LT. JAMES W.
A. FORD,
20TH VA. CAV.

[August 22nd].- Had a fine breeze all day, making good time. . . .
Not as much gale as usual, though the steamer rolled and tossed
about no little. A great many officers were sick. I could not help
laughing at some of them, though I was deathly sick myself, up
and down, to and fro, hither and thither, racking pains, disjointed
bones, agonies internal, that none can comprehend, but those who
have to endure them, fell to our lot while prostrated on our back
with the usual seasickness. O how pitiable and yet how laughable
afterwards.[12]

One of the guards who accompanied the prisoners was Private Alexander
J. Hamilton of the 110th Ohio. He wrote in his diary of the *Crescent City* that
she was "a most miserable ship to rock," and substantiated the conditions
of seasickness on August 21:

I was awakened at 4 a.m. to go on post, it was raining heavily and
the water was running all around and under me. At 5 we pulled up
the anchor and got under way. It was raining and blowing briskly
and some of the boys take their first lessons in seasickness, among
the prisoners below decks it is absolutely horrible.[13]

Forced to endure such misery, compelled the men to hope for exchange,
and that is probably the only thing that sustained them in those conditions.
Finally, arriving at Fortress Monroe on the second day, where all expected to
be relieved of the *Crescent City*, they were disappointed when once again,
they put to sea, the reason given that the movements of the armies of Lee
and Grant impeded exchange. The Union had no intention of exchanging

them. Secretary of the Navy Gideon Welles on August 19 told Lieutenant William B. Eaton, commanding the U.S.S. *Admiral*, to be prepared to meet a convoy containing rebel prisoners on their way to Charleston, and to accompany them the rest of the way, acting as escort.[14]

The officers continued to be misled on the assumption of exchange, the guard on board knowing full well no exchange was planned. Yet the prisoners still expected they would be relieved at Charleston. Joined by a convoy of gunboats, including the *Eutaw*, *Dictator* and the *Admiral*, their floating prison continued on its way to South Carolina, at a speed of about ten knots.

The voyage was uneventful, making good time in the clear weather and calm sea off Cape Fear. The night of August 23-24 was moonlit and starry when First Mate Brown ended his watch at midnight. He could see six or seven miles distant across the water, and kept the ship on its course of southwest by west. They were making much better time than anticipated due to the tail winds.

When his watch ended, and Second Mate Baxter took over, Brown went to bed. Baxter knew the orders and the course, and passed his watch in the wheel house visiting with George Stow, another crew member. All was well, and Baxter didn't bother to take any soundings, certain that the ship was well away from shallow water. Meanwhile, the escort convoy had been left behind, nearly out of sight.

When Captain James Prentiss saw signal rockets in the distance, he became curious. He went on deck to the wheel house and asked Baxter what the signals meant. Baxter replied that the *Admiral* was only signalling to another ship, as an identifying gesture. In actuality, she was signalling the *Crescent City* to slow down. At 3 o'clock, as she rounded the shore of Cape Romain about forty miles north of Charleston, the *Crescent City* ran aground. Baxter was surprised, thinking he was far enough offshore to avoid shallow water.[15]

Aug. 24.- At about 3:30 a.m. our pilot ran us aground off Georgetown Courthouse on the coast of South Carolina. We all believe that the Rebels bribed them to do so. Our convoy had signaled us to stop but to no purpose, she kept on her course till she struck. When daylight came we found our position rather an unpleasant one as we were hard aground almost within rifle shot of the enemy's coast and distant not more than 15 miles from one of his strongholds. We were unable to advance or retreat without becoming a prey to the Rebels or to the water and a very small storm would blow us all to pieces. The Johnnies might at any time bring a small battery to bear on us and knock us into a cocked hat. I was very strongly tempted to shoot the pilot but was restrained by Captain Prentice, who told him he would give him until noon to get the boat off or he would have him shot.[16]

PVT.
ALEXANDER J.
HAMILTON,
110TH OHIO
INF.

Latham and Baxter would actually be court-martialed on these charges, even though Baxter immediately called the captain and set about backing the ship off the bar.[17] However, the *Crescent City* was stuck fast, off Cape Island, in sight of land. The jolt awakened the prisoners, and a hastily planned escape attempt was put into action.

CAPT. THOMAS PINCKNEY, 4TH S.C. CAV.

To my surprise I observed on coming to the open port that we were surrounded by yellow water, which I immediately surmised was from the Santee River, and on going on deck I discovered that we were on Cape Romain Shoal, some forty miles north of Charleston, the Lighthouse immediately in front of us, which the Confederate authorities had long since dismantled, and our convoy out of sight. The roofs of the houses at McClellanville were plainly in view, my own summer house among them. Our ranking officers, I learned were then holding a meeting below, devising a plan for our seizing the ship, and as soon as they learned of my acquaintance with the locality, my counsel was sought . . . I had to inform the Council that the lighthouse apparently so near us was on an island some ten miles from the high land, and there was a navigable channel to the inside of it, which our convoy might enter and recapture us, even after we had gained the Lighthouse island, if the tide was high. It was therefore determined that we should wait until the tide commenced to ebb, then with a desperate rush we should over-power the guard, land our men, and get out of reach of recapture before the next high water.[18]

COL. ABRAM FULKERSON, 63RD TENN. INF.

Great confusion at once ensued among the prisoners and also among the Federal officers. We held a hasty council of war, and determined to make a demand on the captain for the surrender of the vessel. It was a desperate undertaking, as it would have been almost certain destruction if we had attempted to reach the deck under the concentrated fire of one hundred muskets. Still, we made the resolve, and placed in the lead Van H. Manning, the brave and dashing Colonel of the Third Arkansas Infantry. Through him we made the demand upon the captain for surrender, and, to the surprise of some of us, he agreed to surrender the vessel on condition, as I remember, that we would have the officers, crew, and soldiers exchanged at Charleston. My recollection is that we had determined to make a landing in the life-boats at or near Cape Romain light-house. While the preliminaries of surrender were being arranged, a signal gun was fired from one of the escorts, and she quickly came in sight and steamed directly toward our vessel. This untoward event terminated all further negotiations for surrender.[19]

    Within their ranks, two leaders emerged, both of whom had already proved their capabilities as officers on the battlefield. Colonel Abram

Fulkerson of the 63rd Tennessee and twenty-five-year-old Colonel Van H. Manning of the 3rd Arkansas were in the forefront almost immediately as the ones looked toward and consulted by the rest of the prisoners, a position which would continue over the next months. Those two men were later given the credit by several of the Six Hundred as primary reasons why they were able to maintain such a solid and unwavering commitment to principles despite the hardships and tests.[20]

This accidental grounding of the ship sent my spirits away up, and the thought came to me, "Now we can certainly get back to Dixie without the formality of exchange." While I am thinking all this over, Col. Van Manning, 3rd Ark. Inf., came on deck. I hastily told him the situation. He at once said, "Murray, we must take this ship." He went below, a hasty council was held with the prisoners, and it was determined that we should take the ship. It was arranged that Colonels Manning, DeGournay, Abe Fulkerson, and Maj. W.W. Goldsborough should make the demand for the surrender of the ship. If it was declined, those below were to rush the guard at foot of the ladder, get on deck, capture the guard, and go ashore on [Sullivan's] Island. It was a desperate undertaking. It would have been certain death for some of us before we could have captured the guard; yet there was no thought of the consequences of failure, no hesitation as to who should lead. By consent, Col. Van Manning was the leader, and with him we were all ready to chance the fire of a thousand guns. Colonels Manning, Fulkerson, DeGournay, and Major Goldsborough went upon deck and demanded that Captain Webster, commanding the guard, should surrender the ship into our hands at once, otherwise, we would take it. Our men below were all ready to obey the order to rush the guard. Hardly had Colonel Manning made the demand for the surrender of the ship when, to the surprise of all the committee, Captain Webster agreed. . . . While the preliminaries of the surrender were being arranged a signal gun was heard out at sea and soon the gunboats hove in sight. The moment the gunboats came in sight the cowardly attitude of Captain Webster changed to that of impudent defiance. . . . I have always believed and do still believe that Webster made the charge against the first mate of the "Crescent City" for the sole purpose of hiding his abject cowardice in agreeing to surrender the ship to unarmed men.[21]

CAPT. J. OGDEN MURRAY, 11TH VA. CAV.

The crowd was so great that it was impossible to move about rapidly, and quite a number refused to strike a blow for their own rescue, one man stating that it would be impossible to take off our baggage, yet the ball commenced rolling slowly and we had no doubt of success, though it was evident that the Yankees suspected

CAPT. HENRY DICKINSON, 2ND VA. CAV.

us. None of the field officers, except Major Goldsboro, could at first be found, too many of them having found their way days before into the luxuries of the cabin, whence, if they had the disposition, they had not the ability to help us. . . . .During the time we were working to effect our object below decks, the cabin passengers, it seems, were not idle, for they, I learn, made a formal demand upon Captain Prentiss to surrender. . . . But, while we were busy preparing to take the boat, the Yanks were not idle. A signal of distress, an inverted flag, was hoisted, and, just as we thought we were ready for action, a gunboat came in sight. Some of us still favored action, believing that the best swimmers could escape, but others, more cautious or knowing more about gunboats, opposed any action, and while we debated, another and still another gunboat came in sight, so manned as to be able to rake the shore and thus cut off our last hope of escape.

Thus baffled, we sat down and doggedly awaited the return of the tide, which, with the great efforts of the Yanks, after many a hard bump finally got the "Crescent" afloat.[22]

CAPT. JOHN
DUNKLE,
25TH VA. INF.

Most of the prisoners were awake at the time of the accident, and those not awake were aroused by the shock. In a few moments, great confusion prevailed.

The crew and sailors being good fellows, were not much alarmed. The Captain appearing anxious that we should escape, used no means to disengage his boat, but sat silently in the cabin.

The prisoners became bold, and quitting their dismal den, rummaged the boat on every side from deck to hold, and from stern to forecastle. The Yankees soon became alarmed at the boldness of their charge, and suffered the prisoners to heap upon them threats, abuses, and curses. . . . When all things were ready for the surrender, and we were rejoicing in the prospect of soon reaching the land of promise, two gunboats suddenly hove in sight. Imagine our mortification, chagrin, surprise and dismay at this unexpected occurance. . . . The gunboats approached near enough to ascertain who we were, to enquire into the cause of our detention, our business, and other matters, and proffering aid, if desirable.[23]

One fortunate prisoner did make his escape, but his luck was the exception.

CAPT. J. OGDEN
MURRAY,
11TH VA. CAV.

By some means, Colonel Woolfolk, a brave, honorable, and true Confederate officer, had permission to have a stateroom on the ship. Aboard the Crescent City *was an old colored woman who had belonged to the Woolfolk family. . . . She was the stewardess of the ship. She recognized Colonel Woolfolk, her young master, and determined to help him to escape. She took him into her linen room, hid him under the bed, and fed him. She hung out of the stern window of the ship a sheet to make the guard believe he had dropped by that means into the water and gone ashore in the darkness. She kept him concealed on board until after the ship had landed us . . . When the ship reached New York City the old woman smuggled him ashore and gave him money. He succeeded in getting to Canada, from there to England, and back to the South on a blockade runner; and the Yankees never learned how he made his escape until he published it after the war.*[24]

For the rest, the escape attempt ended in failure, and the ship's guard ordered a detail of prisoners to the hold to shovel out coal, lightening and enabling the vessel to get off the sandbar. This, combined with the rising tide, allowed the ship to put back out to sea. She continued her voyage, passing Charleston Bar around 3:00 p.m. on the afternoon of August 24. The next morning, the *Crescent City* steamed into Port Royal.[25]

This harbor is the best on the Southern coast, I expect, being quite commodious, of an average depth of say twenty fathoms, and completely protected except from southeast winds. I found about fifty vessels here of all kinds, including the steam frigate "Wabash", twelve or fourteen gunboats, and a number of tugs and light craft.[26]

CAPT. HENRY
DICKINSON,
2ND VA. CAV.

Aug. 25th.- Weigh anchor and move within the "bar". There are many gunboats and other light crafts in the harbor . . . The captain was placed in arrest and the 2nd mate in irons for intentionally running the boat aground yesterday and giving the Confederates an opportunity to escape. This is very unjust.[27]

1LT. JAMES
W. A. FORD,
20TH VA. CAV.

Court-martial proceedings were immediately convened the following day against Latham and Baxter on board the *Delaware* in Port Royal Harbor. While he waited, Private Hamilton took time between guard duty at the court-martial to record in his diary.

Aug. 25.- At about 6 we got a pilot and about 8 we were at Port Royal. Captain Prentice went ashore, reported to Gen. Foster and preferred charges against the Officers of the boat. The general had the captain and the second mate put in irons . . . .At about 8 a.m. a party of officers came long side of us from the U.S.S. Delaware *to hold a court of inquiry over the officers of the* Crescent. *I was put on board the* Delaware *at 10 to do guard duty, stood there until midnight, came back and went to sleep.*[28]

PVT.
ALEXANDER J.
HAMILTON,
110TH OHIO
INF.

Latham was initially found not guilty by the court. On hearing this, Foster intervened and requested a new verdict, saying, "Such negligence and laxity of discipline are reprehensible in a ship officer at any time. They become criminal when, as in the present instance, the vessel is freighted with prisoners of war, and near a hostile coast."[29] The verdict remained not guilty on all but two counts, and Foster released Latham from custody with an official reprimand. The sentence was not so light for Second Mate Baxter, who was fined one hundred dollars, and confinement in the jail on Hilton Head until the amount was paid.

Meanwhile the prisoners waited, writing letters to pass the time in the miserable hold of the *Crescent City*, and conjectures about their fate in the form of "grape" played havoc with their hopes.

LETTER, 1LT.
SANFORD
BRANCH,
8TH GA. INF.,
ON BOARD
CRESCENT CITY,
TO CHARLOTTE
BRANCH,
AUG. 29, 1864

As I wrote you from Fort D. I was one of the fortunate or unfortunate six hundred sent here from Fort Delaware. Arrived here on last Thursday after a passage of four days. Strange to say I was not sick & now consider myself a first rate sailor. Most of the officers aboard are confident of an early exchange but I am not so sanguine having been disappointed so often. Still I think we stand a better chance of exchange than other prisoners of war confined in the U.S. I am very tired of being on shipboard and hope we may soon be landed. You remember how tired I used to get of the cabin. I am equally so of the forecastle. I think the next two weeks will decide our fate whether exchange or imprisonment for the war. God grant it may be the former . . .[30]

The idleness spurred those restless among them to attempt another escape, and on the night of August 27, several officers made their move.

CAPT. THOMAS
PINCKNEY,
4TH S.C. CAV.

While the Crescent *was lying in Port Royal Harbor, awaiting the Court Martial, some eight of our men attempted to escape by swimming ashore at night. I had talked the matter over with Capt. Perkins (Forrest Cavalry), Lieutenant Allen (Morgan's Cavalry) and had sketched out the route they would have to take to gain our picket posts on the mainland. Could I have gone with them, I could have piloted them through my familiarity with Hilton Head, where I had spent many days on my Grandmother's plantation, and Pinckney Island was the only other land between that and Dixie. But I was so reduced that I did not think I had the strength to gain the shore. Col. Folk and two others were recaptured attempting to get across from Hilton Head Island, and the others on Pinckney Island. The latter having been two days eluding searching parties, and with nothing to eat but green figs and fiddlers, were nearly starved, and had gone to a Yankee picket post and completely deceived them as to their identity, passing themselves off as Federals from Fort Walker whose terms of enlistment had expired, and who refusing to reenlist had wandered off from the Post. They had been fed and were eagerly awaiting a favorable time to surprise the guard, take their boat and row across to our picket post in sight, when they were betrayed by an old negro, whom they had encountered previously, and from whom they had extracted information, and would not agree that Perkins should pistol into silence afterwards, which he had been eager to do. Capt. Ellison of Alabama only succeeded in making his escape, he must have swam eleven miles to reach the Confederate lines.*[31]

Captain George H. Ellison, 3rd Alabama Infantry, from Mobile, succeeded in escaping. He returned to his regiment, and was paroled with his command on May 3, 1865.[32]

On the night of the twenty-seventh Captain Perkins and three others, who had managed to get life-preservers from the cabin, made their arrangements and swam ashore on Hilton Head Island, and from thence to Pinckney Island. Reaching this island they supposed they were on mainland and threw away their life-preservers. They marched across the island and were in sight of our pickets, but supposed by going further to the left they would get safely into our lines. A short swim would have given them liberty, but they actually walked into the enemies' pickets. This adventure was attended with one great danger which deterred many from following them. The harbor, and indeed all the inlets, are full of sharks. Every day whilst we were at anchor the huge, broad-mouthed monsters swam around us, picking up crackers, pieces of meat, etc., and Captain Perkins said he was once lifted out of the water by some large fish, and that he saw a number larger than he was. . . . After the return of Perkins and company, a tug with two small guns sailed, or rather steamed, around us in a small circle every night from dark to daybreak, and in addition to this precaution our vessel changed its position, so that to reach the island would necessitate a swim of one-half mile.[33]

CAPT. HENRY
DICKINSON,
2ND VA. CAV.

[Aug] 27th.- Three officers, Captains Kent, Perkins, and Ellison, having procured life preservers from the cabin escape by night by swimming. After two days and three nights hardships and suffering from hunger and thirst and fatigue, the two former deliberately surrendered to the federal picket, when within 400 yards of our own pickets of which fact, however, they were ignorant at the time. The latter must have made his escape as he has not been heard from since. Such is the desperation to which we are driven by the ill usage of those in charge of us, that many prefer throwing themselves upon the mercy of the waves, or offer themselves a tempting morsel to the immense schools of man-eating shark for the narrow chance of liberty thus offered.[34]

1LT. JAMES
W. A. FORD,
20TH VA. CAV.

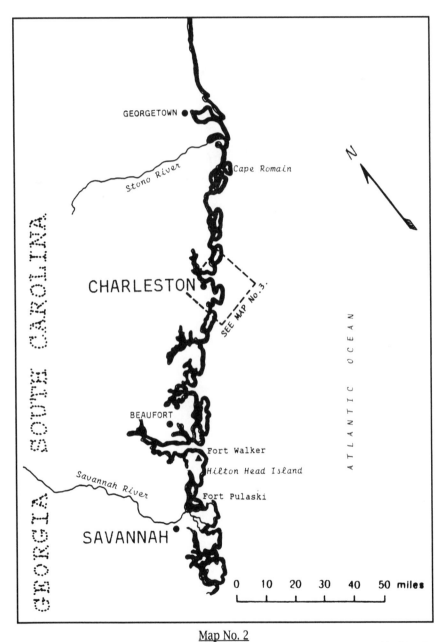

Map No. 2

South Carolina/Georgia Coast

Richard S. Joslyn

Conditions in the hold of the ship, after a week were unbearable, both from a health perspective and in the form of cabin fever. Some, recovering from wounds when they left Fort Delaware, had been unattended since. The twenty or so amputees had been compelled to lie on the floor under the ladder leading from the hold to the upper deck, and were nearly helpless in assisting themselves to the water closet. All were beginning to wonder when the misery would end, when due to either the escape attempt, or a harsh attitude, Captain Webster imposed crueler treatment.

We were then driven in the middle deck or hold, the hatchways were closed, the port holes fastened so as to admit neither light nor air—thus we were entirely excluded from light or fresh air. . . . At this season of the year the climate in the South is excessively hot, so hot, that it can scarcely be borne by Northern or Western persons under ordinary circumstances; much less in our condition—the thermometer being about 96 to 99 degrees.[35]

CAPT. JOHN DUNKLE, 25TH VA. INF.

August 26.- The nights of the 25th and 26th, were the hottest nights we ever experienced, had to fan all night, and our shirts were wet with perspiration. Several men fainting, Capt. Henry Allen, Lieut. David Bronaugh, and Lieut. Carter (a young preacher) . . . We are guarded by 157th Ohio Militia, and a company of deserters, commanded by one Capt. Prentiss, an overbearing tyrranical rascal, who let his men pillage our baggage, rob men of all their clothes, and in one instance one of our men caught a Yankee stealing his hat. He was pointed out to this scoundrel, but he refused to make him give it up. He talked to men as though they were dogs.[36]

CAPT. ALEX BEDFORD, 3RD MO. CAV.

You could hardly turn over when you occupied your position. . . . We were packed as thick as we could lie, and there we had to remain the greater portion of the time, as only those whom the calls of nature demanded, were allowed to leave, and then only one at a time. The place was dark as Erebus, and the air soon became as foeted and as poisonous as the Upas. It was a perfect hell, and nearly as hot. The water that was given us was impure, and some times the stomach would refuse it from its putrid smell. They fed us twice daily, on crackers and raw bacon.[37]

CAPT. JOHN C. GORMAN, 2ND N.C. INF.

The water-closet used by the prisoners was in the wheel-house, to reach which it was necessary to go up the ladder, through the hatch and over the deck. But one prisoner was allowed to go to the closet at a time, and of course there was a great effort made to get a position to avoid delay, and to this end, every morning, nearly all of the 600 would line themselves around the vessel in two ranks. This was in August, and the animal heat, which was greatly augmented by the heat from the smoke-stack, became so intolerable,

COL. ABRAHAM FULKERSON, 63RD TENN. INF.

and the smell of the place so offensive, that it was considered a great privileged to go to the water-closet for a few minutes, where one could get a breath of fresh air and enjoy the spray thrown upon one's body by the paddle-wheel. Of course every man remained there until he was driven out by the sentinel, regardless of the suffering and clamor of his comrades in the hold. By this cruel arrangement it required hours to accommodate the prisoners. Many of them were not able to stand up in ranks till their turn came, owing to their enfeebled condition caused by sea-sickness, which was aggravated by the heated and fetid air which they were compelled to breathe. It frequently happened that men were not able to stand in line till their turn, and were compelled to fall out and rest, when the ranks would immediately close up, and this necessitated their going to the foot of the line, if they still desired the privilege of going on deck. In many instances these people were not able to control themselves, and were compelled to leave ranks and use one end of the hold for their purposes. We were provided with no means for cleaning the vessel, and the Federal officers in charge gave it no attention whatever. When the vessel encountered the rougher waters off Cape Hatteras, its rolling and pitching would dash and splatter this horrid combination of filth from one end of the hold to the other. For eighteen days we were kept in this miserable place, which notwithstanding the filth necessarily accumulating each day, was never cleaned; still we lived and were cheerful, buoyed by the hope of an early exchange and the thought of the loving greeting of the dear ones at home.[38]

CAPT. WALTER
MCRAE,
7TH N.C. INF.

This happy disposition helped to keep us alive in the Crescent's hold. There were several of Morgan's officers aboard, and, though invisible in the darkness, you might hear them calling to one of their mess, a tall cavalry captain, who was a fine story-teller and a clever mimic: "Say, Hammock, tell us about the hair-lipped man. What did he say to Mrs. Gillespie?" etc., and pretty soon would follow shouts of laughter as Hammock progressed with his yarns and imitations. Long afterwards, when many had died and all had starved, and when the scurvy had plowed lines of suffering on every face, when the war in the field was over and we were about returning to face the more heartless war of Reconstruction, Captain Hammock stood before the poor, emaciated crowd, spread out his legs, and, with arms akimbo, personated the "Loyal" Irish woman and said: "Now, yez must all go home and be clever fellies, bekaze the government's trated ye so leniently."[39]

Their sense of humor and hope continued to serve them well, keeping spirits up.

Col. Vannoy Hartrog Manning
3rd Arkansas Infantry.

Col. Abram Fulkerson
63rd Tennessee Infantry.
Captured at Petersburg, Va. 17 June 64.

Capt. Thomas Fear Perkins, Jr.
Co. I, 11th Tennessee Cavalry.
Escaped ten times while imprisoned
with the Six Hundred.

Col. Phillip Perry Brown, Jr.
Commander of the 157th New York
Volunteer Infantry at Fort Pulaski, Ga.

The Immortal Six-Hundred
2Lt. Henry Howe Cook
Co. I, 44th Tennessee Infantry.

The Immortal Six-Hundred
Capt. Lewis Harman
VMI '65
Co. I, 12th Virginia Cavalry.

Some Notables of New Orleans
Capt. Junius Lackland Hempstead
VMI '64
Co. F, 25th Virginia Infantry.
Son of Gov. Stephen Hempstead, Iowa.

North Carolina Troops
Capt. John Lucas Cantwell
Co. F, 3rd North Carolina Infantry.

Not only were the conditions intolerable, but the delay, due to the court-martial, caused a lack of food or water on board for the men during the last week. It was amazing that none died from the lack of water in the heat. Ice was on board the ship, but none was given the prisoners. Also, the ship's hold could have been cleaned while at sea, but Webster refused, not on the grounds that it was impossible to do so, but on the grounds "that it was good enough for rebels."[40] When the exhausted prisoners thought they could take no more, the water ran out, and they were still at sea, while the truce boats met for a third time.

The conduct of the Federals on this occasion was very severe, cruel, and inhuman. Their words were spoken with fierceness and wrath, and their whole deportment betrayed their determination to afflict and punish us.

CAPT. JOHN DUNKLE, 25TH VA. INF.

In a short time they ceased to bring water from the Island, and then ensued a scene of suffering for water, which surpassed all hitherto known. At one time we had no water for forty hours. . . . No pen could convey to the mind an idea of the cruel agony of suffering without water, shut out from light and fresh air in the heat of summer, and confined with a heated steam boiler. . . . Men sank, shrank, begged, wept, mourned, lamented, swore, raved, fainted, and sickened under the dreadful blow. . . . Men of powerful nerve fainted away like children, under the dire effects of the heat. . . . Many bowed on their knees before their cruel tormentors, and begged like children for a single draught of water. . . . Those hours or days of anguish are too detestable to be forced upon the memory; and I shudder, when called upon, to narrate the facts. They often haunt me in my dreams, and make vivid to my mind the shrieks of pain, the groans of misery, the cries of despair, and the wailings of agony of the six hundred.[41]

Finally, they were relieved of this endurance test of suffering when, on August 27, the guard of the ship was changed. The new regiment would be fondly remembered by all 600 as heaven-sent deliverance.

We were almost famished, provisions and water having given out two days before we reached Hilton Head. On one of these days I caught some water in an oilcloth during a rain, and on the other a sailor gave me a cup of hot water. Lt.Col. Carmichael, of the One Hundred and Fifty-seventh New York Regiment, came aboard. He was horrified when he saw our condition, and, expressing much displeasure and regret, earnestly set to work to relieve our deplorable state. A steamer was brought alongside the prison ship and a detail made from the prisoners and from the One Hundred and Fifty-seventh Regiment to cleanse the ship, the prisoners having

2LT. HENRY COOK, 44TH TENN. INF.

*been transferred from it to the steamer. We were supplied with
water and provisions, the soldiers gladly dividing their rations with
us. We were now in the hands of soldiers, not guards.*[42]

The mutual esteem between guards and captives—men willing to die for
their respective principles, no matter what "cause"—would continue in later
months.

**CAPT. ALEX
BEDFORD,
3RD MO. CAV.**

*Aug. 27th.- Our new guard is as kind to us as men could be. They
would do anything in their power to make us comfortable. They
had their orders from General Foster, and could not do much in
that way. They always spoke respectfully to us, and no insults
were offered from any of them. They told us they had smelt our
powder, and some of them had tried Libby prison, and they knew
how to treat a prisoner.*[43]

**CAPT. JAMES
ROBERT
MCMICHAEL,
12TH GA. INF.**

*How wonderful is the goodness of God in preserving my health
while crowded with six hundred in the hole of the Steamer Crescent. Our sufferings there were never surpassed except by the
hundred and forty-six Englishmen who were shut up in the Black
Hole of Calcutta in a room eighteen feet square with only two
small windows on the same side to admit air. On opening this
dungeon ten hours after their imprisonment only twenty-three were
alive. The others had died from breathing impure air. We were
eighteen days in the dark hold of the Steamer Crescent but had
more air, and none died.*[44]

**CAPT. HENRY
DICKINSON,
2ND VA. CAV.**

*A detachment of the One Hundred and Fifty-seven New York
Volunteers, Capt. McWilliams, from this time assumed the guard-
ianship of us, and, though he was stuck up with the importance of
his position, and was unnecessarily rigorous in the discharge of
his orders, his lieutenants were quite polite and respectful as a
general rule; all the non-commissioned officers and staff were not
only very polite, but very kind and attentive to our wants. They
gave us coffee and bread as far as they could, procured hot water
for us without cost, and, notwithstanding orders, allowed us to
come on deck more freely than before. These attentions very much
alleviated our sufferings. About this time all the wounded and
those who were very sick, in all about forty, were transferred to
another boat and carried to Beaufort, where they remained for
some time.*[45]

One of the officers in the 157th New York was twenty-three-year-old
William Saxton of Cincinnatus, New York, in Chenango County. He was a
member of Company C, in charge of the prisoners on the *Crescent City*.

Captain McWilliams of Company G . . . with his company and mine, was sent aboard the Crescent *lying in the harbor, to guard these prisoners. Captain McWilliams being in command assigned me to the task of taking charge of the prisoners' money, of which they had quite an amount. They were not allowed to have this money in their possession, but it was held in trust for them, and they were allowed to purchase good clothing or necessities with it. Sergeant Smith, of Company A, was detailed as purchasing agent. Each day he would go among the prisoners and ascertain if they wished anything, make a list of it, and come and see me if they had sufficient money to their credit to purchase the article, then go ashore and buy what they wanted, bring the bill to me and I would pay it and charge it up to their individual accounts. This necessitated quite a considerable work, but that was the way we treated them.*[46]

2Lt. WILLIAM
SAXTON,
157TH N.Y.
VOL. INF.

The forty men sent to the Federal military hospital at Beaufort, South Carolina were mostly severely wounded officers, some amputees. One of these was Captain John C. Gorman. They were obviously picked at Fort Delaware because they were disabled. Foster wrote to Union exchange agent Colonel William Hoffman, "These men can never be of service to the rebels in the field, and I think that I can exchange them for our well officers."[47]

Beaufort, S.C., Oct. 3, 1864.- On the morning of the 28th of August, the entire 600 were still on board the Crescent *at Hilton Head. Our deplorable condition had been mitigated as far as it was possible, by our new guards, and though we had the privilege of passing from one to the other deck at liberty, the crowd everywhere was still great, and no comfort could be had anywhere. The sick—there were a good many complaining—were stretched everywhere in the way, and there was no prospect whatever that we would be removed ashore. I expected that disease would be soon propagated and many of us would "go up." But the surgeon concluded to land the sick and it was with a light heart that I feebly tottered to the deck of a ferry boat that had come alongside at his bidding. With the sick, was also removed the disabled, some 20 armless or legless unfortunates. We did not know where we were bound, and in truth, I cared not, as I left the deck of that miserable steamer. We were placed under charge of Captain Paul R. Hambrick, of the Veteran Reserve Corps, and our boat headed towards Beaufort, which lay up the Broad River, almost due North from Port Royal, some 15 miles. . . . After two hours steaming, we hove in sight of Beaufort, S.C. spread out on the shore from East to West . . . and as we neared its wharves, I could perceive by its fine mansions and tastily arranged front yards, now in decay, that it was once the abode of the luxurious and the wealthy. It was in fact*

CAPT. JOHN C.
GORMAN,
2ND N.C. INF.

*the summer residence of the wealthy planters on the mainland. . . .
We were landed at the public wharf, which remains intact, and
perhaps has been enlarged and improved for government convenience, and hauled in ambulances to the rebel hospital, where our
crowd are its sole occupants. It is on the front street, facing the
harbor, is a large and commodious two-story residence, with 14
rooms, and was once, no doubt, the homestead of a family of wealth
and ease. . . . Before the Delaware friends left us, we were transferred temporarily to another steamer, to be counted, on our return, to see if we were all present. While on board the other vessel,
our baggage was rifled, trunks, valises and carpet bags pillaged,
and everything taken that pleased the fancy of the thieves. Private blankets, as well as those with the U.S. Brand were taken, and
then they left us. My hearty curse followed them. . . . Woe is their
lot if they ever fall into the hands of the 600 Crescent prisoners.*[48]

It would hardly have been a fair exchange. Some of the Beaufort sick
died later on, unable to rally the strength to recover.

On August 29, by mutual arrangement of Robert Ould and Colonel
Mulford, an exchange of non-combatants was made in Charleston Harbor.
Union General U. S. Grant had made it clear that no more exchanges were
allowed, except in special cases. Therefore, twenty-one assistant surgeons,
ten surgeons, one hospital steward and three chaplains were released. [49]

Sitting in the harbor, the hot, humid days were followed by stormy ones,
in the prime of the hurricane season. The *Crescent City* finally put out to sea
on August 29, heading for Charleston, the prisoners completely unaware of
the reasons for the delay. On September 1, she steamed into Charleston Harbor and anchored under the guns of Battery Gregg. Foster specifically ordered
that the ship be anchored under fire while the stockade on Morris Island was
being completed. The men had ceased to be conventional prisoners of war,
and became hostages in the struggle for Charleston's capitulation.[50]

The prisoners waited anxiously for their release, hoping that the delay
was because truce ships were in the harbor. Colonel Robert Ould had met
with Federal officials, still negotiating the issues about reinstating exchange,
and trying to come to terms. At this time sentence was passed in the court-
martial of Captain Daniel Latham.[51]

As they sat or lay in their bunks in the old steamer, through the open
portholes the prisoners watched the shelling of Charleston from Batteries
Gregg and Wagner. They could plainly see the skyline of the city, every time
a shell fell on Sumter.

1LT. JAMES
W. A. FORD,
20TH VA. CAV.

*[Thursday, Sept. 1st].- Today, the 1st of Autumn, is ushered in
with tidings that make 600 confederate hearts throb with new
animation. We start for Charleston Harbor. All is ready and we
weigh anchor and get under way at 9 o'clock. . . . At 6 p.m. we*

arrived within the bar where many interesting things are visible. Federal Monitors, Gun boats, Blockaders, batteries Sumpter, Moultrie and other batteries and Charleston with blazing cannon and exploding shells all greet our eyes in succession. All feel confident we'll be exchanged in a day or two.

[Sept. 2nd].- The day passes without any developments and we spend the time looking around at the objects of interest and inventing and circulating "grape" to suit all fancies and answering inquiries of the most fastidious. The roaring of artillery and the explosion of shells over the city of Charleston and the faithful walls of Sumpter may be heard and seen all day and night. There is a grandure in the scene and especially at night, which fails of its legitimate effect when accompanied with the sad reality that it is the revelling of hostile fires that hurl the bolts of death and that some friend or fellow creature may be hurried to eternity, a victim to the object that excites the admiration of the distant spectator.[52]

On September 5, a storm blew up, making all aboard nervous as the ship sat exposed in the harbor, amid the Union gunboats.

We were now fairly under fire, I suppose, and here we remained until the seventh of September, listless spectators of the idleness of the vessels around us, almost dead with heat and hunger and thirst, panting for air and liberty, denied every comfort on earth. Day after day we lingered, in hope that each succeeding day would bring us exchange, or even removal to Morris Island, for even the latter, under fire of our own forts, was preferable to the insufferable stench of the Crescent, *added to hot water, a bare modicum of crackers and salt pork, and the daily danger of the equinoctial storm, which might drive us to sea without water or food. Many of the men, I am certain, were almost crazed by the mental and bodily torture they suffered during these long days and nights.*[53]

CAPT. HENRY
DICKINSON,
2ND VA. CAV.

Foster notified Jones on September 5 that he was prepared to put the Six Hundred under fire on Morris Island if the Union prisoners of war were still in Charleston. Jones had pleaded with Confederate authorities to have them removed, but it was impossible after Sherman's destruction of the transportation and supply lines. Foster knew this, but proceeded with his plans of retaliation after Jones notified him on September 6 that he was unable to move the U.S. soldiers immediately.[54]

The waiting continued, the *Crescent City* still under fire, at anchor in the Harbor. An occasional rain shower was the only relief from the sultry heat.

[Sept. 5th].- The spell that lulled our anxious hearts into temporary repose is partially broken. No word or sign of encouragement has greeted our eager expectant senses today. The "deck" was crowded last. night witnessing the shells and rockets flying from the different batteries. It lasted 2 or 3 hours and during the

1LT. JAMES
W. A. FORD,
20TH VA. CAV.

*time the heavens seemed to be brilliant with balls of fire. The sight
was terrible & grand. There is much suffering for water but Providence supplied us abundantly about dusk by means of a cool refreshing rain for which we feel very thankful.*[55]

At last, on September 7, the 600 officers were landed at Morris Island,
where they would say good-bye to the *Crescent City* and the 157th New York
Volunteer Infantry. Now a new experience would test them in a different
way, both mentally and physically.

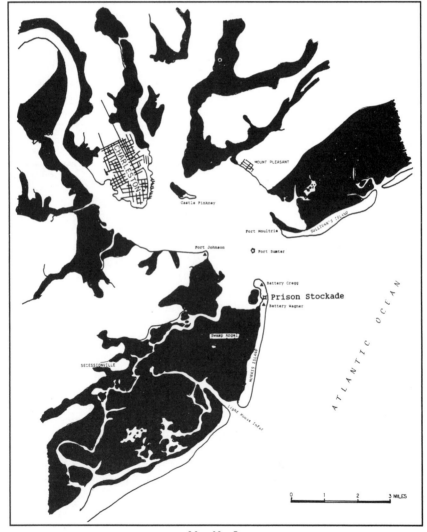

<u>Map No. 3</u>

Richard S. Joslyn

Charleston Harbor, S.C., 1864

CHAPTER SIX

Morris Island

Morris Island is a long sand spit, facing Charleston Harbor for a part of its length and the ocean for the balance. The sea front of the island is a continuous hard sand beach. Immediately in rear of this beach is a strip of low sand hills and hollows—dry, drifting sand with little or no vegetation. This strip of sand dunes was in some places several rods wide, but in others not more than a rod; and the whole of the rest of the island, which in some places is nearly half a mile in width, is simply marsh, with flats here and there above ordinary tides, but all subject to overflow. . . . When you consider that we had always from three to five regiments on duty and that this same ground had been camped on for a year or more, you can form some idea of its fitness as a habitation for four to five thousand men.[1]

MAJ. BENJAMIN THOMPSON, 32ND U.S. COLORED TROOPS

THAT was their destination and as the five hundred and sixty remaining tired, sick, and weary officers waited in the stifling hold of the old steamer, preparations for them were completed in the form of a stockade of logs, consisting of one and one-half acres of sand. Located in the most fired upon area of Morris Island, between Forts Gregg and Wagner, five cartloads of shell fragments had been removed from the area, evidence of the dangerous location chosen. "The ground is covered with iron, and shallow excavations made by the striking and explosion of shells," wrote Union staff officer Major John C. Gray, upon a visit to the fortifications.[2] Around the parapet, in each corner, sentry posts had been constructed with roofs to protect guards from falling shell fragments and debris. The Union forces who would be the guard units, and who had worked on this fortification, were the 54th Massachusetts Volunteer Colored Regiment, under the command of Colonel Edward Needles Hallowell. The regiment had been on the island since occupying Fort Wagner in September 1863, and had bad memories of the disas-

85

trous attack of July 1863. Hallowell had been seriously wounded in the groin and the face, losing an eye. Consequently, his appearance did not endear him to the prisoners, especially combined with his treatment and attitude. He was promoted to colonel when he returned to duty, succeeding Colonel Robert G. Shaw who had been killed at Battery Wagner.

At last, on the morning of September 7, the *Crescent City* steamed into Lighthouse Inlet at the southern end of Morris Island. There she fastened to the wharf, and about noon, disembarked her cargo. The men stumbled out of the hold of the ship, where they had been quartered while the stockade was being finished. None particularly cared what was in store for them, simply glad to be out in the light of day and the fresh air, again on terra firma. Apparently, they were all amused at their appearance after the long eighteen-day confinement and ordeal.

CAPT. WALTER McRAE, 7TH N.C. INF.

On the 7th of September we disembarked at Morris Island and when we finally came out into the light of day and had a look at one another we were astonished to note the ravages made by the terrible heat and the nauseous confinement. One could scarcely recognize his best friends. There were six of us from Wilmington, N.C., all badly damaged. Had we been consigned to any good business man, he would have rejected the cargo and refused to pay the freight.[3]

CAPT. GEORGE W. NELSON, HANOVER ARTY. (VA.)

Our skins, which were much tanned when we started, were bleached as white as possible during this trip.[4]

The 54th Massachusetts arrived to meet their charges at the landing at Lighthouse Inlet on the lower end of Morris Island around 10 o'clock that morning, and lined up to escort the prisoners to the stockade. William Saxton had been ordered to accompany the prisoners with Companies C and G, 157th New York. He was inadvertently left behind at Hilton Head due to a misunderstanding of orders. After spending the better part of the night in a row boat, he caught up to the *Crescent City* after she was out to sea. When she docked at Morris Island, Saxton stood at the gangplank and counted the officers as they disembarked, to be turned over to the charge of the 54th Massachusetts.

The first meeting of captors and captives was awkward. Sizing each other up, guards and prisoners eyed each other cautiously, each forming immediate impressions of the other. The Union troops presented a perfectly uniform set, all dressed alike, conforming perfectly with the military manual. Their charges, on the other hand, having been through up to a year of prison in some cases, looked like anything but military officers. The two would become closely connected in the weeks ahead, not always on good terms, and not always trusting.

Several days before, the Fifty-fourth was assigned to guard this prison camp. On September 7, Colonel Hallowell, with Companies D, E, G, and K marched to the landing, where the steamer "Crescent" soon arrived with the Confederates. The escort was composed entirely of colored soldiers. First came three companies of the Twenty-first United States Colored Troops in column, then the prisoners, flanked on either side by two companies of the Twenty-first in column. In this order the Confederates were taken to the camp.[5]

CAPT. LUIS
EMILIO,
54TH MASS.
INF.

We were met at the wharf by a full regiment of the Sons of Africa, the Fifty-fourth Massachusetts, under command of Colonel Hallowell, son of an abolition silk merchant in Philadelphia. This regiment (whilst the Yanks were getting us off and taking away our blankets, which latter, by the way, they only partially replaced) amused us by exhibiting their proficiency in the manual, and thus, as they supposed, impressing us with a wholesome dread of their prowess. . . . After a time, the dress and manner of [our] officers became loose and careless. As many had no means with which to replenish wardrobes we did not, in this respect, compare favorably with the always neat and tidy Yankee officer. Some of our officers were men of mental culture and refined manners, who would have done themselves honor in any station.[6]

CAPT. HENRY
DICKINSON,
2ND VA. CAV.

This body of five hundred and sixty officers thus placed in our charge was a singular-looking set of soldiers. There were among them tall, lank mountaineers, some typical Southerners of the books,—dark, long-haired, and fierce of aspect,—and a lesser number of city men of jauntier appearance. The major part were common-looking, evidently of the poorer class of Southerners, with a sprinkling of foreigners,—principally Germans and Irish. Hardly any two were dressed alike. There were suits of blue jeans, home-spuns, of butternut, and a few in costumes of gray more or less trimmed. Upon their heads were all sorts of coverings,—straw and slouch hats, and forage caps of gray, blue, or red, decorated with braid. Cavalry boots, shoes, and bootees in all stages of wear were on their feet. Their effects were wrapped in rubber sheets, pieces of carpet, or parts of quilts and comforts. Some had hand-sacks of ancient make. Haversacks of waterproof cloth or cotton hung from their shoulders. Their physical condition was good; but they made a poor showing for chosen leaders of the enemy. It did seem that men of their evident mental and intellectual calibre—with some exceptions—might be supporters of any cause, however wild or hopeless. They were of all grades, from colonels down in rank.[7]

CAPT. LUIS
EMILIO,
54TH MASS.
INF.

Once in line, they were marched the three miles along the beach of Morris Island to the stockade, flanked by soldiers on either side. After the long confinement, many of the prisoners were weak, and collapsed often in the sand. An attempt to help them by the members of the guard was scorned by the officers of the 54th, and the point of bayonets served as an incentive to stay on their feet. Security was tight, and no one was about to give them a chance to escape.

CAPT. JUNIUS L. HEMPSTEAD, 25TH VA. INF.

They have a very military appearance and go through the manual very well indeed. The gangplank was pushed ashore and we disembarked. Were received with high military honors. Two lines of the colored soldiers drawn up on each side of the road. Were marched two miles along a sandy beach. Rain coming down quite lively and we quite wet. Water very scarce. Caught the drippings off of my hat and obtained enough to help me along. They halted us near Battery Wagner and searched us then marched us by detachments to the pen.[8]

CAPT. HENRY DICKINSON, 2ND VA. CAV.

We soon started up the eastern beach of Morris Island, guarded as closely by these negroes as if we were in Confederate lines. The gait was so rapid and we so weak that many of us utterly broke down about one and one-half miles from the wharf, when we halted to rest, and as it just then commenced to raining hard, we eagerly caught water in our hats to drink, having had none for twenty-four hours. The negroes, perceiving this, went to a spring hard by and brought us some very good water.[9]

CAPT. ALEX BEDFORD, 3RD MO. CAV.

September 7th.- We marched two and one-half miles along the eastern shore of the Island and many of our officers gave out owing to their confinement on the boat and want of rations. We passed in front of Fort Wagner, being then in between it and Fort Sumter, we continued in same direction, but a few hundred yards when we run into a pen made of pine poles planted in the ground, about twelve feet in length, making a substantial picket fence with a parapet on it, and mounted thereon was a line of negro sentries. Inside of said pen is a grass rope, about twenty feet from the fence, between this rope and fence we were told by the Colonel of said regiment, was certain death to any of us, except we were escorted by a Yankee officer. Inside of said rope are 160 A-tents. In these we are put, four to the tent. The Yankees fired more than usual since we have been in hearing of this place, we suppose trying to draw fire from our batteries, but got no answer as yet.[10]

CAPT. THOMAS PINCKNEY, 4TH S.C. CAV.

A more disappointed and crestfallen set of men I have never seen, and none of us believed the United States Government was actually going to put its inhumane threat into execution, for how shells from our batteries falling short of Wagner or overshooting Gregg and bursting among our men would help the U.S. Government we failed to see.[11]

A look at the rough map of this region, which so far as I could see, was moderately correct will show how perfectly the enemy had protected Wagner by placing us there. Indeed, it may be said that our situation at no other spot (where a pen of this size could be built) would so effectually silence our forts. We were, then, emphatically acting as breastworks for the enemy, not only shielding them in their breastworks, but enabling them with impunity to haul guns, timber, shell, etc, to Fort Gaines and Fort Gregg, and to work large parties every night on Cummings Point.[12]

CAPT. HENRY
DICKINSON,
2ND VA. CAV.

The threat of being placed under fire became fact. It had been rumored at Fort Delaware, but never expected, all thinking that no civilized nation in the middle nineteenth century would condone such treatment. They steadied themselves for the test and, keeping their courage up, marched to whatever fate awaited.

Everything was done to care for and protect these unfortunate officers whom the fortunes of war placed in our hands except in two particulars,—they were kept in a place within reach of the enemy's fire, and their rations were reduced to conform in quantity to those furnished our officers in Charleston, at first to one half the army ration, and after some time still less.[13]

CAPT. LUIS
EMILIO,
54TH MASS.
INF.

The stockade was to be their keep for forty-five days. Upon reaching the gate, they were halted, counted off by fours to determine tentmates, and assigned a tent in one of the eight rows. They were divided into eight detachments, or companies of seventy-five men each, with a sergeant from the 54th as warden. Rules and regulations were stringent. There could be no gathering in groups of over ten men. This was rather hard when there were 550 officers on an acre-and-a-half sand dune, made smaller by the twenty feet taken up by the dead line. No lights were allowed after taps, although the whole compound was lit as bright as day by a calcium light.[14] Fires were prohibited, since guards cooked the rations. There was to be no loud talking, or calling out to friends across the pen, and men were confined all night to their tents. Any violation of these rules resulted in being fired on by sentries. To be reminded of this constant observation, a battery of Billinghurst-Requa machine guns was trained on the camp, to rake the company streets on a moments notice, certain death to all if ordered.[15]

Under these circumstances, the captives passed their first day on Morris Island.

September Seventh 1864.- I am in Company "D" No. 3. Saw some huge guns one was eighteen feet long and three feet diameter at the breech. We are on the site of the battle field where so many were killed.[16]

CAPT. JUNIUS
HEMPSTEAD,
25TH VA. INF.

*David Garrett . . . Jonathan Arrington, of Campbell Co., of the
Forty-second Infantry, William B. Carder, Fourth Infantry of
Smyth's, and myself joined hands and selected the sixth tent on
First street, Co. A., as our quarters. Our "pen" was made of pine
poles from four to eight inches in diameter, sharpened at top, and
set upright about four feet in the ground, being fully fifteen feet
above ground and so closely set that it was difficult to see between
them. We at first did not know how far they were placed in the
ground, and Captain Perkins and others in the next tent to mine
commenced planning to get out, but they had many difficulties to
overcome. They could get nothing but a few cracker boxes to carry
away the sand and after they dug about nine feet a heavy rain
filled up the hole and that night some scoundrel told the Yanks,
who then let us know that the poles had been put under water
level with a view to prevent mining. Of course this stopped all
mining operations.*[17]

Those individuals who spent their free time thinking about escape, like
Captains Tom Perkins, Leon Jastremski and Holland Coffee, would find no
opportunity here. This was the one prison where no escapes would be
recorded.

The first priority was to take baths, though only tin cups, and basins or
buckets were available. Nearly three weeks in the hold of the *Crescent* made
the simple act of being clean seem special. Clothes were changed, and for
those who had no extra clothing, shirts and pants were borrowed from comrades, while laundry was being washed.[18] Beards and hair were trimmed,
faces scrubbed and shaved, until all felt like civilized men again.

The daily routine was strictly regimented, beginning with roll call at
6:30 or sunrise. The men awoke to drums, fell in line, answered when their
names were called, and dressed ranks to the orders of a sergeant of the 54th
Massachusetts. When all were accounted for, a captain approached and took
the report from each sergeant. Then the prisoners broke ranks and began
their assigned duties, which included policing each company street, raking
the sand smooth, and emptying the barrel sinks, placed at the end of each
tent row for latrines, a menial task imposed by Hallowell, who although
reprimanded for it by superiors, refused to dispense with the indignity.[19]

Rations arrived around 8:00 a.m. and again at 2:00 p.m. Roll call was
repeated at noon and at retreat, thus ending the day. Taps was at 9:00 p.m.,
after which no lights or talking was allowed, nor leaving the tents.

The weather at the time was pleasant with hot days and cool nights. The
sand was a nuisance, and many went barefooted to avoid getting it in their
shoes. However, it was too hot to stand on by the time the sun had been up
a few hours. On windy days it blew and drifted across the prison pen like
snow, stinging faces and collecting in every inconvenient place. Nature added
to their misery in the form of gnats and mosquitoes. These insects were a

constant torture, bringing with their bite the threat of fever. The sound of the surf, seventy-five yards away, was continual and monotonous, only to be heard beyond the stockade wall.

Dressed in summer clothing, which they had worn since leaving Fort Delaware, the men were prepared for the heat. Their blankets were taken from them if they were United States government issue, on the grounds that they were "stolen property."[20] But they were unnecessary anyway in the late summer Carolina sun. The fresh sea breezes were invigorating and restored their health. Soon they regained their tans, and settled into the monotony of a new prison regimen.

Meanwhile, they came to know each other better, many never having met previously. They were a kaleidoscope of nationalities, social status and occupations. Unlike the Union army's rigid caste system of rank, here colonels and lieutenants often treated each other as equals. This casual attitude toward rank was a peculiar feature of the Southern army, where a rich planter may as easily be a private as a major. The diversity of the Southern officer class was also apparent in this cross-section of 600.

Leon Jastremski was a printer in 1861, when he enlisted at age seventeen. Born in France, his father brought the family to Louisiana, along with his Polish ancestry and adopted French middle-class background. Thus young Leon was a peculiar blend of both, with a Southern twist from growing up in Abbeville, Louisiana. Orphaned as a teenager, he joined the army as a private, and rose through the ranks according to ability, becoming captain.[21] As a veteran at age twenty, he sported a goatee and moustache reminiscent of another famous son of Louisiana, General P. G. T. Beauregard. Prison made him restless, and escape plans took up a fair amount of Leon's time.

Surely the most unlikely officer to be found among this small example was Lieutenant Colonel Paul Francois DeGournay. Born into privilege in France as a marquis, his family still owned ancient title to land in Brittany, and he himself had entered the New Orleans upper crust without difficulty, holding the position of editor of the *Picayune* at the beginning of the war. Previous military experience in Cuba, fighting for that country's independence, had given him the military background he needed in 1861, and he raised and equipped an independent company of Zouave artillery. He saved the Confederate government $10,000 by paying the expenses out of his own pocket, buying uniforms, cannon, and equipment. A strong personal sense of honor and justice had led him to the cause for Southern independence, which he upheld all his life.[22]

There were old-line families represented as well, First Families of Virginia and patriot descendents from the colonial heritage, Revolutionary War soldiers and statesmen.

Captain Thomas Pinckney of the 4th South Carolina Cavalry had been a delicate youth. Educated at the University of Virginia, he also attended the Medical College of South Carolina, graduating in the class of 1849. He was commissioned captain when the war began, raising his own company of cavalry, and carrying the sword his father had carried in the War of 1812. Before that, the same sword had ridden into battle with his grandfather, a general in the Revolutionary War, and helped win American Independence. It was captured at Hawes' Shop, Virginia by Lieutenant James H. Ingersoll, of Custer's Division, along with its third generation owner. Pinckney would never see it again.[23]

Two other South Carolinians experienced a strange coincidence, as they had enlisted together at Secessionville, not far away on St. James Island, in 1861 with the 23rd South Carolina Volunteer Infantry. That seemed a lifetime ago. Captain William W. Covington and Lieutenant Moses P. Galloway were neighbors on adjoining farms in their hometown of Bennettsville, South Carolina, and their friendship would sustain them in this peculiar experience. There were sets of brothers present from Kentucky and Virginia. Captains Dave and Robert Logan had joined the same company together as Morgan's Cavalry first formed in 1861. Alexander and Simon Finks of the 10th Virginia were Madison County boys, from the lush pastures of the Blue Ridge Mountains. The Hughes brothers were in different regiments, but shared their fate together on Morris Island, the relationship as family providing comfort.

Those men were for the most part idealists, perfect representatives of the genteel society which had spawned them. They exhibited the qualities considered as standards for which gentlemen were measured in their day. Those among them who were not born into that world were accepted as equals by those who were, and learned its values and principles in their ranks. Exceptions would emerge, and already apparent to their comrades, would betray the true hearts among them. These traitors were referred to by Henry Dickinson, when he wrote on October 18, "Some of our 600 are not gentlemen, . . . and association with better men does not improve them."

Some led ordinary lives before the war. There were carriage makers, farmers, and clerks of every profession. Others were school teachers, and many were students. They were about to undergo an extraordinary experience. Ranging in age from youths of seventeen to a few in their forties, one third of the Six Hundred were barely out of boyhood, rushed into manhood by three years of war. Their youthfulness probably helped them endure the physical privations much easier, plus the fact that they were seasoned by the exposure to several years of military campaigns.

Still they were young men, many like Captain Junius Hempstead. In 1861, he was an eighteen-year-old cadet at the Virginia Military Institute, having matriculated there as a choice of schools by his father, a states' rights man and governor of the state of Iowa. So young Junius travelled east from Dubuque. Once the war started, he upheld the principles of his adopted state, and joined the 25th Virginia Infantry. He was well liked by his men, who petitioned President Jefferson Davis to promote him to captain. Wounded at Second Manassas, with the Stonewall Brigade, he was soon back in action, serving gallantly until captured in the Bloody Angle at Spotsylvania. A dreamer, artistic, and very expressive, the foundation for a career as a writer was laid in his diary entries, recorded between the lines of a book of rhetoric on Morris Island.[24] He found eight other VMI men among the Six Hundred, and they would share many memories and conversations about the "Institute" over the next few months. Undoubtedly his training as a "rat" helped him endure the hardships. He enjoyed listening to the sea, when it was not drowned out by the sound of guns from Batteries Gregg and Wagner, which were in turn answered by Fort Moultrie, Battery Simkins, and the Confederate artillery on James' Island.

They were a special group, destined for a special purpose and they sensed this. When their 600 names were called out at Fort Delaware for the first time, they became a separate entity, to be used to get even with the acts of their government. Such circumstances were unprecedented in nineteenth-century warfare. A captain from among their number took it upon himself to document this outrage, and began gathering information while on Morris Island. Captain John L. Cantwell had fought in the Mexican War as a youth, and was exempt from service in 1861 by his position in the Confederate States District Court of the Cape Fear District. He entered the war as a colonel in the 51st North Carolina, resigning in 1862. He was a man of principle, however, and, returning to the service with a captain's commission, raised a company of the 3rd North Carolina Infantry.[25] As an officer, he was always sensitive to the needs of the men under his command. He constantly requisitioned for fuel, or clothing, and other articles "for the necessity of the men," as he explained on the army forms. A caring and ever vigilant attitude shown like a gemstone in the stockade on that desolate island.

He began to make a list of all his fellow officers, first those from his native North Carolina, getting their statistics, even addresses. Then he expanded his work to a list of all the Six Hundred. He recorded the sick and wounded who were sent to Beaufort, and would meticulously note any particulars of the fates of those with whom he shared the experience. His compassion would never waver throughout the trials that awaited them all.

Immediately after the arrival of the Six Hundred, on September 8, General Foster diligently began shelling Forts Sumter and Moultrie and the city of Charleston. It was the grand finale to what became known as the Third Great Bombardment of Charleston.[26] Most of the men became convinced he was using their presence to stop the guns in the harbor in order to get an advantage and launch an attack by land. Soon, they resigned themselves to the shelling, and the danger it presented.

September 8th.- Firing kept up at intervals yesterday. . . . Other guns are being mounted by the enemy around us, supposed to be with the intention of changing our own fire toward us. While we much deplore the fact that the year of Our Lord 1864 has witnessed a scene so shocking to civilization and enlightment, as hos-

1LT. JAMES
W. A. FORD,
20TH VA. CAV.

tages, and if need be martyrs, for our oppressed and struggling
country's sake, we will bear all without a murmur of reproach.[27]

At first the men, especially the infantry, felt trapped and helpless, and a
sense of panic ensued. There was absolutely no protection from the shells,
which they could see going overhead. Then it became so frequent, their lot in
life so painful and despairing, some seemed hardly to care what happened to
them. Their role in a fratricidal war took on an ominous new meaning.

1LT. JAMES
W. A. FORD,
20TH VA. CAV.

September 9th.- A terrific artillery duel between the Federal bat-
teries and Ft. Moultrie commenced about sun set and continued
until ten o'clock. The shells from "Wagner" (which is about 150
yds. in our rear) passed directly over us and could be seen dis-
tinctly. In a short time our shells in reply are seen to fall and ex-
plode with great accuracy over Fts. Gregg and Chatfield, in our
front. Soon they began to ascend, it seemed more beautifully and
majestically than ever. It being nearly dark and the burning fire
more plainly seen, but instead of falling on Gregg they came di-
rectly over us and burst upon Wagner. This produced no little ex-
citement amongst the 600 confederates confined in a space of not
more than one or one and one-half acres and well it might for if
the faithful gunners at Moultrie should cut their fire 2, 3 or 5
seconds short we should fall the victims. Besides 2 or 3 shells al-
ready have burst from the guns at Wagner prematurely, scatter-
ing fragments through our camp but without injuring any of our
party. A Federal Sargeant (White) looses his leg and has his horse
killed under him. The shelling at W. continued for an hour or longer
when two shells successively burst immediately over our camp
throwing fragments in every direction. Several pieces were thrown
in the enclosure close to several officers. But, thanks to God, no
injury was sustained. Just imagine our position. Tied hands and
feet as it were without the means of defending ourselves and know
not what moment we may be writhing and bleeding under the
effects of the bursting of terrible shell. Thus have passed five or
six hours of painful suspense as perhaps were never passed by the
same number of men before. We can say that we are undoubtably,
emphatically and unequoivically under fire. The barbarous work
has begun. When shall it end?[28]

LETTER, CAPT.
LEON
JASTREMSKI,
10TH LA. INF.,
TO BROTHER
JOHN, SEPT. 11,
1864

Together with a party of 600 Confederate officers, Prisoners of
War, I arrived at this place on the 8th of the present month after a
stay of 18 days on the U.S. Steamer Crescent, *since our departure*
from Fort Delaware. We are encamped between what were for-
merly batteries Gregg and Wagner, and in full range of the Con-
federate batteries. Several shells burst over our encampment night

before last, doing no damage however to any one;—In fact the only harm that was done us by the firing was to prevent us from sleeping for a good part of the night on account of the occassional reports of the artillery. I hope that the military authorities on both sides will reconsider this matter and exchange their prisoners in order that at least if they are to be killed by shot, that it may not be caused by friendly hands. I am in good health and spirits and patiently awaiting an exchange. My love to all the family. Answer soon. Enclose stamps.

P.S. Send me $10.—No more.[29]

What shelling was done was mostly done at night. Some of the shells burst over the stockade and the pieces would fall around, but I don't remember that any of the prisoners were hit. It was rather uncomfortable, though, to lie there and watch the big shells sailing through the air, which we could see at night by the fuse burning, and sometimes burst above us, instead of bursting in or above the Yankee forts 100 yards further on, and then listen at the fragments humming through the air and hear them strike the ground with a dull thud among the tents. We would first hear a distant boom, two miles away towards Charleston, and then begin to look and listen for the shell which was sure to follow that boom. Peter Akers used to say, 'That is trusting too much to the fuse to shoot two miles and expect the shell to burst 100 yards beyond the stockade.'[30]

CAPT. WILLIAM H. MORGAN, 11TH VA. INF.

October 11, 1864.- In this engagement Moultrie fired splendidly, only two or three shots falling too short; the great majority fell into Wagner. Most of our shells were from mortars and looked as if they would fall directly on us, but, whilst we held our breath in anxious expectation, its parabolic course would land it in the fort. Every good shot was applauded by us as loudly as we dared. We were but 250 yards from the spot at which these monster shells were directed, and too little powder or a slight elevation of the mortar might have killed many of us since we were so crowded together. But it was a trial of Southern against Northern gunnery. We were the probable victims and we were willing to see them fight it out. One shell fell near the fort, and afterwards exploded, throwing the screw backwards, endangering us; another fell just twenty feet beyond us, among the negroes, and made them scatter terribly. Unluckily, it did not explode. Two shells exploded over us throwing great and small pieces all about our camp.[31]

CAPT. HENRY DICKINSON, 2ND VA. INF.

9 Sept.- The shell fell all around us, but only a few pieces in our midst. We are in Quarters between batteries Wagner & Gregg— Wagner fires over our heads—Gregg about ½ mile on our left in

2LT. SAMUEL H. HAWES, ORANGE ARTY. (VA.)

front. This retaliation policy may ? be alright, but it is anything
but a pleasant position for those who are operated upon.[32]

It was a hard experience for men of action, all commissioned officers, used to giving orders, not taking them. A few resented the black troops of the 54th being in charge of them; most seem to have put things in perspective. No doubt the artillerymen among them, like Colonel DeGournay and the others who had held the Port Hudson garrison were reminded of those difficult days of bombardment and starvation. Perhaps some familiar with guns, being artillery officers, felt right in their element, and were not too alarmed by the shelling. For others, it began forty-five days of constant pounding and ground-jarring noise, which started almost immediately, on the second day.

CAPT. JOHN DUNKLE, 25TH VA. INF.

Oh, the misery of having the ear constantly filled with such doleful sounds, the misery, the horrible misery, the wretched agony of anticipating death at every moment! The battle-field was pleasure compared with this, for its scenes only lasted a few hours and only occurred a few times in a year; but here death from shells was a continual dread. The mind was continually filled with the horrible prospect of instant death, not only now and then, but every moment. Both day and night, there was no one moment that the mind was free from the dreadful thought . . . exposed to the continual shelling of the Confederate guns and also the Federal guns of Wagner, we lingered on from day to day. Also at the hands of our cruel guards we suffered every indignity and cruel punishment which could be inflicted upon us.[33]

CAPT. HENRY DICKINSON, 2ND VA. CAV.

Our greatest danger in the combat was from a premature explosion of a shell from Wagner, which fired 154 shots directly on our camp and those at Moultrie directly over our heads. Two shells did prematurely explode, throwing huge pieces into our camp, many fragments flying just over our heads, and one of the shells exploded the huge gun, killing a horse and cutting off a man's leg. One of these pieces buried itself in the wall behind my head, whilst a number of pieces fell in a street between us and the fence; another piece struck within two inches of Captain Lewis, five tents distant from us.[34]

CAPT. FRANKLIN C. BARNES, 56TH VA. INF.

The first evening and night the shelling was very heavy but none of us were killed. It seemed our guns got the range and fired over us. One morning while Captain Findley, of Virginia, J. E. Cobb, H. Coffey and myself were in our small tent just after Captain Findley had read a chapter in a Bible, which I now have and in which I placed all the notes of all my travels, a large shell fell right at our feet and covered us all with sand, but fortunately did not explode nor break up our accustomed worship.[35]

In the evening of the second day Wagner opened fire on Moultrie. Soon Gregg opened fire, and the two made the sand island quiver and shake as if it would melt from under us. For several hours this continued, Moultrie remaining silent. Our friends knew that we were staked between Wagner and Gregg. A little after dark a boom from that direction gave notice that old Moultrie would remain silent no longer. I watched the fiery globe as it curved gracefully in the air and descended with frightful rapidity right upon me, as it seemed, but it passed over into the garrison of Wagner. I sat in the door of my tent and watched the battle. The whole heavens were illuminated and the mortar-shells were darting through the heavens in all directions as though the sky were full of meteors. Moultrie had opened with all her mortars, and for some time continued to throw her shells either into Wagner or Gregg. At last one came that looked as if it would surely fall upon me. It came closer and faster, and finally burst right over us, striking several tents, but injuring no one. About one o'clock the firing ceased, and we went to sleep.[36]

2 Lt. Henry H. Cook, 44th Tenn. Inf.

They were under fire from four sides—Sumter and Moultrie to the front and Wagner in the rear, monitors on the seaside, and batteries Simkins and Johnson in the cul-de-sac mouth of the harbor. The heavy guns at Wagner, mostly 30, 100, and 200 pound Parrots, were not as dangerous as the mortars, whose shells, falling short, would land directly in the stockade.

The immediate heavy shelling coincided with both the arrival of the 600 prisoners and reinforcements to the Union army on Morris Island and Hilton Head. Foster had also received word that the Union prisoners of war in Charleston were planning an escape attempt. He intended to aid them by distracting the Confederates with heavy shelling, to commence on Thursday, 6 September.[37]

Foster had notified Jones that he was told by deserters and exchanged prisoners of more Union prisoners of war in Charleston. Jones acknowledged, explaining that it was only temporary due to the necessary move from Andersonville, and the prisoners would be removed as soon as possible.[38] Actually Jones requested the Union prisoners be moved before the 600 officers even arrived on Morris Island, but it was impossible. He further stated that the prisoners were well cared for, and allowed to freely communicate with their army.[39] Indeed there had been no complaint of disruption in the flow of mail and supplies the Union prisoners had received. On September 10, General Jones notified Foster of receiving word that there were Confederate officers under fire from Sumter "because I believe you are retaliating on those officers for a supposed disregard of the usages of civilized warfare in the treatment extended to U.S. officers, prisoners of war, now in this city. Those officers are comfortably housed and receive the treatment due prisoners of war."[40] It was to be understood that this uncivilized method of warfare was abhorrent, and he urged Foster to dispense with his plans.

Prior to these communications, General Foster attempted to notify Jones that the Confederate officers were in the vicinity of Fort Wagner. He suggested a flag of truce be sent to the Confederate commander, accompanied by one of the prisoners, to explain the danger of his comrades if firing continued on Wagner and Gregg. The officer chosen was a young captain, age eighteen. He had attended VMI with Junius Hempstead, though Lewis Harman was a year behind, and became a drill master when the war started. When informed of the intent to send him to General Jones, and for what purpose, Captain Harman said with conviction, "Our lives are offered to our country and it matters little by what shot we fall." He vouched for the decision of all his 559 comrades when he said any prisoner thus sent would tell the Confederates to fire away.[41] Accepting the fact that this would do little good, Foster instead sent Jones the written communication.

If the charges of retaliation were the only reason for locating the men on Morris Island, the officers could have been put under fire elsewhere, such as the siege lines at Petersburg which was much closer to Fort Delaware than Charleston. In the letter to Hallack dated August 18, Foster refers to Jones' placing the officers in Charleston as a matter of simply no choice.[42] The same day he sent correspondence to Admiral Dahlgren requesting more guns be mounted at the batteries of Gregg and Wagner on Morris Island, as well as the new battery constructed and named Chadfield.[43] It seems more than coincidence that their arrival at this particular time and place benefitted the Union shelling on Charleston and its batteries.

Charleston was the best location for the Union prisoners. Rations were good, quarters healthy and spacious. But upon Foster's urging that they be removed, Jones had no choice but to send them to a hastily prepared field near Columbia with poor supply lines.[44]

On September 12, only a few days after the arrival of the Six Hundred in the stockade on Morris Island, the issue of rations arose when Foster received orders describing what the Union prisoners were allowed in Charleston. They were per day as follows:[45]

> Three-quarters pound of fresh meat
> or one-half pound of salt meat
> One-fifth pint rice
> One-half pound of hard bread
> or one-half pint of meal
> one-fifth pint of beans

This was certainly not starvation rations, and the Union officers in confinement in Charleston were not complaining.

LT. LOUIS R. FORTESCUE, U.S. SIGNAL CORPS	*August 18th, 1864.- Rations are rather good at present. They consist of about 3/4 to 1 lb. of fresh meat; 2/3 qt. of corn meal very little salt, 1/2 pt. of flour and about 1 qt. of rice and beans mixed per day. These things we get along with very well if any vegetables*

can be procured but as they are rather high priced and cash rather scarce we are unfortunately compelled very often to go without them. A few boxes from home or our friends the Sanitary boys would be very acceptable at present.

Aug. 24.- We received a visit this morning from three of the Sisters of Charity. These women are really the most humane and benevolent I have met with inside the Confederate lines. They are daily in attendance at our hospital a few blocks from our present quarters. . . . In a conversation I had with one she spoke of the inhumanity of one of our Generals in not allowing a box of medicines to come through that had been sent . . . from some friends.[46]

Our rations consisted of a pint of corn meal, about one-half cupful of cooked rice, and one-half pound of beef and a little salt every 24 hours.[47]	2LT. JAMES M. PAGE, 6TH MICH. CAV.

Those with whom we communicated complained of short rations, which we were not subjected to, for ours were what might be called sufficient, and of fair quality, including frequent issues of meat.	LT. BENJAMIN S. CALEF, 2ND REG. U.S. SHARPSHOOTERS

Three hundred of our officers were in the Marine Hospital, on the same square, which rumor proclaimed to be a very nice place, and as many more were at the Roper Hospital, where I was anxious to go that I might meet and be with my friends. Not receiving any reply to numerous applications for my removal, I had about given up the hope of change, when the welcome order came, and the evening of September 4 found me within its walls . . . We were permitted to burn the gas until nine o'clock p.m., which luxury we fully enjoyed and appreciated, serving as it did to make the evening pass quickly and pleasantly. I should not omit to speak of the long piazza at the front, on which I have spent so many hours with my pipe for my companion.

At Charleston, our money was not taken from us . . . We received our mails more regularly, another inexpressible comfort.[48]

Such was not indicative of the treatment the 600 Confederate officers on Morris island were getting. All mail was withheld for the beginning period on the Island. Their ration was described as "retaliation rations" and barely staved off hunger.[49] Foster sent correspondence to Hallowell which stated that the prisoners were to be fed like the Union prisoners at Andersonville and Salisbury, North Carolina. He included the diet of the Charleston officers as an example for the rations of the Six Hundred and ordered such to be put into effect. There is no correspondence ordering Hallowell to act differently. However, Hallowell held full power over the prisoners, and the Union authorities never monitored his actions. Left up to his own discretion, Hallowell used psychological tactics in an attempt to break down morale.

One particular instance was his pressure to force the prisoners to take the oath of allegiance. General Foster stated that three prisoners had been refused permission on the grounds that "Owing to the peculiar purpose for which they were sent to me I have declined acceding to their request . . . "[50] Yet the prisoners were continually enticed to take the oath, receiving pamphlets on the subject. All refused except the five spoken of by Foster. Despite the constant badgering by Hallowell, had they capitulated they would not have been allowed parole. It would only have served to demoralize them. Hallowell recognized the effect his insistence had. Many prisoners felt he added incentive to give in by withholding food. There is evidence to suggest that Foster had ordered sufficient rations, but Hallowell did not issue such. Those men sent to Beaufort received sufficient rations at the hospital. Certainly Hallowell did not enforce the orders he received, but ran the stockade according to what he felt the prisoners deserved, and this led to mercilessness not necessarily intended by Union authorities.

2LT. WILLIAM WORTH GEORGE, 26TH VA. INF.

For rations we were furnished with three army crackers per day, and a half pint of soup. The crackers were issued in the morning and in the following manner: Two poles, eight or ten feet long were attached one to either side of a cracker box, forming a kind of hand-litter, which was borne by two negroes, one walking in front, the other behind. As the box passed our tents, if no one was ready to receive the crackers, the corporal in charge would throw them to us, giving each his daily allowance.

About noon the half pint of soup was passed. It was called bean soup, but we could never discover any traces of that vegetable in the mixture. In this way we were fed during the forty-four days of our imprisonment in the stockade at Morris Island.[51]

CAPT. JUNIUS L. HEMPSTEAD, 25TH VA. INF.

Saturday, September 24 1864.- Drew for the day 2 hard-tacks and a pint of rice for supper. How I suffer for something to eat. I would eat the crumbs of my table (at home). How long will the misery continue—mercy deliver us from the hands of our enemies. We are like cattle fed and watered in the same manner, only they get enough to eat. We are half-starved.[52]

The rations did not improve, and after several days, Hallowell was questioned about the harsh treatment.

CAPT. WALTER MCRAE, 7TH N.C. INF.

Some of the prisoners, for the sake of the record complained to the colonel. He replied that it was all right; there was meat enough in the meal, bugs and worms, and that if he had his own way he would be only too glad to feed us on greasy rags.[53]

I have before spoken of the lively nature of the bread. Any one who had not seen it would hardly credit the amount of dead animal matter in the shape of white worms, which was in the mush given us. For my own part, I was always too hungry to be dainty—worms, mush and all went to satisfy the cravings of nature. But I knew of several persons, who, attempting to pick them out, having thrown out from fifty to eighty, stopped picking them out, not because the worms were all gone, but because the little bit of mush was going with them.[54]

CAPT. GEORGE
W. NELSON,
HANOVER ARTY.
(VA.)

Sept. 10th.- As the Yankees are continually boasting about how well they feed us, I will attempt to give a correct account of each meal. Roll call one and one-half hours by sun for breakfast, three crackers issued, one tablespoon of rice. . . . Rations for dinner, one-half pint bean soup, two crackers, wormy and full of bugs. Rations for supper, two ounces of bacon, two crackers, wormy as usual.

CAPT. ALEX
BEDFORD,
3RD MO. CAV.

Sept. 11th.- . . . Water full of wiggle-tails today. Rations old salt beef, two ounces, one cracker, wormy as usual.

Sept. 12th.- Rations for breakfast two ounces old salt beef, so badly spoiled that we could not eat half of it. Three crackers, musty and full of worms—not fit for hogs. One of our officers showed his rations of crackers to the Colonel in charge of us (Col. Hallowell, 54th Mass.). His reply was "Do you know that fifty of our officers are now in Charleston, in cells fed on bread and water?" The prisoners wished to know the reason. His reply was "Because they are Yankees."... I am well, but feel weak and hungry, falling off very fast.

Sept. 15th.- Wrote to my wife, very hungry, never any other way.

Sept. 16th.- Am very hungry, every time I sleep I dream of something good to eat. The crackers we get will not make two good mouthfuls, they are so thin and small.[55]

During the first few days when the scanty ration was issued the negroes were so much ashamed that they apologized by saying that it was new to the officer, and he would do better in the future, but it was soon apparent that there was a determination to make us live down to the very lowest limit capable of sustaining life. . . . So extreme was the hunger of some that they dug down with their hands for grass roots for subsistence.[56]

CAPTAIN HENRY
DICKINSON,
2ND VA. CAV.

After about three weeks of this harsh treatment, the rations were further cut to a quarter of the regular amount, and very soon all the officers began to feel the effects in various intestinal disorders and weakness. Added to this was a shortage of water, which they obtained from digging holes in the sand outside the tents and waiting for enough to seep in. One officer, attempting to deepen the well, dug down and found a body of one of the 54th Massachusetts soldiers killed in the assault on Fort Wagner the previous summer. He advised all not to use that particular well in the future.[57]

They fought the war in a different way now—psychologically against degradation and boredom, physically against starvation and sickness. Time became an added enemy. Daily the routine never varied, filled with shelling, hunger, and tension. Added to this was the final act which prisoners of war have always dreaded—humiliation. A great amount of verbal abuse was heaped upon the men, some by the guards, but mostly by Colonel Hallowell and the white officers.[58] On the outside, the men continued to wear a brave face, bearing indignities, insults, and fighting the mental effects of being condemned as "wrong," "traitors," and accused of fighting for slavery. This latter notion came as a surprise to many officers, for they consistently upheld States Rights' and the U.S. Constitution as why the South went to war.[59]

Inside, they felt defenseless, fearful, and sometimes even forgotten. Each bore the universal burden of the Southern fighting man: concern for their homes and loved ones whose land had been invaded by a destructive enemy. As soldiers at the front, they had a certain amount of control over this, at least they were fighting. As prisoners of war, they were helpless, frustrated, and usually uninformed of the war in the field, for they received no newspapers. Their stars had risen with the military success of their young nation, and now their military careers were cut short, all hopes of promotion ended with capture. They were well aware that under the circumstances, they could die for a principle.

They constantly fought the notion that it was a disgrace to be a prisoner of war, comparing their fate to that of Lafayette, Napoleon I and even St. Paul. This kept them from submitting to feelings of inferiority when insulted by guards. Their feelings were hidden from the enemy, but recorded daily in personal journals or discussed among themselves. That baring of their innermost thoughts served as a sort of therapy, and outlet for their frustrations, revealing the sensitivity of a remarkable group of men.

CAPT. ALEX BEDFORD, 3RD MO. CAV.

October 16th.- This has been a day long to be remembered. Starvation has looked us fairly in the face. I have laid down at night and thought what will I come to. Shall I starve here? I have hoped and prayed for better days. I have prayed for my enemies that their hearts might be softened. I believe my prayers have been heard and answered. I am encouraged still to trust in God and all will be well. I have finished reading the Bible through twice since a prisoner.[60]

CAPT. JUNIUS L. HEMPSTEAD, 25TH VA. INF.

Thursday, (Sept) 29th, 1864.- Sun rose in a clear sky. Going to be a pretty day. Drew for breakfast a small piece of meat. Am getting so tired of retaliation ... They are starving us by degrees. ...

It is a mean thing. Dishonorable in both governments to treat prisoners of war. We are so helpless, in the way they do. We fight and die for them and this is the way they treat us. I will never be a military man again as long as I live if I get out of this. I am home sick and want to get home so bad. I have been away from home some long years and would give anything most to see them all.[61]

Most of the prisoners were suffering with acute dysentery. From this terrible complaint not one escaped; but none of our men complained; none murmured against our government. We knew the Richmond authorities were doing all they could for us, and like the dying Caesar, we were too proud to let our Yankee jailors see that we suffered.[62]

CAPT. J. OGDEN
MURRAY,
11TH VA. CAV.

20th Sept.- Still at Morris Island—the rations given us are abominable, rancid meat, with hard crackers in which we can see the worms and bugs crawling through, we are weak and suffering on account of this detestable manner of living—but few of us have blankets, our beds being the ground with scarcely enough straw to hide the sand—Oh how long, how long. Is not this enough to dispirit anyone? Nil desperandum![63]

2LT. SAMUEL H.
HAWES, ORANGE
ARTY. (VA.)

Today, I have been a prisoner for five long months; I have received only one letter from home, dated the twelfth of June, and none from Dixie friends during that time. . . . My friends, my sister and my wife have all been silent, and so long. Are they dead? I hope not, and yet the picture of a desolate hearthstone will often present itself—a home to me no longer. With such fears, how long are the days, and weeks, and months . . . What will history say of this cruelty to us?[64]

CAPT. HENRY
DICKINSON,
2ND VA. CAV.

Sept. 16.- Rapid firing from both sides this evening. Many shells exploding very near our pen. Hunger gnaws at our stomicks. The food being unfit to eat. Time hangs heavy on our hands.[65]

1LT. JAMES
W. A. FORD,
20TH VA. CAV.

September 11, 1864.- I have seldom felt as lonely and never longed more for liberty and to be at home in my life before. The day was very long to me.

CAPT. D.C.
GRAYSON,
10TH VA. INF.

September 21, 1864.- Another day has passed and although time is moving on as rapidly as wheels can carry him, and old age is approaching so fast, how tediously it seems to pass here. I love to number the days with the past, notwithstanding each day but hurries me to the grave, but what is life when deprived of liberty? Oh! how long must we endure such deprivations and submit to Yankee tyranny? God forbid it should be long . . . Rations today . . . Crackers all wormy and meat small and fat, but such is Yankee retaliation, and if it be for the good of my country I willingly yield.[66]

September dragged by, and the heavy shelling continued. The rations worsened, both in quality and amount issued. News was received that Atlanta had fallen to Sherman and surely this was a blow to the prisoners. Guns were fired in salute, which were in turn answered by the batteries at Sumter and Moultrie.[67] The long days of sunlight brought rain, or intense heat, and the prisoners passed time as best they could. On clear windy days they could hear the distant church bells of Charleston. On some nights, the sky was ablaze, illuminated from flames of burning buildings in the city, caused by the incendiary shells fired from Morris Island.[68] Finally, on September 22, they felt the end of retaliation had come when orders were received to pack up and be prepared to leave for exchange.

1LT. JAMES W. A. FORD, 20TH VA. CAV.

Sept. 22nd.- Received orders to bundle up and be ready to move. Many are the conjectures. Are marched to the wharf (3-1/2 miles) and embark on an "Old Schooner" where we remain all night. Two hundred and seventy-five of us placed in the "Hold" of the vessel, filled with dirt and rubbish and abounding in rats of huge dimensions. The space being small and the men were compelled to lie and stand up on each other and in consequence not much sleep was indulged in. Tomorrow is the day fixed for the meeting of the "Two Boats" in the Harbor. We regard this as significant of our early exchange. It is very warm and uncomfortable on board. Mosquitoes raging. My wound and whole system aching intensely caused by the walk from camp. Yet only two crackers and a small portion of meat. [69]

CAPT. JUNIUS HEMPSTEAD, 25TH VA. INF.

Thursday, September 22nd 1864.- We thought we were going to be exchanged. Marched down the beach to the pier and were put on board the steamer General Hooker *and from there transferred to the schooner* Jennie Morton *and put down in a deep dark hold with very little air to breathe. 275 packed in that small space did not have room to lie down and when you did get to sleep the rats would run over you. One ran across my face and the place was so close and stifling I could scarcely breathe. Was so glad when morning came. Was in hopes of being exchanged next day; slept once— about ten feet under. Drew one cracker and some soup, half sand and gravel, to last for the day.* [70]

CAPT. JAMES ROBERT McMICHAEL, 12TH GA. INF.

Thursday, September 22.- Orders were given to pack up get ready to march to wharf—then our hearts leaped with joy; everything looked bright. When we got to the wharf about 1/2 the number were placed on our steamer; the remaining half of us waited patiently in the hot sun until Gen. Hooker *steamed up and received us. We knew nothing of the disposition that had been made with the others, but alas, we soon passed the brig that contained them in its ballast cell, though not a man was seen, and near it lay an old brig damaged by lightning. We were transferred to it and ordered down into the bottom hole where I spent the most miserable night I ever did. . . . We had no air or light except what passed down through the hatchway. I tried in vain to sleep but I had to struggle too hard for breath . . .*[71]

Crowded in the dismal old ship hulls, that night it began to rain, adding to the depression. They hoped for exchange, but most felt it would be like so many previous false alarms. A few hundred yards away, on the truce boats, a handful of selected agents played with the fate of thousands, but none of the Six Hundred would benefit from the bargains. Very few exchanges were made, mostly privates or naval officers, and packages and mail for the prisoners.[72]

Aside from their special purpose in the retaliation game, the Six Hundred were also victims of bad timing. On August 17, before they had left Fort Delaware, Foster notified Halleck that the Confederate authorities were willing to exchange prisoners, man for man, on U.S. terms.[73] While the Six Hundred were en route to Hilton Head, on August 21, Grant interceded and notified Foster that he was not to exchange prisoners under any circumstances.[74] Thus their fate was sealed. Arriving in Port Royal Harbor on August 26, the *Crescent City* was detained while the bickering continued. Major General Ethan Allen Hitchcock, who did much to hamper the efficiency of exchange policies between Ould and Mulford, notified Stanton inaccurately that it was the Confederacy that was making exchange difficult.[75]

Foster gave Dahlgren orders that the *Crescent City* was to be detained in Charleston Harbor under fire of gunboats on September 1, and there she sat for over a week. The only prisoners exchanged were the sick and wounded which Grant begrudgingly allowed, and this was when the forty officers were removed from the *Crescent City* and taken to the U.S. army hospital at Beaufort. For the next few months, special exchanges were made on a select basis, but the remaining officers who were removed to Morris Island all but disappear in the correspondence for the rest of 1864. They appear to have been either completely forgotten or declared ineligible in any exchange bargaining. Yet they waited expectantly to hear that they would be among the lucky men chosen.

Prison stockade on Morris Island where the Six Hundred were confined from September 7, 1864 until they were removed on October 21.

Library of Congress

(View from the Inside)

Library of Congress

(View from the Outside)

Stockade

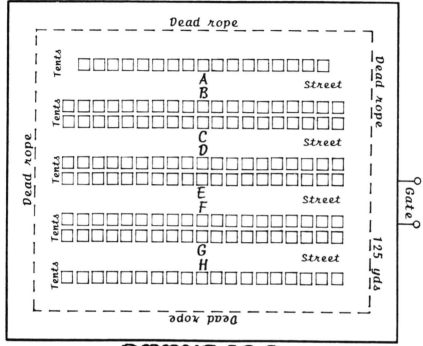

Prison Stockade on Morris Island, S.C.
Taken from a sketch made by Lt. John D. Greever, 50th Virginia Infantry.

CHAPTER SEVEN

Life Under Fire

WHILE the men waited in the hulks of the old schooners, some brainstormed, looking for a chance to escape. The most persistent man among them all in this endeavor was a young captain from Tennessee. He had ridden with both General Nathan Bedford Forrest's and General Joe Wheeler's Cavalry, which proved his mettle. He was also Lieutenant Henry Cook's best friend, the only other man from Franklin, Tennessee among the Six Hundred.

Captain Tom Perkins had become well known by the authorities at every prison he was confined. He first escaped from Camp Chase, where he was imprisoned after his capture at Franklin, Tennessee. Only days later he was recaptured and placed in solitary confinement, shackled with a thirty-five pound ball and chain. At Fort Delaware, he attempted to escape across the Delaware River by swimming through the privy. And he had tried to dig a tunnel in his tent on Morris Island the first day there. Perkins, along with five other adventurous soldiers, concluded that it was then or never when orders were received to march the prisoners back to the stockade. If they could get out of the hold, it was possible to swim to the nearby mainland. One of these determined men was Richard Adams.

1LT. RICHARD
H. ADAMS, JR.,
C.S. ENGINEER
CORPS

On the evening of 23rd Sept. we were ordered back to our prison. Capt. Perkins, Capt. Harman, Capt. Jastremski, Lieut. Fickerson & myself hid ourselves on the Schooner with the intention of making our escape at dark. All went well. All the prisoners went off. The guard followed after one of the negroes (the guard) came in three inches of my head with a huge flat foot. Soon we heard the steamer move off, & my heart beat as high as when the guard passed my hole & did not find me. I felt as though I was free. . . . I crawled out of my hole to get fresh air & also to reconnoitre & see if "land was ahead". Found everything all right . . . then thought it best to keep out of Sight of the crew whom we did not like to trust. I made my way into the pantry & Lumber room & got under a pile of sails. My place was too hot & as I was rather impatient for night & darkness to come on (Knowing they would come back & search for us as soon as the roll was called & we found missing) I began to wander about the room and see what was in it besides ropes, sails, & a great many other things to which I do not know what nautical phrase to apply. I found a barrel of nice ship biscuit & a barrel of Sugar. I ate sugar with the crackers to my hearts' content. Just as I got my fill, a perfect feast, I heard a noise at the hatch. A "little bird" whispered "Rat to your hole" & the "Rat" found a hole. Peeping out with one eye I saw the cook come down to draw supper. He went back, pulled the hatch back & darkness reigned, but only in the part of the schooner we were in. We of course, were wishing forever impatient for Twilight. . . . But said mantle seemed to fall more slowly that evening than I ever saw it. Finally it came & we crawled out of our holes and went "below". Right over the hatchway through which we had to go out the Capt. of the schooner swung his hammock & laid himself down to sleep. We, as noiseless as rats, crawled by him & once more in the "hole" went to the forward hatchway but found the crew all sitting around it taking an evening talk. So we had to wait for them, "cussing the luck", thinking the guard would be back every minute to search for us. One by one they went away. I then went up on deck for another reconnaissance & found the way clear. Then back to report the success of my mission. Tied our clothes on a plank each & were about to launch our barks upon the deep when a boat struck & we heard the guard jump on deck. . . . We knew it was useless to hide so we appointed Lieut. Fickerson to surrender the party which he did with a great deal of Grace & Elegance.[1]

Whilst cooped up below, sweltering with heat, Captain Perkins, of Forrest's Cavalry, found an old saw and with it and a good knife commenced cutting a hole through the boat near the stern, intending to get out on the night of the twenty-third. Though assisted by Captain Harman, Capt. Jastremski, Capt. Fickerson, Capt. Coffee, and Private Dick Adams, they did not get through the thick plank before we were ordered to disembark. They all determined to escape if possible, and accordingly remained on the boat, hiding in the hold, where it was as dark as midnight. Being anchored in lighthouse inlet the distance to Folley Island was only one hundred yards, but that island was closely picketed between the point and Secessionville, and besides the party could not leave the boat until it was dark. Dark came, but the boat's crew sat about the hatches for some time, and during this precious time, one roll had been called; as a result a guard was double-quicked back to the

CAPT. HENRY
DICKINSON,
2ND VA. CAV.

boat, reaching there just in time to meet Perkins coming up the hatchway, naked and preparing to take the swim. All hands except Coffee, who could not be found, soon surrendered, and the guard finally started back, supposing he had escaped. After the guard left, the captain of the schooner discovered Coffee standing as large as life among the crew, with whom he had mingled unobserved, and whom he had assisted in the search for himself.[2]

CAPT. THOMAS
PINCKNEY,
4TH S.C. CAV.

Capt. Coffee of Mississippi, who was an excellent swimmer, concluded if he could get into the water after dark he could easily reach Secessionville, plainly in sight from us up the Inlet, accordingly when the steamer returned to take us back to shore in the afternoon, he concealed himself in a top bunk and "lay low" until the steamer left, and when all was quiet, he crept up on deck, where there was only a boy at the galley fire, with whom he made friends, the men being down in the forecastle playing cards. Everything was favorable if dark would only come, when he would slip down the anchor chain into the water, but the sun certainly appeared to him to stand still, finally it sunk below the horizon, just then he saw the steamer returning. As soon as she came alongside, an officer stepped aboard saying two of the prisoners had escaped and he was going to search the boats for them. He had his lantern in his hand, which Coffee stepped forward to take, offering to show him all over the ship—which he did, calling his attention to the advantages offered by the bunk in which he had concealed himself. On returning to the deck, to proceed to search the other boat, he encountered the Captain who had been ashore, but had hastened back to find out why the steamer had returned, the officer told him his quest. Coffee says his knees smote together, when the Captain pointing at him said he had never seen the man before that carried his lantern, and was not responsible for him! The ruse flashed upon the officer at once, he slapped Coffee on the back, saying, "My good fellow, you played that well, and deserve a better fate, but you are one of the 'Johnnies' I am looking for, so step aboard with me."[3]

The missing men were recaptured and the rest were notified that there would be no exchange. As they were formed in ranks to march back up the beach to the stockade, disappointment was obvious in each countenance, and they saw the flags of the truce ships, their only chance of salvation, departing when the boats drifted apart in the harbor.

CAPT. JAMES
ROBERT
MCMICHAEL,
12TH GA. INF.

Friday, Sept. 23.- We were allowed to come up out of the dark and breathe about 10 o'clock. Flag of truce boats meet and after four hours interview separated. We were high up again at the prospect of being exchanged but soon after the boats parted we

saw guards coming to the wharf to escort us back to the stock-
ade, and as we slowly moved up the beach, I looked around and
every man was silent, head down. I wondered if any crowd march-
ing to the grave of an esteemed friend could have so solemn and
doleful an appearance.[4]

23rd Sept.- Left our place of torture on board of the schooner, and
landed again on Morris Island. Again placed under fire between
batteries Wagner & Gregg. Those having charge of us seem to be
trying the horse experiment with us, that is, to see how little we
can live on—if they keep us at the rate of reduction of rations at
which they have been giving, it will not be long before we are
brought down to the equivalent of one straw per day.[5]

2LT. SAMUEL H.
HAWES, ORANGE
ARTY. (VA.)

[Sept.23rd].- No little excitement prevails this morning in anticipa-
tion of the result of the conference appointed to take place at noon
in the Harbor. As the hour draws near every eye watches with
intense interest the departure of the respective boats for the place
of meeting and as they haul up along side of each other and stand
motionless hour after hour, many and conflicting are the conclu-
sions as to the disposition that will be made of us. The Federal
boat finally moves for its wharf and the Confederate boat stands
still for a few minutes as if waiting its return. Tis then every heart
is filled with inexplicable emotions of delight and one universal
cry is raised "Deliverance Hath Come". But alas, for human judge-
ment! Stern reality crushes out the bright visions of our fancy in a
moment. Disappointment again masks. Our boat weighs anchor
and slowly vanishes from our sight and we resign ourselves to our
fate. We are returned to our stockade heartsick, tired and foot-
sore, but few words are spoken. Thus ends the day from which we
had hoped so much.[6]

1LT. JAMES
W. A. FORD,
20TH VA. CAV.

The move to the old schooners had not been for exchange purposes, but
in order that their quarters could be searched for escape attempts, or articles of contraband.[7]

The month of September drew to a close, without change; the heavy
shelling on Charleston continued. General Sam Jones, concerned for the officers' safety on Morris Island, had threatened to put 600 Union officers on
the ramparts of Fort Sumter if Foster didn't dispense with the retaliation.[8]
Jones further removed the excuse for retaliation, by notifying his superiors
that yellow fever was becoming an epidemic, and all non-combatants and
prisoners of war should be removed to prevent a larger outbreak. Consequently, on October 8, the Union prisoners in Charleston were sent to Florence and Columbia, further inland.

LT. BENJAMIN S. CALEF, 2ND REGT. U.S. SHARPSHOOTERS

About the first of October the yellow-fever made itself known in our midst. That we should be instantly moved not humanity alone but the sanitary condition of the city demanded, and immediate steps were taken toward that end. The order was to me unwelcome, for I knew another place could not be found where so much comfort could be had, so much kindness shown us, as in the Roper Hospital.[9]

Meanwhile, life went on unchanged for the Confederate officers. The only contact they had was with each other, their guards, and Colonel Edward Hallowell. This latter personality would find no good words from any of the prisoners, and indeed showed his contempt for their cause and presence at every opportunity. Hallowell was typical of the white officers of the 54th Massachusetts, an abolitionist with an obsessive hatred for the South. This was observed by Colonel Robert G. Shaw of the 54th upon the regiment's first arrival at Hilton Head the previous summer. In a letter to his mother, Shaw wrote of his disapproval of the burning and wanton destruction ordered by Union authorities. He referred to one officer's zeal as "partly from pure hatred of everything Southern." Consequently, such attitudes made the Union officers unfit for guard duty over innocent prisoners who were due sympathetic treatment under the laws of war. Hallowell treated them as criminals, not honorable men taken in battle.[10]

CAPT. HENRY DICKINSON, 2ND VA. CAV.

Colonel Hallowell, I suppose, fought well at Wagner under Shaw; at least he lost an eye there and another member which is no unimportant part of man's organization. He had a glass eye, which, for the sake of humanity I hope was in part the cause of a hang-dog look, a devilish leer, a fiendish scowl, which would at any time affright Innocence herself, or would cause the strong man, if near him in the dark, to dread the dagger. He was utterly odious and repulsive in manner and looks, . . . and would conform to my idea of one who was determined to prove a villain. I will add that Hallowell also said he wished the "Rebs" would kill one of us for the man killed by the Union shell in Charleston.[11]

CAPT. THOMAS PINCKNEY, 4TH S.C. CAV.

Accordingly Col. Hallowell of the 54th Massachusetts, a phlegmatic dough-faced Yankee, who had succeeded Shaw, strode up to my tent . . . (I) told him he could help all in stockade, as well as myself, if he would investigate the rations that were issued to us, which I said I had no idea the U.S. Government would knowingly force even its prisoners to eat. Epps then produced a plate full of hard tack from our box, and breaking some of them open, I called his attention to the worms therein contained. On seeing which he remarked, "I dare say the Quartermaster is making a good thing out of feeding you prisoners," (some of our men said they had seen 1861 on these boxes, showing they were condemned biscuits, bought cheap for this purpose) but continued he "I don't think you have cause for complaint, as you are getting not only bread, but meat too in those rations!" I felt my hair stand on end at this addition of insult to injury, and made a vow then and there,—in case I ever met that low-bred Yankee again upon this mundane sphere, Well—![12]

Colonel Hallowell, with whom we were brought more in contact with than any other officer,—for the reason he had full control of our pen,—was about the meanest fellow our misfortunes brought us in connection with; in fact, the negroes he commanded were Chesterfields in politeness in contrast with this fellow. After we had been some weeks in the stockade under fire of our own guns, and the starvation rations had begun to tell upon us, this doughty colonel one afternoon came into the stockade, had us draw up in line, and made the following speech which I have never forgotten. He said: "The fate of war has placed you prisoners in my hands, and I will treat you as prisoners. I feel it my bounded duty to fight men who have raised their unhallowed hands against their country's flag. But I will try and treat you as men, since you have fallen into my hands . . . " He treated us like animals, . . . there was nothing this fellow left undone to make us uncomfortable and annoy us; he never let one opportunity pass to show his hatred for the South and her soldiers. And yet in our six hundred prisoners were the sons and grandsons of ancestors who had helped to make American history and consecrate the American flag. . . . One of his smart jokes was to come into our prison pen and say, in his arrogant drawl, "Gentlemen, tomorrow I will have barrels placed in the streets of your inclosure into which you can throw your bones. Of course, I mean your meat bones." This was cruel; it was cowardly to make such jests of our starving condition. He could see daily how the treatment was breaking down and killing our men; he reveled in our terrible condition.[13]

CAPT. J. OGDEN MURRAY, 11TH VA. CAV.

Tuesday 27th (Sept) 1864.- The colonel in charge of us says if he had his way he would make us suck an oiled rag. Hard hearted fellow. His memory will be cherished by all here.[14]

CAPT. JUNIUS HEMPSTEAD, 25TH VA. INF.

The prisoners were divided into eight companies, each under the charge of a different warden, some of whom were insulting and degrading. Despite that less than amiable contact there were instances where the guards actually tried to alleviate the suffering and enjoyed friendly discourse. Understandably, humanity varied with the individual in charge.

Their conduct towards the prisoners was characterized by great cruelty and inhumanity. They heaped any amount of unprovoked abuse upon us. And it appeared to be their chief glory to abuse and maltreat the prisoners . . . to abuse every man in his squad, by

CAPT. JOHN J. DUNKLE, 25TH VA. INF.

calling him a liar, a thief, a coward, a traitor, a rebel, and various other outrageous epithets. No one dared resist this impudence, on pain of being cuffed and taken out to be dealt with in another way.[15]

CAPT. HENRY
DICKINSON,
2ND VA. CAV.

About one-half hour after daybreak, when the whole camp was awake, I heard a sentinel cry out, "Go back there"; a moment after he fired his gun, producing an exclamation of pain. But who was the sufferer? None of us dared then to go and see. In a little time, we slowly made our advances and, feeling our way, found that Captain Henry Board, Detachment D, had started to the spring for water; that the sentinel spoke as he was starting; that he immediately turned back, and, as he was going in his tent the sentinel fired, missing him, but hitting Lt. John Harris, 58th Regt. of Bedford, Va., in the knee. The ball passed through the kneepan and, going into another tent, hit Capt. Blair 1st N.C. Cavalry in the shoulder, though not seriously wounding him. Harris will probably be a cripple for life. This feat of arms amused the negroes wonderfully, one of them remarking, "They run to their holes like rabbits and squirrels." This outrage received no investigation whatever.[16]

CAPT. THOMAS
PINCKNEY,
4TH S.C. CAV.

One of the greatest outrages, practiced upon us occurred one morning when we had been notified to be ready for an early start to the Inlet, our supply of drinking water was limited, these wells not furnishing enough to supply us all at one time, the men each trying to be the first so as to secure a canteen full for our breakfast gathered around the well nearest me, awaiting their turn, when I heard a sentinel from the parapet call out, "Disperse that crowd" and although it was then about sunrise, and they could see perfectly well that our men were only waiting around the wells for water, I saw a Lieutenant point in our direction, and evidently order him to fire on us, which he did, the ball going wide of the mark, but passing through the tents, shot one man through the knee who had not yet arisen, and flattened itself against the rim of a carpet bag, which another man had under his head a tent beyond, fortunately doing no greater damage than leaving a black mark upon his neck.[17]

Another shooting incident occurred on October 14, when the prisoners were ordered to fall into ranks to visit a sutler, the first allowed since the severe rations were issued. A third incident was barely averted by a quick-thinking guard when they were marched to Lighthouse Inlet.

CAPT. HENRY
DICKINSON,
2ND VA. CAV.

Oct. 14th.- More mush today, and the sutler came in and I bought ginger cakes and again traded for beer, made of potato peelings and sour molasses by Captain Dixon. The rush for the sutler was so great that they could scarcely be kept back, and one man, though repeatedly ordered back, disobeyed and was shot at but missed. The sentinel was not in the wrong . . . Hallowell said that all sick and wounded would be exchanged. Someone asked whom the order would include, and explained that there were some wounded in the pen. His reply was characteristic—"Yes, a number will swear they are wounded just to get through."[18]

There was an incident occurred, just as we were leaving the stockade pen on Morris Island. . . . As I said before, it was the general impression, as we marched out of the pen, that we were to be exchanged; and this fact made me feel like telling Colonel Hallowell my opinion of him. He was standing at the prison gate, glaring at us as we passed out. We were marching by fours; in the fours just ahead of me was Capt. Bruce Gibson, Maj. W. W. Goldsborough, and two other officers whose identity I now forget. When I reached Hallowell I halted and said, "You yellow-faced scoundrel, we are going back home now, and I hope and pray to God that it may be my fortune to get my hands on you, that the world may be rid of such a brute." His face turned livid with rage. He shouted out to one of the guards to shoot that man, meaning me; but the guard pointed his gun direct at Capt. Bruce Gibson, and would have killed him but for the order of one of the negro sergeants to put down his gun. By this time the line had passed Hallowell, and Captain Gibson was saved. I never in all my life was so unstrung; my foolish temper had almost cost an innocent life—the life of my best friend. After this incident my temper was kept under control. This was the only conversation I ever had with Hallowell. When he came into our prison pen I got out of his way.[19]

CAPT. J. OGDEN MURRAY, 11TH VA. CAV.

Fortunately, the majority of contact was a positive experience. It is only logical that the Confederate officers would feel comfortable around the black troops. Most had grown up with some contact with the other race, whether as servants, or simply from being in the vicinity of large farms and plantations with field hands. The black troops probably sensed this familiarity also. Actually the relationship between the black guards and the prisoners was less awkward than that of the black troops to their white superior officers, many of whom had little previous contact with blacks outside the military experiment called the 54th Massachusetts Infantry. That would account for the fraternization of guards and captives, and attitudes expressed during captivity. The guards often seemed to sympathize with the feelings toward Hallowell, for apparently they received harsh treatment at his hands also. Overall, the Confederate officers preferred the black guards to the white commanding officers of the 54th.

CAPT. GEORGE
W. NELSON,
HANOVER ARTY.
(VA.)

But black, uncouth, and barbarous as they were, we soon found that they were far preferable to the white officers who commanded them. If physiognomy is an index of character, then surely these officers were villainous. But not one of them, in looks or deeds could compare with their Colonel. I always felt in his presence as if I had suddenly come upon a snake.[20]

CAPT. THOMAS
PINCKNEY,
4TH S.C. CAV.

*Major Emanual, Lts. Gordon, Epps and I occupied one tent, and we were in charge of Sgt. Lennox, who had been a barber in Boston— his business fortunately had accustomed him to wait upon gentlemen, and even under these anomalous circumstances his good manners did not desert him, his duty was to make us fall into line three times a day, count us off and report results to the officer of the day, but he never presumed upon his position to make his authority felt, frequently came into my tent for a talk, but was always most respectful in his behavior . . . On one occasion when Lennox was absent, the sergeant of the next company came round, dispensing bean-soup and hard tack I remonstrated with him on the quality of the rations he was distributing,—"Yes, sir," said he, "they ain't fittin' for a dog to eat, but they are all these **Yankees** are going to give you." He . . . took no pains to conceal the contempt he seemed to feel for our treatment at the hands of his newly made friends.*[21]

CAPT. RICHARD
E. FRAYSER,
C.S. SIGNAL
CORPS

The writer had on his person a finger ring and a $50.00 Confederate note. The two were sold for $10.00 and put in sutler stores, which were purchased at most exhorbitant prices. Sergeant Lennox, who belonged to the 54th Massachusetts regiment, which guarded the Confederates, and whose home was in Boston, was very kind to the writer. With this money Lennox bought bread, molasses and many other things. This he had to do in a most surreptitious manner, for it was a violation of orders, and had it been known, Lennox would have been severely punished.[22]

CAPT. LUIS F.
EMILIO,
54TH MASS.
INF.

Our charges lounged about during the day, visiting friends, or played cards, smoked, and read. There were ingenious fellows who passed much time making chains, crosses, rings, and other ornaments from bone or gutta-percha buttons. Our officers found a number of most agreeable gentlemen among them, who seemed to appreciate such attentions and politenesses as could be extended within the scope of our regulations.[23]

CAPT. GEORGE
W. NELSON,
HANOVER ARTY.
(VA.)

These sergeants were generally kind to us, expressed their sorrow that we had so little to eat. We had a point in common with them, viz: intense hatred of their Colonel. Their hatred of him was equalled only by their fear of him. His treatment of them, for the least violation of orders, or infraction of discipline, was barbarous. He would ride at them, knock and beat them over the head with his sabre, or draw his pistol and shoot at them.[24]

September 8th.- Was aroused this morning at daylight by the Colonel whipping one of his [black] Yankee soldiers for being asleep on the fence . . . Said he was not asleep but just studying.[25]

CAPT. ALEX
BEDFORD,
3RD MO. CAV.

I remember one Sergeant who was in charge of the street upon which the tent I occupied was located. He was formerly a slave of Gen. William A. Blount, and hearing my name, he made inquiries of me and ascertained who I was. Ever afterwards he would do me any act of kindness in his power. In the distribution of the daily rations, the meat being carried around in an empty cracker box and the mush in a large vessel, he would frequently, whenever he could do so without being seen, give me a double portion.[26]

CAPT. CHARLES
BUSBEE,
5TH N.C. INF.

There was some interaction with the white junior officers of the 54th Massachusetts, like Captain Luis Emilio, who were aware that among the Confederate prisoners some had been present at Battery Wagner during the July 1863 attack by their regiment. Curiosity overcame their resentment enough to inquire about the details.

From Major McDonald, Fifty-first North Carolina, who was present in Wagner during the assault of July 18, 1863, very interesting particulars of the affair were obtained. He confirmed the story of Colonel Shaw's death and manner of burial.[27]

CAPT. LUIS
EMILIO,
54TH MASS.
INF.

A Lieutenant, evidently a Spaniard, was inclined to be polite to me, and lent me a few paper back novels. . . . This Lieutenant asked me one day if I had been in that attack on Battery Wagner, July 18th, 1863, there were two of their brother officers whom they had never been able to hear of since that fight, and whether they were killed outright or were in captivity, they had never been able to ascertain. I told him I would investigate the matter as there were probably some among the six hundred who had participated in that battle, and discovered there were two North Carolinians, a [Maj. MacDonald] and Lieutenant Linsay. As soon as the latter learned what I wanted he said I had come to the right man, as he had been in charge of the detail to bury the dead and said he, 'I put that Yankee Col. Shaw just where he deserved to be, in a hole . . .' He further stated that he 'wore the finest boots I ever got hold of, for' pointing to his foot, 'I have been wearing them ever since, and there is not a break in them.' I referred this Yankee Lieutenant the next time I saw him to Lt. Linsay for the information he wanted, but the interview does not seem to have proved satisfactory . . .

CAPT. THOMAS
PINCKNEY,
4TH S.C. CAV.

I well recollect Sgt. Lennox's account of his experiences in that battle. These negro troops it seems had been put in front with the white regiment behind to keep them up. "Why sir," said he, "when they opened fire upon us at such close range they mowed down 1500 of us in about 15 minutes, and I saved myself by taking to that marsh on our flank, where I remained until the fight was over."[28]

The "retaliation" treatment went beyond simply the desire to treat the Confederate officers the same as the Union officers were treated in Charleston. There was no correlation. The attitude was more like a vengeance, an experiment in withholding everything that could possibly give comfort or pleasure to the men, and resembled an endurance test in the sequence of events.

CAPT. THOMAS
PINCKNEY,
4TH S.C. CAV.

But the greatest hardship practiced upon us was withholding for weeks, all express packages and mails, the former consisted largely of provisions we had written home for, by flag of truce steamer; opportunities frequently occurring in this harbor as General Grant had put a stop to all exchanges of prisoners on the Potomac, or other communications, after he was put in command of the U.S. Army.

I shall never forget the spoiled provisions that were thrown out of the warehouse, making a mound upon the back beach, and our letters they must have destroyed as they were never delivered to us. . . . None had been allowed to reach me from home, since my capture in May, and I learned incidentally through one from Cousin M. Huger that my dear mother, to whom I had been writing whenever opportunity offered—had been lying in her grave for more than two months—no letter from home having ever been allowed to reach me.[29]

CAPT. DAVID C.
GRAYSON,
10TH VA. INF.

Oct. 10, 1864.- Nothing yet to relieve the monotony of camp; even rumors have almost ceased, and we are unable to hear anything through the papers, as there are none yet in the pen for more than a week. We truly may be said to be completely isolated from the world—not only deprived of its comforts and pleasures, but shut out from all the beauties of nature and without any knowledge of what is occurring, whilst we have every reason to believe that struggles are of daily occurrence between the armies, the result of which we feel so anxious to know. Oh, what can be more miserable than such a life?[30]

On September 16, General Sam Jones had communicated with Foster on this point of mail and personal packages. The Union prisoners had never complained of being denied their mail or whatever they could receive from home to supplement the provisions of the Confederate authorities. On the other hand, the Confederate prisoners in all Union prisons had not been allowed to send nor receive mail or personal packages. Sutler privileges had been denied as well. Jones relayed his concern specifically regarding the Six Hundred on Morris Island in a memorandum, stating, "Not one letter has been received from the prisoners upon Morris Island. It certainly cannot be of their own inclination that they do not write." It was not until well into October, long after the Union soldiers had been removed from Charleston that Foster agreed to allow the officers on Morris Island to receive any articles.[31]

With so much time to fill, and to avoid dwelling on the constant possibility of death, the officers turned their attention to making life bearable.

Sept.(14th).- Today is my washing day. Being furnished with a tub and soap, I enter upon the new and arduous duty with the zeal and tact of an experienced laundress. I scrub and rinse and wring the much soiled "duds" into white inviting garments. I am surprised at my own success. I can now look forward with pleasure to change of linen. My compassion for the delicate female whose duty it is to bend over the tub week after week in vindication of the cause of decency is very strong at this time.[32]

1LT. JAMES
W. A. FORD,
20TH VA. CAV.

They cunningly found ways to improve on the hard fare their captors offered as sustenance, and learned to use the generosity of their guards to their advantage.

Oct. 13th.- Hunger gnawing at my stomach. Same rations as yesterday, but made the day on two crackers. Capt. Campbell of Tenn. and Lt. Brinkley of Norfolk (these three gentlemen are my tent and mess mates) puts the mush enmasse in a can and fried the whole with fat meat and go it blind . . . The mush is full of worms and bugs and a member of my tent, Capt. Martin of S.C. will be qualified to the fact that he picked out of his rations alone 170 worms and 14 bugs. I threw mine in the Street.[33]

1LT. JAMES
W. A. FORD,
20TH VA. CAV.

Saturday Sept. 17th 1864.- Had coffee for breakfast. Capt. Moore, one of my tentmates, brought some coffee with him and we borrowed an old can and made a fire in it <u>inside</u> of our tent. Made some splendid coffee in about 20 minutes; against orders to build a fire outside—fooled the Yanks that time.

CAPT. JUNIUS
HEMPSTEAD,
25TH VA. INF.

Monday Sept. 19th 1864.- Just finished making coffee. Took four nails and drove them into the barrel stave and covered the stave with sand and set the Coffee Pot on the nails and built a fire under it. As usual, clouds of smoke. My eyes are running with tears. Waiting for our two crackers. As soon as they come will eat our breakfast.

Wednesday September 21st 1864.- Made coffee this morning. The last we will make. Coffee out—am sorry indeed.[34]

CAPT. ALEX
BEDFORD,
3RD MO. CAV.

September 21st.- [Capt.] Benson made the negro Sergeant mad and he said 'By Jesus Christ, I will satisfy this tent for once,' so he gave us a double handful, at least two crackers apiece. That satisfied us and we wish he would get mad again.[35]

Captains John C. Carson of Mississippi and James M. Hobson of North Carolina shared a tent. Carson recognized a friend among General Foster's staff whom he had known socially before the war, in New York. During his confinement in the stockade he took the opportunity to write his old friend to find out if there was anything he could do in the way of alleviating the suffering of Captain Carson and his comrades. The young Union officer regretfully replied no, but he did send a ham as a gift.

(AUTHOR OF
ACCOUNT
UNKNOWN—
COMRADE FROM
ST. JOSEPH, LA.
1899.)

Carson and Capt. Hobson were delighted to get it, and in casting about as to how they would have the ham cooked, they decided to get one of the negro soldier guards to cook it. . . . So they called upon the negro guard, gave him the ham to be cooked and returned that evening, promising to pay him for his trouble. In seasonable time the negro brought to them a large dish covered with a newspaper, stating that this was the ham. The dish was set down before them on the ground, and upon lifting the paper they discovered that the entire body of the ham had been cut out, leaving only the skin and bone.

Carson was so indignant at the robbery perpetrated upon him that he cursed the thief, abusing him roundly. The negro was armed, and was about to attack Mr. Carson, cursing him in turn, When Capt. Hobson leaped upon the negro, bore him down, and caught him by the throat, and being a powerful man and a perfect athlete, he was choking the negro to death in his fury. Just then the sergeant of the guard came up and was about to run his bayonet through Hobson, when the Captain told him that if he touched him he would break the neck of the man he had down. The negro thief cried out to the sergeant, "You let us alone—this white man and me understands each other," and expressing such good nature that Hobson let him up and peace was made, but they had no ham for dinner that day.[36]

Captain Thomas Pinckney had the luxury of his trusty frying pan, a much envied item among the prisoners, and although fires were prohibited, ways were found. It also allowed the pooling of rations to make one meal. The frying pan served as an alternative to the preparation of their paltry fare.

CAPT. THOMAS
PINCKNEY,
4TH S.C. CAV.

Our rations were brought around to us twice a day by two of these sergeants, consisting of a few worm eaten hard tack, a little chunk of bacon one half inch square and a cup of bean soup, per day (the latter three beans to the quart of water, our men said)

*they were received at each tent, and at our leisure the hard tack
was broken up, the worms thrown out, and with the bacon the
mess was passed through the frying pan, and thus made more
palatable.*[37]

The boyish behavior in some instances is a reminder of their youth,
which no doubt helped them cope with the conditions. They used their wits
on the sutler, who was allowed to visit twice a week towards the end of
October. When they discovered the unfair practice of charging the prisoners
higher prices than allowed, getting even occupied their time.

*For some time a sutler drove a cart into the pen semi-weekly and
sold us many things which enabled us to live. His prices were far
above the usual mark of even sutlers. Molasses, fifty cents a pint;
gingerbread or crackers, two for five cents; tobacco at Confederate rates payable in greenbacks, etc. Indeed, he seemed determined
to kill the goose that laid the golden egg. Some of the officers were,
it seems, equal to the occasion, and as all hands had cheated them
by stealing their rations, they stole the sutler's goods to such an
extent that it wouldn't pay to sell to prisoners, and of course he
quit. Those moralists who would blame the officers for doing this
must remember that they have never been prisoners in Yankee
hands. I saw one man steal a handkerchief and in a moment after
offer to trade it to the owner for molasses; another stole a box of
pepper which he said was not good, and the sutler paid him the
money for it.*

CAPT. HENRY
DICKINSON,
2ND VA. CAV

*Following him a new sutler came in who sold at more reasonable
rates. He had little cause to complain of theft, though some of the
officers having gotten their hands in, it was difficult to stop the
habit of lifting.*[38]

*The sergeant of my company, a burly Negro, good-natured . . .
could neither read nor write, and his "roll-call" consisted in counting the number in his command. This was not infrequently a per-
plexing problem, since several men who had been already counted
at one end of the line would slip quietly behind the backs of their
comrades to the other end and be recounted, thus showing the
presence of, perhaps, 105 prisoners instead of the 100 required.
In such an event the good-natured Negro would scratch his head
doubtfully, smile a feeble smile and patiently begin a recount. Now,
perhaps, the movement would be reversed, and the sergant would
find his 105 prisoners shrunk to the number of only 95. Nothing,
however, disturbed his imperturbable good-humor, and with a
broader smile upon his round and shiny black face, he would dis-*

CAPT. HENRY E.
HANDERSON,
9TH LA. INF.

miss us to our breakfasts. In the course of a few weeks we became on the best of terms with our swarthy commander, who often, when off duty, would come into our tents and chat for hours with his charges.[39]

In any circumstance where so many are thrown together in tight quarters, a great deal of tolerance must abound, and the Six Hundred were no exception. Seeing the same faces every minute of every day was monotonous, and there was no escape from the heat. Inside the tents, it was oppressive, and with no shade in the pen, outside was equally intolerable. The hot, sandy ground was only broken in several places with sparse patches of grass.

Games such as chess helped to distract the mind, and reading was a favorite. Most of all, they passed the time writing. Many letters were sent back and forth between friends from Fort Delaware or Johnson's Island. Some received correspondence from their comrades who had been sent to Beaufort, inquiring about the conditions of friends under fire.

2LT. DAVID GORDON, 4TH S.C. CAV.

Went through a monotonous time, in small tent with Maj. Emanuel, and Lt. Epps . . . The weather is extremely hot and a prison life too disagreeable to admit of description.[40]

CAPT. HENRY DICKINSON, 2ND VA. CAV.

Morris Island, Sept. 13, 1864.- Being on Morris Island today without books to read, hungry, and finding it impossible to mingle freely with my friends in their small tents, or to exercise in the streets by reason of the heat; having no comfort or enjoyment (unless it is a comfort to ponder over the cruelties of the United States Government), under these circumstances I have concluded to spend some of my time in jotting down my impressions of prison life as I have seen it.[41]

LETTER, 1LT. WILLIAM N. LEDYARD, 3RD ALA. INF., AT BEAUFORT, SC, TO 1LT. SANFORD BRANCH, 8TH GA. INF., SEPT. 21, 1864

The conflicting reports that we have had of your whereabouts has caused me to delay writing you much longer than I expected or desired. One day we would hear that you had been landed at Morris Island, probably the next that it was at "Hilton Head" and then that you were still aboard the "Crescent." We are pretty comfortably situated here in a good house (once a private residence) with fare some better than that of "Ft. Delaware." My health is very good. I trust that when you write you will be able to give me as good, if not better, account of yourself. Your friends here are all well. If it is perfectly convenient I wish you would pay Lt. Bissell two & 50/100 dollars ($2.50) out of the small amount that you owe me. I borrowed that amount from him at Ft. Delaware and am afraid he will want it before I will have an opportunity to see him myself. The general impression here is that exchange is about "played out."[42]

Being gentlemen, perhaps they complained less than an ordinary cross section of the population would. The tents were designed to sleep two men, but the size of the stockade made four to a tent necessary. Space was further reduced inside the tents by each man's personal baggage. When it rained, all simply got wet. The salt air was humid and uncomfortable, and Captain James McMichael made the observation that, "The gnats are more annoying this morning than shell."[43]

The tents, with straw to cover the sand inside, provided the only source of comfort and privacy, away from the prying eyes of sentries. Here some held religious services, usually conducted by Lieutenant George Finley or Captain Thomas W. Harris of Georgia, both of whom had been inspired by Reverend Handy at Fort Delaware to become men of the cloth. Others, like Henry Dickinson, wrote thorough descriptions of prison life in diaries, or read any book they could borrow from friends. Time was spent in obtaining and copying the list of their own names made by Captain John Cantwell. It was circulated from tent to tent, and compared with several other lists started among their number. Others drew perfectly proportioned diagrams of their prison stockade, down to the exact number of tents on each company street. For those with artistic ability, detailed artwork was executed on scraps of paper with all the patience of an engraver. Every kind of activity was carried on within the small confines of canvas.

CAPT. HENRY DICKINSON, 2ND VA. CAV. *A few gentlemen were chess players of the first order, and one in particular played a good blindfold game. Lieutenant Fry, son of Judge Fry of Wheeling, was the best player I ever saw.... He made some six moves according to the rules generally laid down; he then studied the position, conceived his plan of attack, and rarely checked till he was ready to mate. Though I practiced considerably then, and others said I played a fair game, in playing with Fry I always found myself, after ten or twelve moves, on the defensive, and at each struggle getting more completely hemmed. He looked farther than any man I ever saw, and, though his move at the time did not appear brilliant, its purpose was seen when too late.[44]*

CAPT. JUNIUS HEMPSTEAD, 25TH VA. INF. *Monday September 19th 1864.- ... Gave each of us a little pamphlet. Want us to take the oath I suppose. Read in my Bible. Played ten games of checkers.*

Monday (Sept.) 26th 1864.- Clear day. Very cool in the morning. Hot at noon. ... Played chess today. Beat all.

Tuesday (Sept.) 27th. 1864.- ... Made some tea and then played seven games of chess. Beat me 6 out of the seven. Will write a letter home today. Hope they will get it soon ...[45]

They slept, dreamed of home, and food, and for some, the not so distant days of childhood. The time passed slowly.

2LT. SAMUEL T. ANDERSON, 1ST S.C. CAV.

I laid down feverish and sick. I would frequently during the night awake from a horrible dream, to lay awake brooding over my miserable position—a prisoner of war—until exhausted, nature would send me into the land of dreams only to awake again to the reality and despair that I was indeed a prisoner of war and for how long, God only knew.[46]

2LT. HENRY COOK, 44TH TENN. INF.

Think of starving upon that sandy island, under fire of Moultrie, for forty-two days! In my feverish, fitful dreams I saw all the cool, sparkling springs that my childhood knew, but fate refused me the power to kneel and slake my thirst as of yore. I saw tables loaded with the luxuries of Tennessee, but had not the strength to reach forth my hand and appease my hunger. How both pleasure and frightful visions appear to the dreams of a starving man![47]

CAPT. JOHN DUNKLE, 25TH VA. INF.

The mind was left to think of home, and friends, of fireside, and childhood's bright days, and wonder that humanity had gone forever; and that mercy had hid her face in disgust. It was left to dream of water to quench the thirst, of food to satisfy the stomach, of clothes to clothe the body, of fire to warm the shivering limbs . . .[48]

CAPT. JUNIUS HEMPSTEAD, 25TH VA. INF.

Saturday September 24th 1864.- . . . Battery kept up a fire all night. Slept sound notwithstanding. Awoke quite late. Had dreams of home last night. O! if they were only true.[49]

The men had been lucky so far. Under fire for three weeks, none had been killed. Guards had been killed on the parapet, and outside the stockade. Many Union soldiers were wounded and some killed at Batteries Wagner and Gregg. Shells had fallen among the prisoners, sending geysers of sand in the air, raining down on men standing nearby. Strangely enough those of the Six Hundred in the most obvious place for execution had escaped even a scratch from falling shell fragments. They were convinced only divine Providence had saved them.

Finally, death found the first of their number. But it was not from a random shell, or a hasty sentry that First Lieutenant William P. Callahan died. It was from starvation. His death was unfeelingly reported by his captors.

LETTER, CAPT. THOMAS APPLETON, 54TH MASS. INF., TO LT. COL. W. T. BENNETT, PROVOST MARSHAL GENERAL, SEPT. 30, 1864

I have the honor to report the death of 1st Lieut. W. P. Callahan 25th Tenn Cavalry (Prisoner of War) who died of chronic diarrhea at the Post Field Hospital at Morris Island S.C. Sept. 27, 1864. He was buried at Morris Island and a head board with his name was placed at the head of the grave.[50]

Lieutenant Frank Peake lived in the tent with Captain J. Ogden Murray. He had ridden with General John Hunt Morgan, until he was captured along with many of Morgan's men on the Ohio raid in Syracuse, and had already been in prison over a year. He had been sick, like many of them, but the abdominal cramps intensified on the night of September 27, showing all the symptoms of cholera. Alarmed at his sudden worsening condition, which happened in the middle of the night, Captain Murray and his other tentmates tried to comfort Peake, knowing they could not inform the sentry without risk of being shot, as the rule was not to go outside the tent after dark. So they did what they could for their friend until morning, when the doctor usually came in the pen about 9:00 a.m.

CAPT. J. OGDEN
MURRAY,
11TH VA. CAV.

I went to the hospital tent, as it was called, approaching the doctor in the most polite manner and with the most polite language I could command, related to him Lt. Peake's condition, urging him to go over to see Peake, who, I thought, was in a dying condition, and would die unless he had immediate medical attention. Before this red-headed dispenser of pills replied to my urgent appeal for help, he looked me over from head to foot, then said, 'Can't the man come to my tent.' 'Why of course not, doctor; he cannot stand upon his feet; he is too ill to walk. Could he have come here I surely would not be so urgent in my appeal to you.' 'Well,' he said, 'if he is too bad to walk over here, he must wait until these other fellows here are served; they all need attention.' With this I turned upon my heel and left the doctor's presence in disgust. . . . The boys could hardly credit it. Capt. W. P. Crow, an old friend and companion of Lt. Peake, went over to see the dispenser of opium pills, but met with no more success than I did in inducing the doctor to see our patient. . . . Late in the afternoon the doctor came to our tent, but poor Peake had passed beyond human skill. . . . He lived during the night, suffering the pains of the damned. On the morning of September 29th Capt. Crow and Lt. Dunlap succeeded in getting Colonel Hallowell to remove Lt. Peake from the prison pen to the hospital, just out of range of Sumter's guns. . . . Poor dear Peake! We who knew him loved him for his Christian virtues, manly courage, and gentleness of heart. . . . He lingered for a day or two and died on the afternoon of Oct. 2, 1864. . . . About him stood men in blue; they were enemies, they could not understand, they could not know, the great heart that ceased to beat. In the twilight we dug him a grave in the sands of Morris Island, and laid him to rest.[51]

Both Lieutenants Peake and Callahan died of chronic diarrhea, a condition caused by diet and unsanitary conditions, but easily cured with proper nutrition. Those two losses of their number, so close in time, moved them all. Still another joined his comrades within days.

Second Lieutenant John C. C. Cowper of the 33rd North Carolina had been severely wounded in the lung at Gettysburg, and was confined in the

Seminary hospital there when captured. The wound had never properly healed, and he had been in hospital at almost every prison in which he had been confined. Now the current conditions further prevented healing, pneumonia set in, and he died on October 14, at age twenty-two.[52]

The horrible experience in the hold of the *Crescent City* had brought them all as close as brothers, and now the bond was cemented. They became aware that the most intimate human experience was not only living together, but dying together as well.

Concurrently, their Union counterparts in Charleston had been removed and were on their way to a concentration point in Columbia, South Carolina. General Sam Jones had succeeded in getting permission for their removal around September 21, under the pressure from Foster, and for the safety of the Confederate officers on Morris Island whose imminent danger had alarmed him since September 10.

The Union prisoners, however, were in much better circumstances in Charleston than they would be in the hastily prepared and ill-equipped officers' camp at Columbia. That location was essentially an open field with little shelter. The men realized this, and were not looking forward to the change from comfortable quarters and a good supply of rations.

The new location became known as Camp Sorghum, a name the prisoners coined because of the rations. The camp was strictly for officers. A separate camp for enlisted men was located at Florence, South Carolina.[53]

LT. JOHN WORRELL NORTHROP, 76TH N.Y. INF.

Sunday, October 2nd.- Foggy and chilly this morning; an uncomfortable night though the rain ceased before morning. About 1500 men from Charleston arrive. About 9 a.m. orders came to break camp. We knew we were to go into the stockade the negroes had been building. . . . It is a bad place; the walls of the prison are rough, built of trees from the enclosure, all of which are used except brush and waste pieces, which are scattered mostly in the swamp, those on dry ground having been removed. . . . A brook, larger than that at Andersonville, runs through it, which is to supply water which cannot be obtained without going half knee deep in mud. The stockade contains twenty acres. Instead of sentry boxes there is an embankment outside nearly as high as the wall which the negroes are now finishing. The sentry is to walk this, looking down upon us within.[54]

The prisoners were allowed to buy what little was available for purchase from local citizens who came out to sell. But the administrative confusion experienced by the Confederate government at that time, combined with the disorganized situation at the emergency camp, resulted in poor conditions. The Confederate commander who had to deal with the chaos was General William M. Gardner, who replaced Winder in charge of all the Confederate military prisons east of the Mississippi except Georgia and Florida. He telegraphed Confederate authorities of his dilemma, stating:

*. . . In a camp about five miles from the city (Columbia) are 1300
other officers recently sent from Charleston by Major General Sam
Jones, without my knowledge or consent, and placed by him in charge
of Captain E. A. Semple, whom I had sent there for another purpose,
viz., to superintend the construction of a very large prison, which I
am directed by the Secretary of War to have built. Captain Semple
represents that these officers were thrown suddenly on his hands,
giving him no time for preparation, and that he is in want of almost
everything necessary for their accommodations.*[55]

Finally, one of the prisoners sent a petition, dated November 4, 1864, to
emphasize the need for improvements. The paper was drawn up by Colonel
John Fraser of the 140th Pennsylvania and was addressed to Lieutenant General
William J. Hardee, who replaced Jones on October 5, as the Confederate
commander of the Department of Georgia, South Carolina, and Florida.

*The daily allowance to each officer of this camp consists of one pt.
of unbolted corn meal, one half pint of molasses, one tenth pint of
rice, one fourth of a table spoonful of salt, with occasionally one
fifth of a pint of very bad flour. This allowance our experience has
convinced us does not furnish adequate food for men in our exposed
condition who suffer so much as we do from exposure.*[56]

COL. JOHN
FRASER,
140TH N.Y.
INF.

The Confederate authorities were doing all they could; however, conditions improved at a very slow rate. Jones had been forced to evacuate prisoners from a good situation to a bad one at the insistence of the Union authorities.

Jones had notified Confederate authorities on September 23 that the
Union prisoners must be removed due to yellow fever in the city. Immediate
preparations were begun, and by the first of October, all had left Charleston,
bound for Florence and Columbia. General Foster received a letter from Jones
on October 13 stating there were no longer any Union prisoners in Charleston, and he must remove the 556 officers from Morris Island.[57] Foster ignored the communication and, no longer a risk to Union prisoners, shelling
intensified, reaching a twenty-four-hour crescendo the first weeks of October. The danger to the prison stockade was so obvious, that Union sentinels
were pulled from their posts back into Battery Wagner, abandoning the defenseless prisoners inside the pen. Many of the Confederate officers in the
stockade were reaching the breaking point, and the added stress tested them.
Still none took the oath, swearing they would all go down together rather
than compromise principles. The batteries replied to each other across
Charleston Harbor with a variety of guns then known to the artillery.

*Sunday 16th.- Quite a brisk inter-change of shots is commenced
to-night at 9 o'clock which is more pleasant to the eye than agreeable. At first our shells were thrown with great accuracy, but fi-*

1LT. JAMES
W. A. FORD,
20TH VA. CAV.

nally commenced falling wild and bursting, threw fragments all around us. One piece weighing 2 1/2 lbs. fell in the middle of the street just behind our tent. It made such a horrid noise that each man thought his tent was the doomed one. This last shot put a stop to our firing. The Yanks however keep up their fire on Charleston and Sumpter all night.[58]

1LT. JOHN C. ALLEN, 7TH VA. CAV.

Monday, 17 October.- Very cold. Very heavy firing last night. We were in great danger shells bursting over us and pieces falling amongst us. 1 piece fell just in front of my tent! Not more than 3 ft. from where we were lying. [59]

CAPT. HENRY DICKINSON 2ND VA. CAV.

October 16, 1864.- These mortar shells at night can be seen and heard the moment after fire and, guided by the trail of light, the eye follows them till they explode. The Confederates fired at the flash of the Yankee guns, and frequently cheered lustily. We could distinctly hear the Sumpter lookout warning all hands, "under cover." This duel lasted till 11 o'clock. The [sentries] on the north side left their posts once, but were ordered back. Some of the prisoners became very nervous. Capt. Miner, they say, took to the barrel, whilst all of our mess were affected like most men on the eve of battle. [Battery] Wagner also took a hand, firing over us at Moultrie, whilst Gregg poured a fire into Charleston. This duel was commenced by the "Feds" in the face of the fact, derived from deserters and an escaped prisoner, that all the Yankees had been removed from Charleston.[60]

CAPT. ALEX BEDFORD, 3RD MO. CAV.

October 7th.- Some firing at the city today. Every fifteen minutes a gun starts her deadly missile . . . Rebels shelled the Yankees last night a great many bursting in the right place but after a while they began to burst too close to us. One shell bursted over us, part of the shell on one side and part on the other.

October 8th.- Yankees shelled all last night throwing balls into the city every fifteen minutes. . . . Very cool this evening. Shelling the city is carried on day and night with some new and heavy guns.

October 15th.- Some men counted one hundred and forty worms to the rations, others fifty. I never counted them, would not pay to take them out. I know there were plenty of them. Some men traded their rations of mush for a cracker, others gave it for half a cracker, some few threw it away. I and many others ate it and wished for more. . . . Firing continues day and night in the city.[61]

CAPT. HENRY DICKINSON, 2ND VA. CAV.

October 16, 1864.- At first only Sumter annoyed them with sharpshooters, but finally old Moultrie opened with two heavy mortars, firing wildly, I thought. The shells were spherical case, and after the shell exploded the small balls exploded like pop-crackers, only they were flying in every direction. Being on the prolongation of the line of fire at Chadfield, we were much endangered, the small balls whizzing over us and in some cases going as far as Wagner. Finally a huge shell exploded over us, and the large pieces came buzzing through camp and buried themselves in our midst. One piece struck in my street, another in the next below us, another near the gate, while one hit just behind our tent, so near our heads as to cause us involuntarily to raise up our bodies to avoid it.[62]

October 17th.- . . . Heavy shelling last night. The Yankees shelling Sumter, Sullivan Island and the city. The Island batteries replied vigorously throwing the shells very accurate for a while, but soon lost range and began to throw them too close to be healthy. Some shells bursting over us and the pieces falling all around us and we fearful to move as the sentinels would fire on us if we came out, so we had to stand it. It is an awful situation to be in. I have been under fire many a time, but never before on quarter rations and double fire.[63]

CAPT. ALEX BEDFORD, 3RD MO. CAV.

The shelling continued day and night, without a break, for the first three weeks of October. Rations slightly improved, and life settled into an uncertain waiting for death or deliverance.

Finally, the guns fell silent for a truce, another in the many meetings to compromise for an exchange. The poor rations had been reported by several officers to the provost marshal, and an inquiry was made. It was found that Hallowell had not been issuing what Foster had ordered, and the starvation diet was supplemented. During this lull, mail and boxes from home were allowed to be delivered, and the Ladies Aid Society of Charleston sent much-needed articles over by boat. The officers found this respite from their experience an answer to their prayers.

Oct. 5, 1864.- To-day we received the contributions from Charleston of provisions and tobacco and truly did it make each heart swell with pride, not so much for the article, but to know and feel that there is patriotism in the old land yet, and that we are still thought of by our countrymen, especially the good women, God bless them! [64]

CAPT. DAVID C. GRAYSON, 10TH VA. INF.

Saturday 15th October 1864.- Cloudy and misting of rain. The grape is that the Yanks have been removed from Charleston and that we will leave here soon. God grant it may be so. I received a letter from my wife dated 12th Sept. The first I have got since I left Delaware. Imagine what a pleasure it afforded me to read its precious contents.[65]

2LT. JOSEPH MAUCK, 10TH VA. INF.

CAPT. J. OGDEN MURRAY, 11TH VA. CAV.

Our hearts were made glad by a lot of boxes of tobacco, sweet potatoes, and peanuts our government had sent us under flag of truce. This renewed our strength, and we were all grateful. It was all our government had to send, and it told us the story of want at home, and gave us the cheering, silent news that we were not forgotten by our government and people in our trials and tribulations. For several days we just revelled in good old Rebel sweet potatoes and peanuts, and blew off our misfortunes in the smoke of good old Dixie tobacco. Our cares for the time vanished, and we slept like princes after a banquet. In the early morning the shelling of the island awoke us. The same old monotony settled upon the camp, the negro sentinels surrounded our camp, and the daily roll calls of the Yanks kept us from forgetting we were still prisoners of war on Morris Island . . .[66]

2LT. WILLIAM EPPS, 4TH S.C. CAV.

October 5.- I have not witnessed a more pleasant feeling among the men since I have been a prisoner. A large amount of nourishment from the citizens of Charleston has just arrived and never were provisions more joyfully received. Every man has a smile on his face.[67]

For a few weeks, a sutler was allowed to visit twice a week, and those who had the fortune to have money, finally supplemented their meagre rations with whatever food the sutler sold, preventing any further deaths on Morris Island.

CAPT. HENRY DICKINSON, 2ND VA. CAV.

A Yankee colonel, exchanged, came in the pen and commenced telling what rations he received at Charleston. Colonel Hallowell was with him and exhibited to him the orders requiring that we should be fed as the prisoners in Charleston. The order was not read out and we then found out that someone had been daily cheating us of the rations ordered to us. After this so much complaint was made, and the sick list had increased to such an extent that Doctor Durrant, the surgeon, took the trouble to search into the affair; the result was that following the investigation we received daily about five crackers and one-fourth pound of meat, except one day, when our friends in Charleston sent us something, the Yanks gave us nothing. The Yankees insisted on giving us a gill of soup and cooked rice, although the prisoners in Charleston got daily one-fifth of a pint of raw beans and rice, which, cooked, would make twice the quantity we got.[68]

The weather cooled as the season advanced well into fall. The exposure to the sea air was often cold at night, and no fire was allowed. The men had not received any winter clothing, and confiscated blankets were not returned. Hallowell received orders from Colonel William Gurney, commanding the

Post at Morris Island, to issue blankets to the prisoners on September 9. This order was never carried out.[69] A few still had their own blankets, and tentmates shared their bedding. However, it was unpleasantly damp after the sun set.

October 18, 1864.- To-day has been a cold, rainy day; very uncomfortable to us as prisoners who are destitute of suitable clothing for such changes of weather.[70]

CAPT. DAVID C.
GRAYSON,
10TH VA. INF.

Monday 26th 1864.- Clear day. Very cool in the morning, hot at noon. Have no blanket—slept on the sand. Quite a soft bed but cold. I tell you, hope they will issue some blankets to us for we need them badly. They have promised us some but I have found the Yankees promises pie crust, made to be broken. They tell us so! so! many lies. Never trust a word they say.[71]

CAPT. JUNIUS L.
HEMPSTEAD,
25TH VA. INF.

Thus living on three crackers and two ounces of meat and some warm water, abused, fired upon, shelled, cursed, starved, and rendered miserable in every form, we lingered on for forty-five days in this horrible place.[72]

CAPT. JOHN J.
DUNKLE,
25TH VA. INF.

Toward the end of October, Foster was ordered by his superiors in Washington to dispense with the effort to shell Charleston into submission. He was to take up a defensive position.[73] Now he was saddled with 555 prisoners, who had become a liability. Retaliation was no longer justifiable. They were offered the oath, which only five had agreed to take, but were denied because Foster was "convinced that [they] are unworthy of this measure of leniency in their behalf, and their release would be in opposition to the interest of the service."[74] The simplest solution was to exchange them here in Charleston Harbor, but General Grant had completely stopped all exchanges except for those in the field, which he had extended to Sherman to prevent hampering operations against Atlanta.

It was decided to send them to Fort Pulaski, Georgia, with a detail of the 157th New York as guards, until exchange was reinstated, or retaliation once again enforced. Finally October 21, they once again packed their few precious belongings, and were marched down to the wharf at the southern end of Morris Island, where two schooners awaited them. The company of the 157th in charge of their removal was that of Lieutenant William Saxton:

Oct. 21.- Everything was in readiness to receive the prisoners as the 54th Massachusetts colored regiment marched them down the beach. They were loaded into two dismasted schooners, and took in tow by two steamers, on which the regiment embarked and all convoyed by a gunboat, started for Fort Pulaski at 4 p.m.[75]

When the order came to move out of the stockade pen we thanked God exchange had come at last. We would soon be back in Dixie, away from Hallowell and Foster . . . But, alas, disappointment

CAPT. J. OGDEN
MURRAY,
11TH VA. CAV.

*awaited us; hope was to be ousted from our hearts by despair,
and fate had in store for us a harder ordeal.*[76]

2LT. HENRY H.
COOK,
1ST TENN. INF.

*We staggered or were hauled to the wharf and were placed upon
the little schooners to be towed to Fort Pulaski. The horrors of
Morris Island were not to be compared with what awaited us on
the coast of Georgia. The little funeral ships were on their way to
establish a graveyard upon Cockspur Island.*[77]

Fort Pulaski after Union occupation.
The casemates in the background were those partitioned off for prison quarters for
the Six Hundred.

Courtesy Mrs. Minnie Fitting
Lt. Richard Henry Adams, Jr.
Confederate States Engineer. Photo
taken upon enlistment in 1861, with
5th Alabama Infantry.

Yankee in Gray
Capt. Henry Ebenezer Handerson
Co. B, 9th Louisiana Infantry, part of the
"Louisiana Tigers." Photo taken shortly
after July 1861.

Museum of the Confederacy, Richmond

The Immortal Six Hundred
Lt. Jefferson William Obet Funk
Co. A, 5th Virginia Infantry.

Maj. William W. Goldsborough
1st Maryland Infantry. Later joined 2nd
Maryland Infantry.

Courtesy Mr. Walter Tucker
Lt. Andrew Brooke Cauthorn
Co. C, 26th Virginia Infantry.

The Immortal Six -Hundred
Maj. Lincoln Clarke Leftwich
Staff of Gen. Ben McCulloch. Later joined
C.S. Navy. Captured on a blockade
runner off Wilmington May 1864.

CHAPTER EIGHT

"I Will Make This the Model Military Prison of the United States"

COLONEL Philip Perry Brown received his orders to report with his regiment to Fort Pulaski on October 20, 1864. He and the 157th New York Infantry would accompany some 550 Confederate prisoners of war by steamship from Morris Island.

When the war started, Colonel Brown was a faculty member at Madison University in his native county of Madison, New York. Prior to this, as the son of a Baptist minister, he had been a missionary to the Choctaw Indians for five years. Kind-hearted and compassionate, he seemed the perfect commander for unfortunate prisoners.

While teaching at Madison, he recruited the 157th, mustering the regiment into service in September 1862, in Hamilton, New York. Upon arriving at the battlefront in Virginia, they first camped on the grounds of General Robert E. Lee's mansion at Arlington, and were part of Sigel's Corps in the Army of the Potomac. Victims of Burnside's Mud March from the disastrous Fredericksburg Campaign, and defeated at Chancellorsville in May 1863, the 157th had been on the receiving end of treatment doled out by some of the very men they now were assigned to guard. Thus a respect existed between them and their captives as blooded veterans. They admired the proud spirit of their foes.[1]

After the Virginia Campaign, Colonel Brown and his command were assigned to the Department of the South, headquartered at Hilton Head, South Carolina, on August 23, 1864. Upon his new assignment as commander of a guard unit, he wrote his wife on October 22 to bring their daughter and join him at the garrison for the winter.

Yesterday afternoon I went to Hilton Head to see the General who informed me that we would remain here for the winter, and he approved very highly of my having my family brought here and

COL. PHILIP P. BROWN, 157TH N.Y. INF.

135

now I wish you and Susie to come on here at once to remain with me this winter. I have very fine quarters here very conveniently arranged and we can have a very pleasant time here. . . . You will want your usual winter clothing as we have some pretty cold weather here . . .

I shall be delighted to see you. I have in my front or sitting room, a good fire place with marble mantel piece, a piano, sofa and centre table.

In the sleeping room I have a marble top washstand, large looking glass, closet and drawers. A privy joins the bed rooms so that our rooms are perfectly private. . . . You will find it very pleasant here, Mrs. Carmichael one of the finest of women.[2]

At age forty-one, Brown looked forward to a quiet winter with easy duty and little to do except oversee the care and feeding of a few hundred enemy officers. He would make sure things ran efficiently, as he always took pride in his responsibilities. There would be other officers' wives present for his wife's companionship. The war would seem very far away.

On Morris Island, it was a beautiful, clear morning. The sunshine boosted the spirits of the remaining 549 of the original 600 prisoners as they prepared to march down the sandy beach. Yet there was a definite falter in their step from lack of food, and many suffered from exhaustion. Nevertheless, they were glad to be leaving, as any change was welcome. Surely this time they were going home.

CORP. ALBERT R. BARLOW, 157TH N.Y. INF.

Late in October the union officers having been removed to the rear of Charleston, orders came to send the rebel officers to Fort Pulaski, Ga.

The six hundred confederates had dwindled to five hundred and forty-nine within fifty days after leaving Fort Delaware. They had been under fire forty-five days.

Oct. 21, 1864, the 157th were marched out on the beach and opened ranks. The 54th Massachusetts came down the beach with their prisoners, who moved in between the lines of their new guard. Two dismasted schooners were lying at the wharf at Lighthouse Inlet, into which were marched those rebel officers. The hulks, towed by steamers and convoyed by a large war vessel, proceeded to Fort Pulaski, near the mouth of Savannah River.[3]

CAPT. HENRY DICKINSON, 2ND VA. CAV.

At sunrise, the roll was called with great particularity. Our baggage was either in our hands or had been sent in a wagon to the wharf (by the way, my carpet bag was rifled of some new socks, a book and various other articles), and we were immediately marched out of the pen between long rows of sable soldiers down to the wharf. On the way down many of us were insulted, because it was the last day of the forty-five during which they claimed that, "the bottom rail is now on top." On reaching the wharf we found the One Hundred Fifty-seventh New York, Colonel Brown commander, drawn up in line, and in a few minutes we were marched on board the schooners under guard of the One Hundred and Fifty-seventh New York, thus bidding farewell to the "Nigs" and Morris Island, as we hope, forever. Both schooners were towed outside the bar and the sick and the favorites were placed in a steamer. The One Hundred and Fifty-seventh New York not on guard were put on another steamer and, after much delay, we hoisted anchor and steered southward, the steamers towing the schooners, and a gunboat bringing up the rear. We weighed anchor at 3 p.m.[4]

Early on the morning of the (21st) of October we were drawn up in line, three days' rations were issued, viz; fifteen 'hard tack' and a right good-sized piece of meat. I felt myself a rich man. I remember well the loving looks I cast upon my dear victuals, and the tender care with which I adjusted and carried my trusty old haversack.... The first evening of the journey I fell upon my victuals, and was so hungry that I ate my three days' rations at once. To a question from a friend, 'What will you do for the rest of the time?' I replied: 'I reckon the Lord will provide.' But I made a mistake.[5]

CAPT. GEORGE W. NELSON, HANOVER ARTY. (VA.)

Friday, 21st October 1864.- We left the stockade. Marched to the dock, went on a schooner. Here we met with the 157th N.Y. Vol. again and all seemed proud to see us. We lay off the dock until afternoon then started for Fort Pulaski, Ga. Traveled all night. I slept well all night.[6]

2LT. JOSEPH W. MAUCK, 10TH VA. INF.

The men would have to spend three full days on board ship, and would not receive any more rations. The optimism of an exchange was soon dispelled, when they were informed that only special exchanges were allowed, or exchanges of those captured in the field during Sherman's campaign.

After we learned that we were not to be exchanged we began to speculate as to what the Yanks would do to us, now they had taken us from under fire. The wildest talk that was ever heard was listened to on the transport that night. Lt. Pete Akers said he was sure we were all to be slaughtered, and boots for General Foster and his staff made of our hides. Others said we were to be put to work on river and harbor fortifications; but Captain Hammack, of Kentucky, said a sentinel told him, confidentially, that we were to be slaughtered at Fort Pulaski, packed in salt, and fed to Foster's niggers to make them fight.[7]

CAPT. J. OGDEN MURRAY, 11TH VA. CAV.

They laughed nervously at the jokes, but underneath a feeling of anxiety prevailed, for they did not know what to expect.

The old schooners were the same ones they had been confined in when taken out of the stockade back in September, and Captain Tom Perkins was quick to pick up where he had left off with escape plans. The hole which he and his comrades had started to saw in the old ship's stern was still just as they had left it. The same men who had tried then, made a renewed attempt.

CAPT. HENRY DICKINSON, 2ND VA. CAV.

October 21, 1864.- Being now on our same old dismasted schooner, with a hole almost cut through it, the same party went to work whilst we sailed and now have a place large enough to get through; they have closed it temporarily, waiting for a convenient season. The wind is dead ahead and we only make six miles per hour. It is quite cold below deck, and above the sentinels are shivering in overcoats.

October 22, 1864.- At 8 p.m. the officer commanding, Captain McWilliams, sent for Captain Perkins. Evidently he suspects him, as he demands that he shall accept a parole, which Perkins, very properly, has refused, unless allowed the liberty of the boat. He was ordered to go to his bunk on the middle deck and a sentinel has been placed over him. Perkins has attempted to escape six times and they know him well. A sergeant and guard with lanterns went below and after inspection reported, "All is well," though they actually stepped over the hole.[8]

That night, the schooners were anchored in sight of the Georgia shore, just off Tybee Island. The baggage and those who were sick and needed medical attention were landed. Preparations were made to land the remaining prisoners the next morning at the wharf on Cockspur Island, and march them the short distance to Fort Pulaski, which was visible, its seaward side still bearing the pock marks of the 1862 bombardment. The men who had determined to escape were Captains Tom Perkins, Dick Adams, of Alabama, Holland Coffee of Mississippi, and Lewis Harman of Virginia among the youngest members of the Six Hundred at age eighteen.

1LT. RICHARD H. ADAMS, JR., C.S. ENGINEER CORPS

About 12 oc at night we started out, Capt. Coffee first, Capt. Harman 2nd & myself 3rd. C[offee] & H[arman] gone about 25 minutes, I let myself down in the cold water with my clothes on & no plank to assist me. Away I swam for the shore. Caught C & H & were about to pass them when Harman called to Coffee two or three times then to Jim Hobson whom he thought I was. He being a poor swimmer I thought he was sinking. Just then my clothes became thoroughly saturated & I began to sink & get very chilly. Pulled off my jacket & went under once. The guard on the boat saw us on the water & hailed us. My strength was fast failing as I had to swim against the tide & I yelled for help. My clothes were very heavy & pulling me under. Again I went under & as I came up I had the horrid thought that I was ²/₃ a drowned man. Pulled off my pants & yelled for help again. Thought I was "gone up" and in a watery grave. I had much rather have filled a soldiers grave. . . . Just as I was sinking the 3rd and my last time Capt. Coffee swam up to me & I had presence of mind enough not to catch hold of him. So I assisted him in holding me up by paddling with the little strength I had until a small boat came out for me. I managed to get in with the assistance of Coffee & one of the guard who came out.[9]

At 11:30 p.m. I awoke and soon heard the cry, "Man overboard." The deck was in great confusion, the Yanks evidently believing that one of the guards was the unlucky man. In the meantime the gunboat down the river sent out a boat (we have none). The piteous cries for help were hushed, for the boat had saved him, and the anguish of our guard was ended. . . . In a few minutes Captain Coffee, Captain Harman and Dick Adams were ushered down nearly naked, their few clothes dripping, and as cold, apparently as the North Pole. It is the coldest night of the fall, and I am uncomfortable between decks with two blankets. Soon a sergeant and guard made another search below and found the hole with Perkins at it, just ready to take the plunge; he had escaped from his guard during the confusion and thought then was his only time. The Yankees guarded the hole the balance of the night, while the swimmers' friends rubbed them to get up the circulation, in the meantime learning how it happened they had been discovered. Harman and Adams both started with too many clothes and pulled them off after they started; Dick heard Coffee call for Harman and, thinking he was in distress, replied in too loud a tone, and then, finding that he was discovered, swam rapidly away, breaking himself down, so that he commenced sinking and crying for help. In the meantime Coffee, who was as good as safe, then turned and went to his assistance and held up his head til the boat picked them up.[10]

CAPT. HENRY DICKINSON, 2ND VA. CAV.

During the night, on board the hulk where Co. G were stationed, there was quite a sensation created by the prisoners attempting to escape. They sawed a hole through the counter, or stern of the vessel, and several of them dropped through into the water. Not far distant was the salt marsh and Tybee Island; if they could have reached land they might have gotten away, some of them, certainly. But their calculations were wrong—the strong tide was running out and they were carried rapidly toward the sea.

CORP. ALBERT R. BARLOW, 157TH N.Y. INF.

"Halt! Halt!" sang out Hugh O'Brien. "Shall I shoot the heathen dead, Capt. McWilliams?"

"Don't shoot, Captain. For God's sake don't fire!" came out of the water.

"Keep cool, gentlemen!" called out Capt. McWilliams. Not much like-lihood of sweating in the river. When the patrol boat brought them on board, their teeth rattled like castanets. The dripping fellows asked for something warm, as they went down again into the hold.[11]

The reason none escaped was their dedication to each other. Neither would put self-preservation first, but turned back to comrades in distress, a trait repeated time and time again during the whole of their prison experience. Coffee, though nearly safe himself, knew Adams would drown. When they were all on board the schooner again, it was apparent that Adams was suffering hypothermia from the exposure to water at near freezing temperatures.

1Lt. RICHARD H. ADAMS, JR., C.S. ENGINEER CORPS	*When we got to the schooner I could not move a limb & my jaws were locked. Capt. Jones Christian, Lt. Chandler & Capt. Lemon brought me to life by rubbing me for about an hour before my pulse began to beat . . . I slept soundly until next morning after I came to life but was very weak, but the "merry merry sunshine" drove all the chilly feeling out of me.*[12]

The morning of October 23 was sunny but cool and crisp, as the men marched off the ships. Many had no blankets or coats, only the same summer clothing they had worn since leaving Fort Delaware. What little remained of their uniforms was tattered. Around them for miles were the salt marshes of Cockspur Island, and the desolate landscape gave no hope for rescue, even though Confederate lines defending Savannah were only six miles distant.

For two among their number, the location raised bittersweet feelings, and mixed emotions. Lieutenant Sanford Branch hailed from Savannah. In 1861, he was among the Confederate troops assigned to garrison the Fort, with the Oglethorpe Light Infantry. Then, he and his two brothers, John and Hamilton, had enjoyed the easy duty and gay atmosphere of the early days of the war. Captured at First Manassas In 1861, "Santie" was taken prisoner, but soon exchanged through the efforts of his mother. Now, two years later, his brother John was dead, killed in battle. "Hammie" was wounded, and he himself had been nearly killed at Gettysburg. Those thoughts were on his mind as he marched toward the fort.

The other Savannah man was Captain Harris Kollock Harrison, whose family plantation at Montieth was only miles away. His brother, General George P. Harrison, was serving in Savannah. His thoughts were preoccupied with his wife and children as he followed his comrades toward the red brick walls of Fort Pulaski.

The ships were unloaded separately to provide time for half the men to get inside the fort and situated in casemates, which had been hastily readied for their arrival, the guns having been pulled out and iron bars placed in the windows. The preparations were not even complete, when the first of the Six Hundred arrived through the sally-port.

Fort Pulaski was small by comparison to Fort Delaware. Built on Cockspur Island in the 1850s as part of the same coastal defense system as Fort Delaware and Fort Sumter, it had only been completed in 1860, though it was not garrisoned at that time. Ironically, the engineer who worked on the fort was Robert E. Lee. The Confederate government quickly seized Pulaski in 1861, but did not have sufficient troops to man it. In 1862 it fell somewhat surprisingly to a Union bombardment when it was believed to be impregnable. The results of the bombardment caused a change in the construction of all U.S. fortifications following the war.[13]

The fort, comprising about two acres, is a pentagon-shaped structure of one level of casemates covered by a parapet. At the time the prisoners arrived, the garrison had about forty guns mounted. Surrounding the fort outside the moat were various buildings associated with the garrison's families and a small frame house that served as a hospital barracks. Lieutenant William Saxton marched in with his company, escorting the prisoners. He would live in the casemates on the north side of the fort.

On the inside of the fort the officer's quarters were in casemates on the side that the entrance was and the other part of the fort was arranged in a semi-circle. In these casemates heavy guns had previously been placed, but when it was decided to remove the prisoners there, these heavy guns had been dismounted and were placed side by side on the parade ground in front of the casemates like great logs. The casemates had been fitted up with bunks as quarters for the prisoners and men. When we arrived the carpenter work was not all completed and there was no dividing partition between the regimental quarters and the prisoners' quarters. On the parapet, heavy guns such as 8, 10 and 12-inch Columbiads and Dahlgrens were mounted enbarbette. We had to have guards on the parapet, in front of the prisoners' quarters, on the dock and at various parts of the island. Outside the fort, beyond the moat, on the high part of the glacis, we established a corridor of sentinels that extended entirely along the whole space that was occupied by the prisoners. These sentinels were so instructed, that in walking their beat all faced one way. When they arrived at the end of their beat all turned at the same time. In this manner their eyes could be on all the embrasures and the ditch all the time. The orders to these sentinels were if any prisoner attempted to climb out the embrasures to halt him; if he succeeded in getting out to shoot him at once.[14]

2LT. WILLIAM SAXTON,
157TH N. Y. VOL. INF.

The prisoners were quartered in the old, brick casemates with huge arches vaulted above wooden or brick floors. Some bunks had been constructed, but much remained to be done to make the men fairly comfortable. They were given the whole of the south side of the bastion heavily damaged in the 1862 bombardment. Despite the location, the casemates were dungeon-like, damp and chilly. The wind came directly off the sea, and blew through the gun embrasures in a steady breeze. But the men settled themselves in as best they could, the same messmates staying together who had tented on Morris Island.

CAPT. THOMAS PINCKNEY, 4TH S.C. CAV. *I find the old fort looking much as it did when I saw it last, under very different circumstances, it was then the scene of a gay picnic, given by the elite of Savannah. We were here put under guard of Col. Brown, 157th N.Y. Volunteers, one of the finest regiments I have seen in the Yankee service, and our treatment was in strong contrast to what we had been subjected to under Col. Hallowell of the 54th Mass. We were treated like officers and soldiers, and with all the consideration possible . . . We were quartered in casemates in the Southeast of the fort. I unfortunately had to take a bunk near the door, where I was much exposed to the cold from which we suffered.[15]*

CAPT. HENRY DICKINSON, 2ND VA. CAV. *The fort is a pentagon, each side, something like 100 yards long, being built of brick and surrounded by a moat of sea water from which the water for use is condensed and held in reservoirs under the floors. The walls are just five feet at the portholes, and the supporting columns to the arches are five feet square, making one-half the wall ten feet thick. This wall is about thirty feet high to the parapet, on which at present twenty-six guns are mounted. . . . The officers occupy the whole of the south front, except the arch and gate way and the engine room for condensing water. On the other four sides there are forty-eight casemates, occupied at present by ourselves and the guard. Piles of cannonball are scattered about in the yard, besides broken carriages and eight or ten disarmed guns. Two brass howitzers are kept constantly in front of the officers' quarters pointing towards us.[16]*

Their location was nearly opposite Colonel Brown's quarters across the parade ground, and adjacent to the rooms housing the other garrison officers. The first day was spent settling in, though there were some complaints of having hard plank bunks to sleep on for winter quarters. Later, cloudy and overcast weather added to the gloomy, spartan atmosphere. Regimental carpenters of the 157th were put to work building additional bunks, and tables for the prisoners' use.

There was no complaint upon the arrival of full rations, which had not been allowed for weeks.

2LT. JOSEPH MAUCK, 10TH VA. INF. *Thursday, 27th Oct. 1864.- Rations a little better than common. When they issue crackers we get from 8 to 10, a cup full of soup and as much meat as I want.[17]*

Col. Brown seemed desirous of doing all for us that the government allowed for prisoners of war. Our rations were increased to a sufficiency which had not been the case hitherto, and in place of three or four worm eaten crackers, and bean broth on which we had been rationed on Morris Island, eight or nine good hard tack were issued, and when a complaint was made about their quality he sent us an apology, saying as soon as ovens could be built he would supply us with fresh bread—the greatest treat imagineable.[18]

CAPT. THOMAS PINCKNEY, 4TH S.C. CAV.

The casemates were uncomfortably crowded, measuring 15-by-26-feet on the average and housing twenty-eight men in each, some holding more. The next day, October 24, the other schooner unloaded, and there was a mad scene as everyone tried to find room and board, as well as attend to their personal hygiene and grooming.

About ten oc we were sent ashore & quartered in the fort. Carson came on ahead of me & got good quarters. So the mess consisted of Capt. Jas. K. Polk, Tenn., Lieut. Carson, Miss., Lieut. A. J. Kirkman & myself, Ala. A nice mess but our friend Carson a thundering eater. We have a nice little place, a table, 5 stools, 4 tin cups & wooden spoons, my handiwork, 1 china plate, one water bucket & one coffee pot (a tin bucket) & a molasses jug. I must not omit a box we use as a "Cubbard".... I am the "Bridget" of our little mess viz: "Chief cook & bottle washer".[19]

1LT. RICHARD H. ADAMS, JR., C.S. ENGINEER CORPS

October 24, 1864.- Last night we had tubs brought into our quarters for sinks, and though removed this morning they have left a terrible stench. Today we were escorted out six at a time to the sink. All this day we spent walking around trying to fix up, but the captain of the other schooner discharged his crew and they came pouring into the casemates this evening, hunting for quarters ... We already begin to feel the effects of the damp, cold walls, rendered more damp by the water which is constantly thrown about. Many men have no basins and wash in cups, plates and tubs. If the doors to the casemates were opened during the day, allowing air and sunlight, our sanitary condition would be better, but if this were allowed, by a preconcerted signal, we might rush out in line of battle, overpower the guard and in a few minutes be masters of the fort.[20]

CAPT. HENRY DICKINSON, 2ND VA. CAV

October 24th.- Land and take up our quarters in Fort—very much crowded. Forty two in the casemate I am in.... Capt. P. [Pinckney] and myself have an upper berth which is more comfortable.[21]

2LT. DAVID GORDON, 4TH S.C. CAV.

It was very damp, the next division being used as a washroom, and they kept everything wet. We here reversed the usual style of preparing for the night. Every man put on all the clothes he had,

CAPT. THOMAS PINCKNEY, 4TH S.C. CAV.

slept four in a bunk, and covered with all the blankets we could collect. However, I was well satisfied. I had good company with me, Maj. Emanuel, Lt. Gordon, Lt. Epps, Maj. Zeigler, Capt. Moore occupied one bunk. Captains Carrington, William Carter of Virginia and Lowe of Missouri, Lieutenants Hart, Rodes Massey, and Hawes of the Virginia Artillery completing our little coterie.[22]

CAPT. HENRY DICKINSON, 2ND VA. CAV.

October 26, 1864.- Today bunks are being rapidly constructed, four for each casement, with three tiers to each bunk. . . . Carder and self, Garrett and Arrington, Board and Harris, Dalton and Mitchell of the Forty-second Virginia; Captain William Barnes and Captain Graves of Georgia; Captain Brown, of Virginia, and Lieutenant Bartholemy, are nominally in one mess, though we separate our rations and my three original companions eat with me. During Harris' confinement at hospital, Board, having no blanket, sleeps with two others.[23]

2LT. SAMUEL H. HAWES, ORANGE ARTY. (VA.)

11th Nov. 1864.- Our prison is divided into six divisions—the one in which I reside is smaller than the others. We have eleven states represented—viz: Ten from Virginia—eight from North Carolina— Six from Tennessee, three from Georgia—three from Kentucky— two from Texas—one from Missouri, one from Louisiana—one from Arkansas—one from Alabama making in all forty two men in our Division.[24]

Their spirits were boosted by the entry of Colonel Brown into their quarters, who gave them a short speech, with promises of considerate treatment.

Gentlemen, you shall be treated, while in my custody, humanely. You who have friends within our lines with whom you can correspond may write them at once for money, clothing, and such other articles that will add to your comfort. I will do all for you I can do, consistent with my duty, to make you as comfortable as possible. Myself and my regiment have seen service in the field and know what is due a brave foe. I will make this the model military prison of the United States. I have already made requisition on headquarters for blankets and clothing for you, and full army rations, together with plenty of fuel. All I shall ask is that you obey orders for government of the prison, and such sanitary rules as shall be issued by me.[25]

It sounded too good to be true. Brown's stated intentions compared dramatically to the situation they had left on Morris Island. They were placed on parole on arrival at Pulaski, until an exchange could take place. Finally, somewhat relieved from the anxiety they had felt, most allowed their hopes for exchange to soar once again. Those wishes were reflected in letters home, and journal entries.

October 27, 1864.- The bunks are being completed, and we are beginning to have something like order. Though the ration is quite small, and our quarters very damp, giving almost every man a cold, yet we all feel the effects of a change in the guard. We do not expect to be shot or bayoneted hourly; if we have a just complaint it is heard. We feel more free and independent, and the danger is that the present good treatment may make us forget the past.[26]

CAPT. HENRY C.
DICKINSON,
2ND VA. CAV.

O for a letter from you, my darling, is the burden of my song, and has been for some months—but I know it is not your fault that I don't hear from you. I doubt whether you have any idea where I am. I wrote shortly before leaving Morris Island, and enclosed to my sister, hoping to get a letter to you in some way. Our prospects are better in every respect here than at Morris Island, and I even hope we may again receive each other's letters regularly. I had very little idea, when leaving Johnson's Island for Dixie on the 22nd of April, that the 31st of October would find me in Fort Pulaski Ga. It does seem impossible for me to be exchanged; no matter how fair a start I make, there is always some Jonah in the party to stop the whole business. Well; I am hopeful still, thank God, looking to what the next month or two may do for me—Who knows, I may SEE YOU by Christmas yet! How my heart beats at the very thought - and how I feel like putting my pen down and dreaming over the sweet picture the idea calls up. In spite of all I have been through since this time a year ago, I can hardly regret my imprisonment, because it has shown me, more thoroughly than perhaps I ever could have learned under other circumstances, how completely my heart is yours; the first of this knowledge will be unmeasured happiness in the years which will, I trust, be granted us together, no matter what our circumstances . . . Best love to all. Remember I am aching to hear from you. God bless you my precious one.[27]

LETTER, CAPT.
GEORGE W.
NELSON,
NELSON'S (VA.)
BATTERY, TO
MISS MOLLIE
SCOLLAY,
OCT. 30, 186

October 25, 1864.- Our expectations so far continue to be unrealized, and we find that our condition is but little better than at Morris Island, but today we received the cheering news that 10,000 prisoners are to be exchanged near this point in a few days, which makes us willing to submit to anything cheerfully, hoping that the occasion for our being here is preparatory to be included in the said exchange.[28]

CAPT. DAVID C.
GRAYSON,
10TH VA. INF.

The exchange did not include the Six Hundred. However, two of their number did benefit from a special exchange when Captains Edward J. Hall of Louisiana and Andrew Jackson Lewis of Mississippi received that privilege on November 4.[29] Some felt hopeful that at least two of their number were lucky while others, too disappointed, lost hope altogether.

Their prison was a series of twenty-one casemates, left open between all so as to form an aisle from one end to the other. The bunks, sleeping two, and in some cases, three men on each bare, plank bed, were arranged at either end of each casemate. The entrance to each, which opened onto the parade ground, was closed up by huge doors, resembling a livery stable or carriage house double door. Above those doors, which were kept shut, were two small transom-like windows with shutters, which if left open allowed a small amount of light. There were also sidelights on the doors, covered by outside shutters. The last two prison casemates at the lower end served as a washroom for clothes and bathing purposes, and the latrine, comprised of tubs for sinks. At first there were gratings placed between each individual prison casemate, but they were eventually removed, allowing all the prisoners to mingle freely.

Upon arrival, within a matter of hours, ideas to take the fort were discussed. There was no grating between the prisoners and the quarters of the 157th New York.

2LT. WILLIAM SAXTON, 157TH N.Y. INF.

Oct. 25.- The cook room and mess hall for the men was outside the fort, and at noon all of the men except the guards on post went out to eat, leaving their guns and accoutrements in their quarters. Here occurred an opportunity for the prisoners to have made a rush and overpowered the guards and captured the fort. The partition between the prisoners and men's quarters had not yet been completed. If they had had a leader and would have acted in concert, they could have made the rush, taken possession of the men's guns and accoutrements, overpowered the guards and they would have been masters of the situation ... They saw the opportunity, but while they were talking over the matter and planning what and how to do, the time slipped by and the men had finished their dinner and returned to their quarters, and the opportunity was gone, never to occur again. We saw the danger and had a strong partition erected, and henceforth only half of the companies went to meals at the same time.[30]

Henry Dickinson was one of those involved. He wrote on October 24, "Indeed, a few of us are concocting plans to take the place, but the great difficulty is to ascertain whether we can communicate with Savannah after we have taken it." The opportunity was lost, never again to present itself. Iron grated doors were placed between the first prison casemate and casemates no. 24 and up, separating the prisoners from the quarters of the 157th troops.

Life settled into a regular routine, more pleasant than at Morris Island. The officers were allowed to receive mail and packages from home, the first of which arrived on October 28, and continued regularly for several weeks, a result of agreements between Colonel Robert Ould and General U. S. Grant to alleviate the suffering of prisoners on both sides. That ended with a rescinding order from Halleck, on the technicality that the exchange agent, Lieutenant Colonel W. T. Bennett, was never officially declared an agent.[31]

Colonel Brown allowed the men to buy goods from the sutler, sending one representative from each division (three casemates) as a "businessman" with lists of needs and money from those in his division. The arrangement provided additional foodstuffs to the prison rations, enabling the men to regain some of their health, as well as break the monotony and present the chance for a brief walk. Many, however, continued to develop colds, still not having sufficient blankets, which Brown had requested. The colonel was unaware that his requisition would go unheeded. As the men were still officially on retaliation status, soon all privileges would be stopped, and Brown reprimanded. But for a limited time, through the last week of November they enjoyed mail, supplies from friends and money for sutler privileges.

October 28, 1864.- A bright day for me. We received a mail and at last I got letters from home. Three from my wife and one from Winkler in the same envelope, but the latest date is August thirty-first. However, my mind is relieved, for all are well . . .[32]	CAPT. HENRY DICKINSON, 2ND VA. CAV.
By flag of truce, we received a most welcome supply of boxes and letters from 'Dixie'. I received eight of the latter, the first from home since I left here on the first of May previous. They then came dropping in for three weeks. Also a box from my factors. William C. Bee, bought me a good supply of bread and biscuits, though they were not as much needed as when written for from Morris Island. There was a great loss in all the cooked provisions, which had been kept waiting for more than a month, many of them had been opened before leaving Charleston, the spoiled portions taken out, and the place supplied to some extent by tobacco, which answered in the place of currency with the sutlers here. One box was directed in Aunt Meta's handwriting, containing a welcome supply of potatoes and rice, surmounted by a cake of corn and sorghum.[33]	CAPT. THOMAS PINCKNEY, 4TH S.C. CAV.
Friday, November 4th.- Received another supply of tobacco from Dixie. Capt. Harris received a box from home containing two hams, potatoes, coffee and clothing, also a ten gallon keg of nice Dixie syrup—the greatest treat we have yet had.[34]	CAPT. JAMES ROBERT MCMICHAEL, 12TH GA. INF.
October 28, 1864.- Colonel De Gournay today went to the sutler's, on parole, bought such articles as we desired and finally made arrangements for one man from each division to act as sutler, going out to the sutler's twice in each week. My name is suggested for my division . . .	CAPT. HENRY DICKINSON, 2ND VA. CAV.

October 29, 1864.- Today I went to sutlery with about sixty-five dollars to buy articles for my division, spending the whole evening

*outside the fort, on parole, and getting as much as I could eat and
drink in the shape of cakes, ale, sherry, etc. My purchases seemed
to please the division. The sutler expects a good stock of goods,
and it is understood there will be no restriction on purchases. About
one-half of the men in my division are purchasers, but most of
them on a small scale. Colonel Carmichael is very particular that
the sutler shall sell to us at the same rates he does to their regiment, but I feel sure the sutler dodges this order on articles in
which he can advance with safety. Today, in buying a tin cup
from a Jew of a clerk, the price asked was twenty cents. A private
in the One Hundred and Fifty-seventh, standing by, told the clerk
he was charging me more than he was allowed. Some rough words
passed and the private whipped the clerk in fine style. Of course
we didn't interfere, but the sutler insisted on twenty cents for the
cup, though the private says fifteen cents is the price. It is the first
time I have seen a Yank fight for Rebels' rights.*[35]

CAPT. ALEX
BEDFORD,
3RD MO. CAV.

*October 29th, 'Washday.'- Some of our officers went out to the
sutler's store this evening with the guard. The sutler began to ask
too much for his goods. When a tin cup was priced at twenty cents
the guard told him fifteen cents was the price. Sutler said he had
the right to ask what he pleased for his goods. The guard told him
he had been a prisoner and knew how to treat gentlemen. One
word brought on another and soon a fight ensued whereupon the
guard gave him a complete thrashing.*[36]

That sense of fairness won great respect from the Confederate officers
for their guards, and the relationship between them over the ensuing months
was one of sympathy and compassion.

Each division elected a leader, or "chief" as a representative to discuss
grievances or requests with Colonel Brown. There were six divisions of three
casemates each, and elections were held immediately. A sense of order and
representation was taken very seriously by all the officers. Whether it had
anything to do with the fact that so many of them had been lawyers before
the war, one thing is certain—it is indicative of their love for the political
process, and a keen sense of justice. They spent a considerable amount of
time drawing up rules and regulations to live by, which were presented to
Colonel Brown.

The author of this document of prison government was Lieutenant Colonel Paul F. DeGournay. However, the political process seems to have gone
awry. Before the regulations could be read and agreed upon by the rest of
the officers, they were passed by the chiefs of each division, and sent to
Colonel Brown as accepted. That caused a ruckus in the ranks, and some
hard feelings as well.

November 6, 1864.- Colonel Brown sent for Colonel De Gournay and the other chiefs and said he wished to suggest certain regulations, which he hoped we would make, and he would then approve as to the orders for prison government. I am . . . only a member of a committee to draft resolutions, . . . Colonel De Gournay wrote some rules and called us . . . to hear them read. They are wordy, but all hands of the chiefs have approved them and Captain Dobyns has taken them to copy.

CAPT. HENRY
DICKINSON,
2ND VA. CAV.

November 8, 1864.- Went to sutlery again today. . . . Returned to find that all the prisoners had been in great excitement about the orders prepared by Colonel DeGournay, which by some mistake were sent to Colonel Brown and approved by him before they were presented to the prisoners for their approval. Colonel Manning, Colonel Folk and others got up meetings and voted down the resolutions because they had not been referred to the prisoners, and because of an eighth section, which contains a threat that in case of willful failure to obey the regulations the officer shall be reported to the Yanks. Several meetings were held and many rough things were said.[37]

The officers continued to be divided on the question of the objectionable rules. Until all agreed, Brown suspended sutler privileges. Meanwhile, the dissatisfied parties held new elections, elected new chiefs and presented a new set of representatives to Brown.

November 10, 1864.- Colonel Brown wrote Major Goldsboro and his associates that he had received a note informing him of their appointment as "chief," stated that he had adopted the rules framed by the former committee, and desired to know whether they would cooperate with him in executing these orders. Trouble again. Goldsboro wanted me to say that I was chief and would co-operate in executing the objectionable orders. I refused and told him Barnes was chief. Barnes, as chief, refused to do so and so did [Captain] Nelson and Captain Hammock, so we are equally divided on the question. Many are talking on the subject and night has overtaken us with the matter unsettled. In the meantime none of us can go to the sutler's, because of which many want us to succumb; others say they will not yield a principle for the sake of a sutler.

CAPT. HENRY
DICKINSON,
2ND VA. CAV.

November 11, 1864.- A string of resolutions were prepared by Colonel Manning and presented to all the divisions, defining the powers of chiefs, and stating their opinions on the late resolutions of the committee. Major Goldsboro of First division, Captain Harris of the Second, and Captain Lowe of the Sixth agreed to cooperate with the Federal authorities and were allowed to go to the sutlery. They bought lots of goods; the other three divisions can buy nothing. When the resolutions were presented today the First, Third, Fourth and Fifth voted in favor of them, the Second tabled them and the Sixth presented in lieu of them a proposition to appoint six men to confer with all parties and adjust. . . . So we go. A little squall has drifted us from our bearings, and so many have command of the vessel that we cannot agree upon the right course.[38]

Eventually all was worked out, and prison society evolved into one of harmony. It only took a few weeks for the novelty of new surroundings to wear off, and be replaced by the same monotony that marked each prison the Six Hundred had seen. On November 16, some Northern female visitors, probably from the Union Headquarters at Port Royal on Hilton Head, arrived to visit the garrison troops and "take a look at the Rebs." Ideas of escape were a constant source of schemes. Rations were issued at 8:00 a.m. and 2:00 p.m., and as it had been everywhere, the roll call was a dull feature of the daily routine. The first week the roll was called four times a day, then dropped to three.

Henry Dickinson was number 82 of the 600, and fell in between two North Carolinians, just one man down from Captain John Dunkle, number 80. As each man answered to his number, he turned and walked back into the casemate. It was a tedious practice.[39]

CAPT. HENRY
DICKINSON,
2ND VA. CAV.

November 10, 1864.- We had an extra roll call at 9 o'clock last night and it is to continue as an order. Four roll calls per day in a fort where, if we were spiders, we could hardly crawl out.

November 11, 1864.- The Yanks change the time and number of roll calls again. We have three now, at daylight, 12 o'clock noon and sunset. Spittoons were brought in today and we hope to keep the floors cleaner.[40]

CAPT. DAVID C.
GRAYSON,
10TH VA. INF.

October 29, 1864.- The usual monotony of prison life prevails to an alarming extent now at this place, caused from the absence of any news, and from the present appearance bids fair to continue during the winter, as every preparation for a long stay here is clearly indicated.

October 30, 1864.- Another day has passed without an incident occurring worthy of note. Each day seems to indicate that we need not hope for liberation soon, and the thought of having to remain prisoners during this winter almost threatens to deprive me of reason. But for the delusion of hope how much more miserable I should feel!

November 1, 1864.- The commencement of another month is ushered upon us without bringing any changes, except that the weather is somewhat cooler, and our teeth were relieved from the arduous labor they have performed for near three months in masticating hard tack by a change to soft bread.[41]

Colonel Brown allowed a few men at a time to go out for exercise on the parade ground. At first it was limited to twenty at a time, then increased to forty, as captors gained more trust in their charges. Each day the casemates were swept out by the prisoners, and an orderly and clean environment was expected to be kept. The regulations posted by Brown stated each prisoner was to bathe once a week, but with no hot water available, and no towels to dry with, it was not a pleasant experience.[42] Mail and packages continued to arrive, and the prisoners turned to writing letters home, a chance to inform anxious loved ones of their whereabouts and condition. Friends who had been separated when the men left Fort Delaware were also contacted, and a correspondence was faithfully kept up between inmates of that and other prisons. Captain James McMichael sent money to men of his company at Fort Delaware, as did Henry Dickinson and Captain Thomas W. Harris of Georgia. Harris shared his own money with privates of his company.[43] Many, reaching desperation, sought special exchanges through influential contacts, writing governors, exchange agents, and politicians. Lieutenant John S. Hughes had a brother in the Union army, a prisoner in Richmond. He wrote to Major General Benjamin Butler requesting a special exchange—himself for his own brother. It was denied.

Captain David Terrell Harris of the 21st Georgia had marched away to war in 1861 from his home in Forsyth County. He left behind a childhood sweetheart, whom he married on his only furlough during the whole war in January 1864. Now he continued to keep up an irregular correspondence interrupted by the fortunes of war.

I will again drop you a few lines to inform you where I am. I am at this fort and have been for some time. We are now from under fire and are getting along as well as could be expected. We was under fire on Morris Island six weeks. I have wrote to you regularly ever since I was captured but have never received any answer. I am very anxious to hear from you and from home. If you receive this please answer. Be sure and give me the news. I (will) have to close. This leaves me in good health, truly hoping it will reach you in due time and find you and all enjoying the same blessing. I remain as ever yours until death.[44]

LETTER, CAPT. DAVID T. HARRIS, 21ST GA. INF., TO WIFE, 2 NOVEMBER 1864

The month of November, ushered in by clouds and damp air, heralded the worst winter in decades. A blustery wind whistled through the bars of the small casemate windows, chilling the stone walls, and making the wet air feel colder. The men shivered in their thin clothing and huddled together in their bunks for warmth. The few who had blankets shared them with those who did not, sometimes sleeping three to a bunk. Men slept "spoon fashion," facing their bedfellow's back, knees bent into his for maximum contact. The continual challenge was to keep warm, and endure the boredom and slow passage of time.

CAPT. HENRY
DICKINSON,
2ND VA. CAV.

November 22, 1864.- But little sleep last night. Many officers have but one blanket. Some have none, and all such got up in the night and built a fire out of old boxes and pieces of wood to sit by. This is said by Southern officers to be the cold day long to be remembered. Ice in barrels, puddles, etc., one inch thick; the wind howling furiously; the Yankees furnish us no wood and some of us lie in bed while others trot about to keep warm. The wind broke the rope of the flag staff, and the "old flag" no longer flaps over us.[45]

2LT. WILLIAM
SAXTON,
157TH N.Y.
INF.

The night of November 22 was the coldest and most disagreeable I ever experienced on guard. A regular "norther" came in from the ocean and pierced the very marrow of our bones. It was so cold that the sentinels were relieved every hour, but the poor officer of the guard had no relief and had to be constantly on the go. In the guard house was a roaring fire, but the officer of the guard could not stop to enjoy its warmth, and like St. Paul when he was shipwrecked while being carried a prisoner to Rome, he wished for day.[46]

CAPT. JAMES
ROBERT
MCMICHAEL,
12TH GA. INF.

Wednesday, November 23rd.- Last night was the coldest November night I ever experienced. I had but one blanket to cover with and suffered severely though not so much as other fellow prisoners who had no covering. Today is clear, the sun's rays are beautifully falling on all outside to warm and enliven, but I can only see them through the prison grates. That even is a privilege for which I should be grateful and take comfort in the thought that I too will some day be warmed by its genial rays.[47]

The exposure to the elements broke the health of some officers, who caught colds which quickly developed into pneumonia. Others had never recovered from the malnutrition and unsanitary conditions on Morris Island. Lieutenant Iverson Burney was a victim of the latter. He had been sick and treated at the post hospital on Morris Island. Despite his illness, he was moved to Fort Pulaski, beyond improvement. Finally on November 12, Death made his first appearance at Fort Pulaski.

CAPT. HENRY
DICKINSON,
2ND VA. CAV.

November 12, 1864.- Lieutenant Burney, of the Forty-ninth Georgia Infantry, died at the hospital last night and was buried today. Three of our number attended his remains to the grave. A military escort was furnished by the Yanks and he was decently interred in the Confederate graveyard, just at the northwest corner of the fort.

November 13, 1864.- Two days ago, Lt. George B. Fitzgerald (called by us simply "Fitz" and believed by us to be simply a citizen or at most a private) was taken to the hospital, and this morning announcement was made that "Fitz is dead." He was a confirmed opium eater; a poor, miserable wreck—ragged, filthy, lousy, loathed by all, and pitied by many, who reported sick that they might get opium for him. He has had no blanket, no socks, hardly clothes to cover him; none of us could supply him, and he slept alone, covering himself with an old piece of tent fly. It was known that he was threatened with pneumonia, but the doctor didn't want him at the hospital and wouldn't take him till Lieutenant Findley, myself and others repeatedly insisted. Upon inquiring I find that he was found dead in his bed this morning. Might not a coroner's jury say that he died from neglect? Poor man! Once he had all the comforts wealth could give him. A graduate of West Point; a lieutenant in the old army, mingling with the Lees, McClellands and Grants; . . . beloved by many who admired him for his learning and accomplishments. Today Lieutenant-Colonel Christian, Lieutenant Finley, myself and two other officers attended his remains to the grave, because he was a Southern man, for we knew him only as "Fitz" and he had no friends. The Yanks gave us a military escort and buried him decently.[48]

There have been two deaths at this prison since our arrival. Lt. Fitzgerald of Virginia and a Lieutenant from Georgia. The latter was buried with military honors, a thing quite unusual. And to Col. Brown we owe many thanks for his continued kindness.[49]

2LT. DAVID
GORDON,
4TH S.C. CAV.

Four stoves were installed when the weather turned cold, not only for warmth, but because it was ordered that the prisoners would now do their own cooking. Rations were issued raw, and wood was limited only to the amount necessary for cooking the food, about twelve sticks of pine for each division as the daily allowance. With that limited supply, only one fire a day was built. The stoves were intended to serve over 100 men each for the purpose, and were placed in every third casemate. The insufficiency was immediately noted.

Nov. 1.- They are putting up stoves for us to do our own cooking— 4 for five hundred and fifty men. Not much chance for a meal, I think, but hope for the best.[50]

2LT. DAVID
GORDON,
4TH S.C. CAV.

November 12, 1864.- Many of the men have spent the day in bed to keep warm. It is hard indeed to spend a day in the cold, dark, damp, gloomy prison. The four stoves only warm the few who can get around them. They gave us crackers and some miserable rice soup today.[51]

CAPT. HENRY
DICKINSON,
2ND VA. CAV.

The problem of using the limited number of stoves in the most efficient way was quickly alleviated by designating two men per casemate as a cooking "team." Each team would cook for a week with some men apparently being fairly good chefs.

CAPT. THOMAS
PINCKNEY,
4TH S.C. CAV.

Capt. Lewis and Lt. Ford of the Va. Cavalry completed our mess, and we fared better, in fact I never lived so well in prison. Capt. Lewis, when we could get some sutler's supplies, and he could get access to one of the four cooking stoves, which were provided to warm up the Fort, made such biscuits as equalled old Prince's; and Lt. Ford spent much of his time gambling for the benefit of the mess.[52]

The end of November still found the prisoners hopeful of an exchange. The men could see the truce ships through the casemate windows, meeting in the mouth of the Savannah River, so close and reassuring that it was assumed the time would come shortly when the remainder of the Six Hundred would finally depart for home. The ability to see the ships presented a peculiar mixture of feelings, both hope and frustration, as the sick and wounded were exchanged from all the prisons of North and South. The exchange agents of both sides had finally received permission to alleviate overcrowding only for those expected to die. The Savannah River was the only point of exchange east of the Mississippi by late 1864, as Grant had Lee's forces bottled up at Petersburg, and Charleston still remained under siege.

COL. EDWARD
C. ANDERSON,
CSA, CMDG.
SAVANNAH
BATTERIES

Wednesday Nov. 9, 64.- Col. Hatch and a number of commissioners of exchange came down from Macon this afternoon and are to go down the River in the morning it is supposed to bring up a number of our prisoners confined at Ft. Pulaski.

Thursday, Nov 10.- A flag of truce steamer went down today at eleven a.m. with Capt. Hatch and a number of gentlemen of the ambulance corps. The weather is damp and cloudy with occasional rain showers—The steamer returned at sundown, having accomplished nothing whatever. I am inclined to regard the whole thing a Yankee political trick from first to last. "The Beauregard" is to go down again Tuesday next.

11th.- The truce steamer went down this afternoon to meet Major Mulford, the Yankee agent of exchange and on her return brought the news that our prisoners had arrived from Hilton Head, and would be delivered on the morrow.[53]

CAPT. HENRY
DICKINSON,
2ND VA. CAV.

November 13, 1864.- Tonight we heard a rumor from a sentinel that we are to be exchanged this week, and all are astir. The sick are being exchanged daily in the river one-half mile distant.

November 14, 1864.- Another very cold morning and we had to shiver or lie in bed. The Yanks brought us no wood for our four little stoves yesterday. 'Tis said that the exchange officers were busy all last night, and have exchanged 4,000; as many are on litters it is tedious. We still have rumors that we are to be exchanged in a few days, and it is added that we are to be paroled for sixty days. Un-

necessary, as three-fourths of us have scurvy and the balance diar-
rhea and rheumatism; this cold place, I verily believe, will exchange
many of us in a few weeks. After what we have endured, old Abe's
Christian people need not talk of Southern prisons.[54]

November 12, 1864.- In reporting the occurrence of the day I can
not vary the usual account, which is that all is dull and insipid and
our own imprisonment becoming less endurable by seeing the ex-
change going on almost in a stone's throw of us and hear not a
cheering report in regard to ourselves.

CAPT. DAVID
GRAYSON,
10TH VA. INF.

November 13, 1864.- Today, being Sunday, is more than ordinarily
dull, and the weather being quite chilly I had to spend a portion of
it in bed to keep warm. I saw today two large vessels loaded with
prisoners for exchange go up the Savannah, and it almost caused
me to envy them their fortune.[55]

Sunday 6th Nov. 1864.- Grape that 10,000 sick and wounded are
at Hilton Head for exchange.

2LT. JOSEPH
MAUCK,
10TH VA. INF.

Monday 7th Nov. 1864.- The exchange grape confirmed it com-
mences today, 1000 per day.

Tuesday 8th Nov. 1864.- Can see the exchange boats going up the
Savannah River. Wouldn't care to be a little sick myself.[56]

Unfortunately, because of the retaliation status of the officers at Fort
Pulaski, there would be no exchange. However, a change occurred which
afforded much excitement on November 19, when 197 of the men were called
out to prepare to leave. The prison conditions were too crowded according
to Colonel Brown, who notified General John G. Foster at headquarters on
Hilton Head. There was some room there since the sick had been exchanged,
and it was decided to split the Six Hundred into two prison camps. It may
have been decided for their own best interest, but none of the prisoners
relished the thought of leaving friends behind. At first it was a false assumption that exchange was the reason behind the move, but that quickly
vanished.

November 19, 1864.- At noon we were startled by an order to fall
in line. Out of our quarters a roll of 200 officers, chosen I suppose
by lot, was called, and they were ordered to get ready to leave in
half an hour. There was one of the prison scenes, settling debts,
dodging creditors, dividing partnership articles, rolling up plun-
der, swapping chances of exchange, selling furniture, quizzing and
bidding goodbye. . . . I managed to settle with all who were to
leave, though parties were constantly changing their names and
trading off. I saw one man, Lieutenant Brinkley, unable to buy a
chance for a long time because he couldn't remember the assumed

CAPT. HENRY
DICKINSON,
2ND VA. CAV.

*name of the man whose chance to get to Morris Island he bought.
But in two hours the 200 were called out and parted in sorrow
from many friends and messmates. John Arrington and Peter
Dalton go from my mess; they couldn't give away their chance of
exchange. Captain Lewis gave away his chance and stays. Colonel
Manning, Lieutenant-colonel Christian, Major Emanuel, Captain
Moon, Allen, Frazier, Bailey and many other friends bade farewell
and soon we saw them on a boat and on their way to Hilton Head.*[57]

CAPT. DAVID GRAYSON, 10TH VA. INF.	*November 19, 1864.- At length a change in our situation has been made, for what purpose still remains unknown. Today 200 of our party were separated and taken from us to some other point. The separation was painful, as many were separated from friends and messmates, and all felt warmly attached to each other from having been together so long in prison and having undergone together the trials of retaliation. This change evidently makes the prospect of our exchange look as gloomy as it ever has yet.*[58]
2LT. HENRY H. COOK, 44TH TENN. INF.	*Col. Brown, finding that we were too crowded, sent two hundred of our number to Hilton Head, and among the number Capt. Thomas F. Perkins, for which cause I lost the only officer from my own county, and my truest friend.*[59]
CAPT. ALEX BEDFORD, 3RD MO. CAV.	*November 19th, two o'clock.- All excitement about leaving roll call. About one hundred and fifty called out to leave. Many conjectures about where we were going. In about an hour fifty more were called, I being among the last fifty. . . . About four we were called out to leave for our new home, knowing not where it would be, but soon ascertained we would go to Hilton Head. About four o'clock we left the wharf, at about seven anchored off Hilton Head. All well. Left two of our mess behind.*[60]
2LT. SAMUEL H. HAWES, ORANGE ARTY. (VA.)	*19 Nov. 1864.- Today I feel "desperately blue." Two hundred of our number have been placed on board of Steamer* Canonicus— *our destination is said to be Hilton Head South Carolina where quarters have been provided for us.—This is said to be a sanitary move,—when our names were first called, the more sanguine of our party conjured up delightful visions of exchange, these pleasing hopes were soon nipped in the bud, when our true destination was learned. I was separated from one of my dearest friends, Lt. Rodes Massie, with whom I have been ever since my capture. I shall sadly miss him.*[61]
2LT. JOSEPH MAUCK, 10TH VA. INF.	*Saturday 19th Nov. 1864.- All hands and the cooks ordered to the yard, and to our surprise 200 names were called to leave this place. Mine was one of the No. Half an hour to get ready to start. Much excitement prevails. Some say it is for exchange and others say to go North. All ready and we marched out of the Fort . . .*[62]

We were suddenly called together, and two hundred of us were selected from the others. . . . for some purpose unknown to us—the popular opinion was that we were to be exchanged. So popular was this opinion, that many strong and robust men, with a magnanimity worthy of imitation, proffered their places to their weakly and sickly fellows, and many offered large sums of Confederate money to the select ones to procure their places, and we really supposed that the star of peace was rising, and that the sun of freedom was about to burst upon us and free us from the dominion of Yankees and negroes. But we were destined to see and feel greater agonies and more deplorable miseries than any we had ever known, or ever for a moment fancied.[63]

CAPT. JOHN
DUNKLE,
25TH VA. INF.

The Immortal Six-Hundred
Lt. Col. Emile St. Mesme LeBreton
A.D.C. to Col. Marshall J. Smith, Chief of
Artillery; 4th Louisiana Militia, New Orleans.

The Immortal Six-Hundred
Capt. Thomas Coleman Chandler
VMI '64
Co. K, 47th Virginia Infantry.

The Immortal Six-Hundred
Capt. Harris Kollock Harrison
Co. E, 7th Georgia Cavalry.

Georgia State Archives
Lt. David Terrell Harris, Jr.
Co. E, 21st Georgia Infantry.

Courtesy Mrs. Effie Darden Hamilton
Lt. Joseph Hardy Darden
Co. A, 3rd North Carolina Infantry.

Museum of the Confederacy, Richmond
Capt. Thomas Benton Horton
Co. B, 11th Virginia Infantry.

Courtesy Mr. Michael James
Capt. William N. James
Co. C, 44th Tennessee Infantry.

Courtesy Mrs. C. W. Wallace
Capt. William Jefferson "Jeff" Dumas
Co. K, 53rd Georgia Infantry.

CHAPTER NINE

"What Have I Offended Against Thee, Or Against Thy Servant, Or Against This People, That Ye Have Put Me In Prison?"

Jeremiah 37:18

WITH the loss of messmates and comrades, those left behind readjusted themselves in the casemates, spreading out to take advantage of the vacant space. Once again, monotony set in and the men marked time in various pursuits.

In the casemate with Henry Dickinson were some young entrepreneurs from Bedford, Virginia. First Lieutenants Thomas S. Mitchell and Peter W. Dalton began a thriving pie business. By going to the sutler and buying supplies, they were able to sell the baked product for a profit to fellow prisoners. Captain Thomas Board and Second Lieutenant William Carder, other men of the same mess, brewed beer in a large barrel right next to the bunks, turning a profitable business. Soon there was competition from others whose recipe was carefully guarded.

CAPT. HENRY DICKINSON, 2ND VA. CAV.

November 28, 1864.- The beer per barrel costs—dandelion 60 cents; molasses, say $2.50; yeast 20 cents. It sells for 5 cents per pint. Adding lots of water and but little of the ingredients a barrel never gives out. The making I found out at the sutlery and advised Board to experiment on it; it is a secret known to the whole Yankee nation. The Yanks have plenty of their own outside and never drink Board's, hence the secret does not leak out. Captain Jones, Granby and others have tasted it and swear it is common "corn beer," flavored with sarsaparilla. They have tried to buy the sarsaparilla, but there is none and Board has the credit of manufacturing a Virginia beer, according to his own recipe.

160

November 24, 1864.- During the night Board's beer barrel, near my bed, became so full of gas that he and Dave got up to fix it. When they pulled the plug out the gas, beer and all flew in every direction with a terrible noise, wetting a number of us, frightening some and amusing others who witnessed the repeated efforts of Board and Dave to stop the hole. After a long time quiet was restored, and Dave contented himself with the reflection that his beer was fully advertised, and so it seems, for it sells well today. It is made of molasses, water and a preparation of dandelion, with yeast to work it. It tastes somewhat like sarsaparilla, and Board makes all believe that it is a Virginia recipe. The contest between he and Lieutenant Jones of Second division, in beer, apples, pies and notions is waxing warm.[1]

Once again on a small scale among 313 men the same economic system was employed as it had been at Fort Delaware. As long as boxes and money from the outside came in, the little prison community sustained itself. For those who received no outside funds the haves shared with the have-nots, as First Lieutenant Sanford Branch confirmed:

Your letter of 5th inst. was handed to me by the gentlemanly Provost-Marshall on the afternoon of the sixth. The boxes were delivered early next morning. The eatables were in good condition & were highly appreciated by a number of friends including several sick comrades with whom I shared the chickens & delicacies. Le Beouf was excellent. We have very good facilities for cooking & you know I am very fond of baked potatoes. The tobacco is a very fine article and I think I can dispose of it at a very fair price. The health of our officers is very good. There are very few sick. Gordon Fort has been quite sick but is much better. Remember me kindly to Mortie Davis please say to him that I have authorized several friends here to have packages sent to his care if he will give these his attention I will feel obliged. All letters & packages if not contraband are promptly delivered. Do write often. Love to Hammie & Sarah.[2]

LETTER, 1LT.
SANFORD
BRANCH,
8TH GA. INF.,
TO MOTHER
CHARLOTTE
BRANCH,
NOV. 10, 1864

The boxes spoken of by the men were not small items. They sometimes weighed as much as 200 pounds, filled with food enough to last for a month, unless it was delayed and the food was spoiled. Shipped in wooden crates, the wood from the boxes was used to build small furniture items, or to burn in the stoves.

The sutler, named Bell, was an accommodating man who took checks from men on an honor system, and helped those in financial straits still obtain goods on credit. His kindness proved to be literally "life-saving" as the end of November saw General John G. Foster halt the privilege of mail and boxes.[3]

**CAPT. HENRY
DICKINSON,
2ND VA. CAV.**

November 29, 1864.- Sent a draft of Henry Fry's on Mr. Paul to the sutler and got it cashed, making Henry look as bright as if he were in Dixie. Bell knows neither the drawer or payer on these drafts, but takes them on my say so.[4]

**2LT. HENRY H.
COOK,
44TH TENN.
INF.**

Goldsborough, Fitzhugh, and others from Maryland, and a few from the Confederate States had a little money, and succeeded in getting credit with the sutler of the One Hundred and Fifty-seventh Regiment. My friends were all young men from Middle Tennessee, with no knowledge of commercial affairs, and none of us asked or received credit, though it was known that the sutler, Mr. Bell was one of the kindest of men. . . . During the months of November and December my good friend, Capt. Nicks, often gave me a good piece of meat and bread. He was a man of great industry and energy, and would do any kind of work for those who had money, and he had a kind heart, and divided with me the proceeds of his labor.[5]

Perhaps the largest purchase from the sutler was in paper and pens for writing. Other frequent selling items included vegetables, sweets, and candles. Tobacco was frequently sent in Dixie mails, and the prisoners used it as currency, the Union soldiers especially willing to trade because it was a commodity difficult for them to obtain.

Various entertainments such as games and reading kept the men amused. Some, like Joseph Mauck, plied their trade as jewelry makers and "washwomen" to earn extra money. Gambling soon became popular again, lasting for weeks, until the game tables were closed down after it was discovered that Lieutenant George C. Nash was dealing with marked cards. When things became boring, something to do was always found, and daily life droned on in that way.

**CAPT. HENRY
DICKINSON,
2ND VA. CAV.**

November 14, 1864.- We have had a regular faro bank and several vantoon tables for sometime, and crowds hang around them. One dollar is the limit, I believe. Gambling is a great propensity with most prisoners and many will risk their last cent, probably advanced by some friend as charity.

November 29, 1864.- Gambling is going on at a high rate in prison. Faro, poker and vantoon tables are all around and well attended. Vermin are about the prison in abundance, there being no way to heat water with which to kill them. I wash often and use a little mercurial ointment, but the animals will get on me. Men sit on the barrels or on their bunks and kill lice and nits by the hour.[6]

**CAPT. THOMAS
PINCKNEY,
4TH S.C. CAV.**

A great deprivation was the want of something to read, newspapers were carefully excluded, unless they contained news of the Yankee victories. The few novels I bought, from poor Dave Garrett's stock, were read to pieces, and there are no more to be borrowed. In spite of this, however, I make but indifferent progress in the one book I try to make my daily reading, which was given to me by the colporteur.[7]

December 3, 1864.- The Yanks generally let us alone and we let them alone. Many spend the days and nights till taps in gambling; others abuse the Yanks; others spend their time in picking lice; others cook and eat and others again grumble over their hard fate. Literature is at a terrible discount. No books or papers can be bought, and the stock on hand is very small. A few are studying French or mathematics, but only a few.[8]

CAPT. HENRY
DICKINSON,
2ND VA. CAV.

Dickinson found a supreme whist player in Captain Henry L. Hoover, and the pair was unbeatable in the many games between other messmates, including Henry Fry, Henry Board, Lieutenant Frederick Fousse from Paris, France, and William Carder. Many winter evenings were spent sitting around the small table, wrapped up in blankets against the chill.

The scholarly among their number taught classes. Rodes Massie and Henry Handerson taught Latin and Sciences, while the French from Louisiana, and Lieutenant Fousse taught their native tongue.

Often men would sit or lounge on their bunks, listening to storytellers, like Captain Thornton Hammack, an especial favorite who had a repertoire of Irish jokes and anecdotes. Sometimes the talk took on a somber tone, and reminiscences of home, or experiences in battle filled the idle hours, leading to musings on how their commands were faring in the field.

The conditions were an improvement over Morris Island, but still left a lot to be desired. Hot water was unobtainable, thus washing clothes was not effective against that old army plague the louse, causing constant discomfort. Rations were still insufficient and limited in variety. Many had lost up to one-third of their weight from the ordeal on Morris Island, and food was still a common thought on many minds.

Wed., November 23, 1864.- No change. It appears to us we are still under retaliation for something, but we can bear all the Yankees can put on us, although it is hard to stand.

1LT. JOHN C.
ALLEN,
7TH VA. CAV.

Mon., November 26, 1864.- No change. We have had the statement of several Yankees who were prisoners at Charleston and Andersonville, Ga. and according to their statement they got at least double the rations we get. They say they got a quart of cornmeal and more molasses than they could use & beans or peas, but no meat.[9]

Fort Pulaski is not a pleasant habitation at any time and my recollections of it are not of the brightest hue. It was particularly exasperating to be encased within a dungeon-like hole and gaze while almost starving through the grated casemate window at oysters

SGT. MAJ.
CHARLES M.
BUSBEE,
5TH N.C. INF.

*in abundance clinging to the sides of the moat which surrounded
the fort.* [10]

Colonel Brown addressed the men regularly, giving them a chance to be heard, and they took every opportunity to voice their opinions and needs.

CAPT. HENRY DICKINSON, 2ND VA. CAV. *December 4, 1864.- . . . Col. Brown took occasion to speak fully of his desire to accommodate us with facilities in getting money, boxes, etc. and I believe he is sincere. He spoke of offers made by some to write to their Dixie friends to help any of his regiment captured in the late fight. Said none were captured but that a number were killed and wounded, including McWilliams. . . . Said he desired that we should be more cleanly in prison and if he stopped some of our privileges we might attribute the act to disobedience of his orders on the subject of cleanliness. I felt the imputation was uncalled for, and publicly replied that neatness could not be expected when no facilities were furnished for heating water to kill vermin. Lousy men will not sweep floors. He replied in extenuation that he was doing his best to increase the supply of wood, and so the conference ended.* [11]

Once the prisoners were invited to church services with the garrison, and a group of seventy-five took the opportunity to attend. The sermon was too political for them, dealing with issues related to the war and praying against "the enemy." Most of the officers showed their disapproval by refusing to stand with the congregation, and refrained from attending the garrison services again. Instead, they held their own prayer meetings in one of the casemates, often sharing space with other activities.

CAPT. HENRY DICKINSON, 2ND VA. CAV. *Had Episcopal services in my casemate, no. 32, Capt. Nelson officiating. During the time some men were cooking, others washing, others playing chess, and others sleeping, whilst the surgeon was giving pills.* [12]

The long hours of idleness gave the men much time for mental reflection. They undoubtedly re-evaluated their lives and attitudes toward religion. The armies had experienced surges of religious revivals in 1863 and 1864, and prison was the perfect atmosphere for spiritual hope and renewal. Their belief in God survived, despite the tests they endured, and offered comfort when they felt forgotten and hopeless. Every facet of daily life was seen through the veil of Faith.

The daily routine still consisted of roll calls and inspection of quarters. The U.S. garrison became more secure, and the prisoners noticed a tightening of rules and regulations around the end of November, that coincided with the arrival of the vanguard of Sherman's troops north of Savannah.

November 17, 1864.- Plenty of grape about exchange but no news or letters. The Yanks place another small piece of artillery in front of our quarters. Their men are constantly on the alert. They allow only twenty-five of us out at once though the order says forty, and at night only eight. As a consequence a long string of men stand at the door waiting their time to get out. I found forty-nine waiting and went to bed, getting up at 11 o'clock. . . . I learn that after dark the Yanks turn three pieces located on the parapet on us and a company is always near them ready to resist us. This makes the place much stronger at night than most of us believed.[13]

CAPT. HENRY
DICKINSON,
2ND VA. CAV.

I had to visit each sentinel on duty each hour, to see that he was properly instructed and performing his duty faithfully. I also had to pass through the prisoners' quarters once each hour to see that they were all quiet and subordinate . . . I formed many pleasant acquaintances with them . . . They understood that they were prisoners of war, and that while we treated them as gentlemen, if an attempt to escape was made we would not hesitate a moment to shoot them down.[14]

2LT. WILLIAM
SAXTON,
157TH N.Y.
INF.

The most mentally stressing subject was the condition of the Confederate army in the field, of which they were now denied knowledge, and that preyed on their nerves. They chafed with frustration at their inactive state, knowing they were needed by their commands. Confinement often bred impatience, and fights occurred among some of the prisoners, as tempers flared. One argument between Hugh Dunlap and Rufus Gillespie involved the reputation of the Army of Tennessee, in which Dunlap served. Captain Fitzpatrick of Louisiana and Captain Lewis were mentioned by Henry Dickinson as "still at enmity" for some disagreement. But the altercation between Thornton Hammack and one of the Logan brothers must have been hot, for Alex Bedford recorded in his diary, "No one hurt serious."[15]

The officers were treated to a diversion by the sound of artillery fire in the direction of Savannah, which confirmed their fears of Sherman's progress.

December 1, 1864.- Today went out of the fort to buy articles for my division; found the Yanks much excited about the movements of Sherman and the troops which left here and Hilton Head on the twenty-eighth inst. They report that Sherman has taken Milledgeville, scattered the legislature, whipped the militia (under Cobb), and at last accounts was within seventy-five miles of Savannah.[16]

CAPT. HENRY
DICKINSON,
2ND VA. CAV.

December [10], 1864.- The quiet of our evening was broken into by the bugle sounding the assembly on the Parade a short time after which we heard the Yankees cheering most vociferously, the band striking up the Yankee Doodle. We could not help feeling

CAPT. THOMAS
PINCKNEY,
4TH S.C. CAV.

much depressed, knowing they were exulting over some war news. It soon turned out that Sherman had been heard from, and they reported that he had captured Savannah, which caused many sleepless nights in prison. Gordon, poor fellow, was shivering like a wet dog. I tried to laugh off his nervous apprehensions. He turned upon me and said, "You have no wife and children who will be subjected to the depredations of Sherman's army." It turned out that his scouts had reached the coast, and he wants ammunition and provisions collected at the upper end of Ossabaw Sound. All particulars are carefully kept from us, which is very trying, as we continually hear the distant booming of Artillery in the direction of Red Bluff and Ossabaw.[17]

CAPT. HENRY DICKINSON, 2ND VA. CAV.

December 3, 1864.- They say that Baker and Cobb are in Savannah with 40,000 militia and that Sherman is hard pushed. We receive a Dixie mail today (no letter for me), from which we learn that the Andersonville prisoners are in Savannah, that a part of Early's troops are in Augusta, and that, though the country west of Augusta was cut off from Savannah between the thirteenth and twenty-fourth of November, communication is now open. Sherman will strike for Darien and Port Royal and we think in either case just fight not far from Savannah. God grant that he may be overwhelmed. Tonight the Yanks issued two circulars, one stating the embargo on money letters and boxes is withdrawn and that we can write for either. Colonel Brown is evidently suspicious of the future action of his government, however, as he will neither persuade us to send nor dissuade us from sending for articles.[18]

CAPT. DAVID GRAYSON, 10TH VA. INF.

December 1 and 2, 1864.- Another month has begun without any event transpiring to characterize its entrance. It may be that each and every day now are eventful days in the history of our country, as we have reason to believe from what rumor says of the movements of Sherman, but our knowledge is limited to the prison walls, and we are ignorant of the great events that may be daily occurring as if we were banished from the world. Oh, who can imagine the suspense each and every Confederate officer here must feel when he reflects and is made sensible of how little he may know of the real sufferings and trials of his own immediate friends and relatives may at this moment be subjected to![19]

Another constant concern was their families from whom many had been separated for two years or more. Of course there was the obvious fear of what hardships and dangers a war-torn country was inflicting upon loved ones. But there was something more than that. There was the fear that they were forgotten by their children, or abandoned by sweethearts. Captains Thomas Martin and Andrew McLeod and Lieutenants William Epps and Peru

Benson were being mourned as dead by wives and parents. The erratic delivery of their mail, imposed by retaliation, left them out of touch with loved ones and lives were changed irreparably in some cases. When Captain Andrew McLeod returned home to his farm in Mitchell County, Georgia, he would find his wife remarried, thinking him dead after not hearing anything for so long.

There is evidence to suggest that some men cracked under the mental stress. Lieutenant Thomas Easterling, 5th South Carolina Cavalry, suffered from paranoia and was convinced his fellow prisoners were trying to kill him. He probably was distraught over the death of his brother, killed in battle, and the loss of the family plantation and property.

Their reveries swung from the memories of home and the peaceful life they left, to fears and uncertainty of what they would return to, if they returned at all. The prospect that these could be their last days on earth led to close friendships, and vows were made that would last a lifetime. Captain William Kemp and Lieutenant Bolivar Edwards had been friends before the war. They promised that if they survived, each would name a son for the other.

The apprehension at hearing constant cannonading, combined with the news from home and comrades still in the field, served to frustrate the men even more.

Monday, November 21st.- A large L & N mail has been distributed today. I received a letter from Col. Hardeman telling of more casualties in our old regiment. My first Lieutenant has been severely wounded. No officer left with my company, and I fear few men.[20]

CAPT. JAMES
ROBERT
MCMICHAEL,
12TH GA. INF.

December 2nd.- Boxes and letters were delivered. I received a letter from the loved ones at home informing me that a box and clothing had been sent—which box & C. I had received the last day of Nov. My letter was dated Nov. 8th and brings me the sad intelligence that my poor dear Brother W.B.G. has not been heard from since he fell into the enemies hands wounded. O the horrors of war how sad to contemplate. But if it is the Divine Will we must pray for grace to enable us to submit with patience.[21]

2LT. DAVID
GORDON,
4TH S.C. CAV.

The officers sent to Hilton Head wrote back to Fort Pulaski immediately, in particular to Captain John Cantwell, who specifically showed an interest in their welfare and fate.

Dear Sir: - Agreeable to promise, I embrace this opportunity of writing you a few lines to inform you of our safe arrival at this place, all well. We arrived about seven o'clock the evening of the day we left Fort Pulaski. We are camped about one mile from the town, three in a tent—the same tents we lived in at Morris Island. Lieutenants Henderson, Merchant, and myself are together. Since we have been here we have had a

LETTER, 2LT.
GEORGE M. CRAPON,
3RD N.C. INF.,
AT HILTON HEAD, S.C.,
TO CAPT. JOHN L.
CANTWELL,
3RD N.C. INF.,
NOV. 24, 1864

very disagreeable time. The weather has been quite cold—we had ice last night and night before from a half to one inch thick. You would be amused to see our chimney which we have erected to our tent. The material is sand and grass. We had a fire in it last night for the first time, and made our tent comfortable, notwithstanding it smoked some. Built it higher this morning and hope it will draw better. No news of interest. Give my very best respects to Captains MacRae and Cowan, Lieutenants Gurgannus, Henderson, and Childs and all enquiring friends. My address is Hilton Head, S.C., 3rd Division. Hoping this may reach you safe and find you in good health.[22]

At the same time, exchange became a resurrected topic. More sick and wounded were brought to the Savannah River, and finally optimism paid off for a handful of the Six Hundred when it was announced on December 5 that some would be going home.

CAPT. HENRY
DICKINSON,
2ND VA. CAV.

December 5, 1864.- This evening, to our surprise, Major Mulford's exchange boat touched at this wharf and he came in and issued orders to Lieutenant-Colonel De Gournay, Major Branch, Capt. George Howard, Captain Fitzhugh and Lieutenants Branch and Busbee to get ready at once for special exchange, which they soon accomplished and marched out as happy as lords. In their present condition, all together, I suppose, would not make a good soldier. Lieutenant-Colonel De Gournay, a good man and soldier, is sorely afflicted with heart disease. Fitzhugh was captured during the First Maryland campaign, just as he had made up his company; he has never been in action or even commissioned. We fear this special exchange bodes no good to the rest of us, and yet I am hopeful because Mulford is still here.[23]

SGT. MAJ.
CHARLES M.
BUSBEE,
5TH N.C.

I will state how I got out of Fort Pulaski, as it illustrates the fact that combinations exist in all issues. General W. H. Mulford, who was the Federal Agent of Exchange, entered into negotiations with Colonel W. H. Hatch, the Assistant Agent of Exchange of the Confederate Army (who was afterwards a distinguished member of Congress from Missouri) for the purpose of exchanging the sick prisoners at Charleston and Fort Pulaski respectively. They had a conference on the subject and after agreeing to the exchange of the sick, one said to the other (it matters not which one), "Now if you have any special friends in prison whom you would like especially to get out, why you just add six names to your sick list and I will add six names to mine." The proposition was adopted and so six names of prisoners who were not sick were added to the list. I, fortunately, was one of the six added to the list of those who were to be released from Fort Pulaski. I owed this blessing to Lieu-

*tenant M. J. Allen, who was an Aide on Colonel Hatch's staff. I did
not know Lieutenant Allen nor did he know me, but his interest in
me had been enlisted by a mutual friend, a Mr. Dennis Redmond,
who edited an agricultural paper at Marietta, Ga., and who was a
great friend of my grandmother; and who, when he learned that
I was in prison, had asked Lieutenant O'Brien (who was his intimate friend) to do what he could for me if opportunity offered. . .
      I well remember what I was doing when my name was called out
in Fort Pulaski for exchange. . . . I was playing a game of seven up
with Captain John Cowan of Wilmington, for a cracker. It was a
common game among the prisoners, although the stakes were
high and the victor had extra luxurious living for the day.*[24]

Connections paid off in the exchange of a few, and the truce boats waited
to find out about the negotiations for the exchange of the sick and wounded
in Beaufort, who had been hospitalized from the *Crescent City* on August
28. For the next two weeks, the officers at Fort Pulaski lived in hope, daring
to allow some optimism that they would be among the lucky ones this time.
It was an emotional rollercoaster, fraught with highs and lows.

Finally on December 14, Colonel Mulford returned with a list of thirty
names picked for exchange. Captain Thomas Pinckney was among the number, and he bade farewell to his comrades.

*Reports of our coming exchange are so prevalent I have backed
my opinion with a bottle of wine, on getting through within a week,
which I hope to make Gordon pay me within that time in Dixie. On
the night of the 14th of December, I was rejoiced at hearing I was
wanted outside of the fort, when I learned my hopes were about
being realized. I was ordered to be ready to board a steamer, which
was to carry 100 sick and wounded to Charleston Harbor, for
exchange the next day. So bequeathing my frying pan and blanket to the unfortunates I was leaving behind me, Capt. Howard
and I embarked, and were exchanged in Charleston Harbor the
next day. I have never discovered to whom I am indebted for getting my exchange. Col. John Lay of Beauregard's staff, who interested himself to effect it, or Mr. William Habersham of Savannah,
an old friend of my Brother's who has told me since he dined with
Col. Mulford, while Sherman occupied Savannah, on parting, the
Col. offered his services, which Mr. Habersham declined, but said
he had two friends among the prisoners at the Fort and if an exchange of them could be facilitated he would be much obliged. He
wrote on one of his cards the names of Capt. George Howard, of
the Maryland line, and Capt. Thomas Pinckney, of the South Carolina Cavalry, which seems to account for the fact that Capt. Howard
and I were taken out of the prison to fill up the tale of the one
hundred sick and wounded . . . On entering Charleston Harbor,*

CAPT. THOMAS
PINCKNEY.,
4TH S.C. CAV.

*where our exchange was to take place under flag-of-truce, Col.
Mulford returned our money and watches. He had a package
marked Henry T. Coulter 53rd Va. Infantry and asked me if I knew
of such a person. I replied I did, that he was aboard this very boat,
having come from the hospital. I called him up, when the Col.
expressed the greatest surprise at finding him here, "I have had
every prison in the United States searched for you. You have been
the subject of a special exchange and never until this minute have
I been able to locate you, your man has been at liberty at least
three months." The fact was Coalter had bought out some comrades place [George Miller] to get away from Fort Delaware but
did not think it worth while to go into explanations under present
circumstances.*[25]

2LT. DAVID GORDON, 4TH S.C. CAV.	*Dec. 14th.- Some 30 of Confederate officers are called. Told to prepare to leave immediately—one all supposes on exchange. Capt. Pinckney among the number. I am left alone and in the cold. Things look gloomy but will still hope. Learn that 116 have been sent through.*[26]

CAPT. HENRY DICKINSON, 2ND VA. CAV.	*December 14, 1864.- About 8 p.m. Major Place came into our quarters and read out a list, beginning with Major McCreary, Captain Barnes, Lieutenant-Colonel Daugherty, and ending with several sick, making in all about 31 officers, including all but one at the hospital; he ordered them to get ready to leave at once. About 9 p.m. they are ready to start to Dixie, leaving us sadder than ever. Adjutant Coulter, Captain Crow, Captain Ashton, all friends, and my patient, young Hooberry, of Nashville (who is a mere shadow), are among the lucky ones. I gave Lieutenant Hooberry a letter to my wife, but fear he will never live to see her. We learn that all the Beaufort men, about 45, and a number from Hilton Head are to go, making about 116 in all. Some of us think this looks well for us, others say it looks badly. George Howard writes from Charleston that we shall be exchanged at once; an officer connected with the exchange bureau says differently. So we go, depressed and excited several times each day.*[27]

Those into whose hands fate placed these men were little bothered by
their mental or physical condition. The exchange agents bargained in their
own way, but the 600 officers who had left Fort Delaware were under a
different set of rules. Little could they know that their lives were looked
upon as no more than names or numbers on a roll. Colonel Philip Brown
had been largely responsible for the exchanges of the thirty-one men allowed to leave.

In the Charleston *Daily Courier* on the morning of December 7, a letter
appeared, addressed to Colonel Brown. It was merely a small notice to con-

vey appreciation for humane treatment and civilized behavior, signed by six officers who had experienced such, and the gesture harkened back to the medieval code of the laws of war.

On Board S.S. New York, December 6, 1864.

*Col. P. P. Brown, 157th New York, Commanding
Fort Pulaski*

Colonel—In a few hours we will be free. We wish to anticipate that wished for moment, and before we land to leave you the freely spoken expressions of our respect for you and the lively sense of gratitude with which we will ever remember your kindness.

During the time we have remained prisoners in your hands you have clearly demonstrated the truth of the oft forgotten principle, that duty can always be made compatible with humanity; and while enforcing strictly measures necessary for our safe keeping, you have invariably shown us the courtesy of a gallant soldier and Christian gentleman.

Lieut. Col. Carmichael and Major Place have nobly seconded you, and in fact the conduct of all your officers and men has been such as to make the name of the 157th New York a pleasant reminiscence to all Confederate prisoners from Fort Pulaski. Our long and varied experience of prison treatment makes this, our last stage of captivity, an ever to be remembered epoch.

Allow us, Colonel, to tender you and your command the assurance of our respect and esteem.

P. F. DeGournay, Lieutenant-Colonel Artillery P.A.C.S.
T. P. Branch, Major P.A.C.S.
Inspector General, Gen. Ransom's Staff.
Captain George Howard, 1st Maryland Cavalry.
Captain C. D. Fitzhugh, 1st Virginia Cavalry, Co. K.
Sgt. Major C. M. Busbee, 5th N.C. Infantry.
Lieutenant S. W. Branch, Co. B, 8th Georgia.[28]

Colonel Brown was of course at Fort Pulaski, and knew nothing of the letter, until a few days later when he received a reprimand from Major General John G. Foster's headquarters on Hilton Head Island. The scathing letter informed Brown that he had been notified of the correct treatment of the prisoners repeatedly and they were not to be exchanged or given full rations.

It is perfectly well understood by every officer in this department that these prisoners were sent here for the purpose of retaliation—to be treated in precisely the same manner that our prisoners are treated that are in the hands of the enemy—and for no other reasons whatever.

LETTER, CAPT. WILLIAM BURGER, ASST. ADJT. GEN., TO COL. PHILIP P. BROWN, 157TH N.Y. INF., COMMANDING FT. PULASKI, DEC. 15, 1864

Full instructions were sent you, on the 4th ult. for the care and management of these prisoners, and a corrected copy of your General Orders No. 11 which you were directed to issue and strictly enforce in place of the one you published. This letter alone contained sufficient instructions for your guidance in their management, and was thought to cover all the points . . .

The letter of censure was sent you, not only because you did not treat those prisoners in accordance with your instructions but because you permitted yourself to be complimented by our enemies for conduct that same enemy would scorn to bestow on our prisoners in their hands.

The Maj. Gen. commdg. directs that you immediately acknowledge the receipt of this letter, and state whether you received the letter of instructions of Nov. 4th with the corrected copy of your General Order No. 11.[29]

The General Orders No. 11 referred to consisted of a list of rules to be observed in guarding the prisoners. Among the rigid scheduled daily routine, were several orders which the surgeon Dr. Clymer suggested be dropped due to the undesired effect on health. These changes included leaving the privy accessible all night, and leaving the upper casemate windows open for ventilation. Another provision was the allowance of numbers of the men to take exercise on the parade ground daily. Under the letter of censure, however, these revisions to the rules were denied. The Confederate officers would suffer under another strict provision of General Orders No. 11—it also ordered Brown to cut the rations to one quarter pound of meat per day. Brown acknowledged receipt and promised to comply. He did however warn the prisoners that hard times were ahead.[30]

1LT. JOHN C. ALLEN, 7TH VA. CAV.

Mon., Dec. 12.- Nothing new today. We are cut off from the sutler entirely so that even those who have a little money can't use it and no person is allowed to sell us anything. They arrested one of their men for selling a pie to one of our number.[31]

CAPT. HENRY DICKINSON, 2ND VA. CAV.

December 17, 1864.- Colonel Baker and Major Goldsborough went out today and learned that, owing to wonderful tales of twenty escaped officers from Columbia, we are to be restricted to corn meal and molasses, and cut off from sutlery. This is probably stuff, but many believe it and are buying up all they can to eat.

December 19, 1864.- We had a rumor again today that rations are to be cut down and that we are not to be permitted to go to the sutlery.

December 20, 1864.- Twenty-eight pounds of meat were issued to eighty-four men today—they say for ten days. If so, we shall have hard times.[32]

It was during the last part of December, after the severely cut ration was imposed, that the disloyalty in the ranks first surfaced. Colonel John Baker of the 3rd North Carolina Cavalry had been cautiously watched since leaving Fort Delaware, and was suspected from the beginning by some prisoners as a traitor. Abram Fulkerson referred to Baker and one other as "two mysterious characters . . . some thought they were spies and others thought they would be exchanged on reaching Charleston Harbor, but they were not. They were kept with us throughout the entire retaliatory expedition . . ."[33] They were also blamed for foiling escape attempts on Morris Island, and when the *Crescent City* ran aground. Baker exposed himself to further suspicions by his actions. On November 17, Henry Dickinson wrote, "I learned that Col. Baker of North Carolina remarked today that if anyone was known by him to try to take the fort he would tell on him, and this was said in the presence of a sentinel."[34] Baker had overheard discussions by Colonels Van Manning and Abe Fulkerson in regard to overtaking the garrison.

Their suspicions were well founded. Baker had applied to take the oath of allegiance as early as June 20, 1864. He made three applications, the final on February 13, 1865, all in secret. Baker had done commendable service in 1862, being promoted to a staff officer and cited by his commander Brigadier-General Samuel G. French. Whatever caused him to seek betrayal was a strong force.

Another traitor, undetected by most, was Lieutenant John M. Guyther, also of North Carolina. On November 23, 1864, he wrote Major-General John G. Foster, "I am not a sympathizer in the rebel cause nor have I ever aided it in the smallest degree." In a lengthy and obviously well-thought-out plan, he offered his valuable knowledge to aid Union forces in the taking of Fort Branch near Hamilton, North Carolina. "I can plan its capture without the firing of a gun," he claimed, in exchange for release from prison. Apparently he felt he was under suspicion, and even his life endangered for his infidelity to principles. "There are several officers of the 1st North Carolina Regiment here who have long suspected [me] . . . and they have on several occasions threatened my life." He even requested these six officers be sent north to prison for his own safety. His proposition went unheeded by Union authorities.[35] Of the 313 officers confined at Pulaski, the strict vow not to take the oath under any circumstances remained the cohesive factor, and each loyal officer found strength in his companions' support.

December was filled with news of Sherman's approach to Savannah. Several companies of the 157th left as reinforcements to the Union army, returning with casualties taken at an engagement at the Coosahatchie Bridge, in an unsuccessful attempt by Foster to cut the railroad between Savannah and Charleston.[36] The Confederate prisoners were always on the alert for news of the fighting which they knew was close at hand since they heard the artillery daily beyond the walls of the fort. The Confederate lines were only six miles away.

CAPT. HENRY
DICKINSON,
2ND VA. CAV.

December 2, 1864.- At an early hour this morning we saw three wounded men brought into the fort and soon the fact leaked out that this regiment at least had gotten a flea in its ear at the Bridge fight. The Yanks are very reticent, yet they admit that at last accounts they were pushing their way to the Bridge, but had thirty officers and men of this regiment wounded, out of some 120 who went. Captain McWilliams (the scoundrel who made us drink hot water on the "Cresent") is wounded—some say badly, others slightly. Lieutenant Grant mortally wounded, and three other officers wounded. They say they fought all day on the thirtieth and were fighting yesterday when the wounded left. If Hallowell and his negroes were in the muss we shall be gratified. The only consolation the Yanks have is that deserters now report that Sherman is with in thirty-seven miles of Savannah. They talk in knots, refuse to let even the usual sergeants come in prison tonight, and beyond doubt have been whipped. . . . Some officers imprudently said today, in presence of the sentinels, that they hoped the Coosahatchie expedition would suffer, etc. whereupon the Yanks issued an order to shoot any prisoner who thus insults them.

December 16, 1864.- The Yanks insist that Forts McAllister and Beaulieu have been taken and this evening they say that Thunderbolt "went up" at 12 o'clock noon. They say Sherman's force left Atlanta 61,000 strong, and have lost from all causes 1,400 men, and that he dined yesterday at Hilton Head, having sent rations for 60,000 men to Nassau Sound. They assert that he has his battery within one and a half miles of the Charleston & Savannah railroad and is permitting all cars to go in but none to go out, and that the city must capitulate. We believe none of this and it leaked out today that nothing could be heard from Slocum with two corps. We are awfully impatient and all are excited and disturbed by Sherman.[37]

On December 21 Sherman occupied Savannah. The news arrived in the prison at Fort Pulaski, and was met with both disbelief and concern.

CAPT. DAVID
GRAYSON,
10TH VA. INF.

December 20 to 25, 1864.- Great events have no doubt occurred in the Confederacy during these past several days, but having been not very well I am unable to give such a detailed account of even the meager news we have, but I fear it is a painful truth that our forces have evacuated Savannah, thus making Sherman's movement a glorious victory and placing him upon a better base for aggressive operations in the future than Atlanta was. We are entirely without any definite news of the cause and consequently unprepared to censure, but if some great blunder has been made, it surely exhibits a weakness upon our part that nothing save stubborn facts could have ever made me believe and which will certainly embolden the enemy and encourage the war fever in the North.[38]

December 21, 1864.- Firing heavy again this morning and continued until the high wind prevented us from hearing much. The day was quite cold and windy, and many said it was a very long one. At sunset there were unmistakable signs that the Yanks had good news. Presently the band began to play, three cheers were given and they soon brought us news that Savannah had fallen. They say a captain is the bearer of the news, that the city fell at 5 o'clock this morning, and that the captain walked through the streets. We still can't believe this. It seems preposterous.[39]

CAPT. HENRY DICKINSON, 2ND VA. CAV.

In addition to the despondent news of Savannah's fall, the final hope for an exchange was also lost.

Captain Howard, of Baltimore has talked with Mulford, who says he has orders to exchange, but that General Foster has not yet received the orders and does not think that he is justified in making the delivery. . . . I had a long private talk with Captain Chambers, who has always been favored by the authorities, and expects a special exchange in two or three days. He told me that Mulford intended to exchange us ten days since, but Foster declined to give us up without a direct order, which he is now expecting.

CAPT. HENRY DICKINSON, 2ND VA. CAV.

This month is closing with as little prospect of exchange as ever. All the talk has died away. None of us now hope. We once were very confident that our misery would end this month; now we are preparing to spend the winter here, every mess getting little traps to render themselves comfortable. Many still have scurvy, though the vegetables we have been able to buy have improved us in that respect. Many have dysentery and some will die . . . the best of all is that we have but little to do with the Yankee. He doesn't rub against us here.[40]

The year went into decline, and winter made an early appearance. Ice was frequent on puddles, and cisterns where water was obtained, and it often glazed the damp inside walls of the casemates as well. The sea turned a cold, heartless gray with white cresting waves. Leaden skies blocked any warmth the sun had to offer. Despondency was the dreaded enemy now, as minds grappled with ways to pass the time and keep hope from fading, while bodies fought the cold with every ounce of strength left. Each day they grew as weak as their fading hopes.

November 26, 1864.- Nothing worthy of note has occurred today. If we were to judge by the present daily appearance we would at once conclude that we were banished from the world as we seldom ever hear anything, and never see anything but the walls of

CAPT. DAVID GRAYSON, 10TH VA. INF.

our prison and the limited expanse of heaven that can be viewed from within the walls of the fort.[41]

2LT. HENRY COOK, 44TH TENN. INF.

The embrasures were grated to prevent our escape, and guards were placed upon the banks of the moat in front of us. Our only view was through these grates, and our eyes met naught but the expanse of water, dotted with little barren islands. For many a day I watched the great waves chase each other in and then turn back to the vast ocean. At times a sail-boat or man-of-war would appear in the distance and relieve the monotony of the scene. How eagerly I watched to catch the sight of the topmast sail of a ship that might be approaching the island, hoping that something might happen to relieve our condition![42]

2LT. DAVID GORDON, 4TH S.C. CAV.

Nov. 25th.- This day ten years ago was the happy day of my marriage. Oh! how different this from that day. Then I could look out on the world with a bold free and happy spirit. With nothing to mar my pleasure and everything to contribute to it. But now my sphere is the narrow lunets of Fort Pulaski and can look out on the world only through an embrasure closed with iron grating. Destitute of even the ordinary comforts of life such as clothing and blankets, and deprived of the privilege of getting these from home.[43]

CAPT. DAVID GRAYSON, 10TH VA. INF.

November 22, 1864.- To-day has been exceedingly cold, the wind very high and cutting. All of us have to keep walking and jumping to keep warm. At night we almost freeze: Three of us are sleeping under but one blanket, and ice is upon the ground: one-half of the men are without any blanket.

November 23, 1864.- To-day the weather continues very cold and the men are all suffering, some of them terribly. If we are compelled to pass the winter without any additional blankets it will break down the constitutions of many men and fill early graves.[44]

CAPT. HENRY DICKINSON, 2ND VA. CAV.

December 11, 1864.- It is bitter cold, many of us have but one blanket, some have none, and we sleep but little. The portholes being only partially stopped, the cold would be as great inside as out but for the four cooking stoves, which we are trying to run with old pieces of barrels and boards.

December 12, 1864.- Ice in abundance this morning; the wind is still blowing and it would be called cold even in old Virginia. We are almost without fire and many are trotting up and down the prison to keep the blood circulating.[45]

Enduring in that chilling and desolate cold, the warmth of men's souls kept them alive. In these officers, the remnant of 600, was a compassion for each other which led to the formation of a relief agency, whereby the able-bodied could help those sick and unable to care for themselves. Meagre resources were pooled to provide clothing and food. Through this organization much suffering was alleviated.

We who were true can speak of the comradeship of love to each CAPT. J. OGDEN
other. It was born in suffering, cemented by the brutality of a MURRAY,
civilized government controlled by brutes. Men, as a rule, when 7TH VA. CAV.
suffering, become selfish; but this was not true of the majority of
the six hundred. Of course, there were some selfish men in our
number, but it can be truthfully said . . . there never was a grander
lot of men brought together than the Immortal Six Hundred. The
efforts of one prisoner to relieve the other were sublime.[46]

December 13, 1864.- This morning I suggested to some friends the CAPT. HENRY
propriety of forming an association to provide for the wants of our DICKINSON,
sick and suffering, and Major Ziegler and others encouraged me to 2ND VA. CAV.
get it up. I wrote out a constitution and by-laws, got a number of
friends together and we formed the "Confederate Relief Associa-
tion." Colonel Fulkerson is president; Captain Cantwell, secre-
tary; H. C. Dickinson, treasurer, and Major Jones, Major Ziegler,
Captain Ake . . . are the executive committee. We at once went to
work and, having looked up all the sick, provided shirts and draw-
ers for the needy. I have given all the very sick such food as they
need from my mess and tomorrow we shall meet and collect some
money and provide for their wants. Several are quite sick and
badly clad, poor fellows! Exchange only, I fear, will save some,
but we are determined to help them all we can.[47] *[see appendix]*

Exposure to the damp conditions in the casemates quickly affected the officers' health. The prison halls resounded with coughing and sneezing as most men caught colds. Some cases turned into severe pneumonia and bronchitis, impossible to cure without the improvement of quarters and rations. As the year ground to a halt at Christmas, their worst enemy began to tear at their ranks, though not in the form of enemy soldiers. Disease began to take its toll.

The most prevalent condition of which the prisoners suffered was scurvy, a disease known for centuries, and easily cured. The British navy discovered in the eighteenth century that fresh fruit and vegetables on long ship voyages would allay its effects, and it was naval regulations to issue lemon juice to sailors on extended seafaring expeditions. Scurvy is caused by a simple vitamin deficiency. Too little Vitamin A, which is easily obtainable in fresh fruit and vegetables, causes a breakdown in the collagen of the body's tissues.

Easily prevented, once scurvy takes hold of a man it renders severe debilitation. The prisoners began to see signs of it in their health, and reported it to the surgeon. However, the surgeon was not allowed to treat the men. Antiscorbutics were available, but treatment was denied as part of the retaliation on the men for the lack of medicine available in Confederate prisons. He could only treat the symptoms, not the disease. Therefore he merely prescribed pain killers, mostly in the form of opium, issued indiscriminately. Several of the officers became addicted to the drug. Sympathetic comrades would report sick in order to get opium, which they gave to the addicts rather than watch them suffer withdrawal.

A secondary condition of their diet was diarrhea and dysentery. Malnutrition led to this malady, which caused dehydration and eventually, if not arrested, death.

Winter tightened its grip on the island. The evenings were long and dark, brightened only by the feeble glow of candlelight in the casemates, flickering in the drafty air. The wind moaned around the corners of the battle-scarred fort, making forlorn sounds and emphasizing the frigid and desolate atmosphere. Even though crowded, the solitude of each man was a burden he carried emotionally. On December 22 the coldest day yet experienced greeted the men. Not only was it physically unendurable, but the despairing psychological state of most officers was recorded poignantly in journals and diaries. They faithfully wrote letters home, unaware that most would not be allowed to go through the lines, as part of retaliation. They committed themselves to sweethearts, and the love for wives and children strengthened the determination to live. Probably in some cases, it was what kept them alive.

Deprived of the affection of loved ones, their loneliness was painfully evident, and Christmas Day was anything but a day of rejoicing.

CAPT. J. OGDEN MURRAY, 7TH VA. CAV.
On Christmas day, 1864, the snow on the fort parade ground was four inches deep, and we prisoners of war had neither fire, blankets, nor clothing to shield us from the rigors of the winter weather. Really, it seemed like the elements had joined hands with Stanton and Foster to destroy us. There can be no claim set up by the Federal authorities and General Foster, commanding Department of the South, that the ration given us was the best that could be done for us. If such a claim is made, it is false, for I do know that the storehouse of the fort contained commissary stores going to waste, while we human beings were being starved to death.[48]

CAPT. HENRY DICKINSON, 2ND VA. CAV.
December 24, 1864.- One year ago today I was pushing through the gap at Peaks of Otter, with my home in sight. Then all was health and I anticipated the enjoyment of the Christmas. Now I am almost in rags, in a cold, damp prison, in constant pain with rheumatism. A constitution shattered by exposure, and this Christmas and how many more I know not to be spent under the hated flag, but, whatever we call a blessing, freedom is the pledge of all.

I trust we may be able to evince the justice of our cause by the many privations we are willing to endure.

Christmas Day, 1864.- And a gloomy one it is. Cold, raining and severe. But little money in prison. One-fourth pound of beef, and seven crackers for rations. Added to this the United States mail came this morning and brought the late usual amount of bad news.

At Nashville General Hood has lost 5,000 prisoners on the field, 1,500 sick and wounded, 1,500 stragglers and forty-nine pieces of artillery; his army is scattered and demolished. So says General Thomas' official report. Many are down in the cellar of despondency today. I feel that I shall spend the next Christmas in Dixie. I picked a few vermin this morning, and put on clean clothes. For the first time since I was seven years old I put on woolen drawers to drive away the rheumatism, which, by the way, has almost got the better of me. It dodges about from place to place and I hope may some day dodge away.[49]

December 25, 1864.- To-day is Christmas, a day which is generally hailed with delight; but oh how different it is this year with me; instead of being at home with all the family meeting at the dear old homestead to eat a Christmas dinner, as is a regular custom, and has been in our family ever since I can remember, here I am in prison at Fort Pulaski; and sick in bed with a fair prospect of having a spell of typhoid pneumonia. Oh, how gloomy is the comparison to every other Christmas I have seen during my life. . . . The old year winds up leaving me in trying circumstances, sick, and with but one thin blanket to protect me from the rude blasts of winter and no comforting hand to soothe my pillow, but with a hard board, one blanket, and such a pillow as my change of clothing can make constitute my bed. Oh, how gloomy are my reveries of the happy past, when contemplated under such a cheerless present and such an indefinite future,. Oh, how miserable should I feel were it not for the pleasure afforded me through memory of the loving hearts that are beating at home for me.[50]

CAPT. DAVID
GRAYSON,
10TH VA. INF.

The men were at a low point. The retaliation treatment claimed more lives. Yet their trials were far from over, and conditions would become more severe. The warning of a further reduction in rations caused anxiety. They were already hungry. Some men had lost as much as sixty pounds, and wondered what would keep them from starving to death under less fare.

The retaliation rations Foster ordered were to commence December 26. Colonel Brown received a communication that he was to put into immediate effect 10 ounces of cornmeal a day and unlimited pickles.[51] The pickles were supposed to prevent scurvy, but this is not the best foodstuff to provide. The acidic quality only added to the many health problems.

Corn meal alone has no nutritional value. The men were not even allowed grease for the pans, and were only given water to mix the meal into a mush which was baked in pie pans issued for the purpose. It was brittle and hardly palatable. Sutler privileges and any aid from home was suspended, and the New Year of 1865 began a survival test imposed by Union policy.

Col. Abram Fulkerson, 63rd Tenn. Inf.

Some escaped prisoners from the Confederate prison at Andersonville came through the lines into General Foster's Department, and reported to him that, for more than a month before they escaped, the prisoners at Andersonville had nothing issued to them but corn meal and sorghum, which had caused much suffering and sickness among the prisoners. The unfortunate 600, having been selected and sent to General Foster for retaliatory purposes, an order was issued to place them upon like rations, and the privilege of receiving money, clothing, or provisions from Northern sympathizers be withdrawn. . . . The allowance of corn meal was ten ounces to the man per day, and as sorghum could not be obtained within the Federal lines, it was suggested, in some quarters, that army pickle be substituted. This suggestion was adopted, so that our rations consisted of ten ounces of corn meal, with acid, blood-thinning pickle. The effect of the pickle was to thin the blood, and its use was quickly abandoned by the prisoners; still it was issued to us, day by day, in kegs, which were not opened.[52]

Capt. Henry Dickinson, 2nd Va. Cav.

December 31, 1864.- A raw, cold, drizzling day, and one of damp gloom to all. The threatened ration is at last issued! Ten barrels of corn meal—funky, wormy and sour, and two and one-half kegs of mean pickles, with a little, very little, salt, are ten days' rations for 313 men. No meat, no vegetables—nothing but sour meal and pickles. And this food for men fully one-half of whom have diseased bowels! Well may we be gloomy, for a few weeks at most will terribly thin our ranks. All, however, evince a determination to bear it as long as they can.[53]

Capt. W. W. George, 26th Va. Inf. Battn.

The meal was kiln-dried and had been put up in 1861; so it was four years old. It had turned very dark and was not suitable food for animals—certainly not for human beings.

When taken out of the barrels it was a cemented mass, and would come out in chunks and blocks as large as half a bushel.

Before using it, we would have to rub it in our hands, and sift it through tin cans perforated with a nail. This was to separate the bugs from the meal, when we felt that we could spare the bugs and have enough meal left. One can imagine what our condition was with no food but this for forty-four days.[54]

Brown was ordered to issue to us ten ounces of corn meal and one-half pint of onion pickle each twenty-four hours, as a ration, without salt, meat, grease, or vegetables. Ten ounces of corn meal, one-half pint of pickle—nothing more. No fuel but twelve sticks of pine cord wood for each division of twenty-eight men. The order, he said, was peremptory, leaving him no discretion whatever, and he was powerless in the matter. It must be said of Colonel Brown and his officers that they were gentlemen, and when he made the promise to treat us humanely and kindly he intended to keep his promise to the letter. The officers and men of the 157th New York never failed to show their disgust for General Foster and his brutal corn meal order.... If the corn meal had been good we might have managed to live upon it . . . but the meal was rotten—filled with black weevil bugs and worms. The barrels were branded, "Corn meal, kiln dried from Brandywine Mills, 1861," showing by the brand and date on the barrels that it was four years old; condemned by the quartermaster as unfit food for nigger troops but excellent diet for helpless Confederate prisoners of war.[55]

CAPT. J. OGDEN
MURRAY,
7TH VA. CAV.

Col. Brown was much moved, and his voice was tremulous when he informed us of the new orders, but he attempted to cheer us up, stating that he hoped the cruel treatment would be of short duration. Winter had now fairly set in, and its chilly blasts off the Atlantic wailed mournfully through our open casemate windows, causing the poorly clad prisoners to shiver. It was a damp, nipping, and eager cold, such as no one who experienced it could soon forget.[56]

2LT. HENRY
COOK,
44TH TENN.
INF.

January 2, 1865.- Our new ration of corn meal (sour), pickles and seventy-five loaves of bread went into effect yesterday, and a terrible diet it is. That it will kill some is evident. They have plenty of boxes and money letters in the fort for us, but won't issue them. It is said that this cruel order is Foster's only. I should hope that the representative man of no nation would issue such an order. Our sick at the hospital are fed on bread and water only. I took up a subscription for the sick yesterday and received about ten dollars, though all of us are very poor.[57]

CAPT. HENRY
DICKINSON,
2ND VA. CAV.

Their hearts sank at the thought of life ahead. All knew the one way out was to take the oath of allegiance. Among the Six Hundred existed an unspoken stubbornness to suffer rather than surrender principles and duty. Determination to stick it out bound all together, and the first trial of their vow occurred on December 29.

A steamer docked at the Fort Pulaski wharf, and disembarked its important visitors, one of whom was the Honorable William M. Stone, newly elected governor of Iowa. He was accompanied by a correspondent of the *Dubuque Daily Times*. Stone and his entourage had taken time from his eastern journey to review Iowa troops at Hilton Head, and pay a visit to Lieutenant Junius L. Hempstead, prisoner of war. The visit was a special request from a fellow Iowan, concerned about the former governor's son. The journalist reported his mission to readers in Dubuque as follows:

> *After eight days' visiting among the Iowa troops in Gen. Sherman's grand army, I left Savannah, this morning at 4 o'clock. . . . The immense Fort which Gilmore so splendidly reduced is in full view, being not more than a mile distant, I should guess. On going up quite a party of us staid over night at the Fort. Governor Stone was along, and having been so requested asked to see Lieut. Hempstead of the Rebel Army, now a prisoner of war. . . . He is as many of your readers know a son of Ex-Governor Hempstead of your city, where he received "a bringing up" which must have been somehow vicious, or he would not be in his present predicament. He was comfortably clothed and in good health. He talked an hour or so with the governor and other gentlemen who had been in the Army, and was very communicative about Rebel affairs. He has refused I believe to take the oath of allegiance to the United States. He is quite young . . . but seems to have good sense enough. The Company blamed rather his education, than himself for the fact of his having taken up arms against his county, therefore ruining himself in the estimation of all right thinking men.*[58]

CAPT. HENRY DICKINSON, 2ND VA. CAV.
> *Still very cold, men coughing terribly. Yanks signalling from the fort. Governor Stone of Iowa arrives. Sent for Lieutenant Hempstead, Twenty-fifth Virginia, son of ex-governor of Iowa, and begged him to take the oath. Brown added his persuasions and told him we were to be fed on corn meal and pickles. Hempstead nobly refused.*[59]

Upon his return to the casemate prison, Junius Hempstead received a rousing applause.

CHAPTER TEN

"In Perils By Mine Own Countrymen;
In Perils Among False Brethren."
II Corinthians 11:26

THE year 1865 saw the beginning of the end for the Confederacy. Militarily the South was enclosed from all sides. Charleston still stubbornly held out against Union forces on Hilton Head, Morris Island, and gunboats in the harbor. The threat now was from the rear.

Sherman's forces left Savannah and marched into South Carolina in January with a vengeance. They vowed to make the Palmetto State pay for her role in starting the war. Instead of attacking Charleston, Sherman turned toward the capital at Columbia, and burned it and everything in his path. The Confederate prisons at Florence and Columbia were captured, and the Union prisoners of war freed. By December 1864, all had been exchanged at Charleston Harbor. Brigadier General George P. Harrison was the Confederate commander of the prison in Florence, where 25,000 enlisted men were held. In recognition of his kindness to these prisoners, a special order from the Federal commander gave protection to Harrison's home, in Savannah, Georgia.[1] No Union prisoners of war remained in South Carolina.

Among the Union regiments stationed at Hilton Head Island, in conjunction with Fort Walker and Port Royal, was the 144th New York State Volunteer Infantry, known by the other Union regiments there as "Foster's Pets." This referred to the easy guard duty these men always seemed to pull, far away from the front. For many of these soldiers, the battlefield was a place they had never experienced first-hand. Their orders were mainly to guard Confederate prisoners, stand sentry duty, and build fortifications. One of the privates in this regiment who was directly in charge of the Confederate officers sent here from Pulaski was Daniel B. White, a young recruit who took the bounty and joined in his home county of Delaware, New York. He wrote home to his wife regularly, informing her of his daily routine on guard duty.

PVT. DANIEL
WHITE,
144TH N.Y.
INF.

Saturday, November 19, 1864.- There was a detail out of the regiment of 64 men to go somewhere after Reb prisoners. They went this morning. They say that they are going to put them in the fort for us to guard. If so, it will take a lot of new guards to take care of them.

Sunday, Nov. 20, 1864.- I spoke to you about some reb prisoners coming here. They have come. I believe there is 180 of them, all officers, Captains & Lieutenants, some Lt. Colonels. I spoke to you about them going in the Fort. That is not the case. They are stationed about 20 rods from our camp. There has been a lot of our boys detailed this afternoon to put up tents for them. The tents are set on the ground. It is a hard place to sleep with the ground wet under them and nothing to sleep on. Some have blankets & some have none. They are clothed in all shapes, generally looking pretty rough. It seems hard for them, but they are better provided for than our prisoners would be if in their hands, and at the same time we may see times that we would be glad to have their quarters and be in the 144th at the same time.[2]

One hundred and ninety-seven of the original Six Hundred taken from Fort Pulaski would spend the winter on Hilton Head. Their conditions were different from their brother officers, though still as harsh. In one respect, they fared worse than the Fort Pulaski prisoners—their guard was not as sympathetic. Even Private White only makes cold and unfeeling references to them in his letters home. Upon arriving at Hilton Head in November, the men were quartered in tents on the beach, despite the bitter winter weather and whipping winds. The exposure soon took a toll in sickness and suffering.

2LT. SAMUEL H.
HAWES, ORANGE
ARTY. (VA.)

20 Nov. 1864.- Landed at Hilton Head S.C. and marched to our quarters about one mile from the wharf. We are quartered in A tents, three men to each tent, and are having anything but a pleasant situation, a heavy rain storm having come on before our tents were pitched, thoroughly saturating the ground with water. But few of our number have more than one blanket (some none at all). Therefore I should not say that our sleeping arrangements were of the best sort, and don't suppose that many of our friends would envy us them.[3]

PVT. DANIEL
WHITE,
144TH N.Y.
INF.

Sunday, Nov. 20, 1865.- I think there will be some johnnies that will feel the effects of cold lead if they stay here long. There is lines drawn, and the Rebs have their ground. After they step over that line, our boys are ordered to shoot them.[4]

2LT. JOSEPH
MAUCK,
10TH VA. INF.

Sunday 20th Nov. 1864.- Was landed in the evening. Marched 2 miles where we found quarters in our same old Morris Island tents, was divided into 4 divisions and 3 men to the tent. I was allotted to

the 1st division, Col. Manning for chief. Lieuts. Bell and Long my
tentmates. Rained all night. I slept comfortable.[5]

22nd Nov. 64.- Another night of suffering gone by—the rain storm
abated last evening, and a strong northwest wind sprung up,
making the weather intensely cold. Our sufferings were great. My
hand is so numb that it is with great difficulty that I write.[6]

2LT. SAMUEL H.
HAWES, ORANGE
ARTY. (VA.)

November 22d.- Our mess is P. H. Benson, William H. Allen and
myself (A. M. Bedford). All well. Clear and very cold. Slept cold last
night. Many of our officers nearly froze as they had no blankets. I
loaned one of mine to Capt. Hodges of North Carolina. We have
four roll calls per day. Eight o'clock roll call. Rations, one pint of
good coffee, nine crackers. Two o'clock. Over a pint of good bean
soup, about one and one-half ounces pickled pork. Last night we
got a pint of coffee. One ounce pickled beef, one pint coffee to-
night, and twelve crackers issued for the coming day.[7]

CAPT. ALEX
BEDFORD,
3RD MO. CAV.

Wednesday, Nov. 23, 1864.- It is rather rough writing here this
morning. The ink is froze so I can hardly get enough thawed to
write with. We have had two cold nights. After it stopped raining it
turned cold. Last night it froze so hard that an eight quart pan of
water was froze in a solid cake, and all the wash dishes in camp
that had water in them was froze solid. If there had of been snow
on the ground it would have come up to old Delaware County
nights. You will have to try hard to read this, for it is so cold that
I have to get up and slap my hands to keep warm, and it is about
eleven o'clock in the forenoon, & the sun shines out clear, but the
wind is so cold that the sun does not have an impression.[8]

PVT. DANIEL
WHITE,
144TH N.Y.
INF.

23rd Nov.- I thought that our trials of night before last were se-
vere, but they do not compare in severity with those of last night—
ice formed on the water in our tent. This bringing us to this place
was said to be a sanitary move, but it looks like anything else. now
I have undergone severe exposure in the field, but no hardship
there ever tried me as severely as this. We have passed through (it
seems to me) most of troubles which Pandora's box produced since
being in prison, hunger, thirst, heat, cold, sickness, etc. but we still
hold out—being buoyed up by that great blessing—Hope. This en-
ables a man to stand trouble and trial which would otherwise crush
him out of existence.[9]

2LT. SAMUEL H.
HAWES, ORANGE
ARTY. (VA.)

November 23d.- Slept with my blankets on last night and like to
froze. Rations very short here. Ice one-half inch thick this morn-
ing . . . We got a pint of coffee this morning, the best we will
have issued to us. We will have to buy all we get. I understand

CAPT. ALEX
BEDFORD,
3RD MO. CAV.

we will not be allowed to receive any box or money coming from our friends now.

November 24th.- Clear and cold. Slept with clothing on last night and got very cold. Ice three-fourths inch thick.[10]

After a few days in the tents, it became apparent to the Union authorities that the men could not continue to live in the cold. Arrangements were made to move them inside a stockade, whose two-story, windowless barracks were previously used as cells for convicts. Here, they lived in crowded and austere conditions.

CAPT. JOHN J.
DUNKLE,
25TH VA. INF.

This enclosure contained the barracks of the officers and privates, the cookhouses, hospital, guard house and general headquarters. It contained several acres and was square. . . . On the north and east sides there extended from one end to the other a high plank wall, hiding from the view the outside scenes, and rendering the inside inaccessible to outside intruders. There was but one entrance to this feudal castle, which was a large gate on the east, rigidly guarded. Near the centre was the guard house, a commodious and comfortable structure for the convenience of the guard, both black and white. . . . Near the angle formed by the union of the north and west sides we were situated. We were situated in two buildings, surrounded on three sides by sentinels, and on the fourth by the wall of plank on the north side of the enclosure. . . . We were placed in two similar buildings, one hundred in each. These buildings were built of plank placed one against another, and of course affording light and plenty of fresh air through the openings between the planks. . . . They would have been cool and pleasant in summer, but in winter admitted all the terrors of the cold and freezing atmosphere.

They were probably seventy or eight feet long, and were wide enough to admit an aisle of several feet in the centre, with bunks on each side. The bunks were enclosed on every side by upright planks, thus being formed in small squares with bunks one above another. Each door was so fixed as to be locked if necessary. The entrance to the aisles was closed by two large gates kept securely locked every night.[11]

2LT. SAMUEL H.
HAWES, ORANGE
ARTY. (VA.)

26th Nov./64.- We were today removed from the tents, and placed in quarters on the beach, in the suburbs of Port Royal; these quarters look more like a jail than any prison that I have yet been in, being divided off into small rooms, each to accommodate four men; to each room is a door, with lock upon it. Our fare is very much like that at Morris Island, about enough to keep body and soul together.[12]

November 26th.- Excitement about moving into quarters in town. About eleven, we moved down, halted inside of barracks. Roll call and kept us there until half after four p.m., then put in quarters, room like staterooms on a steamboat six and one-half by six and two bunks, four men in a room. No rations to-day. Always save a day's rations by moving us. Our building is two stories high. The hospital is above us. Our door is made of thick slats about two inches apart with a padlock hanging to it.[13]

CAPT. ALEX
BEDFORD,
3RD MO. CAV.

Saturday 26th Nov. 1864.- Orders to get ready to move. All ready and we marched to Capt. Prat's yard where we found quarters in a building representing a livery stable more than a prison. 4 men allotted to a cell 6 feet square. Lieuts. Bell, Long and Donaghe are my room mates.[14]

2LT. JOSEPH
MAUCK,
10TH VA. INF.

I am living with the Rebs now. Thair is 198 of them hear, and they make me liv with them all the time. I hav charge of one batalion of them. They are all ofisers, from Colonel down to 2 Lt. I hav to call the roal four times a day, and the rest of the time I hav to my self.[15]

PVT. DANIEL
WHITE,
144TH N.Y.
INF.

For a short time the rations were less than desirable, but tolerable. Soon, however, they were ordered to conform to what Union prisoners were being fed and were cut just as the rations at Fort Pulaski, under the same General Orders No. 11.

Hilton Head was the location of Major General John G. Foster's Headquarters, and the prisoners attributed the harsh treatment to being located where the orders originated from. The 144th New York Infantry Regiment was detailed as the guard in charge, under the commandant of the prison, Major Benjamin Thompson who took command in December, relieving Captain Joseph T. Pratt who was with the 144th New York, as provost marshal.[16] The men found Thompson harsh and rigid.

... General Foster, then commanding the Department of the South, took his rebel prisoners down to Hilton Head, put them in prison there, and sent word to the rebel authorities that he would feed them just such food as was given to our officers at Salisbury, North Carolina. This was the first and only retaliation that I know of in our service. It continued for a long time and afterward I had some connection with it. . . . I was very soon assigned to duty as Provost Marshall of the Post, then of the District. All the prisoners were under my care, including the rebel officers who were being retaliated upon . . .[17]

MAJ. BENJAMIN
W. THOMPSON,
32ND U.S.
COLORED
TROOPS

Among the officers designated for Hilton Head was Lieutenant George Finley, who had steadied their faith with daily religious services on Morris Island and at Fort Pulaski. He was approached by Colonel Van Manning, and requested to continue the services. Manning was aware that the men could become demoralized, and lose civilized behavior under severe conditions. Therefore he sought to maintain as normal a routine as possible, and regular Sunday worship constituted a basic part of that.

At Hilton Head were also the "Houdinis" of the Six Hundred, those few who enjoyed escape attempts. Led by Tom Perkins, several immediately tried to dig out of the tent city. They were relocated to the barracks before the tunnel was complete. However, undeterred, they worked day and night, and finally succeeded in getting out, on the very first night that Daniel White walked his post.

PVT. DANIEL WHITE, 144TH N.Y. INF.	*Tuesday, Nov. 29, 1864.- We had bad luck last night. There was 4 of the Reb prisoners escaped from us, & they have not been captured yet. It is now about 3 o'clock in the afternoon. I was on guard last night and shall be tonight again. . . . Those that escaped cut a hole in the floor of their cell and went down through. I have heard since I commenced writing that they have captured them again, but I do not know for certain yet.[18]*

2LT. PETE B. AKERS, 11TH VA. INF.	*Capt. Tom Perkins was one of the most daring brave men I ever knew. He would take the most desperate chance to get away of any man in the prison. He was the most determined of men, yet to his comrades he was as gentle as a woman. He was a man positively without fear, and the men associated with him in his plans to escape were just as brave as himself. After a few days in the log barracks, Perkins and a party set about planning to escape. With nothing but pen knives for tools these men succeeded in cutting through two of the thick logs that formed the floor of their cell. On November 29, just after the clock at the provost-marshal's office struck ten, Colonel Folk, of North Carolina; Capt. Tom Perkins, and Lieutenant Kilmartin left their cell and safely passed the guard line of the prison. At midnight Captain Campbell, Lieutenant Cason, and Lieutenant Brinkley followed.[19]*

Clamoring over the high plank fence, their confidence soared that they had passed the worst of the obstacles, when, suddenly, they were confronted with a second high plank fence, surmounted by a parapet with a guard walking his beat. Somehow they managed to elude him and get over the second fence. Finding themselves in a field, they stumbled upon a sentry and in trying to outflank him, on their hands and knees, lost their direction in a large swamp. After floundering around in the dark, they finally came out on the road to Mitchellville. Their clothes were covered in mud, and apparently the inhabitants of that settlement did not know whether they were Union or Confederate, and cared little. As daylight approached, they hid in the woods, lying low until night.

They started out in the dark to hunt the right road south. They had gone from their hiding place but a mile or two when they came onto a negro cabin. Being almost famished for water, they concluded to stop and ask for water. One of the party started for the cabin, but before he reached the door a negro woman came out with a bucket in her hand, leaving the door open behind her. In the light they saw a negro cavalry sergeant in the room. They at once retreated back into the road. They had not gone a mile from this cabin when they found they were on the outskirts of a village, which proved to be Mitchellville. Again they retreated a mile or so back. Now hunger and thirst began to tell upon them, and they were compelled to stop for a rest. They were completely broken down. They hid in some bushes and fell asleep from exhaustion.

When they awoke they were chilled, numbed, and in great pain, which made it difficult for them to walk. They, however, again took up the line of march, as they thought, to the south. They staggered on for some time.... Now a new trouble presented itself to them. Their wet clothing became heavy and uncomfortable. Hunger and thirst was wearing them out, and they dare not go out from their hiding, in daylight, to seek food. In looking into the haversack they found about a spoonful of wet corn meal for each man, and this was divided amongst them. When night came the boys again began their march. Captain Campbell, who was a scout of note, took up a position on the road, that he might ascertain by the travel in which direction the town lay. They had all gotten together and were about to start, when two cavalrymen galloped into sight.... After these horsemen passed the boys fell in behind them, trusting to fate to discover to them the outer picket post towards Charleston. After a long tramp they discovered they were going in the wrong direction, and were compelled to seek shelter in a swamp to keep from being picked up by a company of infantry coming towards them.

It was concluded best to await the coming of some lone person on the road, and go boldly out to him and ask for information. They were too weak to walk far, so they just laid down in the swamp grass and soon fell asleep, and did not awake until late the next day, when they found their limbs so swollen and numb they could hardly walk, and then only with great pain. Yet they had no idea of going back to prison. From their place of hiding in the swamp they saw a clump of timber. This they safely reached and in its shelter remained the day and night. Next morning after they had reached the timber, Lieutenant Hugh Brinkly was discovered by some negro wood choppers, who informed the white soldiers of

2Lt. Pete B. Akers, 11th Va. Inf.

the presence of a white man in the woods, dodging about amongst the trees.

While our boys were in custody of the 144th New York Volunteers, who had captured them and treated them kindly, a Confederate deserter came up to ask about the capture. He was dressed in citizen's clothes. After looking at our boys for some moments this scoundrel pulled a pistol out of his belt and, pointing it at Captain Campbell's head, deliberately pulled the trigger, and would have killed Campbell but for the timely aid of one of the 144th New York, who knocked the pistol out of the fellow's hand. This fellow was acting as spy for the Western Yankee army, and had recognized Captain Campbell as one of the Wheeler scouts.[20]

At Hilton Head it became apparent that many deserters were ready to betray any of the Six Hundred. The prison there, unlike Pulaski, was full of prisoners from other categories, including Union deserters, thieves, and convicts, who had no loyalty to the Confederate officers placed among them. Fort Walker was garrisoned by several regiments, being the U.S. Headquarters of the Department of the South, and, consequently, many types of visitors and civilians frequented the site.

There were women "schoolmarms" from the local area, who had come down from the North with good intentions to educate the displaced blacks, and hovered around the Union soldiers stationed at the fort. These Boston abolitionists and "philanthropists" were affiliated with what became known as the "Port Royal Experiment," later to be the model for Freedman's Bureaus. Many of the Confederate officers were disgusted by the miscegenation of the teachers with their black charges, and the black soldiers. At Port Royal were also recently freed refugees from plantations on the island, who were dependent upon the garrison.[21]

To all these gawkers, the prisoners were a source of curiosity, and sustained much abuse and humiliation while out in the prison yard for those hours allowed to cook rations and exercise. The additional embarrassment of being on exhibit for degradation added to their already miserable existence.[22]

Private White was more cautious after his venture with Tom Perkins, who continued to give White fits of paranoia concerning another escape. White exhibited the poor self esteem and nervousness common to green troops, good reason for the officers to be cautious of him, as they knew first hand how inexperienced soldiers made trigger-happy guards.

2Lt. Samuel H. Hawes, Orange Arty. (Va.)	*30th Nov. 1864.- Those having us in charge seem to be trying to make our position as uncomfortable as possible. Night before last six of our number effected their escape—This has exasperated the "Yanks" very much, who are trying to use us as severely as possible as a retaliatory measure.*[23]

Thursday, Nov. 24, 1864.- I have just been informed that I shall have to guard prisoners tonight, and if any of them walk over the dead line in front of me, there will be one less to fight some other day.[24]

PVT. DANIEL
WHITE, 144TH
N.Y. INF.

Their barracks were under the constant surveillance of a sentry who walked the center aisle, and often used his position of authority to extremes, not allowing talking, or any remarks of a personal opinion. When expressing any anti-Union sentiment, the officers were often threatened at gunpoint.

December 31st.- We have the privilege of all being out during the day, which is a great privilege, more than we have had for some-time. We are closed up half hour by sun, and opened about the same time next morning. Our officers were talking the other night, when the negro guard ordered them to hush them damned lies or he would do some shooting. They spoke a few words like they did not hear. He brought down his gun and told them to dry-up, which they did.

CAPT. ALEX
BEDFORD,
3RD MO. CAV.

January 5th.- Nigs on guard and very saucy, need killing. We have to give the road to them, they threaten to bayonet us. They prom-enade the room all night. We don't crowd them, but would kill the saucy ones, if we had a half chance. Some I pity, as they are so dissipated. One told us that Sherman's army ran him down and shot at him, and forced him into service. They [Sherman's men] said that Wheeler's cavalry was killing all that returned, or he would have gone home. He wished he was at home then.[25]

After the escape attempt, the men were marched back to prison where they were put in close confinement for a few days. Soon they rejoined their comrades in the barracks. Shortly boredom overtook the Hilton Head pris-oners just as it did their comrades at Fort Pulaski. The weather was the same too—cold and wind and ice. The retaliation rations of corn meal and pickles, issued once every ten days, were imposed sooner here than at Pulaski, and no officer was as kind as Colonel Brown in trying to warn the men. Hunger began to gnaw at them, and pain from scurvy nagged at their joints daily. On December 15, just as thirty-one men left Fort Pulaski for exchange, twenty-seven left Hilton Head.

Desperation set in, as men tried to bribe guards to buy supplies, after that privilege was revoked.

The meal, as shown on the marks of the barrel, was kiln dried in New York in 1861, and issued to us in the winter of 64 and 65. It was mouldy, much of it rotten and swarmed with vermin, so that most of it would crawl away if not confined. The flour was little if any better. The pickles only sharpened the appetites the remain-ing rations could not satisfy, and the main use of the pickle issue

CAPT. GEORGE
FINLEY,
56TH VA. INF.

was to eat out the staves of the casks the scant supply of wood
furnished us . . . this was an unusually cold winter . . . when water
would freeze in our bunks.[26]

2LT. JOSEPH
MAUCK,
10TH VA. INF.

*Thursday, 15th Dec. 1864.- Meat rations stopped and no wood to
boil our soup. Consequently we are reduced to bread and water. I
sent my last and highly prized ring out by a Yank to sell for me, in
order to get something to eat. It was one I had fully determined to
reserve for my Wife, though [hunger] will cause man to do many
things. He sold it for 3 dollars, but I did not receive but fifty cents
of the money.*[27]

2LT. WILLIAM
EPPS,
4TH S.C. CAV.

*Dec. 20.- Corn meal and pickles instead of molasses. . . . The Yanks
say they are retaliating on us for some of their officers who were
treated badly at Columbia, South Carolina. Some of them who
made their escape from Columbia arrived here a few days ago.
Some of them said they were very roughly treated while others of
the same party said they were treated well.*[28]

2LT. PETE
AKERS,
11TH VA. INF.

*It is not retaliation that this is done, for it is nothing but brutality!
If the Federal prisoners in Confederate hands were treated in this
same manner, there is not an officer in the detachment who would
be cowardly enough to murmur. Let facts as they stand be truly
stated. Since these officers have been undergoing this treatment,
a large number of Federal escaped officers have visited them. In
every case they have been questioned in regard to their treatment
and no man paints as dark a picture as here drawn. They all say
they received meal, meat, syrup and peas. Give the Confederate
captives these, and they would at once consider themselves fortunate men.*

*It was a brutal mind that conceived the corn meal and pickle diet.
It was the brutal hand of Foster that executed it upon helpless
prisoners of war. On this diet of corn meal, with no meat or vegetables, scurvy soon came to add to our suffering, and acute dysentery was prevalent among our men. It took stout hearts to bear
the burden put upon us. Many of our number physically gave way
under the cruelty, but in spite of it all our men bore it with dignity
and courage.*[29]

CAPT. JOHN J.
DUNKLE,
25TH VA. INF.

*Here our treatment . . . far exceeded in cruelty any we had hith-
erto experienced. Indeed we had imagined that the cup of human
sufferings could not be fuller, and that the soul was susceptible of
no greater miseries than those which we had previously felt.*

*The cornmeal had been ground for two years, as appeared from
the brand on the barrels, and in this time had become quite stale,*

so much so that it was both sour and bitter, and to such a great degree did it possess these qualities, that to a stomach not wholly given up to hunger and starvation, it would not have been in any ways edible . . . The meal was given raw and unbaked, and no utensils or cooking vessels of any kind were given us in which we might prepare our food.[30]

December 10th.- Very cold this morning. How do men do without blankets? I nearly froze with two over me and one under and a gum cloth. We have no fire, only a little in the yard for cooking purposes. Only twenty allowed out at the time from each division. . . . They give us no blankets nor fire. Our prison is getting worse. Very cold for this climate.

CAPT. ALEX BEDFORD, 3RD MO. CAV.

December 12th.- Very cold weather. We suffered severe to-day. All slept cold. Col. Manning talked to the provost-marshal about our treatment but did not affect anything. Hardly any meat issued to us. We shivered all day, could not exercise as we were under a hospital with our sick and wounded and can't go out doors only twenty at a time and have to do our own cooking out there. I can't do the subject justice.

December 21st.- We had corn meal issued to-day. They say we will get ten ounces corn meal and four ounces bread per day and some pickle in the place of meat or molasses. Can man live on corn meal and pickle? No way to bake it, nothing to cook in, and no wood to burn. We are without fire in an open barn of a house eighty feet long and twenty-five feet wide for one hundred and eight men. Who can love a Yankee, after such treatment? We got one-tenth pint grits, that is a pint to ten men. Who can live on that? We are for retaliation and they are using us.[31]

Despair set in, and it was only through letters and other diversions that the men could escape the miserable conditions and surroundings. For those as lucky as First Lieutenant James Cobb, who corresponded almost daily with a lady friend in Baltimore, letters from friends and loved ones helped them endure. Lieutenant Cobb and Cora Williams had agreed to set aside one hour on Sunday evenings and write to each other, a ritual accompanied by each other's photograph and the knowledge that at that very moment their thoughts were the same. The emotions kept in restraint by captivity were freely poured forth.

You indulge a little sarcasm in your letter of Nov. 29th and I am not sure but a little scolding on my part would be a just return. But I can't scold now—it is Sunday evening, the hour we have agreed should be devoted to pleasant, hopeful thoughts—& I know yours must be such at this moment—the

LETTER, 1LT. JAMES E. COBB, 5TH TX. INF., TO MISS CORA WILLIAMS, 11 DECEMBER 1864 *picture tells me so. It is gratifying, I assure you, to know there is a time, regularly recurring, when your thoughts are with me. I seem to realize the communion & feel the influence of your presence. You desire me to suggest how such hours shall be employed when I am no longer where a letter will reach me. They must be mine still, & I wish your thoughts & feelings to be preserved. You can do this by means of a journal in which entrances are fully & freely made, and hereafter when the happier times shall have come, you can give it to me to be treasured up with what is, in my esteem, the most valuable of possessions—your letters. Promise me to do this, will you? I would be ever more pleased if you would commence at once & enter a thought—now and then, as you may feel inclined. The regret you speak of, that so much of the best part of our lives is passing under such sad circumstances, I can but feel very keenly, strive as I may against the weakness of useless repining. But the most trying situation to me—my imprisonment—has had its bless-ings, & I often feel "it is all for the best." I sincerely hope it may prove so in the ultimate result. But fears will come, fears that I know not how to define, and which will not always be "done at my bidding." You could exercise them effectually, but situated as I am, & it is likely I shall be for an indefinite period yet to come, I have not courage to ask at your hand the exercise of such power. If I only was sure you understand my meaning—that you know me thoroughly, I would try to be content & for the rest "in patience to abide." I was going to say something of that faith you have in your friend—I can only say that my interest in that faith—I wish you to preserve under all circumstances. Trying ones may be at hand—separation without tidings save at large intervals.*[32]

Change for the better did not come, and Christmas found the men at the depths of depression. The long winter nights were often spent lying awake, or in conversation about their circumstances, searching for some cause to hope. The cold forced many to walk the length of the prison barracks to keep warm.

Thoughts turned to home, and loved ones, and many letters were writ-ten with no guarantee of delivery, saying as much as the one page limit would allow.

2LT. SAMUEL H. HAWES, ORANGE ARTY. (VA.)

25th Dec/64- Our rations are worse now than ever, our bread rations being cut down still lower and a few pickles being given us, which only increases our appetites for food which we are not allowed to have. They say that we have permission to buy what we may want from the sutler, but at the same time withhold our money from us. A sad day for Xmas is this. Our number was a little increased yesterday by prisoners captured at Fort McAllister by Sherman. We have suffered most intensely from cold during the last few days.[33]

You will know, my dear Cora, that every letter from you gives me very great pleasure, but the last received, yours of the 19th inst. I have no words to describe the gratification—the ardent feelings it awakened. It's tone so frank & of such earnest trust delights and touches me, & it is a rebuke too, to those doubts and fears that I have suffered at times to disturb me. I give these to the mind, henceforth to be indulged no more. I have not received the other letter you speak of intending to mail. Several of your last contained stamps, but only one with money, Oct. 26th, ever reached me. We are not permitted to have funds or boxes sent to us, & let me again beg you to think no more of trying to send anything until you know that this order is revoked. I have spent the morning in looking over and reading portions of "Words of Jesus." The little book was handed to me last night.—I thank you with many thanks. As a Christmas present from you will affectionately cherish it.—I trust to receive many, many times, full measure of consolation from the inspirational utterances of the "Faithful Promise." Oh! that each of us, dear Cora, may seize fast hold upon His promises, & so order our lives that if we should not meet on earth, we will meet when troubles come not,—& parting is no more! Then, indeed, may we regard these present afflictions as "light" & recognize "disguised love" in them all. You are perhaps even now giving me my portion of this Christmas Sabbath, & it is cheering I assure you to feel that you are near me even in thought. I would that I could give to you the full, free letter my inclinations prompt me to write, but since this cannot be, I must ask of you what you bid me do—think of all you would have me to say, & imagine it said. To you I have devoted the greatest portion of the day, & so I feel happier thus to have spent Christmas than if I had suffered Memory to busy herself with the past,—as I am perhaps too prone to do. And I do earnestly hope that ere another Christmas shall have come, the longings of this one will have been displaced by full fruition![34]

LETTER, 1LT.
JAMES E. COBB,
5TH TX. INF.,
TO MISS CORA
WILLIAMS,
25 DECEMBER
1864

Sunday 25th Dec. 1864.- And this is Christmas day. Oh how different it is from those I've spent in former years, nothing to eat except a little mush and pickles.[35]

2LT. JOSEPH
MAUCK,
10TH VA. INF.

Captain Tom Perkins and friends had not given up on escaping. It was too tempting to be so close to friendly land and not try. Again, he was joined by the previous five companions, plus Captain Kitchin of North Carolina, Lieutenants Emmett Depriest, Pete Akers, and two new arrivals captured at Savannah. Next time the arrangements would be different, to prevent a fiasco with directions as before. The plan was to send out a scouting party, lay the route of escape, then return to the prison to get the others.

2LT. PETER
AKERS,
11TH VA. INF.

This being arranged, one evening just after the five o'clock roll call of the prison was made, Captain Campbell, arrayed in the uniform of a Yankee lieutenant, with Captain Perkins and Sergeant Denham in the uniform of privates (how they procured them no one has ever known), walked boldly out of the prison, passed the sentinel, and reached the outer guard about the prison before being halted. When the sentinel at the outer gate halted them Captain Campbell said, "I am Lt. Thomas, 22nd New York Volunteers. My men and myself got inside of your post line looking for the well." The guard saluted Campbell and they passed out the gate.

While getting the proper direction our boys stumbled on some Yankee soldiers cooking supper. Captain Campbell saluted them, asked several questions, said good night, and started with his two comrades down the road. Now that this danger was past another problem presented itself: how to pass the provost-marshal's office guard, and officers that would most likely be sitting on the porch at the office. The boys put on a bold front, walked slowly down the road past the office, saluted the guard and a group of officers sitting on the porch, they thinking Campbell was what his uniform made him look—a Yankee officer of the newly arrived troops from the East. The boys went into the town of Hilton Head, mixed with the troops, talked with the officers, learning all they could that would help them on their final trip.[36]

After a few more misadventures in the dark, Captain Perkins found a local slave who knew the area. A deal was struck for whiskey if the slave would meet him and his companions at the boat dock the next night, and take them across the river, where they could find the Confederate pickets. Time and place was agreed upon, and Perkins hastened back to his comrades, feeling pretty cocky at his success. With details taken care of, the band started toward prison, where they would successfully sneak back in.

2LT. PETER
AKERS,
11TH VA. INF.

On the way down the road Capt. Tom Perkins collapsed. The corn meal and pickle diet had broken him up. From the time the boys left prison they had walked over twenty miles. After a rest of an hour or so Perkins revived, and our fellows started back to prison to communicate the information gained to their comrades. They got as near the prison as they could before daylight without discovery. They then hid until good daylight, then walked boldly into the Yankee guard's barracks, next to our prison. They had wonderful stories to tell us on their return to prison. They had been out of the barracks for over thirteen hours—never missed even by the sergeant who called the prison roll. But later in the day some spy in the prison communicated the story of the boys to the provost-marshal. He was dumbfounded as to how our boys got hold of the uniforms; it was real funny to see the agitation of the pro-vost-marshal-general when he found he had been outwitted by the cunning of the "Reb."[37]

January brought the same cold and severe winter to Hilton Head that characterized Fort Pulaski. Pneumonia, colds, and other maladies further weakened the already famished men, who were at the mercy of "the best government the world ever saw."

The weather was exceedingly cold, so freezing cold, that many of the prisoners froze their feet, hands and ears, and some other parts of the body. It must be remembered that the season of the year was mid winter, and though we were in South Carolina, we were upon the beach, and so near the ocean, that we received the benefit of all the chilling winter blasts which constantly pervade the ocean. The chilling winds here were the fiercest I ever felt, and fiercer than those of Virginia. It must also be kept in mind that the house in which we were confined was so open as to admit large quantities of these chilling and freezing blasts.[38]

CAPT. JOHN J. DUNKLE, 25TH VA. INF.

January 17.- My birthday—twenty two years of age. We are still suffering from cold and hunger. My feet have been frost bitten and pain me considerably. A great many others of my fellow pris-oners are suffering in a worse condition. No fire is allowed us at night, and during the day, only enough to cook our small rations. It is astonishing that any government will treat prisoners of war as we are treated.[39]

2LT. WILLIAM EPPS, 4TH S.C. CAV.

January 14th.- Cool weather. Three years ago I was sworn into the Confederate service. We still live on corn meal and pickles. The Provost-Marshal says, he would reduce us to less, if he thought we could live. The object is to just spare life. I think sometimes it is better to starve men to death, than treat them this way.[40]

CAPT. ALEX BEDFORD, 3RD MO. CAV.

Wednesday, 4th January 1865.- No news of interest. 25 of the 1st lot captured officers ordered into the other prison and 25 of the late captured to fill their places. This caused a great deal of dissat-isfaction. The grape is that the late captured officers are to re-ceive full rations and we are to be kept on the same.[41]

2LT. JOSEPH MAUCK, 10TH VA. INF.

28th Jany/65.- All prisoners at this port with the exception of our party (called the retaliation party) were today sent to Northern prisons.[42]

2LT. SAMUEL H. HAWES, ORANGE ARTY. (VA.)

It is not at all wonderful that we suffered all the wretchedness of despair, and the anguish of misery, while freezing in a land flow-ing with milk and honey. . . . It indeed seemed that we were de-

CAPT. JOHN J. DUNKLE, 25TH VA. INF.

serted by God and man, and had been given over to demons and devils to be tormented.

Many men, in order to keep from freezing, trudged the floor at short intervals from morning to night, and from night until morning. This had to be resorted to in many cases to keep from freezing. The feet were cold for many days and nights together.[43]

Along with the officers of the Six Hundred, those taken prisoner when Savannah fell were also brought there. Among them was General George P. Harrison, Jr. He was also the nephew of Captain Harris K. Harrison, one of the Six Hundred exchanged from Fort Pulaski on December 15. The general arrived on Christmas Eve, 1864, along with forty-eight other officers, and over 500 men captured when Fort McAllister and Savannah fell. Harrison was so disturbed by the condition of the men at Hilton Head, that he urged officials in Richmond to pursue some way to alleviate the pitiful circumstances caused by retaliation. His letter graphically described the situation:

> *Prisoners' Barracks,*
> *Hilton Head, S.C. January 9, 1865.*

Hon. Julian Hartridge, Richmond, Va.

My Dear Sir: You will see from where this is written that I am a prisoner of war, captured about a month since at my home by General Sherman's forces on their advance to Savannah. I reached this place about two weeks since with about 600 prisoners. With the officers I was sent to the prison on this island, where 200 Confederate officers are confined and upon retaliatory treatment. Having shared their privations, hardships, and sufferings for two months, I propose to give you, and through you the authorities of the Government, some what in detail what we have been called to endure and what these 200 officers are still enduring. (Sherman's prisoners are now drawing better rations, in other respects the same treatment.) . . . No fire is allowed in these buildings. At about 5 p.m. is roll-call, when the inmates are all locked in until 7 a.m. next morning. The cold here is severe. Once since my arrival water would be ice in a moment after it touched the floor. Many of these officers are in rags, scarce enough clothing to cover their nakedness. Many, well nigh shoeless, lay at nights upon a rough, naked board, and in some instances two cover with one blanket, with their hips covered with a rough, horny scab from their nightly contact with their bedless bunks. To avoid freezing to death when the weather is cold much of the night is spent running up and down the building to keep up the circulation. This is done by almost the entire prison. The daily allowance to each man is one pint of stale meal, about two spoonsful of which is husk and weevils, four ounces of bread, and one-fourth pint of pickles. Three

*camp-kettles are allowed to each prison as cooking utensils. One stick
of green wood about eight feet long and eight inches in diameter for
fuel. The cooking is done in the open yard by the prisoners. Old coffee pots, tin kettles, frying-pans—in a word, everything upon which a
hoecake can be baked or in which water can be boiled is brought into
requisition and used thus. Two or three of a mess pick up their bunch
of chips, cup of meal, etc., select a place, open a hole in the sand, pile
it around the edge to keep off the wind. Into this the chips are deposited, the fire applied, down drops an officer, his mouth near the coals,
and blows until sufficient fire is kindled to prepare his mush or
hoecake. From the scanty supply of provisions and wood only two
meals are taken per day. It is not uncommon for officers to cut the
wood for the hospital for the privilege of picking up and using the
chips. I have seen a little piece of dirty grease carefully picked out of
the sand, carefully cleaned and put away for use . . .* [44]

It took tremendous courage and loyalty to endure the conditions. The
oath of allegiance would end the misery—but that meant giving up principles and betraying their country. Still, some men found the severity too
much. For them, taking the oath was a ticket to easier living, maybe even an
escape from death. Surprisingly, only seven men at the Hilton Head prison
took the oath. Their comrades were outraged. For the majority remaining
who held out against betrayal, these seven were seen as the lowest form of
humanity. It was a divisive act, tightening the group against taking the oath
while making outcasts of those who did.

*On January 20, 1865, Col. Van Manning received positive infor-
mation from one of the guards that Lieut. J. W. Davis, 20th Va.
Cav., was going to take the oath of allegiance and had made application to take it and be released. A meeting of prisoners was
called to meet in Capt. Tom Perkins' cell, and a committee appointed to wait on Lieutenant Davis and invite him to come before
the prisoners and refute, if he could, the charge Colonel Manning
had made. Davis promptly accepted the committee's invitation,
came before the prisoners, and solemnly declared on honor that
he had made no application to take the oath, and had never had
such idea. When Colonel Manning read a copy of the application
to him he broke down, admitted the truth, and became very defiant. Colonel Manning suggested to the meeting that, as Lieutenant Davis had premeditatedly intended to dishonor his uniform of
the Confederate States Army and insult by such act his brother
officers, prisoners of war, that the bars and buttons be cut from
his coat, and his coat turned inside out, and that he be ostracized
by his fellow prisoners. This suggestion was quickly carried out by
Tom Perkins and Pete Akers. Colonel Manning suggested to Davis
that he get the provost-marshal to remove him from the prison at*

2LT. PETE
AKERS,
11TH VA. INF.

once, as the prisoners were not in good temper to tolerate or over-
look his insult to them by taking the oath. Like a whipped cur
Davis ran and put himself under care of the guard, who soon had
the fellow out of our prison.[45]

    The act had repercussions for the offended officers. Davis reported that
Manning had plans to lead a group of officers in an escape, which involved
killing the guard. The Union authorities believed Davis, and punished the
six. They would be treated severely by being put in cells with common criminals, an act forbidden by the laws of war toward soldiers.

2LT. PETE
AKERS,
11TH VA. CAV.

*The committee that called the meeting and disgraced Davis, were
taken from our barracks and locked up in a cell in the Yankee
convict prison, where criminals of all sorts were confined,—men
who had broken the laws of God and man. These refined gentlemen, Confederate officers, prisoners of war, were locked up with
criminals without the least investigation, by the provost-marshal,
of the charges Davis made against them. These gentlemen were
all put in one cell, not over three feet wide and six feet long, and
there they were kept, in this cramped condition, for seven days
and nights. From five o'clock in the afternoon until ten o'clock in
the morning their cell door was closed and not allowed to be opened
except by order of the provost-marshal.*

*It almost shudders me to think of this little hell on earth. It was a
pig-sty, no less. The position of the men was painful, the vermin
intolerable, while the stench arising from it was almost beyond
human endurance. In the building were ten cells. In this cell all the
men could not lay down at once, comfortably, but by tight squeezing they could lay spoon fashion. . . . The cell floor was made of
heavy pine logs, smoothed with the axe, from which the rough
knots were not cut very close. They had no blankets, and the hard
logs was not a downy bed. . . . Just above the cell in which our
comrades were confined was a room in which . . . convicts were
confined. Most of them were negroes with ball and chain; there
was only one white man in the prison at the time, and he was
charged with committing a rape upon a lady of Georgia. . . . The
other prisoners not only reviled the officers, but took particular
pleasure in abusing the virtue of the Southern ladies. Daily they
polluted the ears of our comrades with the vilest epithets such
scoundrels could utter about our Southern women. They even cut
a hole through the floor and spit upon our men, and when the
prison authorities were complained to about this indignity they
simply smiled and made no effort to stop it; they even rather encouraged these vile scoundrels in their meanness and insults to
our helpless men. It should be stated that there were two excep-*

tions—and commendable for negroes. Without the assistance of these two negroes, our officers would have suffered inconceivably.

Davis, the deserter, one day did worse than spit upon our men in the cell. Our men protested to the sergeant who had charge of the convict room, but he would take no notice of the protest. Finally the conduct of the convicts . . . became so unbearable that Colonel Manning got the sergeant to ask Lieutenant Thompson, U.S.A., assistant provost-marshal, to come and see him, which he did. Our men protested against such insults as the convicts perpetrated upon them, but Thompson simply ordered the cell door closed, and paid no further attention to the protest.

Finally the provost-marshal-general made a general inspection of the convict prison, with his assistant, Thompson. When the door of the cell in which our men were confined was opened Colonel Gurney asked Thompson why those Confederate prisoners of war were confined in convict cells. Thompson . . . then lied by saying the men had formed a conspiracy to escape and murder the guard. Colonel Manning at once denounced Lieutenant Thompson as a liar. . . . When Colonel Gurney heard Colonel Manning's story, he ordered Thompson to instantly remove the prisoners from the filthy cells to a room on the floor above, where they were confined seventeen days. . . . This fellow, Thompson, inflicted upon Colonel Manning all the little mean indignities he dared without Colonel Gurney finding him out. These brave men never allowed this fellow to see how much he really made them suffer.[46]

Sunday, Jan. 22, 1865.- They have 6 of the officers locked up in a cell for stripping one of their officers that they supposed had taken the oath of Alegience. The cells are made of logs, and the floor is made out of logs about 10 inches through, split in four parts, and all the edges are laid up so it makes a rib bed. The cells are about 4 ft. one way & 8 the other. The logs are laid so that the ocupant has to lay croswise on the sharp edges.[47]

PVT. DANIEL WHITE, 144TH N.Y. INF.

The officers spent seventeen days in close confinement, and were not released until February 15. The behavior of Thompson toward the Confederate officers in regards to their quarters was obviously one of callous indifference. However, Thompson was reprimanded for allowing the conditions by Lieutenant Colonel Stewart Woodford, the exchange agent. Woodford wrote, "I would respectfully call your attention to the filthy condition of the quarters of the Rebel Prisoners of War in your custody and hereby direct that you take immediate measures to correct this evil." Thompson's reply was that he found the quarters "in good condition."[48]

The continuing trial that tested them the most was starvation. The corn meal-and-pickle ration drove the men to find anything available to eat, and led to desperate acts.

CAPT. WILLIAM
B. BALLANTINE,
2ND FLA. INF.

One day I saw one of our men sitting very quietly in one corner of the room. Thinking he was sick, I went over to speak to him and do whatever I could for his comfort. I found he had a long string in his hand, on which he had a fish-hook baited with a grain of corn. This he dropped through a chink in the floor. . . . For a while I thought the poor fellow was crazy, but when he yanked in a rat the problem of why he was quiet was solved. He caught rats and ate them to keep from starving.[49]

PVT. DANIEL
WHITE,
144TH N.Y.
INF.

Sunday, Jan. 22, 1865.- Our Rebs are all going to die if they are kept here. I think they leave pretty fast. They ocasionaly get hold of a cat or dog, and dress them & cook & eat them. They are meat hungry I think.[50]

2LT. JOSEPH
MAUCK,
10TH VA. INF.

Tuesday 3rd Jan. 1865.- The one eyed bob tailed cat went up today. Cats are all the go now a days.

Saturday 7th Jan. 1865.- Rats are now in demand.[51]

CAPT. JOHN J.
DUNKLE,
25TH VA. INF.

It was thought a streak of the finest fortune to be so lucky as to procure a small rat. Though horrible to the thoughts of men in good society, and decidedly offensive to the taste, they made a savory meal, and as much desired as a dainty meal at home. Cats played around the prison on our first going there, but they were soon slain, and eaten with the same avidity as if they were fine beef.[52]

CAPT. FRANKLIN
C. BARNES,
56TH VA. INF.

Lieutenant Samuel H. Hawes, of Richmond, narrowly missed a feast on a fat dog, which came about thus: Some of his comrades boasted of having had rat stews; and he did have an invitation to a cat supper. Capt. Perkins caught a cat, killed and cooked it for his mess of four. One of the mess, as a special favor, sent Lieutenant Hawes an invitation to the feast, and he accepted to the extent of looking at them as they ate. It was very kind to invite him, but he couldn't "go" cat. It was suggested that as he was so squeamish about cat, maybe he would take some "Ponto" stew if offered.

Ponto was a beautiful half-grown, well-fed, fat setter puppy, belonging to the Federal officer in charge of our guard. This young dog came to our quarters every day to have a frolic with the prisoners. Hawes agreed to accept invitation and to eat some of the dog supper when prepared, for the puppy was young, cleanly washed, fat and healthy.

Perkins thereupon agreed to catch and kill "Ponto" and prepare the feast. The next morning the dog came bounding into the prison yard as soon as the gate was opened, as was his habit, but most

positively declined all of Perkins' advances, notwithstanding his
friendship heretofore. As soon as he looked into Perkins' eyes doubt
took possession of him. Ponto sniffed danger in the air, tucked tail
and ran for the gate, and foreswore his prison friends ever after.[53]

Even the acts of eating cats and dogs did not alleviate the pain and suffering from scurvy and other diseases. While there had been some men exchanged on the reason of being sick and wounded, by the end of January all the prisoners were sick to a degree, some worse than others. Yet they would not be considered for exchange. They were allowed to write letters, and many tried in vain to enlist some favor from government officials and friends to relieve their misery. The treatment of Captain William Bailey is particularly touching.

I have the honor to address you on a subject which directly con-
cerns myself, but may result to the advantage of some of your
friends. My object is to get a parole of sixty days visit to my home
within the Confederate lines with the view of getting a Federal
officer of the same rank sent back on parole to be specially ex-
changed for me. In consideration of this favor I will pledge myself
to distribute any reasonable amount agreed upon between us,
among the sick Federal prisoners who are now confined in the
South. I have been a prisoner since the battle of Gettysburg, July
4th, 63, When I was severely wounded. Owing to the long confine-
ment and a predisposition to consumption my health has failed
and I do not believe that I can live much longer. . . . I can give you
no further security under present circumstances for the perfor-
mance of the above promise than my word of honor, and can only
refer you to my old friends . . . Messrs. H. L Ritch and Co. and Mes.
J. L. Smallwood of New York City. I would be pleased to hear from
you, or have an interview at the earliest practicable moment.[54]

LETTER, CAPT.
WILLIAM BAILEY,
5TH FLA. INF.,
TO COL. T.L
WOODFORD,
FEDERAL AGENT
OF EXCHANGE,
25 DECEMBER
1864

Captain Bailey's request was denied, and he lingered on until he died on March 3, 1865 at Hilton Head. His official cause of death is listed as inflammation of the lungs. A family friend requested that his grave be marked for removal.

Your letter of the 8th inst. conveying to me the sad intelligence of
the death of Capt. Wm. Bailey of one of the Fla. Regt. was rec'd
today. I thank you for your kindness in acquainting me so promptly
with the painful fact. Capt. B. was known to me in "better days" as
a noble hearted gentleman, and his death will be a sad blow not
only to a lovely and devoted wife and little ones, but to the many
warm friends he left in his sunny home. May I ask of you in behalf
of an aged parent and his afflicted family, that you will cause
some mark to be placed on his grave so that at some future day,
his friends may be enabled to remove his remains to Fla? Your
compliance with my request will greatly be obliged.
Please answer.[55]

LETTER,
WILLIAM R.
HAYWARD,
CAMBRIDGE,
MD., TO MAJ.
B. W.
THOMPSON,
PROVOST
MARSHAL
GEN'L,
18 MARCH
1865

Confederate Veteran Magazine
1Lt. James Edward Cobb
Joined Co. F, 5th Texas Infantry, July 11, 1861. Captured at Gettysburg.

Museum of the Confederacy, Richmond
1Lt. Alexander Jackson Kirkman
4th Alabama Cavalry.
A student at Heidelberg University when the war started, he came home on a blockade runner to join the army.

National Archives

Deserters' jail and prison
where the six Confederate officers were held for cutting the buttons off the coat of Lt. John Davis for taking the oath.

Courtesy Mr. Carl Mark Barker
Capt. Samuel J. Johnson
Co. E, 25th Tennessee Infantry.

Museum of the Confederacy, Richmond
Capt. James H. Polk
Co. E, 6th Tennessee Cavalry
(Wheeler's).

Courtesy Mr. T. C. Greever
1Lt. John Dudley Greever
Co. C, 50th Virginia Infantry.

North Carolina Troops
Lt. Col. Tazewell Lee Hargrove
44th North Carolina Infantry.

Upon hearing of Bailey's death, his family requested special permission to bring the body home to Florida. General Sam Jones, commanding the Department of Florida, submitted the request to U.S. Brigadier General Eliakim P. Scammon, commander at Hilton Head:

> At the request of relatives of the late Capt. William Bailey C.S.A. who, it is reported has recently died at Hilton Head whilst a prisoner of war, I have permitted the bearer of this, Mr. A. Hopkins, a citizen of this place, to go under flag of truce to your lines, and with your permission into Jacksonville, to recover if he can the body of the deceased and if practicable bring it to his family.
>
> I will appreciate any aid you may give Mr. Hopkins to carry out the object of his visit.[56]

The letter was returned with "Disapproved" written on it. Even in death, Captain Bailey remained a prisoner at Hilton Head Island.

The winter of 1865 slowly rolled toward spring, and the men found their health waning. Alex Bedford noticed his eyesight failing, eventually unable to see at night to read. Still he wrote to his wife faithfully, several times a week. Most were so weak they could not walk without feeling dizzy and exhausted. Joseph Mauck had such problems with loose teeth and diseased gums from scurvy that he could no longer chew the coarse meal and was able to trade it to a sympathetic guard for soft white bread. Some lives hung by a slender thread just as a change in command brought attention to the suffering.

CAPT. ALEX BEDFORD, 3RD MO. CAV.

January 27th.- Clear and very cold. I have been quite sick, but feel much better. Had my washing done for the first time in twelve months. We drew four ounces of pickled beef and four ounces of Irish potatoes this evening, the first we have had since the 14th of December; making forty-four days living on ten ounces of cornmeal, spoiled at that, four ounces of bread or flour, and a few pickles; two ounces of salt for ten days. Hard living, nearly half the men sick and would have died had it not been for the Yankee surgeon informing Gen. Foster, if he did not increase the rations, it was no use to give medicine, as they all would die. The order soon came for us to receive the above rations. Lieut. Campbell is very sick and they say will die.[57]

It was Foster's own suggestion that the Six Hundred be exchanged because "there seems no necessity of keeping them for the original purpose for which they were sent, as General Hardee has stated that it was not the intention to expose our prisoners to the fire on Charleston. . . . I respectfully request to be informed, if you see fit to grant this request, to what point they are to be shipped." The correspondence was addressed to Major General Henry W. Halleck on January 8, 1865. There was no reply.[58]

CHAPTER ELEVEN

"Murder of the Most Terrible Kind"

AT Fort Pulaski they survived, taking life day by day, ration by ration. Each man dealt in his own way with the ordeal of retaliation, and helped those whose mental outlook turned bleak. The emotional battering of prison life, combined with the physical abuse of starvation and the elements, worked against the will to live, and induced hopelessness. Many simply longed for death and the release it would provide, while brother officers coaxed them to cling to life.

Lt. Billy Funk, 5th Regt., Stonewall Brigade, one of our number, was little more than a boy in years when he joined the Confederate Army in 1861. A gallant, brave boy, he was captured May 12, 1864, at the battle of Spotsylvania Court House, reaching Fort Delaware prison just in time to be selected as one of the six hundred. . . . Upon Lieutenant Funk the rigors of retaliation worked very hard, and soon completely broke him down. But never a complaint escaped his lips, and he bore his suffering like a hero. Lieut. Tom S. Doyle, a noble fellow, Funk's messmate and regimental comrade, with us all, did all we could to help him and keep him alive, giving him part of our scanty corn meal ration and all the white bread given us, which was just two ounces. (This white bread was not added to our corn-meal-pickle ration until late in February.) In his suffering with dysentery and scurvy Funk lost heart and nerve, slowly starving to death.[1]

CAPT. J. OGDEN MURRAY, 11TH VA. CAV.

Not only were blankets and clothing not issued, but we were not allowed to receive what friends had sent us. We had only so much fuel as was needed for cooking. Can a more miserable state of existence be imagined than this? Starved almost to the point of death, a prey to disease, the blood in the veins so thin that the

CAPT. GEORGE W. NELSON, HANOVER ARTY. (VA.)

207

least cold sent a shiver through the whole frame! . . . Add to this the knowledge on our part that a few steps off were those who lived in plenty and comfort! I remember one instance that, suffering as I was myself, touched me to the heart. One poor fellow, who had grown so weak as not to be able to get off his bunk, said to his "chum": "I can't stand this any longer, I must die." "O, no," said the other, "cheer up, man, rations will be issued again in two days, and I reckon they will certainly give us something to eat then— live until then anyhow." The poor fellow continued to live until the day for issuing rations, but it brought no change—the same short pint of damaged meal and pickle, and nothing more. As soon as the poor fellow heard this, he told his friend not to beg him any more, for he could not live any longer, and the next evening he died.[2]

MAJ. DAVID B. COULTER, 12TH ARK. INF.

During the time we were kept there, my casemates were G[eorge] W. Carter of Arkadelphia and Capt. Dobyns. A good many of the officers died from starvation. My bunk-mate Carter was naturally a delicate man and he was sure he was going to die. He told me so and refused to get up from his bed. I had a gutta-percha ring that was made by some of the boys in prison. One night I took this ring and went down to the Yankee guard who was separated from us by an iron railing, and offered to trade him the ring for a piece of meat. One Yankee told me that he had a little piece of meat but that it was not worth the ring. I told him to take the ring and give me the meat. He gave me about one half pound of raw bacon. I went back to my bunk and told Carter to get up, that I had him some meat. He looked at the meat, put his arms around my neck and cried like a child. He told me that I had saved his life. Ravenously he ate the meat raw and he did not die but lived for several years after the war.[3]

CAPT. J. OGDEN MURRAY, 11TH VA. CAV.

I recall the dreadful sights of misery in that Fort Pulaski prison— loved comrades starving to death, dying with that terrible disease scurvy, and the great government of the United States responsible for all this wanton cruelty; and yet no effort was made to alleviate or curtail it. Who will ever forget grand old Capt. John Lucas Cantwell—Gentle, kind, true; never tiring of helping his sick comrades. Capt. Ed Chambers carried out the command "love thy neighbor as thyself." Lewis Harman, generous with whatever he had. Lt. Tom S. Doyle and Capt. J. L. Hempstead, doing all men could do to better the condition of their sick comrades. Capt. Hempstead—gentle as a woman, brave as the lion, a courtly knight of the old school, his heart went out in sympathy to his suffering comrades, his generous hand relieved their wants from his scanty ration. LeBreton, of Louisiana, gentle, kind, suf-

fering without a murmur. Capt. Will Page Carter—"We can suf-
fer, men, for principle; we cannot surrender without dishonor," I
heard him say to those comrades about him who were not able
to leave their bunks . . . It was sad, it was heart-breaking, to see
the suffering of our men in the Fort Pulaski prison. One thing
that often impressed me was the heroic conduct of our men un-
der the ordeal. Before taps, every night, some of our comrades
would get together in one of the casemates of the prison and sing
the old familiar songs of the South, seeming for the time to for-
get the pains of retaliation and their hunger.[4]

Young men, once vigorous, lay prostrate with the diseases of old age—
rheumatism, pneumonia and bronchitis. The sound of coughing and labored
breathing filled the room, disturbing the sleep of all. Scurvy and dysentery
existed in the extreme, causing debility and making life unendurable. In advanced stages, as many officers had it by the end of January 1865, scurvy
symptoms are similar to those of hemophilia. The blood vessels simply dis-
integrate, spilling blood into the body. The joints are particularly affected,
as the blood swells them and prevents movement, causing excruciating pain.
Most became blind to some degree, their pallid faces like ghosts from the
anemia induced by scurvy. In the harsh conditions they clung to each other
for comfort, suffering patiently.[5]

In letters home, they often kept the facts of their ordeal to themselves,
partially because their letters were censored, but also because they did not
want wives and mothers to know the true extent of the suffering.

Writing to his wife Malissa, Captain Moses Bradford only touched on his
condition. "I have suffered a great deal with cold. I have but one very light
Blanket and never feel the heat of fire. . . . I have but little news that I can
write." Though he complains and mentions his health, in actuality, he was
dying as he wrote, "Hope this will find you all in good health. My health is
very bad, I am very weak. We have been living on 10 ounces of meal and 4
ounces of Baker's Bread, and have that only per day. This is 15 days on it. . . .
O how I wish I had such as my dogs used to have. . . . If you have not sent the
money or things that [I] wrote to you for, you need not do so for we are not
permitted to receive anything without permission of Gen. Wessell. Give my
love to all. Yours till death. M. J. Bradford."[6]

Those among them with medical training, one of whom was Captain Henry
Handerson, appealed to Colonel Brown to allow them to help their own.

In the course of a month the effects of insufficient food began to   **CAPT. HENRY**
show themselves in a daily increasing sick-list, which soon assumed   **HANDERSON,**
alarming proportions. Accordingly a mass-meeting of the prison-   **9TH LA. INF.**
ers was held, and a committee appointed to visit Col. Brown and
endeavor to effect some amelioration of our condition. Of this com-
mittee I formed one, and one Sunday evening we were conducted
to Col. Brown's quarters, where we found him sitting by a cheerful

*grate fire, surrounded, apparently, by all the comforts of home.
On stating to him the purpose of our mission, the colonel, with
considerable emotion, replied substantially: "Gentlemen, I feel very
sorry for you, and have done all that I could to prevent the enforcement of this order. But I am bound to obey my orders, and
can do nothing for you." We then asked if he could not, at least,
furnish us with sufficient lumber to enable us to partition off a
portion of the casemates as a hospital, so as to enable us to separate the sick from the well. Again he replied: "Gentlemen, I can do
nothing, absolutely nothing," and with heavy hearts we retired to
our gloomy quarters.*[7]

2LT. HENRY
COOK,
44TH TENN.
INF.

*If our condition was horrible on Morris Island, it was much more
so here. Many were unable to walk; others meandered through
the vaults like living skeletons, gazing into each others' faces with
a listless, vacant stare, plainly indicating that they were border-
ing upon imbecility or lunacy. That dreadful disease, the scurvy,
was raging fearfully, so that the mouths were in a fearful condition, their gums decaying and sloughing off and their teeth falling
out; while others had the disease in a more dangerous form, their
arms and legs swelling, mortifying, and becoming black. Black
spots appeared upon the arms and legs of some, looking as though
the veins and arteries had decomposed, separated, and spilled the
blood in the flesh.*[8]

CAPT. GEORGE
W. NELSON,
HANOVER ARTY.
(VA.)

*Our diet soon induced scurvy. This loathsome disease, in addition
to the pangs of hunger, made life almost insupportable. The disease first made its appearance in the mouth, loosening the teeth,
and in many cases making the gums a mass of black, putrid flesh.
It next attacked the limbs, appearing first in little spots, like blood
blisters. One of them, after being broken, would become a hard,
dark-colored knot. These spots would increase until the whole limb
was covered, by which time the muscles would have contracted
and the limb be drawn beyond all power of a straightening. I have
seen cases where not only the legs and arms but the back was thus
affected. Another feature of the disease was the fainting produced
by very slight exercise. I have walked down the prison, and stumbled
upon men lying on the floor to all appearance dead, having fainted
and fallen while exerting themselves to get to the sinks.*[9]

CAPT. WILLIAM
H. MORGAN,
11TH VA. INF

*In consequence of this inhuman order, there was a great deal of
sickness and many deaths among the prisoners. "Starved to death,"
said the Yankee surgeon who attended the sick, "medicine will do
them no good." . . . Many a poor fellow, in attempting to make his
way to the sinks, would fall fainting to the ground. I remember, in
one day, assisting three of these unfortunates to rise from the
ground and back to their bunks.*[10]

*During this awful scourge I was stricken with pneumonia. A Yan-
kee doctor gave me treatment, being kept right there in the afore-
said quarters on a bunk of plank with a few blankets. I do not
know how long I lay there, nor when I left.*[11]

CAPT. THOMAS
B. MARTIN,
HOLCOMB'S
LEGION, S.C. INF.

*When the wolf, hunger, takes hold of a man, all that is human in
the man disappears. He will, in his hunger, eat anything. I most
fully understand, after my personal experience, why those poor
fellows on the late expedition to the North Pole did eat each other,
and thought it no crime. No person knows what hunger is, what it
really means, unless they have had an experience in starvation's
grasp. It is impossible to explain how we lived through the terrible
ordeal of fire and starvation. Those were horrible days—days which
most thoroughly convinced me that nothing but actual experiment
can determine how much starvation, hunger, and bad treatment
a human being can stand.*[12]

CAPT. J. OGDEN
MURRAY,
11TH VA. CAV.

*January 2, 1865.- Yesterday I made no memorandum of passing
events because it was "the" cold day of the winter, which the Yanks
celebrated by refusing to furnish any wood. All day and all night
many of us walked to keep up the circulation, or shivered in our
scanty covering. On Saturday night it commenced turning rapidly
cold, and on the first morning of the New Year, long icicles were
visible and the pump (which we now use) was frozen up. It continued all day and last night it was still dead cold. Many men slept
none and looked haggard and woebegone. Having a moderate
share, I slept very badly. How could men endure such a night with
only one blanket for two, as a number are situated here?*[13]

CAPT. HENRY
DICKINSON,
2ND VA. CAV.

*Some of the boys had no blankets, and we all slept on bare boards.
It was so cold that the boys who had no blankets had to walk all
night to keep from freezing. The next morning they would crawl
into the bunk someone else had occupied during the night and
would sleep that day. It seems to me that I can hear those poor
fellows yet—walking, walking up and down on that brick floor.*[14]

MAJ. DAVID B.
COULTER,
12TH ARK. INF.

*January 8, 1865.- We suffered terribly today; the weather was
very cold and damp, with an east wind. All who can have wrapped
up in blankets. The coughing and limping continues. No wood was
furnished us, and as a consequence we shall not be able to cook
our sour meal tomorrow. Somehow, the supply of wood is shortest
on cold days. . . . Last night two cats were captured and to my
surprise were èaten today. I was not so fortunate as to eat any of
it, as the owners found too many just tasting the cat; it smelt very
fine, however, and I know I could have "gone for a leg." Another*

CAPT. HENRY C.
DICKINSON,
2ND VA. CAV.

cat was captured today and will be cooked when we get wood! Several of us agreed tonight that we would take some steps about the wood question and, if possible, the doctor, tomorrow, though it is a delicate question to tell a Yank his doctor is worthless.[15]

CAPT. GEORGE
W. NELSON,
HANOVER ARTY.
(VA.)

Fortunately for some of us, there were a great many cats about the prison. As may be imagined, we were glad enough to eat them. I have been partner in the killing and eating of three, and besides friends have frequently given me a share of their cat. We cooked ours two ways. One we fried in his own fat for breakfast—another we baked with a stuffing and gravy made of some corn meal—the other we also fried. The last was a kitten—was tender and nice. A compassionate Yankee soldier gave it to me. I was cooking at the stove by the grating which separated us from the guard. This soldier hailed me : "I say, are you one of them fellers that eats cats?" I replied, "Yes." "Well, here is one I'll shove thro' if you want it." " 'Shove it thro,'" I answered. In a very few minutes the kitten was in frying order. Our guards were not allowed to relieve our suffering, but they frequently expressed their sympathy.[16]

CAPT. J. OGDEN
MURRAY,
11TH VA. CAV.

One day I had the good fortune to catch a big fat cat. Capt. Thornton Hammack, 49th Ky. Regt. skinned the animal for me, and dressed it for the pan. In an old tin can I made soup of part of the cat for Funk, and, after threats and coaxing, I prevailed upon him to drink some of the soup. The effect upon him was magical. It revived him in spirits and for a time counteracted the effects of the scurvy. As long as I could get him rat and cat meat he showed signs of improvement; but the cats gave out, and the rats I could not catch . . . so poor Billy Funk lapsed back into his former condition.[17]

Despite the terrible conditions, the Southern soldiers still kept their sense of humor, and there were many amusing incidents. No doubt the ability to laugh at the absurd events induced by their situation helped keep them alive.

CAPT. HENRY
HANDERSON,
9TH LA. INF.

Col. Brown's little daughter, who with her mother shared his quarters, was the happy possesor of a beautiful white cat, which gaily decked out with a blue ribbon, was wont to sun herself upon the parade-ground, and occasionally even wandered into the casemates of the unfortunate Confederate prisoners, where she was warmly received and freely petted. Suddenly poor pussy disappeared, and no inquiries sufficed to determine the cause of her absence. About this time I was invited by some of my comrades to join them in a "swell" dinner, with the intimation that a piece of good-luck had enabled them to prepare quite a feast for the occasion. Hungry and curious, at the appointed time I joined my friends, and we sat down to an impromptu table, loaded with corn-bread, pickles, and the piece de resistance, an appetizing looking roast, which I took for a rabbit. To my horror, however, as the host was proceeding to carve the mysterious dish, some practical joker in the party whispered in audible tones "mee-ow" and the secret was out! The disappearance of Col. Brown's white cat was fully explained. Hungry as I was, I could not persuade myself to taste of poor pussy.[18]

January 10, 1865.- Still cold and damp, and the men very gloomy. A friend caught and gave to me a large boar cat. Burgess, of Louisiana, agreed to prepare and cook Tommy on shares and soon had his jacket off, finding him very fat.

CAPT. HENRY DICKINSON, 2ND VA. CAV.

January 11, 1865.- Burgess roasted the big cat today and we found that hunger had removed so many prejudices we, the owners, got a small share. I found the ribs and part of the back elegant food, and the gravy was splendid sop. Cats are now firmly established in our affection, and I long to get where either bacon or cats are abundant.[19]

Our men became as expert as cats at catching rats. If a rodent poked his nose out of his hole some fellow would nab him like a cat. We had cleaned out all the cats about the fort but one. He was a pet of Colonel Brown's wife; she begged us not to disturb him, so Tom came in our prison perfectly free from danger, although I must say that about Christmas Day the temptation was very great to make a Christmas roast of Tom.[20]

CAPT. J. OGDEN MURRAY, 11TH VA. CAV.

The pain of living in these conditions, the frustration and boredom, led to emotional feelings hard to contain. The heartbreak of watching comrades dying a slow, painful death, deliberately imposed by a cruel government order, spawned bitter feelings. The outrage was recorded in the spontaneous words of young soldiers, who never dreamed of such helplessness when they left home to fight in an idealistic war.

December 31, 1864.- Arguing the question of morals with Lewis today, we thought it best to swallow the oath whenever we were reduced to such a condition by this treatment that death must shortly ensue, and then we will go for them. . . . This gloomy day I close a sad and suffering year, with no hope of life through another unless released, but with the conviction that the Yankee nation is one of utter depravity, unfit to mingle with civilized people and unworthy of a name on earth. From one man only, General Scammon, have I received the kindness and courtesy due a gentleman—and he is the exception. I may not be permitted to live to see the close of another year, but, however long or short my life, I

CAPT. HENRY DICKINSON, 2ND VA. CAV.

would spend it in exterminating the race so that my little ones may never see such fiends. They have outraged civilization, religion, the Bible, humanity, and, as my last curse of this year is upon them, so I expect will be the last curse of my life.[21]

1LT. JOHN C. ALLEN, 7TH VA. CAV.

Jan. 6.- The privates who are here with us drew meat today for 5 days, but we are still the subjects of the most severe retaliation and of course look for nothing better from a man who is no more than a brute. Such a one is Gen. Foster.[22]

CAPT. DAVID GRAYSON, 10TH VA. INF.

January, 1865. This has been a month that will ever be remembered in the history of my life. The suffering witnessed and experienced is etched in fire upon my mind, and the additional hatred formed for the Yankee nation can never be reconciled. The officers here at Fort Pulaski have undergone the petty spirit of retaliation inflicted upon them by the jealousy of a downfallen and degraded Nation, with an equanimity of temper and resolution of purpose that must excite the admiration of even our enemies, to see the determination we evince in maintaining principles in which not only interest but honor is at stake.[23]

CAPT. HENRY DICKINSON, 2ND VA. CAV.

December 22, 1864.- What Southern woman does not feel life to be almost a burden, when she lives in daily expectation of learning of the loss of a brother, son or husband? How many noble females have Lincoln and his minions rendered desolate for life? How many seats by the fireside are vacant? How many familiar faces are seen no more? How many languish in hospitals or hobble on the streets? How many are dying in the Northern dens? How many are sleeping on the field of battle? How many widows and orphans will there be? How much poverty and crime? How much ignorance? How has civilization even turned back in her career? One word from Lincoln and his man Seward would have averted all this.

It has been awfully cold all day and we have had but little wood for the four stoves. Just think, you New England philanthropists, of four cooking stoves to quarters 200 yards long; over 100 windows without glass; the thermometer far below freezing; many of us sick, some without a single blanket, many with but one; all of us with threadbare clothes; . . . prohibited from receiving money, clothes, or food from our friends. Will your historians of this war admit that such things occurred in the United States?[24]

CAPT. JAMES ROBERT MCMICHAEL, 12TH GA. INF.

Sunday, February 12, 1865.- Since the first of January we have not been upon an equal footing with other prisoners of war and our privations and sufferings have been very great. Truly have we suffered for our country. Some could not endure the trials and have slept the sleep of death. Many others for want of attention will do likewise soon.

God forbid that either Government should ever again become so infuriated, so blinded to the sense of humanity as to practice such inhumane and barbarous treatment upon guiltless prisoners. Our hall has been a hospital since my last writing, and the patients were deprived of the sick rations. After retreat the doors and windows are all closed and midnight darkness reigns until reveille.[25]

January 25th.- Rec'd a letter from Capt. Pinckney who has been exchanged, he says our chances for exchange are gloomy. I have been without meat for 22 days and feel like I could eat cat, dog or anything—it is telling a fearful tale among my fellow prisoners— Scurvy and other chronic diseases are prevailing to an alarming extent—It is murder of the most terrible kind and I don't think it has any parallel.[26]

2LT. DAVID
GORDON,
4TH S.C. CAV.

The consequence of all this was that the prisoners died like sheep. Whatever the immediate cause of their death, that cause was induced by starvation, and over the dead bodies of nine-tenths of those brave, true men there can be given but one true verdict: "Death by starvation."[27]

CAPT. GEORGE
W. NELSON,
HANOVER ARTY.
(VA.)

Life was in eclipse. The struggle continued daily to decide if it would emerge. Their damaged constitutions could no longer keep at bay the life-threatening forces brought on by denial of the basic sustenance of survival.

During the forty-three days of the corn meal and pickle ration, nine men died. One of these was Captain Moses Bradford who, nursed by comrades, succumbed to death on February 13, after weeks of suffering. Four more would follow shortly after. Funerals were held with either Captain Thomas W. Harris or Lieutenant George "Wash" Nelson presiding. However, most of the men were too weak to attend the many graveside services, which came for days in a row.

February 1, 1865.- On the 28th inst. Lieutenant Burgin, of North Carolina, died from dysentery at the hospital; We have had cold weather and as much gloom as ever hung over the same number of men for so long a time. Over 100 men are now sick, and scurvy in its worst form is among us... The scurvy sores on the bodies of those around me are terrible sights.

CAPT. HENRY
DICKINSON,
2ND VA. CAV.

February 5, 1865.- Yesterday Lieutenant Legg, of the Fiftieth Virginia Infantry, died; he was buried today. In a few days others must follow him.

February 14, 1865.- Whilst the friends of Captain Bradford were out burying him, Capt. Alex King, of the Fiftieth Virginia Infantry, died. He and Captain Bradford had been in the hospital since the 8th inst.

February 15, 1865.- A party of us, mostly Virginians, attended the burial of our friend, Captain King; but one Yankee was present— Rowe, our guard. The religious services were conducted by Captain Harris of the Georgia regiment. This is the seventh man buried by us since our arrival; at least five of them were victims of Yankee cruelty. None of them were perhaps equals of Captain King, who, besides being a good soldier, possessed rare literary attainments and might have been an ornament to south West Virginia. At the hospital we saw at least two more of our number who must die.[28]

Soon the guards of the garrison stayed away from the horrible sights inside the casemates, and were seldom seen, except on their posts of duty on the parapet and parade ground. Brown refused all petitions to have him visit the cells and see the conditions, on the reason that it pained him because he could do nothing about it.[29] When he made his inspections, he rushed through the prison aisle, as if to escape the suffering he was forced to behold. Some of the guards told Captain Dickinson, Murray, and others that Brown had requested to be sent back to the front rather than starve men to death.[30]

CAPT. J. OGDEN MURRAY, 11TH VA. CAV.
There were lots of good fellows in the 157th New York Volunteers. . . . Often, when they were on duty about the prison some of them would put a loaf of bread or piece of meat on the end of their bayonets and dare any Rebel to take it off, always holding their guns in such position that the meat or bread could be taken off by the prisoners. These men took this method of helping us and getting around the orders. They dare not openly disobey. There was one officer in this regiment who deserves well of every Fort Pulaski prisoner. He was Major Place, quarter-master of post. His kindness to the prisoners will ever be remembered by us all of the Fort Pulaski detachment. On one occasion this kind hearted fellow took a lot of his men fishing with seines in the Savannah River about the fort. At night, after their return, Major Place gave Capt. Ed Chambers, of Alabama, one of the prisoners, a barrel of the fish he and his men had caught during the day. "These," he said, "Captain Chambers, distribute to your sick men who can not get about."[31]

CAPT. HENRY E. HANDERSON, 9TH LA. INF.
One week an order would be issued authorizing prisoners to receive money, books and articles of clothing from their friends, and promising safe delivery for all articles thus forwarded. Of course

we all wrote immediately for various necessaries. The next week, perhaps, the order would be countermanded, and all donations for the comfort of the prisoners positively prohibited. This occurred so often, and with so little apparent cause, that we were kept in a constant state of anxiety, fearing that the donations of our friends would be forwarded, and then either confiscated or lost. . . . I had written to my father for a cheap edition of Herodotus to pass away the weary hours of the winter. It was sent, and reaching Hilton Head about the time of one of these embargos, was stopped at that place, and, as I supposed, was lost. One night, however, soon after I had gone to bed and when I had fallen into a doze, I was awakened by feeling some person pulling slightly at my blanket, and turning hastily to that side I caught sight in the dim light of the casemate of a figure hastily retreating and disappearing in the darkness. Smiling to myself at the idiocy of a man who should undertake to rob me of anything valuable, I quietly turned over again and went to sleep. On arising in the morning what was my surprise to find my Herodotus tucked safely under my blanket, but nothing to give any clue as to the route by which it had come. Of course I felt it must have been brought by my nocturnal visitor, but it was some time before I knew that the latter was the Lieut. Col. [Carmichael] of the regiment in charge of the fort. . . . Happening to be at Hilton Head on official business, he saw my Herodotus at headquarters, and slipping it quietly in his pocket conveyed it to me anonymously and secretly—an act of generous kindness for which, I regret to say, circumstances never permitted me to return my thanks.[32]

I want to say a few words for Colonel Brown's wife. One day, in a fit of desperation, I wrote Colonel Brown a note, asking him to grant me an interview. To my surprise, on the following day he granted it. A sergeant conducted me to his office quarters. The Colonel received me politely. I told him I had an uncle in St. Louis, St. Andrew Murray, who would gladly aid me with money if I were allowed to communicate with him. His reply was, "Sir, I, personally, would be glad to grant your request; but I am sorry indeed I can not, under my orders, do so. I am powerless." For a few moments he left the office. The lady who had been present during the interview was Colonel Brown's wife. Turning to me she said, "Write your draft on your uncle; you shall have the money." This kind, noble lady . . . gave me, as I left the office, a paper containing two large slices of bread, butter, and ham. I took them to my sick comrade, Billy Funk.[33]

CAPT. J. OGDEN MURRAY, 11TH VA. CAV.

CAPT. HENRY
DICKINSON,
2ND VA. CAV.

February 8, 1865.- Colonel Brown, whom I think sympathizes with us deeply, has managed to turn over to us some condemned vegetables and some sago. The latter will make soup for the sick for a week. He has also managed to have the sickest men in prison put on sick rations.

February 11, 1865.- Tonight Colonel Brown sent us 2,500 fish of the mullet species and such scaling and frying I never saw. The treat was relished by all, and those who, for the first time in forty-two days, tasted meat were wild with joy.[34]

Colonel Brown had apparently been contacting some authorities regarding the situation. On January 8, Major General John G. Foster requested an exchange of the Confederate officers, addressed to Major General Halleck, who in turn passed it up the chain of command to Grant. Toward the end of January, Foster was relieved of his duties in the Department of the South, and replaced by General Quincy A. Gillmore, who had been in command at Hilton Head in 1862. Until Gillmore took complete charge, Major General Cuvier Grover would command from the headquarters in Savannah. On February 16, Gillmore again petitioned for exchanging the remainder of the Six Hundred, and was informed by Grant that he had granted Foster permission to exchange these officers January 5. Why they were not exchanged is inexplicable. It would be six weeks or more from the time permission was given to exchange the men, and the time they actually would leave Fort Pulaski. Although Foster initiated the request to exchange, he purposefully ignored the instructions granting the permission.

Another possible explanation for ending the retaliation was the fact that the U.S. Congress was well aware of Foster's actions, and some House members did not approve. Congress had been debating the official stance of the government on retaliation and on January 27, 1865 Senator Henderson from Kansas made this statement on the subject:

Permit me to ask . . . under what authority the retaliation practiced by General Foster, of which he speaks, was adopted before Congress acted upon the subject. If Congress has entire power over the question and Congress has not directed retaliation to be exercised, how could an officer in the field undertake to say that he would retaliate in the way . . . stated? . . . never would I consent to the slow system of destroying life by starvation or by cruelty in any form.[35]

2LT. HENRY
COOK,
44TH TENN.
INF.

Some two or three weeks after the occupation of Savannah by the Federal forces Col. Brown came into our prison, appearing to be much excited and overcome with emotion. He told us that Gen. Foster had been relieved, and that Gen. Gilmore had just sailed from New York to take his place. He stated that Gen. Grover, now in command at Savannah, would command the department until Gen. Gilmore's arrival, and that he would go at once to Savannah and represent to him our sad condition. In a few days the colonel returned from Savannah with five or six medical officers, who went through the prison and made a close inspection. When they came to my bunk I was nursing . . . several other officers who were unable to walk or assist themselves in any way. I myself was able to stand up and walk for a few minutes at a time. I asked them why medical officers should come into the prison, and one of them replied: "We wish to see how much longer you can live under this treatment." Of course I was displeased at this apparently flippant and heartless remark, but I learned from others that the inspectors were really kind and humane, and were shocked and horrified at our condition. One of them stated that he would not have believed a Federal officer guilty of such horrible brutality if he had not seen it himself. One stated that in all his experience he had never seen a place so horrible or known of men being treated with such brutality.[36]

February 12, 1865.- A medical director made his appearance with a number of subs; we learned that General Foster has been relieved and that our situation under Gilmore, his successor, will be much better. The medical director declares that our situation is terrible, and says he will insist on a more generous diet.[37]

CAPT. HENRY
DICKINSON,
2ND VA. CAV.

After remaining in this condition until about February, 1865, we were visited by one of the chief surgeons of the U.S. Army, who I was informed, said if this treatment lasted for one month longer that there would be none of the prisoners left to tell the tale. An immediate change was therefore ordered, and much better rations were given us, but alas, it was too late for many who had borne bravely up only to fall at the gate of relief.[38]

2LT. DAVID
GORDON,
4TH S.C. CAV.

The medical officers sent their findings to General Grover, who had also received a letter from some of the officers in prison, including Colonel De Gournay, Lieutenant Colonel LeBreton and Captain Cantwell. He insisted upon an improvement immediately, and notified Foster's headquarters of his findings.

HEADQUARTERS DISTRICT OF SAVANNAH
Savannah, Ga., Feb. 7, 1865

Assistant Adjutant-General,
Headquarters Department of the South.

My medical director yesterday inspected the condition of the Rebel prisoners confined at Fort Pulaski, and represents that they are in a condition of great suffering and exhaustion for want of sufficient food and clothing; also, that they have scurvy to considerable extent.

He recommends, as a necessary sanitary measure, that they be at once put on full prison rations, and also, that they be allowed to receive necessary articles of clothing from friends. I would respectfully endorse the surgeon's recommendations, and ask authority to take such steps as may be necessary to relieve actual sickness and suffering.

C. Grover, Brev. Maj. Gen. Commanding[39]

Despite this warning, the situation at Fort Pulaski did not change. The suffering continued. A new surgeon arrived around mid February, who at once admitted the sick to the hospital, and began to improve the medical care of the men. The will to live devised drastic attempts to escape.

CAPT. HENRY
DICKINSON,
2ND VA. CAV.

February 1, 1865.- We hear no rumors of improved diet and still have the pickles and sour corn meal. Cats can no longer be gotten. None of us have money. Neither money nor clothes are allowed to come in, and we are in a deplorable fix. Our physician, Dr. Craw, who is believed to be a scoundrel without feeling or good sense, is today to be relieved by Doctor ———, who seems to have feeling for us; I hope he will partially alleviate our sufferings . . . The condition of many in the prison is truly lamentable. They are carried about by their friends and the tubs they use as sinks are very offensive . . . I have been sick and in bed for a week, and feel like my days are numbered. I suffer with a terrible dysentery and am very weak. My friends are attentive and under the new doctor I am trying tea and crackers and other medicines, which already make me feel better.

In closing this book I must express the opinion that no prisoners in a civilized country ever received more barbarous treatment than we have for the last thirty days.[40]

COL. WILLIAM
E. STEWART,
15TH ARK. INF.

I was taken very sick, and one day I was removed, wrapped in a blanket—I could hardly see, taste, or smell—carried in a horse cart from the fort to what was intended for a hospital. It was a small house I suppose, a quarter of a mile from the fort. I found about eight or ten sick prisoners. We had beds and a fire—the same rations, only the bread was in loaves, and the corn meal was baked in large cakes. After awhile I began to improve and could walk about.

The night I escaped from the Island, a salute in honor of the fall of Charleston was fired . . . I think it is called ten miles from the Island to the South Carolina shore—that is the route we took.

Hatcher and myself roomed together; the new doctor came to the hospital where we were; he looked at and examined the prisoners, and he told Hatcher and myself that we were well enough to go back to the fort, and that he would send us back. Neither one of us was well and we were very weak. I told Hatcher that if in our condition we went back to the damp fort, we would surely die— that we must get away that night or get killed in attempting it. He agreed with me. There were sentinels, then a boat guard and a gunboat not far from the island. We gathered up a haversack full of scraps of bread, and had a canteen full of water and were preparing for our trip. About the time we were ready to leave the doctor came in on us. I pretended that the things were in such a condition, because I was hunting for a letter. The doctor did not suspicion us and in a short time left, so now we were ready. I shall never forget a poor fellow named Davis from Florida. I gave him my uniform suit; he was very ill and could not walk. He asked us to take him along, but, of course, he could not go and we left the house. It was, I reckon, 8:30 or 9 o'clock at night.

We crawled out of the house and through the grass until we got to the shore. We had to go past guards and we could hear the sentries on the boat wharf. We went up the shore towards the fort hunting for a boat . . . we prowled around and in a little while found a small canoe, about large enough for one man—a very light and frail affair. I hardly think the boat was ten feet long and she was very narrow. I told Hatcher to untie the boat; he crawled in the grass to the bow of the boat, and then crawled back to me and said the boat was chained and locked. I asked him if he had any keys; he said he left his keys at the hospital . . . I told him to stay in the grass and I would go back to the hospital and get a file and cold chisel. I went back and brought them. We filed away and it seemed to us that you could hear the noise one hundred yards; finally we filed through the link; then we got two stones and put a hat over the chisel and drove the chisel into the link until it was opened wide enough to let the chain be parted . . . We soon launched the little craft and Hatcher got in the middle and I took a seat in the stern . . . We concluded that if we could pass the boat guard, and not be discovered by the gunboat, we would escape. We paddled lightly, were not seen, and then we went at it with all our might . . . After a while we got out of sight of everything, and then we concluded that we were going to sea, and that we would be swamped and drowned, but we kept on and finally came to land on our right.[41]

Hatcher was Henry Dickinson's bunkmate, who had visited the hospital several times to see "Hatchie" as he was called, and the two had talked of escaping together.

CAPT. HENRY
DICKINSON,
2ND VA. CAV.

February 19, 1865.- Whilst near the hospital I saw Major Stewart and Lieutenant Hatcher, who are convalescent. The latter gave me a ring for my wife and promised to let me know tomorrow whether the boats at the wharf are guarded. He stated that he and Major Stewart were thinking of an escape attempt, and asked whether a parole of honor could be implied. I replied I thought not, but, as both were weak and their escape would affect the sick, I advised that neither try it.

February 20, 1865.- This morning it was ascertained that Major Stewart and Lieutenant Hatcher had both escaped from the hospital during the night and made away in a small rowboat. It seems that the Yanks notified them yesterday that they must either act as nurses on parole or else go into prison, and this hurried them off. One more day and I should have gone with them, if Hatcher had sent me the information he promised yesterday.[42]

CAPT. J. OGDEN
MURRAY,
7TH VA. CAV.

Christmas Eve night, December 24, 1864, was one of the coldest nights, I think, we had to endure while at Fort Pulaski prison. I was lying in my bunk, praying that God would let me go to sleep and never awake in life. Yes, I was begging God to let me die and end my torture. I was cold and hungry, no blanket to cover me, no fire to warm me. As I turned over in my bunk, to warm the side of my body exposed to the cold, one of the boards fell from the bunk, and I got out to replace it, that I might lie down. In fixing the board in its place, by the dim light of the prison lamp, I saw beneath my bunk a trap door. For a few moments I felt dazed and really believed I was but dreaming. After a little while I gathered my wits, and this thought came to me: "Providence has answered your prayer; through this door you can reach liberty." Little sleep came to me after this discovery. I laid all sorts of plans only to brush them aside. At daylight I awoke my comrade, Dave Prewitt, of Kentucky, and communicated to him my discovery. I can, in my mind, recall the look of pity Prewitt gave me after he had heard my story. It was a look that plainly said, "Poor Murray, he's gone; the cruelty was too much for him." But when he saw the door, like myself he concluded Providence made it especially for our escape.[43]

After debating between themselves, presenting and dismissing numerous plans, Murray and Prewitt decided to get some advice. Captain Ed Chambers had been an engineer, and was familiar with the construction of forts. After a consultation with Chambers, however, the pair were despondent. He explained that the fort's foundation consisted of large blocks of granite, which would be impossible to cut through.

CAPT. J. OGDEN
MURRAY,
7TH VA. CAV.

When we finished this interview with Captain Chambers our hearts were way down below zero. For a few hours we brooded over the matter saying very little of it to each other. December 25th Prewitt and myself sat on the side of my bunk, talking of the good fat turkeys and luscious hams they were eating at his home in Kentucky, and how we could enjoy the turkey bones, if we had them, when suddenly Prewitt turned to me and said, "Ogden, lets try and get to where those turkeys and good things are; lets go down through that trapdoor and find a way out of this hole." It was all done in a moment. Down in that hole we went, up to our armpits in water and mud; and the coldest water I ever dropped into. We groped about in the dark, feeling our way around the wall, but could find no opening. We did however, find out that the foundation was brick, set in cement good and hard. After this discovery we found also that the wall at the water line was much wider than it was next to the floor. We got out by Prewitt getting on my shoulders and pulling himself out by the floor; then he pulled me out. Prewitt had two pair of pants, and part of an old blanket. He put on the pants and loaned me the blanket to keep me from freezing while my pants dried. I do positively believe I had to tell my comrades six million lies about how I fell down in one of the cisterns that some one left open. We gave Captain Chambers full details of our exploration below, but his advice was to stop our foolishness before we took cold and died. While talking to Chambers, he said: "If you had a good hard saw to cut out the cement, and a bar to pry out the bricks you might, in months of hard work, cut from one air chamber to the other until you cut outside of the guard line"—but this was doubtful. Well, this settled it, and we determined to cut that wall. We got hold of an eighteen-inch stove poker; Prewitt had an old dinner knife of which we made a saw; Billy Funk agreed to watch for the coming of the guard or officer of the day, and that night, December 25, 1864, we began what seemed to be a hopeless task.[44]

Murray and Prewitt were joined in their efforts by Captains Ed Chambers, Thomas N. Kent, and Wylie Hunter Griffin, and Lieutenants William H. Chew, and Hugh Dunlap. One night they were caught coming out of the floor, by Rufus Gillespie, a private, and took him into their confidence out of necessity. Every night they worked in pairs on the foundation wall of the fort, waist deep in freezing water, nearly starved. Persistence in digging out the brick mortar over a period of weeks eventually paid off, and a tunnel was made the length of eight casemates. Finally on February 28, 1865, the last brick was removed.

We had cut through forty two brick walls that were eight feet thick, making a cut through just 336 feet of solid brick walls, with that old case knife and poker. At last we were done and fixed upon the night of February 28, 1865, to say good bye to our Yankee cap- CAPT. J. OGDEN MURRAY, 7TH VA. CAV.

*tors. . . . By saving an ounce or two of corn meal each day, from
our rations, we had considerable pone to sustain us until we could
cross over the Savannah River and find friends from whom we
could obtain food. At 11 p.m. we began our exit. Captain Griffin
was the first man below. Lieutenant Chew followed, then Captain
Kent, then Dunlap, then Gillespie, Prewitt, then myself. When we
had all gotten below, Captain Chambers could not, he said, get
through the trap door, so we left him behind. . . . The night was
dark, and a drizzling rain was falling. All went well with us through
the tunnel until we reached the trapdoor in the casemate at the
end of our tunnel, which we were to ascend through to the casemate above. When we attempted to remove the door we found, to
our consternation, that it was weighted down by some very heavy
weight. It was a dilemma we had not counted on. We knew we
could not cut through another wall by daylight, so we concluded
to force up that door at all risks. Four or five of us got under it,
pushing with our hands and heads until Dave Prewitt could get
the poker under the edge of the door. When he pried down on the
poker he started the heavy body on the door to moving. Well, I
have heard the artillery of Jackson in the Valley; I heard the roar
of the guns at Gettysburg; I have heard the heavenly thunders of
the Rocky Mountains; but I say to you, all these sounds combined
were but pop-gun reports when compared to the noise those barrels made above our heads rolling over the casemate floor; and
yet, strange as it may be, the noise did not disturb the slumbers of
a whole company of the 157th New York Volunteers, asleep in the
very next casemate. After waiting for a time, to hear if the noise
alarmed the sentinels about the fort, we began to ask each other,
"Shall we go back or go on?" (We could not see each other's faces
in the darkness, yet I feel confident they would have been a study
for an artist's pencil.)*[45]

The vote was to go on, and all climbed out of the trapdoor and into what
was the quartermaster's department. They scrambled out the casemate window, using a rope they had made from old pieces of cloth and blankets.

CAPT. J. OGDEN
MURRAY,
7TH VA. CAV.

*I was delegated to remain and get rid of the rope. While the others
were going down the rope I found an open barrel of brown sugar,
ate bountifully of it and filled my coat and pants pockets. I forgot,
in my hungry greediness, that I would be compelled to swim though
the waters of the moat to reach the bank. When Gillespie, the last
man to leave the fort before me, slid down the rope into the water
he made as much noise as a whale, and I believe now he was then
doing his best to attract the attention of the sentinel. I saw him
finally go over the moat bank, I then followed down the rope, landed
safely in the water, and had reached the moat bank when, just as*

I started to climb up the bank, the midnight relief came in sight. I was compelled to roll back into the water and remain until the guard passed on. After getting over the bank into the swamp I found the boys awaiting my coming. But I want to relate that the moat water dissolved all my sugar and left me in a sticky condition. I had tugged at the rope, but could not get it to budge, so left it hanging out of the casemate window.[46]

Freedom was just yards away. A plan was devised to grab the sentinel, silence him, and make for the boats at the wharf. Just as Prewitt and Murray were about to make the move, Gillespie cried out for the guard not to shoot. All was lost, and any chance of escape forgotten as the whole garrison became aroused.

Why Gillespie betrayed us has always been a mystery to me. He worked just as hard as any one of our party to cut the tunnel through the walls, and ate his corn meal and pickle with us. I can only account for his conduct on the ground that when it came to killing the sentinel over the boats he thought, if the escape failed, we would all be shot; and this broke his nerve and made him shout as he did. Afterward, shame of his conduct made him take the oath, that he would not be put in the cell with us.[47]

CAPT. J. OGDEN
MURRAY,
7TH VA. CAV.

February 27, 1865.- Two hours before day this morning we were wakened by hearing several shots, and soon the Yanks came and called the roll. Captain Griffin, Captain Kent, Lieutenant [?], Lieutenant George, Lieutenant Kendall, Lieutenant Chew, Private Gillespie and Murray all came up missing. Early in January they had cut through the walls under nine casements down to No. 8 for the purpose of getting commissaries; finding that they might escape through the window in No. 8, they had foregone the commissary and last night being foggy made the attempt. They crossed the moat successfully by wading, but it seems on reaching the wharf they were discovered and fired upon by a number of sentinels at the water battery. Several guns snapped, and, though nobody was hurt, all hands were captured and brought to the guardhouse. The roll was again called at day-break and sunrise, and the Yankee officers all came in bedraggled and muddy. The hole was soon found, of course, and we had a stirring morning generally. . . . This evening we saw two of the number who attempted to escape under close guard at the guardhouse. Their clothes were still wet, and we have learned that they are to remain in close confinement.[48]

CAPT. HENRY
DICKINSON,
2ND VA. CAV

The men were manacled and confined in a dark, cold cell, and not allowed any dry clothing for five days. The guard, who out of curiosity to know how they ever got out, offered them a good drink of whiskey each. For

Immortal Six-Hundred
Lt. Charles P. Mallett
3rd North Carolina Infantry.

Clark's North Carolina Regiments
Lt. Robert B. Carr
Co. A., 43rd North Carolina
Inf. Carr died at Hilton Head on June 1, 1865.

Clark's North Carolina Regiments
Col. George Nathaniel Folk
6th North Carolina Cavalry.

Clark's North Carolina Regiments
Lt. James Marcellus Hobson
2nd North Carolina Infantry.
His son, Richmond Pearson Hobson,
became a hero in the Spanish American War.

Courtesy Dr. Charles Kellum
Lt. Thomas Jefferson Gurr
Co. B, 51st Georgia Infantry.

Courtesy Mr. James W. Benton
Lt. Peter Gooding Benton
Co. C, 11th Missouri Infantry.

Immortal Six-Hundred
Lt. Hopkins Hardin
Co. C, 19th Virginia Infantry.

this they told their story, and received the whiskey, but no dry clothing.[49]

Late in February better rations were allowed, and the slow road to recovery began. Prison life took on again the daily chore of alleviating boredom. Spring brought renewed hope and more tolerable weather, and the men emerged from their hibernation of suffering to seek hobbies and entertainments to pass the time. Letters from home and sutler privileges buoyed their spirits. Henry Dickinson planned an escape attempt by dressing in Union uniform, but was discovered and the pants taken away. However, he would not betray the Union guard who had furnished them for him.

CAPT. HENRY DICKINSON, 2ND VA. CAV.

February 22, 1865.- Fry, Hoover, Fannin and others are getting up a grand chess club. There are over ninety players, but only thirty-two can belong to the club. Any outsider may challenge a member and if he beats him four in seven games take his place. I have challenged Major Jones.

February 23, 1865.- Today Hoover played with me agreeing to check me with kings, castles and pawns. I beat the game in eight moves. Chess is certainly a great rage, and many games are played with great skill.[50]

CAPT. WILLIAM H. MORGAN, 11TH VA. INF.

While at Fort Pulaski the "Lee Chess Club" got out a paper, in pen and ink, foolscap size; I was one of the scribes and preserved a copy.[51]

CAPT. HENRY DICKINSON, 2ND VA. CAV.

February 28, 1865.- Today the Lee club commenced publishing a weekly paper, to be written and circulated. By request I am a contributor and wrote a letter from Hatcher to Zeke detailing the incidents of his escape. Tonight we had the usual dance at the lower end and for the first time I participated. We have plenty of fiddlers in prison and some play well.[52]

For prisoners of war, February was a month of heavy debate over their fate. The 600 Confederate officers knew nothing about what had transpired in the United States Senate, or what political moves on the chess board of exchange had been made.

The Hampton Peace Conference on February 2, 1865, at Fortress Monroe brought the first hope in weeks to the men at Hilton Head and Fort Pulaski. The privates and officers captured at Savannah were all sent north, leaving the remnants of the Six Hundred behind. News finally came that a general exchange had been approved.

General Gillmore was reinstated in command of the Department of the South on February 11, 1865, the same position he held in 1861. An improvement in rations followed on February 16 when meat was added for the next ten days' ration, and letters were allowed to be received.

On February 14, 1865, Colonel William Hoffman, the Union agent for exchange, asked General U. S. Grant to exchange the officers at Fort Pulaski.

Hoffman was informed that Union General John G. Foster had been given permission for this on January 5. Once again Grant acknowledged his approval to exchange the men.[53]

General Gillmore notified the Confederate commander of the Department of South Carolina, Lieutenant General William J. Hardee, that Grant had authorized all Confederate officers confined in the Department of the South to be exchanged according to the original equivalents of the cartel agreed upon in 1862. Now that all military objectives had been met by the North, the sidestepping of issues to prevent conformity with the cartel was unnecessary, and it was accepted once again. Besides that, the Lincoln Administration was coming under tremendous pressure from the public to reinstate exchange. Newspapers, hostile to Grant's stubbornness, also played a role in the decision.

A communication from Gillmore informed Hardee to send Robert Ould, the Confederate agent, to meet Union agent Colonel Woodford on February 16, in Charleston harbor for the purpose of exchanging the prisoners.[54]

Finally the retaliation was over.

CHAPTER TWELVE

"They that had fought so well
Came through the jaws of Death
Back from the jaws of Hell,—
All that was left of them,
Left of six hundred."

Alfred Lord Tennyson

THE 157th New York Volunteer Infantry, under Colonel Philip P. Brown, was ordered to the front, and left Fort Pulaski on February 22, 1865. The Confederate officers under their charge were anxious about their parting, fearing the new command would be harsh and abusive.

The troops who took the place of the 157th was the 175th New York Volunteer Infantry. They were under the command of Colonel Edward L. Molineaux, detached from the 159th New York, who was less than pleased with the assignment.

COL. EDWARD MOLINEAUX, 175TH N.Y. INF.

Febry. 21.- The if . . . has come to pass & behold me here on this dull lonely marsh island of Cockspur as Commander of Fort Pulaski & Tybee. Pleasant society, comfortable rooms, books & comrades, brigade & regiment far away & no associates except some 300 Conf. Officers & 100 privates prisoners of war & a garrison of 250 men. . . . I cannot understand my being taken away from my Brigade & given this miserable command. Genl. Grover insists that his order was for a "General" Officer—the telegraph operator says it read "good" officer. However I am promised that it will be but for a short time so patience, patience. I find my head is annoying me more than ever & begin seriously to think of resigning & I believe I would be justifiable in so doing. There is no active work before us & if I am only to be used for this contemptible work of jailor surely I can be spared to look after my health & business.[1]

230

The 175th New York Volunteer Infantry was mostly composed of very young and raw recruits, many of them paid substitutes, and consisted of every conceivable nationality. The Confederates cautiously befriended their new guards, most of whom were eager to meet Southerners for the first time.

The One Hundred and Fifty-seventh New York Regiment left us to join Sherman's Army. It was natural that we should regret their departure. For more than three months they had not been guilty of one unkind act or word. Under the most trying circumstances they had done all they dared to alleviate our sufferings. We now fell into the hands of Gen. Molineaux. His command was composed of all the nations and tongues of the earth, except English, Scotch, and Irish. We could not understand them and they could not understand us. They greatly feared us, and we feared them more, and the beginning was not propitious.[2]

2LT. HENRY COOK, 44TH TENN. INF.

February 17, 1865.- Our new guards are very rough in appearance, seem to be filthy black and of all nations and tongues, but they are old soldiers. They seem wanting in exact discipline and are loose and lounging. The officers exhibit great curiosity to see and talk with us, and already the rules of Colonel Brown have been infringed. Give prisoners an inch and they will take two ells.[3]

CAPT. HENRY DICKINSON, 2ND VA. CAV.

In this regiment there were a great many youths in their teens. I remarked on this in a conversation with a Yankee sergeant, who stated that these boys were put into the army by their fathers for the sake of the large bounties paid, which, in many cases amounted to $2,000 and over, and that these fathers were using the money to buy homes and lands for themselves. Just like a Yankee—he would sell his own flesh and blood for money![4]

1LT. WILLIAM H. MORGAN, 11TH VA. INF.

The new command ran a paranoid garrison, determined to prevent any more escape attempts or successes. Molineaux took extremely strict precautions, posting more artillery with the muzzles trained on the prisoners. Suddenly the surveillance and vigilance became strangling.

February 21, 1865.- This is my birthday; I am 35 years of age. I was quite sick last night with my bowels, but with the aid of opium I am better. It is a cold, cheerless day. The Yanks will let us have no coal for the buckets in which we make fire, and I went to bed to keep warm. Our guards are exceptionally strict about calling the roll, let scarcely anybody out to the sutlery, let only a limited number go to the sinks and otherwise show that they are awfully out of humor about the late escape.

CAPT. HENRY DICKINSON, 2ND VA. CAV.

Today they sent a man in from the hospital who had to be lifted along; they feared he would escape.[5]

February 22, 1865.- No celebration of Washington's birthday. The One-Hundred and Seventy-fifth have shown themselves very dif-

*ferent guards from the One Hundred and Fifty-seventh. They seem
terribly apprehensive of our escape. They are hauling all the boats
to one place and seemingly do not trust to the fort. We learn that
none of the sick at the hospital are allowed anything but bread
and tea; some of them sent to me today to raise some money to
buy food, but there is no money in prison.*[6]

Col. Edward
L. Molineaux,
175th N.Y.
Inf.

*Febry. 26.- Last night some of the Confederate officers attempted
a skillful but unsuccessful escape—by working an old vent hole
into the subterranean chambers they dug another vent into the
Commissary's casemate, then by a rope dropped into the ditch,
swam the moat & eluded the sentries under cover of a dense fog.—
They found the boats all guarded & were all recaptured—eight
attempted it.—thin men who could squeeze through the holes. In
consequence of this I have taken additional precautions & keep
guard among them constantly & their quarters are visited daily &
nightly every fifteen minutes by an officer.*

*I fear surprise being attempted & as our garrison is very small &
composed of recruits I have had a six pounder taken to pieces at
night & placed in Handy & Wilson's room with canister ready also
some hand grenades so that if the prisoners surprise the guards &
overpower them I can open an unexpected fire upon them from
my quarters. Every man & officer sleeps on his arms.*[7]

Capt. Henry
Dickinson,
2nd Va. Cav.

*February 27, 1865.- The guards in the fort were increased from
five to fourteen and a large number were placed outside, taking
one-half the whole regiment. At 11 o'clock the artillery in front of
our quarters was manned and ammunition conspicuously placed
near it. The half of the regiment not on guard was placed in front
of us. We were called out of our quarters and a thorough search
for gunboats, torpedoes, saws, files, ropes, etc. was made. During
the search the water battery fired two shells, I suppose to frighten
us. Sentinels, three in all, were put in our quarters to walk back
and forth, which would be excusable if there were no fort and we
numbered 3,000 instead of 300. No regiment ever before showed
such a dread of 300 unarmed and sick men.*[8]

2Lt. Henry
Cook,
44th Tenn.
Inf.

*The next morning all of us who were able to walk were ordered
from the casemates and formed in line upon the parade ground.
The garrison was drawn up in line about forty yards in front of
us. Two brass field pieces were placed in position and manned.
The garrison was ordered to load, which it did in the usual way.
We had seen several deserters shot, which was done in about this
manner, and we had read of the slaughter of the Mamelukes—but
what did all this mean? I must confess that I was without fear; I*

did not care what it meant. Suffering had left us without fear; We were soon ordered back to the casemates. The General only intended to intimidate us and show us the danger there might be in an effort to escape.[9]

Despite the rigid measures, the guard was not unkind, and Molineaux was not intentionally cruel.

Some of the Confederate officers I find to be perfect gentlemen & others quite the contrary. Two who were in the outside hospital on parole of honor & under treatment escaped. . . . The prisoners amuse themselves in various ways some by making rings, chains, crosses from gutta percha inlaid with silver or gold & beautifully carved. At the present time I am having a Corps badge made as a relic by them. One of them has a collection of seashells & is adding to them as I allow him to go to the shore under guard to collect— He is a poor delicate fellow & I think his health is impaired by long imprisonment. He is a gentlemanly, quiet man & I am glad to alleviate his suffering as I am for any of them.[10]

COL. EDWARD
L. MOLINEAUX,
175TH N.Y.
INF.

While the decision to make retaliation an official policy was only recently passed by Congress, those who had just survived their seventh month of its unofficial effects were notified that it was over. Word was received about the general exchange ordered by Grant, and Molineaux was informed by the arrival of Major Benjamin Thompson from Hilton Head on February 28 that the prisoners were to be immediately exchanged. Preparations were begun to pack up the men and leave Fort Pulaski. The cautious optimism expressed by the long-suffering Confederate officers could not be contained.

About the first of March we heard that we were to be exchanged, and were directed to be in readiness to leave at any time. We were satisfied that the orders had been received, as the officers and men came among us and offered the oath of allegiance to those who wished to remain in the United States until the close of the war. I heard that five or six accepted the offer . . . none of my personal friends did it. . . . It was on the morning of March 4, 1865, that Gen. Molineaux entered the prison and informed us that orders had been received to send us to the James River to be exchanged. We made ready to leave the fort, but were almost unwilling to leave, notwithstanding the fact that it had been to us the scene of so much sorrow and affliction. About it lay the remains of those who were dear to us, who had died from starvation. How altered the appearance of the prison! When we entered we were too much crowded; now, upon the eve of leaving, the passageways were almost deserted.[11]

2LT. HENRY
COOK,
44TH TENN.
INF.

CAPT. HENRY
DICKINSON,
2ND VA. CAV.

March 2, 1865.- Cloudy and damp, and my rheumatism troubles me. It is understood that we will leave in a day or two for exchange. Our guard must be anxious for us to leave; they are required to do duty two nights in succession, sleeping during the day. They have fifteen guards at the wharf, where Colonel Brown had none.[12]

CAPT. GEORGE
W. NELSON,
HANOVER ARTY.
(VA.)

The 3rd of March, 1865, dawned upon us laden with rumors of a speedy exchange. The wings of hope had been so often clipped by disappointment, one would have thought it impossible for her to rise very high. "Hope springs", etc., received no denial in our case. Each man was more or less excited. Strong protestations of belief that nothing would come of it were heard on all sides. But the anxiety manifested in turning the rumor over and over, the criticisms upon the source from which it came, and especially the tenacity with which they clung to it in spite of professed disbelief, showed that in the hearts of all the hope that deliverance was at hand had taken deep root.[13]

March 4, 1865, was cloudy as the *Ashland* lay at the wharf near Fort Pulaski. A two-masted, square rigger, the ship was even smaller than the *Crescent City*.[14] She had arrived to take the prisoners to Hilton Head, where they would pick up the remainder of the 200 waiting there. The retaliation was over, or so they were told. They had paid a dear price for their loyalty. Nine of the men confined at Fort Pulaski were dead, and lay buried in unmarked graves outside the fort. Only eight had taken the oath at Hilton Head, and six at Pulaski. Four were left behind, their condition so delicate that they could not travel. They would die in the days and weeks ahead. Most who were still alive were barely conscious and unable to walk. They left on stretchers, in a state of stupor, and would not even remember their leaving. Others, on crutches, limped under their own power to the boat, unable to straighten out their deformed legs, whose muscles were drawn from scurvy. Once proud soldiers leading gallantly arrayed troops now could barely walk without assistance.

CAPT. GEORGE
W. NELSON,
HANOVER ARTY.
(VA.)

On the 4th the order came to be ready to start in two hours. Soon after one of our ranking officers was told by one of the officials that an order was just received from Grant to exchange us immediately. We were wild with hope. The chilling despair which had settled upon us for months seemed to rise at once. All were busy packing their few articles. Cheerful talk and hearty laughter was heard all through the prison. 'Well, old fellow, off for Dixie at last,' was said as often as one friend met another. The alacrity with which the sick and crippled dragged themselves about was wonderful. Soon the drum beat, the line was formed and the roll called. 'Forward, march!' Two by two we passed through the entrance to the Fort, over the moat, and then Fort Pulaski was left behind us forever![15]

Early on the morning of March 4, 1865, Captain Sexton, with a guard, came to our cell, opened the door, and ordered us to fall into line. We marched down to the fort wharf, where we found the small steamer "Ashland" with the other prisoners, (our comrades) on board. We were placed in the forward part of the ship's deck, and I heard Sexton tell the captain of the guard, "I hardly think it necessary to iron these fellows. They won't jump overboard, but they need close watching." "Grape" was rife amongst the prisoners. The Yankees said we were to be exchanged at Fortress Monroe, and sent from there up the river to Richmond. I do not think our fellows took any stock in the "grape" of exchange. Most of them were in such physical condition that they did not care what became of them.[16]

CAPT. J. OGDEN MURRAY, 11TH VA. CAV.

Upon the hard benches lay the helpless forms of many of our comrades in the last stages of that most horrible disease, scurvy. We embarked upon the vessel "Ashland", and were crowded into the hold of the ship and lay down upon the floor. The helpless were brought down upon stretchers and placed upon the floor. We were very much crowded. More than half of our number were unable to help themselves, and all soon became seasick. As I looked upon the scene, the densely packed mass of suffering humanity, I wondered if a Massachusetts slaver had ever presented a scene so horrible.[17]

2LT. HENRY COOK, 44TH TENN. INF.

For the 160 men at Hilton Head, the same preparations were being made to leave. So certain was the belief of exchange, that messmates said their farewells, and wished each other luck. Diaries at both prisons became autograph albums, where addresses were swapped and the sentiments reflected the affections of one man for another:[18]

Soon the change which has so long been desired will be realized. We are soon to meet with dear friends, from whom we have long been separated—We expect much pure and unalloyed happiness—We expect to realize our brightest dreams of perfect bliss—Such as may be felt, but cannot be described—But, my much esteemed Friend, Let us remember, that we cannot escape the many trials ills and vexations of this life—The sweetest morsel of pleasure will be mingled with the bitterness of some new want—Thus it will be through this life—All its pleasures are worst than vanities. There is but one thing that will give solid comfort while pilgrims here on earth—And that is faith in Christ and love to our fellow man.

S. G. Adamson
2Lt Co. G 11 Texas Cav.
Hilton Head S.C.
March the 2nd 1865

****

U.S. Military Prison.
H. Head S.C. March 3rd 1865.

Lt. Mauck;

It affords me no little pleasure to leave with you under existing circumstances some expression of friendship which I feel for every Confederate officer who has been with us in this department for the last six months, and has continued here to the end. The memory of the mean treatment received at the hands of the Yankees since our arrival here unavoidably will be as lasting as life, and altho the heathens may be forgiven by Him, who hath said "vengeance belongeth to me and I will recompense" yet I can never forget nor forgive.

May your plans for the future meet with no unforeseen obstacle to their happy consummation and may your "shadow never grow less," is the sincere wish of Yr. friend, A. R. Humes

****

Special Prison
Hilton Head, S.C.

Friend Mauck

With what joy and pleasure unrestrained do I clasp the opportunity of giving utterance to my feelings, in expressing my regard for you. It is useless to enumerate the infamous barbarities and deprivations, which you have so magnanimously combatted. You have been totally excommunicated from the participation of domestic enjoyments—aloof from your accustomed sphere, and singled out as a mark for the shaft of calumny and vituperation. Despite all these indignities, which have been so eagerly heaped upon you, I have ever found your deportment, immutable and unerring. A reputation so untarnished in its bearings, that every True Confederate should be emulous of. Now that everything portends an approaching long-looked for exchange, which will doubtless result in our separation; it may be that the sight of a friend's autograph will not prove altogether unwelcome to you. With this slight assurance, at least have I written. Accept, in conclusion the well-wishes of your Fellow Sufferer. When peace and quiet again smile upon our now distracted land, and your thoughts have occasion to revert to Prison scenes on Hilton Head, think of

Your True Friend
Jno. R. Cason
Lieut. 17th Miss.

Address
Watson, Miss.

****

Military Prison
Hilton Head, S.C.
March 3rd 1865.

My Dear Finley,

You have my thanks for the friendship reflected in your wish for a line commemorative of our acquaintance, and the remarkable experience of our prison-life. Amid troubles too unusual to be properly appreciated without experimental knowledge, I have most gratefully enjoyed the intimacy of our association, and the influence of your warm, Christian bearing. The recollection of your character—happily cherished by the bounds of our acquaintance—I trust will serve me as no ordinary stimulus to range myself, as has already been your inestimable fortune—under the banner of the great Prince of Pilgrims & to this end, I beg to ask your interception at the mediatorial throne.

Very truly your friend,

Hamburg   Van H. Manning.[19]
Ark.

****

Capt. J. R. McMichael.

Dear Mc: I'm indebted to fate's dark decree,
For the friendship of heart I can hope for in thee;
For had fortune smiled on, the misfortune that fell,
Allotting to each war's dark prison cell
Would ne'er have been ours; and a stranger to thee,
I Still would have been:-thou the same unto me.
Yet we've met, and I feel there's a charm in the tone
Of a name that so nearly accords with my own.
A tie that will bind while life's fleeting day
Of mine from the earth is fast fading away.

Then Mc, when this war of destruction shall cease
And earth shall re-echo the plaudits of peace,
As you glide roughly on, o'er life's troubled sea,
Remember the friend you can find but in me.
Remember the trials of sorrow, and care,
As "prisoners of war" we together did share:
Oft look at these lines, a memorial they'll be
Of the best friend earth ever gave unto thee.

Jas. R. McCallum[20]
Capt. Co. D 63rd Tenn. Vol. Inf.
Address: Knoxville, Tenn.

****

When the *Ashland* loaded the rest of its cargo of 173 men at Hilton Head, she was so overloaded, and rocked so dangerously, that the commander refused to sail. A larger ship was necessary, and the men were transferred from the 837-ton ship to the *Illinois,* much larger at 2,123 tons. She was already carrying prisoners taken by Sherman at Savannah, so consequently the overcrowded conditions were unalleviated. Spirits were high as they left the wharf, home only days away. Comrades exchanged greetings with the Pulaski contingent, and old friends were glad to be together again.

CAPT. GEORGE
W. NELSON,
HANOVER ARTY.
(VA.)

We reached Hilton Head without anything remarkable happening. Then we took on our party which had been sent there at the beginning of the retaliation, or "Meal and Pickles," as we used to call it. This party had undergone the same treatment. The greeting between friends was: "How are you, old fellow, ain't dead yet? You are hard to kill." "I'm mighty glad to see you. Have some pickles—or here is some sour meal if you prefer it." The boat in which we started was now so crowded that there was not room for all to sit down. It was so overloaded, and rolled so, that the Captain refused to put to sea unless a larger ship was given to him. Accordingly we were transferred to the ship "Illinois." The sick, about half our number, occupied the lower deck—the rest of us were packed away in the "hole." But no combination of circumstances could depress us as long as we believed we were "bound for Dixie." So we laughed at our close quarters, at ourselves and each other, when sea sick. We were almost run away with lice, but we off shirts and skirmished with these varmints with the "vim" inspired by "bound for Dixie."[21]

2LT. JOSEPH
MAUCK,
10TH VA. INF.

Saturday, March 4th, 1865.- A day long to be remembered. President Lincoln again takes his seat for another 4 years. About 3 o'clock p.m. We rec'd orders to get ready in fifteen minutes to move. Soon we were on the march to the dock. Which place we reached very tired and fatigued as all were heavy laden with their baggage. Soon we went on board the U.S. Steamer Ashland, *where we met with our Pulaski friends, but found many of them in a suffering condition and one, Lt. Eastham, missing was left at Pulaski in a dying condition. We did not remain on the boat* Ashland *before we went on a first class steamer the* Illinois, *on this boat we found much more comfortable quarters than we did on the* Ashland. *Lay off the dock all night. I feel very unwell, but rested well at night.*[22]

CAPT. HENRY
DICKINSON,
2ND VA. CAV.

March 5, 1865.- This morning we learned that my friend, Captain Bailey, of Florida, is dying with pneumonia. We left five at Fort Pulaski to die. At 11 a.m. we weighed anchor and found the sea rather rough. The sick could not get up; nearly all were seasick, and as we had no buckets or tubs, our quarters became intolerably filthy. The sick relieved their stomachs and bowels in the pas-

sages through which we walked. The Yankee doctor paid no attention to the sick and many of them prayed for death.[23]

We left quite a number at Pulaski and Hilton Head, who were expected to die. Being thought past all hope of recovery, they were left behind. I learned from Capt. Perkins that they had received about the same treatment as ourselves, and their appearance indicated the truth of his statement. He related to me that he had made his escape and had been recaptured and placed in a box or cage just large enough for him to sit upright, and kept there for more than a week.[24]

2LT. HENRY
COOK,
44TH TENN.
INF.

Sunday March 5th 1865.- Early this morning I learned that Lts. Cameron and Foly of our party taken the oath and remained at Hilton Head. Also 10 of the officers from Fort Pulaski taken the oath & got off at Hilton Head. About 12 o'clock we hoisted anchor and off for Dixie soon we were out on the deep blue sea & its waves running high. Many of the party soon became seasick & soon they would call for "Enoch". We continued our journey all the afternoon & all night—I rested well most of the time.[25]

2LT. JOSEPH
MAUCK,
10TH VA. INF.

Within sight of exchange, it was strange that several took the oath, thinking to alleviate the conditions. The chance had been offered upon leaving Pulaski and Hilton Head. Only seventeen men "swallowed the yaller dog" as it was referred to. Once again among their loyal comrades, they took some abuse for the dishonorable act.

March 18, 1865.- I mentioned Capt. Kelly's defection. He left our party at Hilton Head, choosing not to return to the South. I did not see him & you may imagine my surprise and grief when I learned what he had done. If I had been called to assist at his burial I would have grieved for him, but his memory and many recollections of pleasant intercourse with him, would have remained for me to cherish through the coming years; but now—well—I will forget if possible his very existence.[26]

LETTER, 1LT.
JAMES E. COBB,
5TH TEXAS INF.,
TO MISS CORA
WILLIAMS

March 4, 1865.- We started at 11 o'clock and soon after Captain Halliburton and Covington and Douglass were severally called out and went above to join Colonel Baker and Captain Kelly, as was supposed to swallow the oath. We jeered and hissed the party till we were hoarse and nothing but bayonets prevented us from kicking them.

CAPT. HENRY
DICKINSON,
2ND VA. CAV.

During the passage to Hilton Head it was ascertained that Captain Mulvaney, of South Carolina, and Private Gillespie, of Texas, had slipped off into the oath-taking crowd, and soon after Captains Craft and Miner, of Missouri, followed them. At Hilton Head they were joined by Private Adkins, of Kentucky, of our crowd, and Lieutenant Foly, of Mississippi, and Cameron, of Tennessee, of the Hilton Head crowd. Together with Davis and Doyle, of Virginia, who went sometime since, this makes in all fourteen who have sold their birthrights for a mess of pottage.[27]

The plan was to exchange them at Charleston, according to correspondence between Grant and Union exchange agent William Hoffman.[28] Grant notified Halleck on February 22 to have all prisoners of war forwarded to City Point for exchange, as Charleston had fallen to the Union. That was the destination of the Six Hundred when they left on March 4, 1864. Fate dealt them a blow on the sixth when Grant suddenly notified Hoffman to discontinue delivering prisoners to City Point, presumably because of the military operations around Richmond. Yet, the Six Hundred were already well on their way to Richmond, passing Cape Hatteras that very day.

COL. ABRAM
FULKERSON,
63RD TENN.
INF.

We were told that the Federal authorities considered that we had been punished enough, and that orders had been issued for our exchange at Charleston, S.C. On reaching the harbor we were informed that General Hardee, who had been in command at Charleston for some time, had just evacuated the city and was retreating before the advancing army of General Sherman. It was then said we would be exchanged at Wilmington, N.C. When we reached there, General Butler's army on transports, with a fleet of war vessels, were making preparations to storm Fort Fisher, and we were again disappointed. The Illinois was then ordered to Fortress Monroe, with orders, we were told, to proceed up James River to the regular place of exchange, and to exchange us there. On arriving at Fort Monroe, our vessel streamed on up to Norfolk, and anchored off the city about the middle of an afternoon, and remained there until the next morning.

We arose early the next morning with light hearts and joyous expectation of being exchanged on the James, and of landing in dear old Richmond that day, but, instead, we were on the very eve of our most distressing and heart-breaking disappointment. About ten o'clock the "Illinois" weighed anchor, and with every one on deck, steamed down the river, and it was not long before we came in sight of the mouth of the James. It soon became obvious that the vessel was not steering for the James, at least we thought it was not, and all eyes were upon the prow, and the gravest apprehensions were excited in our minds.[29]

CAPT. HENRY
DICKINSON,
2ND VA. CAV.

March 9, 1865.- [Last] evening we saw a boatload of our prisoners going up for exchange. At an early hour we moved up to Norfolk Harbor and spent the day. Three or four of our crowd were allowed to go ashore under guard, but Major Weymouth, formerly of Point Lookout, kicked up a fuss and others who aimed to go were prohibited. Some ladies and gentlemen came aboard to see personal friends.[30]

On the 8th of March a large steamer, crowded with prisoners from Fort Delaware, passed us, bound for Richmond. They passed close enough for us to recognize each other, and many were the joyful greetings. But we did not move up the James River; hour after hour we lay at anchor. In the evening a number of medical officers came on board and went through the ship. They gave each prisoner a careful examination, and then left. We did not know the object of their visit at the time, but soon learned that we were not to be exchanged, but sent to Fort Delaware, as the medical officers had reported that our condition was so horrible that we ought not to be sent to Richmond. The ship proceeded to Norfolk to take on coal, from which place we were taken to Fort Delaware.[31]

2LT. HENRY COOK, 44TH TENN. INF.

We then called upon the captain and asked him to tell us the worst. He very frankly informed us that he had received orders to return the prisoners to Fort Delaware; that active operations had commenced at Petersburg that morning by an attack upon Fort Steadman by General Lee's army, and that no prisoners would be exchanged on the James as long as active operations continued. This was disappointment's greatest shock. Hope, that had sustained us in every peril, now forsook us, and our hearts sank within us. All was despondency and gloom.[32]

COL ABRAM FULKERSON, 63RD TENN. INF.

This proved too cruel a shock for some of the prisoners who weakened by disease and sickness, and seeing that they were bound for another Federal prison, gave up all hope and died aboard ship. . . . Why this move was made I never knew, but I suppose that after seeing our terrible condition that they were ashamed of their own wickedness and did not want any one in Dixie to see our condition, sick, ragged, and forlorn as we were, a very picture of Death masquerading in rags.[33]

2LT. DAVID GORDON, 4TH S.C. CAV.

Something had gone awry in the agreement to exchange the Six Hundred. There were prisoners exchanged at City Point, despite the excuse of the Confederate attack on Fort Stedman. On March 21, two weeks after they left Norfolk, Mulford enquired of Grant the decision concerning the officers at Fort Pulaski. Grant telegraphed back on the same day, "I do not know what has been done with the officers at Fort Pulaski. I sent orders to have them delivered to Charleston. Gilmore wrote me that . . . he had sent a flag to find an enemy to deliver the prisoners to. I have heard nothing since."[34]

Bureaucracy, poor communications between commanders and government officials, and the constant "revolving door" policy of the Union to shift commanders within the Department of the South all played their part. Apparently the remaining 430 officers who originally composed the Six Hundred were lost in the shuffle, and their priority over any other prisoners of war to be exchanged was not recognized. Or, as the men believed, their condition was an embarrassment to Union officials.

On arriving at Fort Monroe, the ship of eager and hopeful prisoners was told to proceed to Norfolk, and here with Dixie in sight, the anxious officers could no longer contain their desire for freedom. Escape attempts were contemplated and attempted.

CAPT. HENRY
DICKINSON,
2ND VA. CAV.

March 10, 1865.- We loaded coal all day and awaited orders. More ladies came aboard and we received intelligence that Johnston has been fighting Sherman successfully. About dark the hint reached the boat that we were not to be exchanged. Captain Harris, of Georgia, at once donned a Yankee dress, boldly walked up among the coal hands and a few minutes afterwards, as the tug left, jumped aboard; however, a "galvanized" suspected and then betrayed him. On landing at Portsmouth all hands were counted and the captain was fairly caught and carried to the town jail, where he stayed till 2 p.m. Then, under escort of eight men, he was reconveyed to the boat, and orders were given that he should not come above for any purpose. About 10 a.m. we were towed out to near Fort Norfolk, and again cast anchor. Clear and bitter cold, though it was awfully hot below and the stench insufferable. . . . Several are in a dying condition.[35]

CAPT. WILLIAM
H. MORGAN,
11TH VA. INF.

Our hearts sank within us; visions of exchange, of home and friends, vanished in a twinkling. Doomed to further incarceration in a detestable Yankee prison, when we had expected in a few short hours to be free and with friends! With hope, aye, certainly of relief, dashed to the ground, our feelings may be better imagined than expressed in words. . . . The Yankee guards on board the ship were at once on the alert, and with harsh and insolent commands, ordered and compelled, at point of bayonet, all the prisoners to get off the deck, and would not allow, after this, more than six or eight men on deck at a time; sentinels with loaded guns and fixed bayonets stood at the hatchways above us, and there was no chance to take the ship. One scoundrel threatened to shoot me as I stood at the foot of the ladder, with my hand on it, awaiting my turn to go on deck. He said to me in an insolent tone, "Take your hand off that ladder." I did so, then he said, "If you are an officer, why don't you dress like an officer?" I replied, "It is none of your business how I dress." Then he said, "Damn you, I will shoot you," bringing down his cocked gun on me, when I stepped back out of sight, thinking "discretion the better part of valor." How much the seventy men in the plot regretted not putting that plot into execution can never be told.[36]

March 11, 1865.- Weighed anchor again this morning, and put off for Fort Delaware without explanation or apparent reason. What are Yankee promises worth? They know that we now require watching and all are crowded down below, two being allowed above at once. We who had formed an organization at Pulaski met and discussed our situation. Finding that we had only ninety tons of coal, the amount the vessel required per diem, and provisions being scarce, we declined to take the boat, which we could have done easily, notwithstanding the two pieces of artillery aboard which were loaded in our sight. If we beached the boat, all of our sick must at the least suffer terribly; if we tried the ocean, our coal was too short to reach a friendly port—so on we sailed to Fort Delaware.[37]

CAPT. HENRY
DICKINSON,
2ND VA. CAV.

We now regaled our credulous minds with the happy thought that next morning we would go to Dixie, but imagine our pain and dejection, mortification and misery, to see the boat turn her head and steam off towards the ocean, and as we passed the picket boat the cry was, who are you, what is your freight, where are you bound? The answer was, "The Illinois, loaded with prisoners, bound to Fort Delaware."[38]

CAPT. JOHN
DUNKLE,
25TH VA. INF.

CHAPTER THIRTEEN

"Our Comrades Scarcely Knew Us, So Changed Were Our Features"

THE *Illinois* sailed on through the darkness. The news that, after all their misery and tribulations, they would come full circle back to the hell from which they had started served as the last blow to many, and two died on the voyage. To the horror of their comrades, they were not kept on board until reaching the Jersey shore, but were buried at sea within sight of land, leaving no marked grave to mourn, or chance for removal to their Southern homes.

2LT. JOSEPH MAUCK, 10TH VA. INF.

Saturday, March 11th 1865.- All on board became very despondent and gave up the exchange. Sailed all day and night until about 3 o'clock in the morning when we anchored in the brake water. Lieuts. Edwards and Dillard of our party died during the night. Also a private soldier.... I am still improving on the trip but in rather low spirits.[1]

CAPT. HENRY DICKINSON, 2ND VA. CAV.

March 11, 1865.- At sunset Lieutenant Edwards, of Norfolk, died in his bunk. That morning he was at Death's very door, and his friends begged that he might be sent ashore, but the Yankees were inexorable. Soon after dark I heard someone say that Lieutenant Edwards would be buried at sea, but as we were sailing in sight of land and must reach Delaware Breakwater before midnight, I believed it to be an idle rumor. At 9 o'clock, though, I found out that he was really being buried. Captain Harris, who usually reads the burial service for us, and Lieutenant Mosely, a nurse, were the only ones permitted to attend. I ran up and found a corporal who had the curiosity to see the burial, and after some persuasion he took me along. And thus only three of the poor fellow's companions in suffering were permitted to pay the last tribute of respect to his memory. I found the corpse on the deck. A heavy bar of iron had been placed firmly between his legs and two of the boat hands

244

were sewing his blankets tightly around him. Whilst sewing up the head, I saw one of them get a knife and cut off, as I supposed, a piece of blanket on each side of the head, but Mosely, who was nearer, says he knows it was the ears of the corpse; they threw them overboard. I suppose this was some superstition of the ignorant sailors; at any rate, the ears were certainly cut off. Before the body was entirely sewed up the two boatmen commenced cursing and quarreling, and I thought they would have a regular knockdown over the corpse. When ready for burial, Mosely and myself laid the body on a plank, which we extended over the guards so that, by a slight inclination of the plank, the body would slide into the sea. Captain Harris read the solemn burial service, the Yankee officers smoking and talking and swaggering around us, and thus we committed our friend's remains to the deep. May God pardon our wicked persecutors for this hasty and unnecessary burial, during which we were so shocked by their levity and profanity. I soon went to bed, for we were then in the breakwater and at anchor, the lights being visible during the burial. At 2 o'clock I was awakened by someone saying that Lieutenant Dillard, of Arkansas, a particular friend, was dying. I put on my shoes, and stepping to his bunk some twenty feet distant, found that he also was "sleeping the sleep that knows no waking." His bunk mate, a private, who, poor fellow, had no other place to go to, very unwillingly yielded up his place, saying he reckoned he was not in the way. Captain Carson and myself, after we had satisfied ourselves that he was really dead, quietly stretched out the limbs, closed the eyes and covered the body with his blanket. We pursued this course to prevent the Yankees from again shocking our sense of propriety by another burial in sight of land. Again I went to sleep, and again I was awakened with the declaration that another man was dead. . . . Thus we spent the long night in the midst of disease and death, with none to pity who could relieve us. Though under the protecting care of the "best government on earth" we were only "damaged Rebels." I shall never forget the night, and may I be struck dumb if I ever join hands with a nation whose agents have thus cruelly persecuted me and my friends.[2]

The thought and hope of escape had never quite left four of the officers, who had persisted in attempts to gain freedom since leaving Fort Delaware seven months earlier. Captains Leon Jastremski and Tom Perkins, together with Lieutenants Emmett Depriest and Cicero Allen, found a friend in one member of the crew.

The vessel put to sea and after dark I went on the upper deck for fresh air. I was soon approached by an Irishman, who was of the crew and was a Southern sympathizer. He said to me: "They're treating you like dogs. I'd get away if I were you."

CAPT. LEON
JASTREMSKI,
10TH LA. INF.

I replied to him that I would do so if he could show me how, and that I had already made four fruitless attempts. He then told me that in the forward part of the deck, where I was quartered, I would find a hatch through which I could descend to the forepart of the hold, where the anchor chains and sail duck, ropes, etc., were stored. That if I concluded to make the attempt and would let him know, after a while—after the prisoners would be landed at Fort Delaware, the day following—he would bring me food for the trip to New York, where the transport was to go to take on supplies. That before reaching New York he would come down to supply me with clothes and to give me a few dollars. "Then," he concluded, "if you're smart, you'll be able to get back South." I thanked him and told him that I would let him know as he suggested. Thereupon, I went down for a consultation with some friends. Three of them agreed to make the attempt with me. They were: Capt. Thomas F. Perkins, 11th Tenn. Cav.; Capt. Emmett E. Depriest, 23rd Va. Inf., and Lieut. Cicero M. Allen (a Louisianian), 2nd Ark. Cav. We decided not to inform my Irish friend, for fear that by some indiscretion he might have our attempt revealed. We swapped clothes with other friends, gathered some crackers and canteens of water, some matches and candles, and arranged with some of the Georgians to personify us at roll calls, and after bidding our friends good-bye and receiving their warm wishes for our success, we went down to the designated place of concealment. We fixed places to lie in with the aid of candle light but soon afterwards Captain Perkins, who had been suffering with flux, was violently seized with pains in the bowels and his ailment grew more pronounced, to an extent that caused us to insist upon his return to the deck above us and seek the assistance of the surgeon. The gallant fellow urged his right to risk his life in the endeavor, and that the responsibility rested wholly upon himself. We finally resolved to inform him that we could not agree to his view and that we had rather abandon the attempt than witness his increasing sufferings and danger, and that we would proceed to do so. He then consented to be assisted up the hatch. We then fell into a sleep from which we awoke by the cessation of the vessel's rolling and pitching, and the rumblings above indicating that we were at Fort Delaware and that the prisoners were being landed. For several hours we lay upon the anxious bench, but when the vessel began to move once more we felt that our absence had not been observed and that we had only to fear a telegram to search the vessel on her arrival at New York. At times during the rest of the voyage we would light the candle for an instant, eat some crackers and go back to sleep. Finally we were awakened by the firing of a cannon and soon after the ship's motion told us that we were in New York harbor.[3]

For those of the Six Hundred who arrived back at Fort Delaware on March 12, at 10:00 a.m., it re-echoed the feelings many felt a year ago upon their first arrival. Yet, after the astounding journey from which they were returning, even this place would offer a certain sense of relief. Seventy-five men were carried off the boat, unable to walk, underweight, and some already in the grip of death. They filled the hospital to the extent that others who should also have gone there were sent to the barracks due to lack of space. Their condition was appalling to those who had seen them leave seven months prior, with thoughts of home in their hearts, smiles on their faces, and health still good.

Sunday March 12th 1865.- Daylight found us running up the Delaware River, about 12 o'clock we came in sight of the Old Fort. The place we left on the 20th of Aug. Soon we anchored and was taken ashore on tug boats, there being not sufficient water to let the "Illinois" up to the landing. Here we came in contact with Gen. Schoepf, Capt. Ahl, Lieut. Wolf, Sergt. Randolph, Johnny and many others of the Blue coats. About three hours was consumed in landing all of us and counting and searching then came as usual before going into our quarters. Finally we marched in where we met many familiar faces. All seemed much relieved although in a Northern prison.[4]

2LT. JOSEPH MAUCK, 10TH VA. INF.

March 12, 1865.- At sunrise we weighed anchor and at 10 a.m. again anchored in the stream opposite Fort Delaware, which place I bade farewell to, as I thought forever, nearly seven months ago. Soon a tug came alongside and they commenced releasing us from the stench of the hole; a great rush was made to be first, but Carder and self got on the tug on the second trip. Landing, we were drawn up in line and the old game of counting commenced. We recognized Schoepf and Wolfe, each of whom must have indulged very freely in lager beer during the winter. Randolph, "Johnny" and other familiars were on hand, but the Ohio militia are gone and old soldiers are on guard. After counting and marching us for some two hours (during which our poor sick, to the number I suppose of 125, were carried in stretchers and ambulances to the hospital), we were finally searched for money, artillery and torpedoes. During the search I luckily saw my brother and Robert Jeter, and, being near them, I had an opportunity, by casting one eye on the guard, to have quite a talk.[5]

CAPT. HENRY DICKINSON, 2ND VA. CAV.

The prisoners at the fort had largely increased in numbers during our absence. They were in comparatively good health, and the contrast between their appearance and that of the emaciated, haggard and ragged survivors of the 600 was most marked. The

COL. ABRAM FULKERSON, 63RD TENN. INF.

photographs of sick soldiers, after their return from Confederate prisons, taken by the United States Sanitary Commission, and industriously and widely distributed for the purpose of firing the Northern heart, would have brought a blush of shame to the Northern cheek, if they could have seen a photograph of the group of Confederate prisoners, taken on their return to Fort Delaware.[6]

CAPT. ROBERT
E. PARK,
12TH ALA. INF.

March 13th.- About 100 officers and 1,000 men have been sent off for exchange, and 500 officers arrived from Fort Pulaksi, near Savannah, and Hilton Head, South Carolina. These sickly, limping, miserable looking men were chosen from the prisoners last August to be sent to Sullivan's Island near Charleston, and placed under fire of the Confederate batteries, in retaliation, it was said for the placing of Federal prisoners in the city under the fire of the Yankee batteries . . . in August 600 were sent and subjected to the harshest treatment, exposed in the sickly, malarial season to the severest hardships. For forty-three days they lived on ten ounces of meal and four ounces of pickles per day. Not a vegetable nor a pound of meat was issued to them, and consequently that depressing and dreaded disease (scurvy) became general among them. Their lean, emaciated persons were covered with livid spots of various sizes, occasioned by effusion of blood under the cuticle. They looked pale, languid and low spirited, and suffered from general exhaustion, pains in the limbs, spongy and bleeding gums. All this was caused by their rigid confinement and want of nourishing food. They were not given food sufficient to supply the elements necessary to repair the natural waste of the system. Nearly one out of every six died from this inhuman treatment, and on their arrival at Fort Delaware, for the second time, over one hundred out of five hundred were sent to the hospital. The feet and legs of many were so drawn by the fearful disease as to compel them to walk on their toes, their heels being unable to touch the ground, and they used either sticks in each hand, or a rude crutch, sometimes two of them, to aid them in hobbling along. Several, unable to walk at all, were carried on stretchers to the hospital. Our hard fare and rough treatment at Fort Delaware has been princely compared with that inflicted upon these scurvy-afflicted Fort Pulaski sufferers. Captain Thomas W. Harris, a Methodist minister, of the Twelfth Georgia infantry; Lieutenant W. H. Chew, of Seventh Georgia cavalry—both old collegemates of mine; Captain A. C. Gibson, of the Fourth Georgia; Captain J. W. Fannin, of the Sixty-first Alabama, formerly a private of my company, and Captain L. S. Chitwood, of Fifth Alabama, among the new arrivals, are all old acquaintances and friends of mine.[7]

Wednesday March 15, 1865.- Last Sunday 450 officers arrived from South Carolina. They are the same that were sent from here last summer. Of the remaining 150 about 30 have died, 20 taken the oath and 100 been exchanged. Their sufferings have been awful. By way of retaliation they were kept upon one pint of miserable wormy sour meal and pickles per day for 45 days. Some actually starved to death upon this diet. Many others have been afflicted with scurvy in its worst form, some still dying from its effects, and all whom I have seen show their bad treatment plainly. At one time one-half their number were unable to rise from their beds. This diet was continued even after many had been sent to the hospital in little better than a dying condition. . . . Amongst the number returned here are all my old friends and acquaintances, Charley Brand my old messmate.[8]

ADJT. FRANCIS
A. BOYLE,
32ND N.C. INF.

We were marched into the same place we had left more than six months before. I had no idea what a miserable looking set of men we were until contrasted with the Fort Delaware prisoners—our old companions. I thought they were the fattest, best dressed set of men I had ever seen. That they looked thus to me, will excite no surprise when I describe my own appearance. A flannel shirt, low in the neck, was my only under-garment. An old overcoat, once white, was doing duty as shirt, coat and vest; part of an old handkerchief tied around my head served as a hat; breeches I had none—an antiquated pair of red flannel drawers endeavored, but with small success, to fill their place. I was very thin and poor and was lame, scurvy having drawn the muscles of my right leg. When I add that I was in better condition, both in flesh and dress than many of our crowd, some idea can be formed of the appearance we made.[9]

CAPT. GEORGE
W. NELSON,
HANOVER ARTY.
(VA.)

The writer, with others in the officer's quarters, was at the gate when these same veterans arrived. Many of them were carried in on stretchers. . . . One of the returned prisoners, brought in on stretchers, was a gallant lieutenant of Morgan's cavalry, from Lexington, Ky. The brave veteran was almost dead, and as we gathered around to greet him, his eyes filled with tears at the sight of his old comrades, and he said, "Never mind, boys; I will tell Gen. Breckinridge all about our inhuman treatment;" and this threat seemed to give him relief.[10]

K. F.
PEDDICORD,
PALMYRA, MO.

The first I can call to mind I was back at Fort Delaware prison. I was so thin and changed when I got back there that my Lieutenants and friends I left there did not at first recognize me. I recognize the hand of Providence and the worth of good friends while recuperating from so serious a condition.[11]

CAPT. THOMAS
B. MARTIN,
HOLCOMB'S
LEGION,
S.C. INF.

CAPT. JOHN
DUNKLE,
25TH VA. INF.

We exhibited the appearance of having been treated with extreme cruelty and excessive horror. Our comrades scarcely knew us, so changed were our features, and so haggard were our countenances. Our number, too, was changed from what it had been, for we now only numbered one-third we had at first. Many of us had diseases from which we never recovered. Some died in a short time, some lived longer, and some linger invalids still [1869].[12]

On March 21, Colonel William Mulford was still inquiring where the Six Hundred officers were, whom he had been notified by Grant to exchange so long ago. He once again asked Grant for information, to which he replied that he did not know where the prisoners were.[13] There is no further official correspondence pertaining to the Six Hundred, and the unfortunate officers were to endure more months of imprisonment, which further reduced their number by twenty-three deaths in the dismal climate of Fort Delaware. For those sent to the hospital, the treatment did little to improve them. Captain Robert Park was in the hospital at the time, and described them thus, "The officers from Hilton Head and Fort Pulaski, afflicted with scurvy, are constantly complaining of hunger, and wishing for meal hour to arrive. The poor fellows . . . are a sad sight, as they walk in their hospital garb of shirt and drawers (which are oftentimes either too large and long, or too tight and short for the wearers) . . . How necessary a few vegetables are to these helpless sufferers. The 'best Government the world ever saw,' however, is either too poor or too mean to furnish them."[14]

Those well enough to return to the barracks were taken into the care of old comrades, brother officers who gave them clothes, held concerts to raise money, and tendered acts of kindness and goodwill which characterized the prison environment among the officers. The minstrel show was one fund raiser both prisoners as well as guards enjoyed. This was probably the most popular theatrical entertainment of its day, a forerunner to the vaudeville shows of the early 1900's. The prisoners enacted satirical skits based on the daily occurrences of prison life, the amusing along with the unjust actions of the authorities. General Schoepf permitted the entertainment to be held in the messhall, which was attended by Federal officers as well as fellow prisoners. Admission was fifty cents, though the prisoners unable to pay were given complimentary tickets. As much as three hundred dollars was raised per night, some in currency, some in tobacco which amounted to currency inside the prison.[15]

CAPT. J. OGDEN
MURRAY,
11TH VA. CAV.

There were in our prison gamblers, barbers, tailors, laundrymen, workers in rubber, and a minstrel troop, which gave performances in the mess hall of the prison when the commandant gave the permission. The proceeds from these shows went to relieve our sick comrades in the prison hospital. Sutler's checks was the currency of the prison, and these checks were taken at the mess house

door for admission to the show. General Schoepf and his staff of-
ten attended these shows. Pete B. Akers as the tambourine, and
J. Ogden Murray as bones, were the star performers of the show,
with Capt. Ed Chambers as the manager.[16]

The boxes of clothing and provisions, sent to the prisoners by North-
ern friends, were opened and inspected before they were deliv-
ered, and it often happened that the contents were appropriated
by the inspectors, and old clothes and army rations sometimes
substituted. Of course, these petty peculations greatly annoyed the
prisoners, and they protested vigorously to captain Ahl, and it
was believed that if he had laid the complaint before General
Schoepf, the pernicious practice would have been checked.

COL. ABRAM
FULKERSON,
63RD TENN.
INF.

The farce of opening the boxes outside the prison, the daily box
call on the platform overlooking the pen, and the amusing scenes
that occurred inside the pen when the recipients opened their boxes
and found old clothes and prison rations in place of the fine things
sent them, were reproduced on the stage by the minstrel com-
pany, to the delight of the prisoners and the chagrin of the Fed-
eral officers present. It was a splendid take off, and must have
been productive of good results. A portion of these exhibitions were
used in supplying the sick in the hospitals with delicacies and things
necessary to their comfort, and in aiding officers in the pen who
had no friends North to send them money or clothing, and the
balance was divided among the members of the troupe. This or-
ganization was, in fact, a charitable institution, for, besides af-
fording pleasure and amusement to the prison public, in my opin-
ion it was the means of saving many lives.

Lieutenant Peter Akers, of Lynchburg, Va., was the star of the com-
pany, and his ceaseless flow of spirit, his wit, humor, and inex-
haustible fund of anecdotes added immensely to the character
and enjoyment of the exhibitions, and he did more, probably, to
give life, spirit, and success to the laudable enterprise than any
man in the prison, and for his noble efforts in this behalf, Pete has
and deserves the gratitude of his fellow sufferers.[17]

March 31, 1865.- Captain Chambers and self first raised a small
subscription and bought some potatoes; finally the Christian As-
sociation voted us $70.00, and Pete Akers, Major Otey and other
musicians have had two negro concerts, getting some 160 pounds
of chewing tobacco, and about $100.00 in money. Captain Cham-
bers is expending it for onions and potatoes to be given scurvy
men, and now, thanks to these efforts, I think all in the pen are
improving. I wish I could say the same of the hospital, but, alas,
Death has been busy there and there are other martyrs to the
cause.[18]

CAPT. HENRY
DICKINSON,
2ND VA. CAV.

CAPT. GEORGE
W. NELSON,
HANOVER ARTY.
(VA.)

The prisoners came to our rescue, gave us clothes, subscribed money, and bought vegetables for us. For a long time after our arrival, whenever any one was about to throw away an old crumb or piece of meat or worn out garment, some bystander would call out: "Don't throw that away, give it to some of the poor Pulaski prisoners."[19]

The relocation to Delaware was like stepping back into mid-winter. Once again the men had to brave the cold, damp climate of severe weather. The end of March brought the first signs of spring, and prison life picked up where it had left off, seven months earlier.

The men were allowed to send and receive mail, and many contacted old friends in the North for money. The Confederate government and Ladies Aid Societies all sent clothing and personal articles. Letters were written immediately to notify family and loved ones of the relocation.

LETTER, CAPT.
GEORGE W.
NELSON,
HANOVER
ARTY. (VA.),
FORT
DELAWARE,
TO
MISS MOLLIE
SCOLLAY,
13 MARCH
1865

I arrived here from Fort Pulaski yesterday. . . . imagine my joy at learning that the mail route to you is open. I tried until there was no use in trying to communicate with you. I wonder if you have given me credit for the efforts I have made to get letters to you, and for the trouble I have been in for fear you would'nt get them & would'nt know what to think of me? I assure you this has been my greatest trial. Bodily suffering weighs little when the great hope of the heart is in the balance. I have heard of you now & then, through Jennie & other friends, as being well and in her last Jennie sent me a scrap of one of your letters to her, the handwriting & the name by themselves are treasures to me. We left Pulaski expecting to land at City Point but with such a Jonah as myself along the party might have known we would stop at Delaware or some such safe place. Well I suppose I will be exchanged one of these days. Sometimes I think if I were one of those generous people we read about in books, I would write to you not to waste your youth & beauty on me, but, my own love, I can't find any where in my heart, so selfish is it, any such inclination. As soon as I get fixed here again, get some big paper, stamps, etc. I shall write to you to make up for lost time. Won't you second me? Best love to all. May God bless you dearest.[20]

Due to the addition of more inmates since their departure, the Six Hundred were unable to be assigned their old quarters in the Bull Pen, located outside the fort. It was necessary to readjust messmates, and fit in where space allowed.

2LT. JOSEPH
MAUCK,
10TH VA. INF.

Monday March 13th 1865.- On arriving in the Bull Pen yesterday we found our old Division '25' crowded. Consequently we had to take up lodging in '34' where I found it tolerable comfortable as it too is crowded and Lt. Bell and myself had to take a lower bunk. Today I occupied my time in writing letters and visiting my friends.[21]

March 12, 1865.- We were soon marched into the officers' pen and rammed into 34, 35, 36, and 37 till we were too thick to thrive, but many scattered off with old friends, and self and Carder found a miserable bunk in Division 35, between Toney Davis and Captain Carter on one side, and Captain Patterson and Lieutenant Coon on the other. D. Garrett and Board have not been congenial for a long time, and for reasons not necessary to mention, I thought, with Board, that the old mess had better dissolve. So Carder and I still hang together, he cooking and I furnishing, whilst Board and Garrett split off, each to himself. . . . We got some dinner soon after entering the pen, fixed up a little, caught many a louse and talked with old friends.[22]

CAPT. HENRY
DICKINSON,
2ND VA. CAV.

March 22nd 1865.- Cold and blustery day, the proceeds of the concert given out. Tobacco to the destitute, potatoes and oranges to the sick. Also clothing issued from the Confederate Government. I drew a jacket and pair pants.

2LT. JOSEPH
MAUCK,
10TH VA. INF.

March 23rd 1865.- Spent most of the day in putting a set of buttons on my jacket and doing other work to it. . . . Changed the pockets in my pants, went to Prayer meeting in 25 at night.[23]

Life fell into a routine, but it was to be short-lived. As long as it lasted, all seemed satisfied, improving in health, telling their tale to old friends, enjoying a status of celebrities among the prisoners. Frequent visits to the sutler supplied many with pen and paper for writing, and blank books were bought for use as autograph albums. Collecting each other's names, addresses, and commands became a popular custom, and promises of lifelong friendships were sealed. The usual boredom and searches for ways to pass the time occupied many minds. For Captain Wash Nelson, it was most pleasantly spent thinking of Mollie, eighteen months after his capture.

Division 34 Fort Delaware
March 31st 1865

Two letters and a package, all from you, my darling Mollie, make me so happy this morning that I hardly remember that I am yet a prisoner. To find you still my own darling, after not having heard from you for so long, is such sweet comfort, not that I ever doubted you. I think I would die if I did that, but then to have again your own true word for it is joy indeed. I am so sorry you won't get a letter from me as soon as you expect. I was so completely out of everything on getting here, that I had to beg the materials for the one I wrote, and begging being something I have not yet learned to do with a good grace, I determined to wait until I received assistance from some of my friends, that has come and now I am ready & able to write whenever I will, so after the receipt of this, you needn't expect long intervals between my

letters. The articles you sent me are ever acceptable on their own ac-
count, and you know how I value them for the sender's sake: they fit
and suit me exactly. I must tell you, not to risk anything more to me by
mail; this was given me with the express understanding that all pack-
ages sent by mail would in future be confiscated. I am so delighted at
receiving this token from my beloved, that I don't bother about the
future, all I ask or wish of the mail is that it will bring me very often
such sweet letters as I got this morning . . . You asked how I have been
and how I managed to pass away the time. I have not been really sick
since I left here last August. I had a touch of scurvy, but I just deter-
mined I would not give up to it, and a kind Providence enabled me to
stave it off. Many of our poor fellows, who are now dead, would, I
believe, be with us now if they had had more strength of will. I passed
the time, while it was daylight, in reading, playing chess, whist, etc.
And when the long evenings came, I used to button my great coat up,
pull the cape over my head, and treat myself to a long, sweet interview
with thought and memory; some of these days, when we are together,
I will tell you who was the beginning, continuance, and end of all my
reveries . . . I will tell you many of the happy thoughts which, come
what might, kept me always in good spirits. . . . Love to all. God bless
you my precious one. Your devoted Wash.[24]

Although no visitors were allowed to see the prisoners, there were instances of Northerners visiting the members of the garrison troops. For purposes of curious entertainment, occasionally visitors, including young ladies, were allowed to walk along the parapet of the fort, which gave them
the opportunity to watch the officers below, going about their daily rou-
tines. It had unexpected results for Captain Thomas Chandler, of the 47th
Virginia Infantry. At age twenty-one, the view of young ladies afforded him
no little pleasure, as it did many of the bachelor officers "on display."

CAPT. JAMES M.
CARRINGTON,
CHARLOTTESVILLE
ARTY. (VA.)

After his return from Morris Island and Fort Pulaski to Fort Dela-
ware, [Capt. Chandler] was in bad condition, as may well be imag-
ined from the treatment to which he had been subjected. While
laboring under this disability, a number of young ladies from Phila-
delphia, actuated by curiosity to see a pen of rebels, came to Fort
Delaware and by permission of the General then commanding,
their curiosity was gratified. The rebel boys, from the pen beneath,
enjoyed the sight of the young women on the stockade above them
as much as they enjoyed the strange sight below. One thoughtful
and kind hearted young lady, before she left Philadelphia, and
perhaps thinking of the story of mother Eve and father Adam,
selected the biggest red apple she could find, and with great art
cut a hole in the top of it, taking out the core, and in the vacancy
within, thereby produced, she deposited a piece of paper with ten
dollars enclosed. Whether she was attracted by the homeliness or

the beauty and the flashing eyes of this dirty and ragged but still game and aristocratic Confederate soldier, the writer does not know, but he does know Chandler. The young lady pitched this apple over into a mass of two or three thousand Confederate prisoners, nearly starving, and who had not seen an apple for twelve months, and Chandler, with his usual good luck and energy, caught it in his hand, or mouth, and without present romance, commenced to devour it. He ate everything but the tissue paper, and was about to eat that, but it occurred to him there might be some trick in it; he didn't know the young lady as well as he did afterwards. He carefully unrolled the piece of paper and, to his amazement, discovered a ten dollar bill and the name and address of the young lady written upon the tissue paper. The story goes that if he had had boots he would have jumped out of them, but was barefooted! If he had had a pair of breeches, he would have jumped out of them; but the story goes that he had nothing but drawers on. Anyhow, he went back to his bunk, greatly rejoiced, and wrote the sweetest letter he says he ever wrote back to this lady, and in due course of mail a tender and elegant response was received. This correspondence continued, and Chandler was in love before he was released.[25]

The relative monotony of prison life was shattered by the news of Richmond's fall, and Lee's surrender of the Army of Northern Virginia on April 9 at Appomattox Court House. It was devastating to the morale of the prisoners, necessitating an emotional and anguishing decision to be made by the Virginians. Now that their home state had surrendered, how were they to handle the consequences? Were they obligated to maintain loyalty to the Confederacy as long as there was an army in the field? Meetings were held, and the issue debated, resulting in divided opinions. Union authorities expected them to surrender, by taking the oath of allegiance to the United States. Most of the Six Hundred, as was typical, refused.

The second concern of the officers was their personal fate. Would they be tried as traitors and executed? According to the Lieber Code, which was official policy, such a trial was legal.

They were helpless while they waited, in a dismal prison, to learn the answer. The courage and bravery it took to prepare themselves for what would be, was bolstered by prayer, and the love of those at home.

April 11, 1865.- This day's gloom I shall never forget. All outside was rejoicing, cannon booming. Inside, many shed tears; friends could not look into each other's faces. With many all hope was gone—we had reached the crisis where we had no country. After this day the high tone of the prison could not be sustained. Too many now thought only of home and were ready at the first moment to take the oath.[26]

CAPT. HENRY
DICKINSON,
2ND VA. CAV.

CAPT. WILLIAM
MORGAN,
11TH VA. INF.

When General Lee surrendered at Appomattox on the 9th of April, 1865, the prisoners were very much depressed, and almost the last hope of the establishment of the independence of the South vanished. A meeting of the Virginia officers was held to consult as to what was best to be done. Gen. Jos. E. Johnston was still in the field with an army in North Carolina, and Gen. Kirby Smith, commanding the Trans-Mississippi Department, was in Texas with a few thousand men. Whether we would abandon all hope and get out of prison as soon as possible by taking the oath of allegiance to the United States Government, which was offered, or await future events, were the questions discussed.[27]

CAPT. JAMES R.
MCMICHAEL,
12TH GA. INF.

April 11th.- Bad news. Gen. Lee has been forced to surrender his army to Gen. Grant. Woe be to the Confederacy! Now for the first time I consider our cause hopeless.[28]

CAPT. ALEX
BEDFORD,
3RD MO. CAV.

April 11th.- Oh, we hear such bad news, Gen. R. E. Lee, has surrendered his army to U. S. Grant. What will become of us nobody knows. Many conjectures about our punishment. It is enough to know our army has gone and our cause hopeless. Are we wrong? I think not, but we are overpowered. I cannot see the error of our way yet. God help us is my prayer, and submit to our fate.[29]

The anxiety was further deepened when news was received of Lincoln's assassination on April 14. It had been promised that field officers would be exchanged and the members of the Six Hundred would be the first to go. They were called out, with their baggage, but after waiting shortly, were ordered back to the barracks, never an explanation given. Even the sick in the hospital were dismissed, despite their condition, and ordered back into the crowded officers' barracks. Apparently, there had been a change of heart on the part of the North, and in retaliation for Lincoln's assassination, all chances of exchange, reception of mail and boxes, and regular rations were cancelled.

2LT. JOSEPH
MAUCK,
10TH VA. INF.

Saturday April 15th 1865.- Great consternation with the Yankees— early in the morning news came to the Island of the assassination of Pres. Lincoln and Sec. Seward. Lincoln died it is said, at 4 a.m. Sec. Seward yet alive but recovery said to be doubtful, several others were severely wounded at Mr. S. house at the same time with himself. Our men treated very insultingly by the Yankees. All that were out on parole were sent to the barracks—general confusion.[30]

CAPT. ALEX
BEDFORD,
3RD MO. CAV.

April 15th.- All well. Cloudy and raining. All astonished at seeing the flag at half mast this morning. News soon came of the death of President Abraham Lincoln. No one believed it at first, but soon found out it was a stern reality and all seemed to regret it, as they thought it worse for us. . . . . A barbarous deed.[31]

CAPT. WILLIAM MORGAN, 11TH VA. INF.

When the news of the assassination of Lincoln, which occurred on the night of the 14th of April, 1865, reached Fort Delaware the next morning, there was great excitement among the Yankee guards and prisoners also. The Yankee soldiers looked mad and vindictive, and the guards were doubled. Visions of retaliatory measures—banishment to Dry Tortugas, or worse—rose up before the Confederate officers. If retaliation was resorted to, no one knew how many Southern lives it would take to appease the wrath and vengeance of the North. If lots were cast for the victims, no one knew who would draw the black ballots. While all were discussing these questions in all seriousness, Peter Akers, the wit of the prison, broke the tension with the remark, "it was hard on old Abe to go through the war and then get bushwhacked in a theater."[32]

CAPT. HENRY DICKINSON, 2ND VA. CAV.

Then came the news that Lincoln had been assassinated and Seward probably would die. Guns were fired at half-hour intervals. For days and days the authorities promised and were evidently ready for mischief to us. We gave them no cause—we had not been responsible for the assassination; it was not our way of conducting war. We preserved our propriety by a dignified silence. At once, and for ten long days, all mails were stopped, all on parole to the island were sent inside and strict orders given to shoot any man who expressed joy. Even the games of ball, etc., were stopped for several days in our pen.

On the tenth day of April an order from the secretary of war was posted in prison, authorizing prisoners to receive clothing and food from their friends. I immediately wrote to Mrs. Edgerton, who, on the thirteenth started me a box weighing 200 pounds containing ham, eggs, cheese, sugar, butter, coffee, peaches and many other good things. The order of the tenth was annulled before the box was delivered, for nothing was delivered for two weeks after Lincoln's death, and during the time my box was confiscated. Many others shared the same fate. The Yanks pretend that all such things are for use of the hospital, but it is notorious that the sick get nothing except the simplest, poorest diet. The Yankee officials, as I believe, almost support themselves in this way, and yet, hypocritical race, we Southerners only are guilty of ill-treatment to prisoners.[33]

April brought shock after shock. The Confederacy had no good news of military successes. General Joseph E. Johnston surrendered to Major General William T. Sherman at Bennett's Farm near Durham, North Carolina, and the prisoners' last resolve to refrain from taking the oath, offered to them daily, was waning. Only a few kept the faith. After all they had suffered, putting their lives on the line and willing to starve, it was almost impossible to admit defeat now. The fear of how Confederate officers would be dealt with by a victorious and vengeful government was a constant dread.

CAPT. JAMES R.
MCMICHAEL,
12TH GA. INF.

April 20th.- My birthday. This is the thirtieth anniversary of my existence and nearly the close of a long, dark, and miserable year in prison. How long, O Lord, will this gloomy, crowded, and horrible cell be my place of abode. How long will this sad heart, burdened with sin and full of grief be deprived of the privilege of weeping or rejoicing with the dear ones at home. The fall of our capital and the surrender of our armies has banished the hope so long cherished for the independence of our Confederacy, and soon the U.S. authorities will rule the entire South. O how humiliating the thought of failing to gain that liberty for which so many have bled and died. Do, Lord, look in mercy upon the families of our deceased soldiers and now O most merciful heavenly Father to Thee do I ascribe all honor and praise for the many privileges enjoyed through all the days of my unprofitable life. Many as good by nature and far better by practice have been taken from time to eternity and yet I am a living monument of thy amazing goodness.[34]

2LT. JOSEPH
MAUCK,
10TH VA. INF.

Wednesday April 26th 1865.- We were all called out and the roll called to see how many there was that was willing to take the oath. The roll was called as far down as the G's, with the result as follows—yeas 243 and nays 279. They closed for today and finish tomorrow.[35]

CAPT. HENRY
DICKINSON,
2ND VA. CAV.

Finally, on the twenty-sixth of April, a roll of all was made out and each was solemnly asked whether he was willing to take the oath. Those willing seemed anxious to make it popular. They said what was true, that on the day previous all the privates save a corporal's guard had taken the "pup." Many of us tried arguments, persuasion and ridicule. In vain we urged them to remember that Lee was not the cause, that two out of three armies still existed, and must be sustained. They were determined to take care of themselves. They talked everywhere of the great majority they would have, and said the few left would have no other chance and would be hung or banished. As the roll was called, those refusing said "No" so defiantly that the authorities more than once threatened. Those willing generally answered "Here" and then, as they passed Captain ———, said "Yes" in a low tone; many indicated by their manners, etc.—anything else but a conscience at ease. Many field officers set the example; others refused to speak out. A very considerable number said no and immediately after made written applications to have the vote changed, and some actually wrote these applications before they voted. The morale of the pen was evidently gone, gone, gone. A count showed that out of 1900 officers only 600 had refused, of whom perhaps 200 had in less than

forty-eight hours made application to change their vote. Lieuten-
ant-Colonel Casey, Captains Wright and James, Lieutenant Carder,
Waldron and J. Waldron, J. Harris, Johnson, Howard, and Captain
Board all consented to take the oath. Lieutenant Tom Watts, Lieu-
tenant Latham, self and Lieutenant Rucker and, I believe also,
Lieutenant Hiram Burks refused. So much for Bedford men.[36]

Sunday April 30 1865.- The roll was all called again to correct
mistakes. There was a meeting of Virginia officers in Div. 34. Those
who had said No—to exchange views as to the answer we should
give if we were again called on to say whether or not we would
take the oath. Several appropriate speeches were made and all
save one thought it best to take the oath.[37]

2LT. JOSEPH
MAUCK,
10TH VA. INF.

During the four remaining days of April this vote was the great
topic of conversation, and a good deal of bitter, angry feeling was
engendered by violent men on both sides. The one side argued
that as Lee had surrendered and Johnson had agreed with Sherman
for terms which involved the surrender of all the troops remain-
ing, we could do no harm to the cause. Others said that we had
been given for the war by our states, that if some were now to take
the oath they could not get home without being tried for treason,
and that therefore the war continued and we were deserters. The
truth was between the two extremes. . . . We had just received
information of the formal surrender by General Johnston of all
his forces. Were we released from allegiance to the Confederate
states? This question troubled many. The Virginians, who up to
this time had refused to take the oath, determined to have a meet-
ing and consult. We met at 11 a.m. on Sunday. I was first called up
and spoke for perhaps one-half hour. I argued that it was yet too
soon to act, that the plans of Mr. Davis were not known and that
he alone could release us. Captain Carrington, Captain McCue,
Captain Swan, Captain Halsey, and many others followed, all think-
ing that the peculiar condition of Virginia demanded that we should
now take the oath and go home. The meeting adjourned for din-
ner; in the evening I was called to the chair and our meeting opened
with prayer. It was a most solemn convocation. No intemperate
language was used, but real eloquence, which was prompted by
our hopeless condition, caused many to shed tears. I shall never
forget this meeting. We passed no resolutions, we left each to act
for himself, but we were brought nearer together. We felt that we
were brothers in adversity, and there was a tacit understanding
that all of us would go home eventually and try to redeem old
Virginia.[38]

CAPT. HENRY
DICKINSON,
2ND VA. CAV.

2LT. JOSEPH
MAUCK,
10TH VA. INF.

Tuesday May 2 1865.- We were called upon again today to answer yes or no to the question, will you take the oath or not. I answered this time in the affirmative thinking it useless to hold out any longer. 159 officers here out of 2252 have refused to take the oath.[39]

It was not only the Virginians struggling with the decision, but all the officers. On May 3, those who still refused the oath met in Division 22 for a consultation. Despite the threats of exile from the country, many urged their comrades not to submit. Colonel Van Manning, who made "an excellent speech, full of fire and stirring eloquence" shored up the defiance of many. Still, it was an emotional and heart-breaking situation for men of pride to endure. The decision was on James Cobb's mind when he wrote his usual letter to Cora Williams:

LETTER, 1LT.
JAMES E. COBB
TO MISS CORA
WILLIAMS,
MAY 2, 1865

. . . Not only the privates, but all the officers except one hundred and fifty nine, have signified their willingness to take the oath. The rolls are being prepared, & are to be sent to Washington without delay; & it is thought that those taking the oath will soon be released. I am of the number who refuse. I have tried to view the matter in the proper light, & to disregard in my decision every consideration except a conscientious discharge of duty. If I have erred I cannot at least be accused of permitting motives of a personal comfort to influence me. At the same time, I do not reproach those whose action is different from my own; my best friends are of the number. I frankly confess my belief that the cause I love & have fought for, is hopeless—dying, but until the agony is over & its death anthem sung, I do not feel at liberty to abandon it. Overhanging the future is a pall, through which scarcely a ray of light comes to my sight.[40]

Davis and his cabinet were captured in Georgia, and little hope remained of any military success in the West. By the end of May, even very few of the original Six Hundred were holding out against taking the oath. Their journals and letters record the deep sense of honor and unselfishness they felt at the difficult decision, as they poured out their souls in silent words.

LETTER, CAPT.
GEORGE W.
NELSON,
HANOVER ARTY.
(VA.), DIV. 38,
FT. DELAWARE,
TO MOLLIE
SCOLLAY,
MAY 3, 1865

The events of the last few days have worked a great change among the officers confined here. The surrender of Johnston's Army, together with the voluntary surrender of one or two members of President Davis' Cabinet have combined to force upon us the conclusion that the Southern Confederacy is indeed a thing of the past. I need not tell you how I in common with others from our dear old state struggled against this conviction, hoped against hope, it is sufficient to say that I don't believe there is a man in the prison who has a reasonable belief that the Confederacy now exists. We have had meetings of the representatives of the different states in here, and the most solemn, most affecting meeting at which I was ever present was that of the Virginia delegation day before yesterday. The state of things was discussed from every point of view, opinions were fully and freely interchanged, and the conclusion arrived at that our government no longer existed in fact, that therefore our obligations to it were at an end, and our honor could in no way be compromised by any course we might pursue with regard to it. Then came up the question "What is our duty under the circumstances?" And the opinion was almost unanimous that we ought to return to our homes and to our loved ones, to support and to comfort them. Under this state of things on the following day our names were called for the third time to know whether we were willing to take the oath of Allegiance to the United States—the result was that out of 2300 officers only 161 said "No"— I myself am with the majority. I acted with the approval of both my reason and my conscience as well as with the advice of my friends and brother officers. God alone knows the struggle I have had with my pride, but I have overcome it, and I feel that I have done what was right. And now, beloved, may I look to you, whom I love a thousand times better than all else in the world for a little comfort—for the cheering word that you will sustain me in the path of duty and conscience? Ah! my darling, if you only knew the rack I have been upon from the fear that by a false step now I might lose you forever, you would have some idea of how I love you—God bless you always. If you love me write immediately. Love to all. Your devoted Wash.[41]

On the second of May the authorities again brought in their roll and submitted the question whether we would then take the oath. This time almost all the Virginians said yes. Tom Watts, myself and four or five others from Virginia still held out. I asked for time to consider, and stated that I hoped soon to be able to decide. This was refused me, and it was hinted that this might be the last chance. I would not take counsel of my fears. . . . My friends begged me not to run the risk of being left nearly alone and then perhaps tried for treason, but upon a count it was found one hundred and sixty-two officers that day refused to accept the oath.[42]

CAPT. HENRY
DICKINSON,
2ND VA. CAV.

April 25th.- I am now for the first time in a U.S. hospital, sick with remittent fever.

April 26th. Hospital Ward.- I am yet quite sick. Today a U.S. officer comes in and offers the oath. Most all take it. I refuse.

May 2nd, 1863.- Since last writing Gen. Johnston has surrendered all the Confederate forces east of the Chattahoochee River. It appears from what we hear that our government has ceased to exist.

CAPT. JAMES R.
MCMICHAEL,
12TH GA. INF.

Most all the prisoners are taking the oath and being released. I am at a loss to know what to do. I want to know what action my state has taken. I have taken the oath of allegiance to the C.S. Government and I must be convinced beyond a doubt that it has failed before I can abandon it. We are told that those who refuse to take the oath will be kept in prison and put to hard labor. I am determined not to act hastily or unthoughtfully. I am improving and hope soon to be well again.

Sunday, May 7th, 1865.- I am again in the barracks with my mess. My health has greatly improved, yet it is bad; but I will not complain for I deserve nothing good. I have now made up my mind to take the oath of allegiance to the U.S. Government and return (with a consciousness of having done my duty) to share the fate of my country and parents. We all consider our Confederacy a failure and it is for me to say whether I will take the oath and become a citizen of the U.S. or remain in prison or be banished. I hope my course will not be condemned by my friends at home for it is love for them that actuates me.[43]

2LT. WILLIAM EPPS, 4TH S.C. CAV.

May 2.- Oath again presented to those who refused a few days ago. All consent to take it except one hundred ten who still feel it their duty to remain in prison for the sake of our beloved country, the Confederacy. After neglecting my dear mother and family for four years and suffering the hardships of a soldier's life and twelve months and seven days of prison life for what I thought was a just cause, but thinking all hope of success is gone now, I consent to submit to the will of a victorious people, to return home with a sad heart and a conquered spirit, subject to the mercy of a powerful enemy.[44]

CAPT. ALEX BEDFORD, 3RD MO. CAV.

May 7th.- All well. Clear and beautiful. Heard of the surrender of Gen. Kirby Smith to the United States forces. All of the Confederate army is gone and we must have peace now. Had grape today of the Hilton Head prisoners. Heard to be sent to Richmond for retaliation. I hardly think it so as we have suffered death twice already.[45]

CAPT. HENRY DICKINSON, 2ND VA. CAV.

On the fourth [May] we had news of Dick Taylor's surrender and of the voluntary surrender of Secretary Mallory. This shook our faith very much. On the fifth Mrs. Edgerton, who never deceived me, wrote that "Joe" and "Kirby" had undoubtedly followed the example set them early in April. Thus was my last prop gone and on the seventh I wrote to Mrs. Edgerton that I saw no necessity to hold out longer, and that painful as it was to succumb I must at last say that I would now take the oath if offered.

May 15, 1865.- I am at sea without a compass, owing no allegiance, but, as I wish to go back to Virginia, I shall take the oath of allegiance to the United States as soon as it is offered.

May 16, 1865.- Received a letter from Mrs. Edgerton, telling me that I must act in a few days, and again offering to do what she could to get me out. I wrote that I would now take the oath, and if she could get me out on those conditions to do so. Information reached here that orders would soon be received releasing only those who had applied, so I at once formally wrote Captain Ahl that I would accept the oath. This was a bitter pill. Today a number of us were called out and received some old checks, drafts, etc., sent us at Fort Pulaski. I got a draft on Bank of America for $50.00, dated December 5, 1864, sent by father. The sutler refused to cash it on account of date.

May 18, 1865.- A formal paper gotten up by those who have heretofore refused the oath, and self, Captain Henderson and some sixty others signed it. It is to be sent to Ahl, and asks that we be put upon the roll as willing to accept the amnesty proclamation.[46]

Taking the oath was the only way the officers could possibly hope to be released. The letters do not always convey the pressure the men were under. Knowing their mail was read and censored by authorities, the writers tend to skirt issues. In his letters to Mollie, Wash Nelson tried to explain his peculiar position. Taking the oath was seen as letting down those at home, and he sought reassurance from his fiancee that what he did was acceptable:

Dick tells me that he wrote to H— yesterday, so you and she will get letters explaining our position at the same time. Of course, dearest, I could not say all I would have liked to say, could not, under circumstances where others would see them, urge motives which should be known to you and me alone, and plead my cause in that way which my own heart dictated and which would perhaps have given you a better idea of the pressure under which I acted than all the facts & arguments I might advance. One thing I will state on this subject now, and then I will leave it until I hear from my last to you. We have the fullest assurance that not one single Confederate Officer will be paroled from Prison; this comes from high authority in Washington. I know the report you heard with regard to the Point Lookout officers to be untrue, because those officers have been HERE for nearly a week, and are in our fix exactly. You are right, my love, in saying that we have been schooled to bear disappointment; there is only one hope in my life with regard to which I can not for a moment bear the idea of disappointment, and when sometimes my reason tells me I ought to take into account all the uncertainty of this mortal life, and

LETTER, CAPT. GEORGE W. NELSON TO MISS MOLLEY SCOLLAY, MAY 4, 1865 *ought to be prepared at least to endure disappointment even in this hope, my heart boiling with indignant love says, "no-" if it must come let it come and kill me all at once, to think of it is a living death . . . Your devoted Wash.*[47]

Nor was taking the oath a guarantee of immediate release. Of the men who took the oath on May 3, 1865, very few had left by June 1. Days after swallowing his pride and pledging not to take up arms against the United States, Wash Nelson still found himself in prison, impatient and depressed, sustained only by his love for Mollie:

LETTER, CAPT. GEORGE W. NELSON TO MISS MOLLEY SCOLLAY, MAY 10, 1865

Still at Fort Delaware, my darling, and no sign of being away from it soon that I can see, and oh! how long and how tiresome the days are getting! I thought I had patience to stand almost anything, but I find the continual expectation, and the never coming reality of release almost too much for me. I look across the river, see the green fields, sometimes fancy I hear the breeze rustling through the trees, or snuff the peach and cherry blossoms from the distance, but instead of being soothed by the gentle influence of so much beauty, I chafe like a caged tiger for freedom to roam at will . . . My space is so limited I have to write in riddles—apply the key of your heart to all I say and you will understand me, for the plain English of it all is—I love you with an intensity that I almost tremble at, and long to see you with an agony of impatience, and I believe, O sweet comforter, that you love me. Love to all. May God bless you. Write often to your loving, devoted Wash.[48]

By June 1865, most of the prisoners had taken the oath, and on June 16 all officers under the grade of major were allowed to leave the stark gray walls of Fort Delaware on their way home to an uncertain future.The United States Government refused to pay their transportation, so some walked, while others had written friends for train fare. In an order dated June 2, General Grant declared that upon taking the oath, each prisoner would be furnished transportation to the nearest port or rail station to his home. The rest of the way, which was still hundreds of miles in some cases, was covered on foot, often dangerous and difficult.[49]

Life for those detained in prison, the field officers and the few who had not taken the oath, became lax and not unpleasant. The enlisted soldiers had left, and only a small number of men remained, waiting for the formality of release.

Among these field officers who continued to refuse amnesty was Lieutenant Colonel Tazewell Hargrove, of the 44th North Carolina Infantry. Wounded by six bayonet thrusts at the South Anna Bridge where he was captured in 1864, he suffered so severely in prison that fellow inmate Lieutenant Samuel Parham had written a special request for his exchange, fearing more months

in prison would result in Hargrove's death.[50] Still the colonel remained steadfast against the oath. He was urged by his father, and Captain George Finley,
who was exchanged in May, to reconsider, and Finley wrote Hargrove of his
acceptance of their fate, on May 25, 1865:

*Dear Colonel. I reached home safe and sound just a while ago &
will leave to your imagination to picture the joy of meeting with
those from whom I have been so long separated. . . . Glad as I am
to be at home once more it is with a sad heart I look upon the
condition of affairs. Indeed Colonel we had no idea in prison of
what is the real status. . . . There is no law, no order anywhere.
Every man is the guardian of his own interests. . . . There is much
I would like to tell you but I do not wish to sadden your already
sad hours & do not suppose you would receive it. . . . Honest hearts,
cool heads & stout arms with willing hands are sadly needed. Will
you pardon me for joining your father in the opinion that you
ought to come home? I do not flatter myself that I can influence
you much & have far too high a regard for you to wish you to take
any step contrary to your own sense of propriety. . . . Your mother,
your father, all your friends think you can not possibly accomplish anything by remaining longer a prisoner. Bitter as it is nearly
everybody has taken the oath. Not one thing can be done without
it. . . . Genl. Lee's advice to all is to take the oath & come back as
soon as possible . . .*[51]

LETTER, CAPT.
GEORGE W.
FINLEY TO COL
TAZEWELL L.
HARGROVE

Tazewell Hargrove, along with the remaining field officers complied on
July 24, 1865, and was released.

The Six Hundred joined their comrades in history as part of a brief,
short-lived legacy known as the Confederate States of America. Captain Henry
Dickinson recorded their epitaph in his journal before they left, on March
30, 1865:

*And thus is the tale of the 600 told—fourteen have taken the oath,
some 125 have been exchanged, one Captain Board is in close confinement, 7 have escaped, 21 have died, 5 were left behind to die,
while the balance of us, sick or under the weather, have been thrown
in here without money to "root, hog, or die."*[52]

When the first roll was called upon arrival back at Fort Delaware, only
295 of the original Six Hundred could physically stand to answer the call.
Statistically, forty-four died of the ordeal, thirteen lie in unmarked graves at
Fort Pulaski, five died at Hilton Head, and twenty-three lie buried at Finn's
Point in New Jersey, having succumbed to their condition within days after
the arrival back on March 11. Two died aboard the *Illinois*, and two died
immediately after reaching home. Seventeen took the oath of allegiance before an army in the field officially surrendered. Seven escaped, all of whom

returned immediately to their regiments and finished out the war in the service of their country. Of those exchanged in December 1864, a handful had returned to their regiments, several had died, and most had gone home too unfit for duty.

They faded into the ranks of ex-soldiers in the South, and began the heartbreaking trial of rebuilding their beloved land. After one, and for some two years imprisonment, like Rip Van Winkle, they found upon release a changed world.

CHAPTER FOURTEEN

Homecomings

IN the immediate years following the war, life was hard for those men who had been soldiers for the South, especially former officers.

For the Six Hundred, a variety of fates awaited. For most, their health was damaged, making recovery a long process. Some would not recover, but return home to die from the effects of retaliation. Almost every man of them had been wounded, whether slightly or severely. Many lived long lives, and others died young of accidents and misfortune. They came home to find themselves fathers of small children they had never seen, husbands to brides they had left up to two years before, or sons of parents who had died in their absence.

In many cases, their farms were destroyed, and the necessity of starting over amid ruin greeted their arrival. Many were in their mid-twenties, anxious to marry sweethearts and pick up life where the war had interrupted, as much as three years prior. They were distressed at their inability to marry because of financial difficulties, and the loss of their livelihoods when they entered the army. Often their former jobs as clerks and teachers had been filled by Northerners who had come south to seek opportunities amid the misfortunes of others. As many were lawyers, or civil servants before the war, they were denied those positions under the oppressive military occupation of Reconstruction. They could not vote or hold office, even though quite often these men were the most educated and qualified to do so.

When Grover Cleveland became President of the United States in 1886, Southerners were appointed to two of his cabinet positions, the first time since the war that the South was given more than token representation. Several of the Six Hundred benefitted under the sympathetic administration, acquiring appointments in the Post Office, Government Printing Office, and other government agencies. But that was to be twenty years in the future.

* * *

267

Captain Alexander M. Bedford was among the first to leave Fort Delaware, being released on May 30, 1865. He arrived home in Missouri to find divided sentiment, even in the Presbyterian church he had belonged to before the war. His Confederate service was unacceptable to some. "They would not let me be a member without I acknowledge I had done wrong and was sorry for it . . . Gabriel will blow his horn a thousand years before I will do it. I had been in the Rebel army three years and nine months."

Bedford instead helped three fellow Methodists build a new church. His friends insisted it be called "Bedford Chapel" to honor him and the time and materiel he had contributed to its construction. Impressed with the care he had witnessed among those of the Six Hundred who were Masons, he joined that order in 1866. Then he fulfilled a promise he had made on Morris Island:

When I was blind and on starvation and made my promise to the Lord, I never thought of preaching, building churches, teaching in Sunday Schools and every other good thing. I promised the Lord if I was spared to get home to my wife and six children that I would be a better man. I . . . was near death's door. I had been working at making rings to get a little money to buy something to eat but I went blind and could work no more for two months . . . When I returned home I called in my family and we kneeled and had prayer for I wanted to fill my promise I made to the Lord.[1]

Bedford served as pastor of the Methodist Episcopal Church South in Savannah, Missouri until his death in December 1912.

* * *

When Henry Dickinson came home, he was forced to find a new profession. Since he could not practice law, he first worked in his father's saltmaking business, then turned to banking, putting to use the bookkeeping talents he had learned in prison as sutler of his division. He became one of the incorporators and first president of the Kanawha Valley Bank. He was also elected mayor of Charleston, West Virginia, where his family had moved during his absence, and where he settled after the war. His post-war career was successful, and he was well liked by all in the community. He died in 1871 at age forty-one, just as life finally rewarded him.[2]

Captain Thomas Pinckney rejoined the 4th South Carolina in April 1865, after hearing that all paroled prisoners were declared exchanged. He arrived poorly mounted on the only horse he could obtain, for which he paid the dear sum of over $2,700.00. His old company numbered only ten men, and it was one of the most fit for duty under the command of Wade Hampton. In one of the last engagements of which the 4th took part, Pinckney's mount fell with him, breaking its rider's leg, thus ending his military career in the Confederate army once and for all.[3]

Upon arriving back at his rice plantation outside Charleston, Pinckney found "El Dorado" vandalized and inhabited by his former servants. His beautiful library was ransacked, and books littered the yard. Although heart-broken, he started anew, first by persuading federal authorities to aid him in reclaiming his property. Then he and a friend hunted game and sold the meat on the streets of Charleston forty-two miles away, to make a living. After years of adversity, he finally recovered his rice plantation, and became a prominent planter. Uninterested in political attentions for himself despite the urging of others, he worked to get Wade Hampton elected governor of South Carolina, and put his energy into benefitting his state. He was known by all as a kind and amiable man with a good sense of humor. Married twice, he had seven children, of whom only a son and a daughter survived. He corresponded for years with the Union lieutenant who took his sword upon his capture, trying to recover it as it was a family heirloom. Ingersoll offered to sell it to him, which Pinckney refused. Mrs. Carol Pinckney, wife of Captain Pinckney's great-grandson:

> *It was a matter of honor that officer's swords should be returned— gentleman to gentleman . . . It was quite dear to him, but I guess HONOR was most dear! Each generation had passed the sword down with the injunction that 'it should never be drawn in a private quarrel nor stay in its scabbard when its country called for it.'*[4]

Years later, after the captain's death, his great-grandson managed to buy the sword from a relics dealer in Ohio. "So Capt. Tom's great-grandson owns the sword—Finally!"[5]

The other South Carolinians did not suffer the property loss of Pinckney, but Lieutenant Samuel Anderson summed up his lengthy absence in his last diary entry, dated June 1865: "Home at last. First time I have seen my wife since the day we were married, 1862."[6] Lieutenants William Epps and David Gordon arrived home around the first part of July. Captain Thomas Martin did not arrive home to Fair Forest, South Carolina until August. Upon entering the yard, he was met by a family who had mourned him as dead for six months, never having received any letters.[7]

Of the seven who escaped, all reported back to their regiments. Once past the salt marshes around Tybee Island, Major William E. Stewart and Lieutenant William Hatcher were fortunate enough to find a local man who had a son at Fort Delaware. He was willing to help them and took them across the Savannah River to the mainland and the Georgia Central Railroad. By an incredible coincidence they ran into a fellow prisoner, Lieutenant Sanford Branch, who had been exchanged in December. They spent the night with him, then left for Waynesboro, Georgia. Making their way to Augusta, they spent a week in that city recovering and reporting to the local Confederate military authorities. One day Hatcher was informed to report to Richmond, and saying good-bye to Stewart, they parted, not to meet again until nearly twenty years later in Baltimore. Several days later, Major Stewart was ordered to the Trans-Mississippi Department. Arriving just as the command was surrendering, he pressed on toward Mexico. When he reached San Antonio, he heard that the Union was paroling Confederate officers, and he surrendered at Columbus, Texas in September 1865, one of the last men paroled.[8]

Leon Jastremski, Cicero Allen, and Emmett Depriest landed at New York Harbor on March 12, 1865, and began their journey home from there.

CAPT. LEON JASTREMSKI, 10TH LA. INF.

We soon crossed Broadway and hastened to go down into a cellar saloon and eating place. We called for cocktails and had a substantial meal. We were in rags and looked like tramps. Fourteen dollars in greenbacks was our aggregate wealth. We went to a cheap lodging house and got a room under assumed names. There we gazed at each other and rejoiced at being free men again. Allen had been a prisoner for fifteen months and DePriest and I ten months. It was then Sunday, March 13, 1865.

The next day we found friends who gave us clothes and money. DePriest left us to go to Baltimore, where he expected to meet friends, and Allen and myself concluded to stay a few days longer to recuperate.[9]

Of these three men, Jastremski became the most famous. He and Allen returned to the army, where Lieutenant General Richard Taylor gave them thirty days furlough immediately. Returning home to Abbeville, Louisiana, Jastremski found a ravaged land which only led to further despondency and gloom. Not a home in that section of Louisiana had been spared. He found nothing left for himself, no way to earn even a meal, "too poor to buy it, too proud to beg for it, and too honest to steal it."[10]

He left Abbeville and went to his brother John's home in Baton Rouge where he was greeted with tears and open arms. To their horror, he was torn from his family by a company of the 93rd U.S. Colored troops and taken to Franklin, Louisiana. Once again a prisoner of war, he was able to sign a parole form and be released from his duty as a Confederate officer.

Jastremski was destined to become quite prominent in Baton Rouge. He founded a newspaper, *The Louisiana Review* and became mayor of the city from 1876-1881. During his term in office, he was instrumental in relocating the capital back to Baton Rouge, from New Orleans where Union Major General Benjamin F. Butler had moved the seat of government in 1862 when he burned the state house. The old capitol was restored and is still to be seen today, a fine representation of Gothic architecture. Leon was also active in veterans' affairs, becoming General of the Louisiana Division of the United Confederate Veterans organization. He was consul to Peru among other titles serving his state and the South. He died in 1908 while campaigning for governor of Louisiana.[11]

Another Louisianian who survived the retaliation experience was Colonel Paul F. deGournay. With nothing left for him in New Orleans, he returned to France for two years. Upon his decision to come back to America, as consul for France, he settled in Baltimore, where he led a quiet scholarly life with his wife and daughter. His time was spent teaching French, and translating French works into English. Yet, he never forgot the South and the Cause he sacrificed for. He was involved in veterans' organizations, and wrote articles for various newspapers, mostly about the war, and Port Hudson in particular, which he felt had always been overrated by the North, underrated by the South, and overlooked by history. He refused to discuss his prison experience and avoided any details. Shortly before his death, he wrote, "I will not write the history of those weary months—eighteen fell to my share—of humiliation, sufferings and privation spent in various Northern prisons, but will leave that dark record in obscurity. Let bygones be bygones; the war is over, and if I have come in contact with petty tyrants, cowardly sneaks, and fanatical idiots, it has been my fortune to fall in with not a few noble-minded, generous enemies, who treated a fallen foe with the true soldier's courtesy and kindness."[12] He died in 1904 and was buried in the Confederate section of Loudoun Park Cemetery in Baltimore, five graves away from Major William W. Goldsborough, a fellow sufferer at Morris Island and Fort Pulaski.[13]

* * *

Among the Virginians returning home in 1865, Captain George Finley walked over 100 miles to get home, nearly blind from the deprivations he had endured. His prison experience convinced him to serve God, and the following year, after recovering his health, he entered Union Theological Seminary, becoming a Presbyterian minister of several churches in the Valley of Virginia. His last charge was Tinkling Spring Presbyterian Church in Augusta County. He was very close to those with whom he had suffered so much, and kept close contacts, preaching some of the funerals of former comrades.[14]

Wash Nelson returned to Hanover County, Virginia in poor health, unable to earn a living. He married Molley Scollay in October 1865, and they lived with her parents in Shepherdstown, West Virginia. Nelson felt the call to the ministry, and also attended seminary, becoming an Episcopal minister. He and Molley suffered the tragic loss of several children at early ages. He eventually settled down in Warrenton, Virginia, as pastor of St. James Episcopal Church.

John Ogden Murray would be the best remembered of the Six Hundred, and an instrumental force in keeping the brotherhood forged in suffering together. He returned to Winchester, Virginia, and like his comrades, struggled to earn a living. Eventually he became successful as a contributing author for various newspapers. In 1891, at a meeting with Colonel Van Manning, then a congressman, and U.S. Speaker of the House Charles Crisp, Murray recalled their days of suffering together among the Six Hundred. Both urged Murray to preserve the history of their stubborn reluctance to yield their principles. He agreed, and no sooner undertook the task than both Manning and Crisp died.

On his own, Murray began trying to locate the survivors of the Six Hundred, who had become scattered across the nation. Through advertisements, hundreds of letters, and the list John Cantwell made on Morris Island, many comrades were located. Murray began writing *The Immortal Six-Hundred* and it was published in 1905, preserving the group's legacy as the only published account besides two diaries. After the book became well known, more comrades came forward. He wrote several books on subjects of the war, including one on Women of the South and a small volume on Jefferson Davis. The same year, surviving members of the famous band formed an organization among themselves, and titled it the Society of the Immortal Six Hundred, with Murray as secretary and Junius Hempstead as president. The purpose was to honor the role the Six Hundred played in the history of the Confederate soldier. They had been meeting at United Confederate Veteran Reunions for years, but with their numbers dwindling, they preferred a separate organization for membership.[15] Each surviving member was honored with a bronze medal, struck specifically for the Society. The tight bond forged in suffering remained firm until death.

The Six Hundred were famous across the South, and for a twenty-year period from about 1895 until 1915, many articles on local and national levels were written about them. Murray had planned for his book to be a fund raiser for a memorial to be placed on Morris Island, so the world would not forget their peculiar and horrible experience. However, his dream went unrealized.

In 1908, at the urging of John N. Southern, an attorney from Missouri, Murray was encouraged to introduce a bill to the U.S. Senate citing their treatment as a violation of international prisoner of war rules. In that year there were forty-two living members of the Six Hundred, and it was hoped some government compensation could be won for them in their twilight years, a half a century after the ordeal. The suggestion was also prompted by a bill in the U.S. Congress to award $2.00 a day to Union veterans who had been prisoners of war. Encouraged by Virginia Senator James Hay, Murray worked diligently for six years before the bill was heard by the Committee on War Claims on March 28, 1914.

At the hearing, Murray pleaded before the committee members that unless the issue of retaliation was addressed, it would remain a blot on the record of the United States, and in case of another war, the same situation could occur against American prisoners of war. With the First World War merely months away, the discussion was timely. However, the committee seemed unwilling to believe the Six Hundred were ever placed under fire by order of Secretary of War Edwin M. Stanton. There can be no doubt that Stanton knew of the plan. The U.S. Congress was aware of Foster's actions during the debate on the retaliation policy.

Despite Murray's references to official correspondence, coupled with depositions from comrades, the bill was killed in committee. This unwillingness to admit that the United States engaged in retaliation was reflected in a document issued by the government called, "Selected Topics Connected With the Laws of Warfare as of August 1, 1914." In regard to retaliation, it blatantly stated that "instances occurred in this country during the Revolutionary War, as well as during the War of 1812; But there was no instance in which retaliation, beyond the measure of severe confinement, took place in respect to prisoners of war."[16]

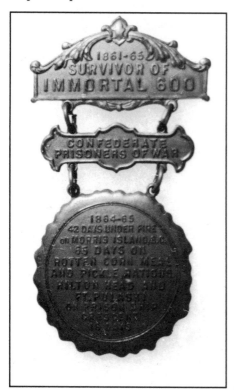

Courtesy Mr. T. C. Greever
Medal of the Society of the Immortal Six Hundred.

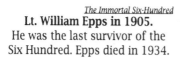
The Immortal Six-Hundred
Lt. William Epps in 1905.
He was the last survivor of the Six Hundred. Epps died in 1934.

Another reason for the bill's defeat lay in the power of the Union veterans' organization, the Grand Army of the Republic (GAR). Composed of 400,000 Union veterans, its political might was formidable, even damaging Cleveland's presidency for his magnanimity towards ex-Confederate soldiers. The GAR staunchly opposed any compensation to Confederate veterans, while at the same time drawing pensions paid for by taxes from those same veterans. The amount requested by the ex-Confederate officers for crimes against prisoners of war was a $5,000.00 claim to be paid by the U.S. government to each of the survivors of the Six Hundred or to their heirs. When the former U.S. provost marshal on Hilton Head, Benjamin Thompson, heard about it, he wrote a letter to the editor of his local newspaper in Minneapolis, blatantly denying any wrongdoing:

> The orders about the rations were explicit. Serve the same kind and quantity of food that is being given our men in Salisbury. Thus we had the menu from week to week, and from it directed the diet of the prisoners. When we received word that Salisbury was serving a pint of cornmeal per day and a pickle as an appetizer, the provost marshal general promptly decided not to give the pickle, and none were issued. The retaliation was strictly confined to the rations . . . The best proof of their treatment was that in all those months not a man died, and when they left Hilton Head the 600 were all able to march. They were as healthy looking as if they had been faring sumptuously.[17]

Thompson was writing forty-seven years after the fact, either living in a state of denial for the cruelty, or suffering from delusions. As with many war claims, the bill to compensate the Six Hundred was defeated.[18]

Junius Hempstead was dedicated to the brother officers with whom he had shared the honor of being one of the Six Hundred. He returned to Dubuque, Iowa in 1865, a twenty-two-year-old veteran, and spent several months recovering his health. In November 1865, he wrote to Captain John Cantwell, "I am doing nothing at present but loaf at home."[19] At first he seemed at a loss as to what to do with his life. He entered into the profession of bookkeeping, then began a writing career. In the same letter to Cantwell, he speaks of a book he wrote about the Six Hundred and their prison experience. After reading sensationalized Northern accounts of Andersonville, Hempstead was particularly outraged, and he wrote in November 1865, "I am so much obliged to you for the list of names and it is done up in your usual neat hand. . . . I have some three hundred and fifty pages and with the list will make four hundred." He decided "not to publish immediately for it is rather strong for the times and I would be run from the country. . . . I have not written it for any other purpose than to show the other side of the question. I cannot sit by and hear of Andersonville and other Southern prisons and hear them run down our brave South, when they themselves have acted a hundred times more brutally."[20] For some reason, this book was never published. He wrote poetry and fiction, enjoying a modest career as a writer. But a sense of restlessness and dissatisfaction plagued Hempstead. After living in New Orleans, Chicago, and Texas, he moved to Jennings, Louisiana. Several of his literary works dealt with the war, and reflected the sensitivity of a man who had suffered and faced death, hinting that his imprisonment may have colored his outlook. In one of his last works, *The Deschanos*, about the early years of the war, a character reflects upon an individual's impact on the scheme of things with these words:

I am alone in the world—a man here and there that drops out of existence does not count in the reckoning of numbers. He is here, he is there, and then he is gone—just a ripple in life—nothing more.[21]

Hempstead was also bitter toward his old school, the Virginia Military Institute. In correspondence with John Ogden Murray, he shared his feelings that the Institute had ignored the contributions of those who would have been the graduating classes during the war, and excluding them from the school directory as alumni. "They state I was at the V.M.I. so short a time. The word alumnus means a graduate. I am sure it was not my fault. I would have taken the four years course had the war not commenced. I was fitting myself for a Civil and topographical engineer. . . . The fourth class suffered by far (in dead and wounded) and fighting qualities more than the other three classes that went from the V.M.I."[22] The point was argued before the Alumni Association, and eventually the school directory included all students who attended the Institute, even for a day.

He was elected president of the Society of the Immortal Six Hundred, serving for over five years in that office. He married and had four children. Sometime before 1880, he became estranged from his family, and moved to Louisiana, where he resided part of the year at a boarding house in New Orleans. He spent summers with a sister and brother in Jennings, a lonely, reclusive veteran whose life centered around veterans associations and the Society. He died in September 1920, penniless, and was buried in an unmarked grave in Jennings. Murray died a year later in 1921, and the driving forces of the Society were both gone. The remaining survivors continued to keep the organization alive, the last "immortal," Lieutenant William Epps, of the 4th S.C. Cavalry dying in 1934.

Aside from Hempstead and Murray, the most important person to the history of the Six Hundred was Captain John Cantwell. After all, he had started the union of kindred spirits by compiling the first list of prisoner names on Morris Island, a document which served as the tie that binds. After returning to Wilmington, North Carolina, Cantwell was not idle. He organized the first Confederate Veterans unit in the South in 1866 with the founding of the 3rd North Carolina Infantry Association, which preceded the United Confederate Veterans. His unceasing commitment to the story of the Six Hundred was lauded years later by a fellow Wilmingtonian, Captain Walter McRae, who remembered their trial by starvation:

*But of all these things and much more—the many attempts at es-
cape, always betrayed, the sickness, the wounds, the deaths, the organized efforts for mutual help, though there was little to give except
sympathy and literally a cup of cold water for His sake, the names,
rank, command, and native States of all the six hundred—are they
not written and minutely set forth in Col. John L. Cantwell's book of
statistics and notes which he began to collect from the start and which,
with untiring zeal and great patience, he continued to enlarge and
perfect on the spot and down even to the present day and which he
preserved, Heaven knows how, amid all the chances and changes of
our prison life, so that it furnishes the only authentic statement of
those trying times which is now extant. . . . Glancing over this little
book, the eye rests on this pathetic sentence: 'Was not allowed to mark
the graves of brother officers at Fort Pulaski, though headboards
were prepared (by the prisoners) for all the dead.' What need of any
further comment?*[23]

For the Georgians who returned to a state devastated by Sherman's army,
the hardships of rebuilding the land would be a long and painful process.
James McMichael went back to the family farm in Buena Vista, Georgia. After
recovering from the physical debilities of retaliation, he chose a future career as a physician-farmer, attending the Medical College of the University
of Georgia at Athens. In 1866 he was married and settled into a comfortable
life spent between two residences, one in Schley County and the family farm
in Marion County, Georgia. At the insistence of friends he served a term in
the legislature after Carpetbag rule ended, from 1886-1887.[24]

Young Tom Chandler was released from Fort Delaware on June 16, 1865,
along with most of the Virginians, and returned to the Shenandoah Valley.
He spent a few years working as a clerk at the Homestead, a popular nineteenth-century spa in the mountains of Virginia which is well known today.
Then he returned to his family land in Bowling Green, Virginia and settled
into farming. Six years after retrieving an apple tossed from a prison parapet, he married Miss Virginia Alsop of Philadelphia whose address he had
found inside. After thirty years of wedded bliss she, like most of the wives
of the Six Hundred, preceded her husband in death, and Captain Chandler
moved to Washington, D.C. where he became the proprietor of Callahan's, a
then-famous restaurant of that city.[25] He and Murray continued a friendship
and visited regularly, along with Bruce Gibson and James M. Carrington, all
of whom lived within the area between Washington D.C. and Winchester,
Virginia. In 1910, Chandler returned to Hilton Head, Morris Island, and Fort
Pulaski, on a curiosity visit. Retracing the grounds of the experience served
as a catharsis, and he wrote Murray of his emotional experience. The letter
was printed in the Society minutes of 1911:

*After the Mobile Reunion, 1910, I determined to indulge my desire of
years, to visit Morris Island, Hilton Head and Fort Pulaski, to look*

upon the grounds and places made sacred by your sufferings, and deaths of our beloved comrades. We alone know . . . On the 23rd day of July I landed in Charleston, S.C. After a day of rest, I procured a steam launch, with guide and sailed down to Fort Sumter. Then over to Morris Island . . . As I stood upon the site of the prison pen, time in her flight seemed to stop, and again I was there with you all, the Negro guards were there, their brutal Commander, Hallowell, was there, the noise of the guns from the Yankee forts sounded in my ears. I could hear the shell of our own gun bursting over our heads. I could see the four hard-tack crackers and one ounce of meat dealt out to us as the daily ration. I could see you suffering men digging in the sand to quench your thirst with the insipid water oozing from the sand. I could hear the brutal laugh of Hallowell and his niggers as they gloated over your suffering. But my heart swelled in pride at your dignified and manly bearing and your faith in God and the cause we loved, and I said in silent prayer from my heart, "Thank God, I was one of the 600, and these are my true comrades, Confederate soldiers, who will die for principles sake." I awoke from this reverie of the past, and from the ideal came back to the real life.

The wind storms coming from the ocean have torn the site of our prison pen and the ocean has washed the sands where stood our prison tents, into gullys. The two Batteries, Waggoner and Gregg, between which were our prison stockade, are gone, only a trace left of them . . . I went down the beach to find the old wharf and the schooner hulks where we were landed from the ship on that September morning 46 years ago. Closing my eyes, I saw emaciated men huddled aboard those old schooner hulks, I saw the march up the Beach, where the torture of fire and starvation was to begin in the stockade pen. My heart turned in bitterness for those who caused all our pain. God forgive me. My heart beat in hate against them before I left the Island. I gathered from the site of our prison pen some shells, that I could bring you each one. Not for hate sake, nor to rekindle in your hearts uncharity. But that you might all keep this souvenir and recall to your children and grandchildren those days when your manhood was tried by fire. At Hilton Head, I could hardly locate the site of our prison pen. Houses are built over the spot, peace and contentment live now, where once cruelty tortured its victims . . . I left the scenes of our torture, sailing back to Charleston . . . From Charleston, I took Court steamer, and went to Savannah, Ga., from there I went down the River to Cockspur Island, where at the River's mouth is located Fort Pulaski. As I landed on the wharf of the Fort, vision of the November day came to me . . . Exhibiting my pass and permit to visit the Fort, the old sargent could not help but ask why I visited this forsaken spot. As I walked with him through the Fort casemates, the diet of corn-

meal and acid pickle came back to me. I could see in my vision, the shrunken forms of my dear old comrades, dying of starvation and that dread disease, scurvy . . . While the sargent was showing me over the Fort, we came to one of the casemates, "There," he said, "is where some of the prisoners cut a tunnel under the fort, and got out into the swamps, and would have gotten away, but just as two of the number were about to capture the sentinel over the boats, a man named Gillespie yelled out and betrayed them." Then the old sergeant took me over to the dark cell where these men, who attempted to escape, were confined, and said, "I believe those fellows would have murdered the sentinel had they not been betrayed by their comrade." After looking over the cell, I said, "Sergeant, I was one of those 600." Well if you could have seen the expression on his face—grasping my hand he said, "Rebel or Yankee, I will say you were all noble brave men to suffer as you did, when you could have taken the oath and ended it all."

So you see comrades, the man that was true unto the end of those terrible days, has the respect of even his enemies and the whole world. Courage loves courage, and manhood is recognized by all who can feel the humanity God gave us all.[26]

The majority of the men of the Six Hundred went on to claim fame as state or national politicians, bankers, successful planters, or at the least prominent citizens. Some went west to Texas and California, becoming scattered across the country, bound only by seven months spent in a confinement and torture which no other living soul could know or identify with.

The seventeen who took the oath tell a different tale. Ostracized and denounced by their loyal comrades, their betrayal haunted them the rest of their lives, a black mark on their record. They carefully avoided meetings with the other Six Hundred at reunions. Colonel Jonathan Baker left the country and went to the West Indies following the war.[27] At a United Confederate Veteran convention in St. Louis, J. Ogden Murray recognized Captain John Kelly across the room. "He slunk out of the hotel without speaking. The only one of the oath takers I ever met," recalled Murray in a letter to John Cantwell in 1901.[28]

*   *   *

How did their war-time experience affect the rest of their lives? In the ways they related their experience as reminiscences, it varies. Many refused or were reluctant to talk about their prison time. Others were vocal, writing post-war articles. Two wrote books describing the conditions as a refute to Northern allegations of cruelty at Southern prisons. The restless among their number went west, drifting or moving from place to place, and have been difficult to evaluate.

They left a legacy to a South who, in the post-war years, needed heroes in that atmosphere of defeat and humiliation. The gallant band of 600 became synonymous with a stubborn unwillingness to yield principle, honor, and duty, even in the advent of a torturous death, and were celebrated in ceremony and literature in all Southern states.

They kept their modesty. At a United Confederate Veterans' Reunion in Houston, Texas in 1920, then Society President Captain David Grayson was the subject of a newspaper article, praising the courage of the Six Hundred. He implied they were only doing their duty as Confederate soldiers, stating, "We claim no especial credit for the action of our men under this severe trial, as we feel that it was only typical of what any 600 who might have been selected anywhere in the South would have done."[29]

One thing is consistent: Most of the men left epitaphs as generous, kind and caring citizens. Their names are still to be found as streets, buildings, or towns in the localities where they lived. Is it coincidence that so many such men were chosen at random to undergo retaliation, or did the experience itself make them more sensitive and aware of the needs of others? It is impossible to know from this point in history but it is proven by their actions and the testimony of others who knew them that they led exemplary lives after the war, remaining an inspiration to those whose lives they touched, as well as to each other.

Some realized as horrible as their experience was, death would probably have claimed more of their number had they remained in active service. Being line officers and field officers, their presence on the battlefield was in the most dangerous place—at the head of their command. Approximately 24 percent of the field officers in the Army of Northern Virginia died in combat, compared to the less than 10 percent mortality rate of the Six Hundred.[30]

It is irrefutable that the harsh prison conditions shortened some lives. Years after the war, men of the Six Hundred complained of the susceptibility of respiratory ailments induced by the winter at Fort Pulaski and Hilton Head. Some had lost teeth from scurvy, and swore their gums never fully recovered. The number of men cited as crippled or who died of pneumonia and tuberculosis at relatively young ages obviously were casualties of prison and not only wounds.

For the most part, they remained faithful to their principles, and never apologized or felt anything but right for casting their lot with the Confederacy. Some remained bitter for the harsh treatment. Most resumed their role as American citizens and bore no malice. But all felt a twinge of pain that their own countrymen had treated them so badly. They never seem to have blamed the Union soldiers who were guards, but held the United States government and Union high command directly responsible for carrying out the orders of retaliation to such a punishing degree.

EPILOGUE

TO the casual visitor who goes to Fort Delaware, now a state park, the fort appears as a somewhat dilapidated example of a by-gone means of defense. Additions for each successive war since the nineteenth century have left the old structure looking a bit confused as to its real identity. The parade ground and vacant, staring casemates, like the eyesockets of a skull, yield no voluntary information about the men whose lives passed through and touched here. The compound surrounding the bastion which consisted of the wooden barracks where privates and officers lived is long gone. The tears, suffering, and immense pain that the men of the South experienced are only touched upon in a few interpretive exhibits. Park staff and occasional living history weekends valiantly strive to give the visitor a sense of life there for those Southern boys of history. Still, the real story is barely conveyed.

As for the Six Hundred, they are considered an obscure event. Only by knowing what happened here and using a focused imagination can a visitor glimpse through time the scenes played out on its grounds 130 years ago.

* * *

On Cockspur Island off the Georgia coast, the salt marshes are still the same. Major William E. Stewart and Lieutenant William H. Hatcher would have no trouble finding their route across them today. One long road leads out from the Georgia mainland to Fort Pulaski. For the beach goers who continue on past the entrance to the fort out to Tybee, a look back will give them a glance of an old brick wall pockmarked with shell holes from a war long past. The black casemate windows can be discerned if searched for.

For those who do stop and drive out to the fort, pleasantly kept grounds and a new visitor center immaculately maintained by Federal funds orient observers to the history of the military significance of the post, and the 1862 battle when Union forces captured the fort. The visitors' center boasts many well designed displays of the short defensive role of Fort Pulaski. Strangely missing is any indication that it was ever a prison, comparable to

280

a German concentration camp of eighty years later, though its life as a prison was longer than that as a military objective. There is no mention of the Six Hundred and the ordeal they endured.

Fort Pulaski is a wonderfully preserved example of the coastal defense system designed in the nineteenth century. Unlike Fort Delaware it was never modified, having been declared a dinosaur during the 1862 occupation. Children climb on cannon on the parapets, casemates near the sally port are furnished and displayed as they were in 1862, and occasional living history programs present the fort when troops had little worry over being attacked. One would get the impression that nothing unpleasant ever occurred there.

The casemates in the south wall of the fort are open to the wandering visitor. Three tiered wooden bunks with blankets stand against the brick walls. The windows have rusty iron bars, and the outer wall is pockmarked. A quiet and dark atmosphere greets the visitor. In one corner is a small plaque, "The Immortal Six Hundred." A few sentences dismiss the history of these particular rooms, and relate an escape. Otherwise, little betrays that in these prison cells so much occurred to change the lives of a few and leave such a legacy. Yet it was here that Henry Dickinson and his friends played cards, James McMichael sat and wrote by lamplight in his diary, and J. Ogden Murray planned an escape attempt, while some paced the prison floors to keep warm. Here men sang through long winter nights to keep up the spirits of comrades who were on the verge of starving to death. Letters to and from home, journals, tears, laughter, and conversations were all part of the life here. Their words echo down the decades, and the scenes they vividly describe can be imagined. In the now deserted casemate prison, a chill passes over the visitor. It is possible to reach back across a century and for one brief moment feel their presence.

The spirits of those who died never left, for their cemetery outside the fort walls is unmarked. Headboards were made by Captains Dickinson, Cantwell, and other prisoners, but they were not allowed to be erected. So they lie beside a paved lot, where cars and buses callously disturb their rest, their presence unsuspected. It is here that Alex King was buried by friends on a cold day, hundreds of miles from his Virginia hills. Captain Moses Bradford too lies in these salt marshes, never having seen his family again after pleading to see that they were safely removed from their home when Federal troops ordered their evacuation from Missouri. Along with these men lie eleven others who died together and rest together forever, innocent victims of retaliation.

* * *

Forty-five miles from Tybee toward Charleston is Hilton Head Island. Fort Walker and the busy military depot of Port Royal no longer exist, swallowed up by beach houses and golf courses of the wealthy vacationers who "developed" the area thirty years ago. Only the ghosts of the past haunt the woods between the suburban lots.

Farther up the Carolina coast lies Charleston. From Fort Moultrie, across Charleston Harbor lies Morris Island. Now, just as in 1864, it is a desolate uninhabited spit of flat land. Beyond its low trees can be seen Lighthouse Inlet, one-third the way to Hilton Head. The observer clearly recognizes the exposed and defenseless position of the captives under fire from batteries at Moultrie, Sumter, and Wagner. The outline of a modern Charleston replaces the one battered by Federal shells, but the proximity is still just as it was in 1864. The intense bombardment of flying shells and crashing noise is gone. Only the cries of diving seabirds approaching Fort Sumter break the stillness.

The three graves on Morris Island now occupy a watery place of rest. Subsequent beach erosion and the sands of time have obliterated all traces of the stockade, batteries, and the men who were players and pawns in the struggle for Charleston.

For those who go to these places, and know about the men whose existence briefly touched them, their presence can be felt. They want to be remembered, and what happened to them never be forgotten. They were Americans too. The blame placed on the Confederate government concerning treatment of prisoners of war was unfair. Union prisoner Edward Wellington Boate summed up the feelings of many Northern soldiers when he wrote of the United States' refusal to exchange:

> A policy like this is the quintessence of inhumanity, a disgrace to the Administration which carried it out, and a blot upon the country. You rulers who make the charge that the rebels intentionally killed off our men, when I can honestly swear they were doing every thing in their power to sustain us, do not lay this flattering unction to your souls. You abandoned your brave men in the hour of their cruelest need. They fought for the Union, and you reached no hand out to save the old faithful, loyal, and devoted servants of the country. You may try to shift the blame from your own shoulders, but posterity will saddle the responsibility where it justly belongs.[1]

In 1930, at age eighty-seven, Lieutenant William Epps was interviewed by a newspaper reporter from Charleston, South Carolina. He was asked to tell his story of the part he played as a Confederate soldier. The interviewer inquired how Epps felt about his citizenship and patriotism, sixty-five years after being imprisoned as one of the Six Hundred:

> I am not untrue to my country. Every drop of my blood is pure American, and today, if America needed me, I should gladly give the few remaining years of my life to her service. The American flag is my flag. My fore-fathers followed it to the end of their lives. My heart still thrills to see its beautiful folds unfurl, but with that thrill comes an unspeakable sadness; for it was the Stars and Stripes that floated over Morris Island, Pulaski, and Fort Delaware.[2]

Appendix A

THE CARTEL OF JULY 22, 1862

The undersigned, having been commissioned by the authorities they respectively represent to make arrangements for a general exchange of prisoners of war, have agreed to the following articles:

ARTICLE 1. It is hereby agreed and stipulated that all prisoners of war held by either party, including those taken on private armed vessels known as privateers, shall be discharged upon the conditions and terms following:

Prisoners to be exchanged man for man and officer for officer; privateers to be placed upon the footing of officers and men of the navy.

Men and officers of lower grades may be exchanged for officers of a higher grade, and men and officers of different services may be exchanged according to the following scale of equivalents:

A general commanding-in-chief or an admiral shall be exchanged for officers of equal rank, or for sixty privates or common seamen.

A flag-officer or major-general shall be exchanged for officers of equal rank, or for forty privates or common seamen.

A commodore carrying a broad pennant or a brigadier-general shall be exchanged for officers of equal rank, or twenty privates or common seamen.

A captain in the navy or a colonel shall be exchanged for officers of equal rank, or for fifteen privates or common seamen.

A lieutenant-colonel or a commander in the navy shall be exchanged for officers of equal rank, or for ten privates or common seamen.

A lieutenant-commander or a major shall be exchanged for officers of equal rank, or eight privates or common seamen.

A lieutenant or a master in the navy or a captain in the army or marines shall be exchanged for officers of equal rank, or six privates or common seamen.

Masters' mates in the navy or lieutenants and ensigns in the army shall be exchanged for officers of equal rank, or four privates or common seamen.

Midshipmen, warrant-officers in the navy, masters of merchant vessels, and commanders of privateers shall be exchanged for officers of equal rank, or three privates or common seamen.

Second captains, lieutenants, or mates of merchant vessels or privateers, and all petty officers in the navy, and all non-commissioned officers in the army or marines shall be severally exchanged for persons of equal rank, or for two privates or common seamen, and private soldiers or common seamen shall be exchanged for each other, man for man.

ARTICLE 2. Local, State, civil, and militia rank held by persons not in actual military service will not be recognized, the basis of exchange being the grade actually held in the naval and military service of the respective parties.

ARTICLE 3. If citizens held by either party on charges of disloyalty or any alleged civil offense are exchanged, it shall only be for citizens. Captured sutlers, teamsters, and all civilians in the actual service of either party to be exchanged for persons in similar position.

ARTICLE 4. All prisoners of war to be discharged on parole in ten days after their capture, and the prisoners now held and those hereafter taken to be transported to the points mutually agreed upon at the expense of the capturing party. The surplus prisoners not exchanged shall not be permitted to take up arms again, nor to serve as military police or constabulary force in any fort, garrison, or field-work held by either of the respective parties, nor as guards of prisons, depots, or stores, nor to discharge any duty usually performed by soldiers, until exchanged under the provisions of this cartel. The exchange is not to be considered complete until the officer or soldier exchanged for has been actually restored to the lines to which he belongs.

ARTICLE 5. Each party, upon the discharge of prisoners of the other party, is authorized to discharge an equal number of their own officers or men from parole, furnishing at the same time to the other party a list of their prisoners discharged and of their own officers and men relieved from parole, thus enabling each party to relieve from parole such of their own officers and men as the party may choose. The lists thus mutually furnished will keep both parties advised of the true condition of the exchange of prisoners.

ARTICLE 6. The stipulations and provisions above mentioned to be of binding obligation during the continuance of the war, it matters not which party may have the surplus of prisoners, the great principles involved being, first, an equitable exchange of prisoners, man for man, officer for officer, or officers of higher grade exchanged for officers of lower grade or for privates according to the scale of equivalents; second, that privateers and officers and men of different services may be exchanged according to the same scale of equivalents; third, that all prisoners, of whatever arm of service, are to be exchanged or paroled in ten days from the time of their capture, if it be practicable to transfer them to their own lines in that time; if not, as soon thereafter as practicable; fourth, that no officer, soldier, or employee, in the service of either party, is to be considered as exchanged and absolved from his parole until his equivalent has actually reached the lines of his friends; fifth, that the parole forbids the performance of field, garrison, police, or guard, or constabulary duty.

ARTICLE 7. All prisoners of war now held on either side and all prisoners hereafter taken shall be sent with all reasonable dispatch to A. M. Aiken's, below Dutch Gap, on the James River, Va., or to Vicksburg, on the Mississippi River, in the state of Mississippi, and there exchanged or paroled until such exchange can be effected, notice being previously given by each party of the number of prisoners it will send and the time when they will be delivered at those points respectively; and in case the vicissitudes of war shall change the military relations of the places designated in this article to the contending parties so as to render the same inconvenient for the delivery and exchange of prisoners, other places bearing as nearly as may be the present local relations of said places to the lines of said parties shall be by mutual agreement substituted. But nothing in this article contained shall prevent the commanders of two opposing armies from exchanging prisoners or releasing them on parole from other points mutually agreed on by said commanders.

ARTICLE 8. For the purpose of carrying into effect the foregoing articles of agreement each party will appoint two agents, to be called agents for the exchange of prisoners of war, whose duty it shall be to communicate with each other by correspondence and otherwise, to prepare the lists of prisoners, to attend to the delivery of the prisoners at the places agreed on and carry out promptly, effectually, and in good faith all the details and provisions of the said articles of agreement.

ARTICLE 9. And in case any misunderstanding shall arise in regard to any clause or stipulation in the foregoing articles it is mutually agreed that such misunderstanding shall not interrupt the release of prisoners on parole, as herein provided, but shall be made the subject of friendly explanations in order that the object of this agreement may neither be defeated nor postponed

D. H. Hill,	John A. Dix,
Major General C. S. Army	Major General

APPENDIX B

FIFTY UNION OFFICERS
Exchanged August 3, 1864 in Charleston Harbor, SC

Name	Rank	Regiment
Heckman, Charles A.	Brig. Gen.	U.S. Army
Scammon, Eliakim P.	Brig. Gen.	U.S. Army
Seymour, Truman	Brig. Gen.	U.S. Army
Shaler, Alexander	Brig. Gen.	U.S. Army
Wessells, Henry W.	Brig. Gen.	U.S. Army
Bolinger, Henry C.	COL	7 PA Res
Brown, Hiram L.	COL	145 PA Inf
Dana, Edmund L.	COL	143 PA Inf
Fardella, Enrico	COL	85 NY Inf
Grover, Ira G.	COL	7 IN Inf
Harriman, Walter	COL	11 NH Inf
Hawkins, Isaac R.	COL	7 TN Cav (US)
LaGrange, Oscar H.	COL	1 WS Cav
Lee, Horace C.	COL	27 MA Inf
Lehmann, Theodore F.	COL	103 PA Inf
White, Richard	COL	55 PA Inf
Baldwin, Clark B.	LTC	1 MA Inf
Bartholomew, Walter G.	LTC	27 MA Inf
Burnham, John N.	LTC	16 CT Inf
Cook, William R.	LTC	2 TN Cav (US)
Dickerson, Christopher J.	LTC	10 MI Inf
Fellows, John F.	LTC	17 MA Inf
Frambles, Granville A.	LTC	59 OH Inf
Glenn, William H.	LTC	89 OH Inf

Hayes, Edwin L.	LTC	100 OH Inf
Higinbotham, Thomas H.	LTC	65 NY Inf
Hunter, Henry B.	LTC	123 OH Inf
Joslin, George C.	LTC	15 MA Inf
Lasselle, William P.	LTC	9 IN Inf
Maxwell, Wilson C.	LTC	103 PA Inf
Mayhew, James D.	LTC	8 KY Inf (US)
McMackin, Warren E.	LTC	21 IL Inf
Miles, David	LTC	79 PA Inf
Moffitt, Stephen	LTC	96 NY Inf
Olcott, Egbert	LTC	121 NY Inf
Polsley, John J.	LTC	7 WV Cav
Rodgers, Andrew F.	LTC	80 IL Inf
Spofford, John P.	LTC	97 NY Inf
Stewart, James W.	LTC	2 IN Cav
Swift, Frederick W.	LTC	17 MI Inf
Taylor, Alexander W.	LTC	101 PA Inf
Baker, William F.	MAJ	10 USC Inf
Bates, Erastus N.	MAJ	18 IL Inf
Beeres, Charles H.	MAJ	16 IL Cav
Carpenter, Daniel A.	MAJ	2 TN Inf (US)
Clark, John E.	MAJ	5 MI Cav Crandall
Walter	MAJ	85 NY Inf
Grant, Horace D.	MAJ	4 MI Cav
Hall, Josiah	MAJ	1 VT Cav
Johnson, James H.	MAJ	11 TN Cav (US)

FIFTY CONFEDERATE OFFICERS,
Exchanged August 3, 1864 in Charleston Harbor, SC

Name	Rank	Regiment
Gardner, Franklin	Maj. Gen.	C.S. Army
Johnson, Edward	Maj. Gen.	C.S. Army
Archer, James J.	Brig. Gen.	C.S. Army
Steuart, George Henry	Brig. Gen.	C.S. Army
Thompson, M. Jeff	Brig. Gen.	C.S. Army
Barbour, William M.	COL	37 NC Inf
Brown, Joseph N.	COL	14 SC Inf

Carter, Richard Welby	COL	1 VA Cav
Caudill, Benjamin Everett	COL	13 KY Cav
Cobb, Norvell	COL	44 VA Inf
Duke, Basil Wilson	COL	2 KY Cav
Ferguson, Milton J.	COL	16 VA Cav
Forney, William Henry	COL	10 AL Inf
Hanks, J. M.	COL	Buford's KY brigade
Jaquess, John A.	COL	1st LA Regulars
Morgan, Richard C.	COL	Morgan's KY Cav
Peebles, William Hubbard	COL	44 GA Inf
Pell, James A.	COL	6 CS Cav
Vandeventer, Alexander S.	COL	50 VA Inf
Ward, William W.	COL	9 TN Cav

Brewer, James Fielding	LTC	1 (Carter's) TN Cav
Caldwell, John William	LTC	1 KY Cav
Carson, John Thomas	LTC	12 GA Inf
Davant, Phillip Edwin	LTC	38 GA Inf
Davidson, William Lee	LTC	7 NC Inf
Dupree, Alcee	LTC	Gen. Gardner's Staff
Ennett, William Thomas	LTC	3 NC Inf
Fitzgerald, John Paterson	LTC	23 VA Inf
Groce, J. E.	LTC	Gen. Wharton's staff
Haynes, Charles Lewis	LTC	27 VA Inf
Jackson, Thomas C.	LTC	G. T. Anderson's brigade
Martz, Douglass Henry Lee	LTC	10 VA Inf
Parsley, William Murdock	LTC	3 NC Inf
Patton, Oliver A.	LTC	Patton's KY Partisan Rangers
Smith, Marshall Joseph	LTC	Crescent Regt.LA Inf
Swingley, A. L.	LTC	Forrest's brigade
Tucker, Joseph Thomas	LTC	11 KY Cav
Warley, Frederick Fraser	LTC	2 SC Arty.

Anderson, David W.	MAJ	44 VA Inf
Henry, E. M.	MAJ	Hunter's Cav
Highley, Horace A.	MAJ	Gen. Bragg's staff
Manning, William Henry	MAJ	6 LA Inf
Nash, Edwin Acton	MAJ	4 GA Inf
Perkins, Lynnville J.	MAJ	50 VA Inf
Sanders, Edward J.	MAJ	9 MS Cav
Smith, George H.	MAJ	Gen. Wheeler's staff
Steele, Theophilus	MAJ	7 KY Cav
Upshaw, Thomas Edward	MAJ	13 VA Cav
Webber, Thomas B.	MAJ	2 KY (Morgan's) Cav
Wilson, J. Moore	MAJ	7 LA Inf

Appendix C

IMMORTAL SIX HUNDRED
NUMBER OF OFFICERS FROM EACH STATE *

STATE	In the Stockade at Morris Island	Sent to Beaufort, SC	STATE TOTAL
Maryland	6		6
Virginia	172	14	186
North Carolina	104	7	111
South Carolina	22	2	24
Georgia	59	1	60
Florida	9	1	10
Alabama	22	4	26
Mississippi	19	2	21
Louisiana	27	4	31
Texas	5		5
Arkansas	23	4	27
Missouri	8		8
Kentucky	34	1	35
Tennessee	<u>48</u>	2	<u>50</u>
TOTAL	558	42	600

*from List compiled by Capt. John Cantwell.

Appendix D

IMMORTAL SIX HUNDRED
Officers Who Died from Captivity.

Name	Rank	Regiment	Death Date	Cause
Morris Island, SC				
Callahan, William P.	1LT	25 TN Inf	27 Sep 64	chronic diarrhea
Peake, Frank P.	2LT	Byrnes KY Arty.	2 Oct 64	chronic diarrhea
Cowper, John C.C.	2LT	33 NC Inf	7 Oct 64	pneumonia
Beaufort Hosp., SC				
Bryan, Robert C.	2LT	2 TN Cav	8 Oct 64	chronic diarrhea
Ft.Pulaski, GA				
Burney, Iverson L.	1LT	49 GA Inf	12 Nov 64	chronic diarrhea
Fitzgerald, George B.	CPT	12 VA Cav	13 Nov 64	chronic diarrhea
Lane, Christopher C.	3LT	3 NC Inf	8 Dec 64	chronic diarrhea
Burgin, John M.	2LT	22 NC Inf	28 Jan 65	chronic diarrhea
Legg, Russell W.	2LT	50 VA Inf	7 Feb 65	chronic diarrhea
Bradford, Moses J.	CPT	10 MO Inf	13 Feb 65	chronic diarrhea
King, Alex M.	CPT	50 VA Inf	15 Feb 65	scurvy
Rosenbalm, Eli A.	2LT	37 VA Inf	18 Feb 65	dysentery
Goodloe, Thomas J.	1LT	44 TN Inf	27 Feb 65	chronic diarrhea
Brumley, Ozniah R.	CPT	20 NC Inf	4 Mch 65	pneumonia
Eastham, Chapman B.	1LT	10 VA Inf	6 Mch 65	chronic diarrhea
Ganoyway, Jonathan T.	2LT	50 VA Inf	10 Mch 65	chronic dysentery
Tolbert, John H.	CPT	5 FL Inf	14 Mch 65	chronic dysentery

Hilton Head, SC

Campbell, Watson C.	2LT	25 TN	Inf	18 Feb	65	chronic diarrhea
Long, John	2LT	10 VA	Inf	22 Feb	65	chronic diarrhea
Bailey, William	CPT	5 FL	Inf	3 Mch	65	pneumonia
Carr, Robert B.	1LT	43 NC	Inf	3 Jul	65	chronic diarrhea

At sea, on board steamer Illinois

Edwards, Alexander W.	1LT	15 VA	Cav	11/12 Mch 65	———
Dillard, Robert Y.	2LT	16 AR	Inf	11/12 Mch 65	———

Ft.Delaware, DE

Lyons, Peter C.	1LT	18 GA	Inf	13 Mch	65	chronic diarrhea
Coggin, Jeremiah	3LT	23 NC	Inf	14 Mch	65	chronic diarrhea
Chisholm, John N.	CPT	9 AL	Inf	16 Mch	65	chronic diarrhea
Boddie, Elijah	1LT	7 TN	Inf	18 Mch	65	acute diarrhea
Earp, Harris E.	1LT	24 NC	Inf	21 Mch	65	scurvy
Guthrie, William L.	CPT	23 VA	Inf	22 Mch	65	scurvy
Gowan, Benjamin A.	3LT	51 NC	Inf	22 Mch	65	acute dysentery
Alderson, William H.	2LT	6 TN	Cav	30 Mch	65	erysipelas
Lipps, Jonas A.	CPT	50 VA	Inf	6 Apr	65	scurvy
Morris, James D.	2LT	8 KY	Cav	7 Apr	65	erysipelas
Knox, William C.	2LT	4 TN	Cav	12 Apr	65	scurvy
Ledford, Jesse	1LT	25 TN	Inf	1 May	65	acute dysentery
Carson, Leroy P.	CPT	35 TN	Inf	18 May	65	pneumonia
Funk, Jefferson Wm. O.	1LT	5 VA	Inf	26 May	65	chronic diarrhea
Dodson, William B.	2LT	5 VA	Cav	1 Jun	65	fever
King, John E.	2LT	3 NC	Inf	15 Jun	65	chronic dysentery
Mitchell, Thomas S.	1LT	42 VA	Inf	16/17 Jun	65	chronic diarrhea

Hosp., Augusta, GA

Farrar, Absalom H.	2LT	13 MS	Inf	1 Feb 65	———

At home

Brown, Bezaliel G.	CPT	7 VA	Inf	– Jul 65	———
Kelly, Thomas E.	1LT	5 LA	Inf	16 Sep 65	———
Crow, William P.	1LT	6 KY	Cav	12 Nov 65	———

APPENDIX E

CONFEDERATE RELIEF ASSOCIATION
OF FORT PULASKI, 1864.
Confederate States Officers' Prison Barracks,
Fort Pulaski, Ga., December 13, 1864.

Elected officers:
Col. A. Fulkerson, president
Major MacCreary, vice-president
Capt. H. C. Dickinson, treasurer
Capt. J. L. Cantwell, secretary

Members of the Executive Committee from Divisions 1, 2, 3, 4, and 5.
Major David Jones
Capt. J. G. Knox
Capt. Peter Ake
Capt. Campbell
Major Martin G. Ziegler

WHEREAS, it has been suggested that a number of our brother officers, confined with us as prisoners of war at Fort Pulaski, are deprived of some absolute necessaries of life, by reason of their inability to communicate with their homes and friends; and

WHEREAS, some of such officers, by reason of the diseases incident to prison life, are exposed to much suffering and in danger of neglect if left to the care of individuals, and

WHEREAS, we recognize the binding obligation on us, as Confederate officers, to search for and relieve the distress of all worthy officers and soldiers of our common country; now the more effectually to carry out our purpose we, whose names are signed to this paper,

DO HEREBY ORGANIZE "The Confederate Relief Association," adopt the following constitution and by-laws for our government, and pledge ourselves, as individuals, from time to time, when called on by the proper officers of the "Association," to aid in sustaining it to the extent of our ability.

CONSTITUTION

FIRST ARTICLE. The officers of the Confederate Relief Association shall consist of a president, a vice-president, a treasurer, a secretary, and an executive committee of one man from each of the five divisions into which we are at present formed. Each of these officers shall be elected viva voce, and shall continue in office till a change in our situation or condition renders a new election necessary.

SECOND ARTICLE. It shall be the duty of the president to convene this Association when in his opinion it may be necessary. He shall preside at all the meetings, shall call on the Association for contributions to the treasurer, and shall detail, upon the suggestion of either member of the executive committee, nurses for the sick, and where practicable may command the medical services of any member of the society who may have been a physician.

THIRD ARTICLE. The vice-president shall preside during the absence or sickness of the president and is charged with the duty of assisting the president, as far as necessary, in all his duties.

FOURTH ARTICLE. The secretary shall keep a record of all the proceedings, including a balance sheet of weekly receipts and expenditures, and shall countersign all orders for the expenditure of money.

FIFTH ARTICLE. The treasurer shall receive and keep all moneys of the Association with an account of the same, and shall pay such moneys upon the order of either member of the executive committee countersigned by the secretary.

SIXTH ARTICLE. The executive committee shall be the active body of this Association, it being expected that they will search out all cases of sickness or suffering in this prison or any Confederate hospital connected with it, and report the same to the president; that they shall frequently meet on the call of the ranking officer of the committee to devise means for the aid and comfort of sick or suffering officers, and that when relief is necessary for any man in the division of either member of the said committee, he shall procure the same by a requisition upon the treasurer countersigned by the secretary.

APPENDIX F

THE MEN OF THE SIX HUNDRED

An Alphabetical Roster

CAPTURED

Abernathy, Sidney S.	1LT	Co. D, 30th NC Inf Regt	Kelly's Ford, VA	7 Nov 63
Adams, Richard H., Jr.	1LT	C.S. Engineer Corps	near Columbia, TN	25 Sep 63
Adams, William H.	2LT	Co. K, 51st TN Inf Regt	Ringgold, GA	25 Nov 63
Adamson, Simon G.	2LT	Co. G, 11th TX Cav Regt	McMinnville, TN	4 Oct 63
Adkins, Samuel S.	2LT	Co. B, 5th KY Mtd Inf Regt	West Liberty, OH	16 Jul 63
Ake, Peter	CPT	Co. A, 3rd MO Cav Regt	Helena, AR	3 Nov 63
Akers, Peter B.	2LT	Co. A, 11th VA Inf Regt	Milford Station, VA	21 May 64
Albright, George N.	2LT	Co. F, 6th NC Inf Regt	Rappahannock Sta., VA	7 Nov 63
Alderson, William H.	2LT	Co. F, 6th TN Cav Regt (Wheeler's)	Columbia, TN	11 Oct 63
Aldridge, Marcus L.	2LT	Co. B, 3rd KY Cav Regt	Cheshire, OH	20 Jul 63
Alexander, William J.	CPT	Co. A, 37th NC Inf Regt	Gettysburg, PA	3 Jul 63
Alfriend, Peyton	CPT	Co. A, 3rd VA Inf Bn Res.	Petersburg, VA	9 Jun 64
Allen, Cicero M.	2LT	Co. C, 2nd AR Cav Regt	Cold Water Ford, MS	3 Nov 63
Allen, Henry A.	CPT	Co. K, 9th VA Inf Regt	Gettysburg, PA	3 Jul 63
Allen, James H.	2LT	Co. A, 45th VA Inf Regt	Logan Co., (W)VA	9 Dec 63
Allen, John C.	1LT	Co. C, 7th VA Cav Regt	near Romney, (W)VA	2 Feb 64
Allen, John M.	2LT	Co. B, 29th MS Inf Regt	Chickamauga, GA	20 Sep 63
Allen, John P.	CPT	Co. H, 55th GA Inf Regt	Cumberland Gap, TN	9 Sep 63
Allen, Thomas M.	1LT	Co. E, 4th NC Inf Regt	Gettysburg, PA	4 Jul 63
Allen, William E.	2LT	Co. I, 60th TN Mtd Inf Regt	Big Black River, MS	17 May 63
Allen, William H.	2LT	Co. E, 49th AL Inf Regt	Port Hudson, LA	9 Jul 63
Allen, Wyatt B.	1LT	Co. I, 6th NC Inf Regt	Rappahannock Sta., VA	7 Nov 63
Allensworth, Stephen P.	2LT	Co. E, 2nd KY Cav Regt (Duke's)	Salineville, OH	26 Jul 63
Allison, Montreville B.	2LT	Co. H, 62nd NC Inf Regt	Cumberland Gap, TN	9 Sep 63
Anderson, Samuel T.	2LT	Co. D, 1st SC Cav Regt	Martinsburg, (W)VA	19 Jul 63
Anderson, William T.	1LT	Co. A, 5th NC Inf Regt	Spotsylvania C.H., VA	12 May 64
Andis, Earl C.	1LT	Co. F, 4th VA Inf Regt	Morton's Ford, VA	6 Feb 64

Andrews, Henry C.	2LT	Co. G, 28th NC Inf Regt	Spotsylvania C.H., VA	12 May 64
Andrews, James J.	1LT	Co. F, 4th AL Cav Regt (Rodney's)	Florence, AL	30 Nov 63
Angell, Anderson R.	1LT	Co. K, 42nd VA Inf Regt	Spotsylvania C.H., VA	12 May 64
Angell, John G.	CPT	Co. A, 5th LA Inf Regt	Rappahannock Sta., VA	7 Nov 63
Appleberry, Thomas A.	2LT	Co. F, 44th VA Inf Regt	Spotsylvania C.H., VA	12 May 64
Arbuckle, David	CPT	Co. I, 17th AR Inf Regt (Griffith's)	Port Hudson, LA	9 Jul 63
Armstead, Thomas S.	1LT	Co. E, 8th FL Inf Regt	The Wilderness, VA	6 May 64
Armstrong, Andrew J.	1LT	Co. I, 46th AL Inf Regt	Champion Hill, MS	16 May 63
Arnold, Bonaparte	2LT	Co. C, 28th TN Inf Regt	Huntsville, AL	24 Feb 64
Arrants, John G. S.	2LT	Co. E, 63rd TN Inf Regt	Petersburg, VA	17 Jun 64
Arrington, John	1LT	Co. I, 42nd VA Inf Regt	Spotsylvania C.H., VA	12 May 64
Asbury, William B.	1LT	Co. H, 16th VA Cav Regt	Wayne Co., (W)VA	15 Feb 64
Ashton, John D.	CPT	Co. M, 4th GA Cav Regt (Clinch's)	Summerville, GA	10 Sep 63
Atkinson, Robert W.	CPT	Co. E, 2nd NC Cav Regt	Hanover C.H., VA	29 May 64
Austin, John B.	CPT	Co. F, 2nd KY Cav Regt (Duke's)	Dickson Co., TN	27 Oct 63
Avant, William R.	2LT	Co. I, 61st GA Inf Regt	Gettysburg, PA	1 Jul 63
Avent, George W.	1LT	Co. D, 35th NC Inf Regt	Petersburg, VA	17 Jun 64
Bailey, William, Jr.	CPT	Co. G, 5th FL Inf Regt	Gettysburg, PA	2 Jul 63
Baker, Henry	CPT	Co. G, 3rd CS Cav Regt	near Chattanooga, TN	20 Jul 63
Baker, John A..	COL	F&S, 3rd NC Cav Regt	Petersburg, VA	21 Jun 64
Ballantine, William D.	CPT	Co. A, 2nd FL Inf Regt	Gettysburg, PA	2 Jul 63
Barnes, Francis C.	2LT	Co. K, 6th VA Inf Regt	Gettysburg, PA	3 Jul 63
Barnes, William W.	CPT	Co. A, 9th GA Art Bn	Cumberland Gap, TN	9 Sep 63
Barrett, Charles L.	1LT	Co. B, 3th MS Inf Regt (Claiborne's)	Port Hudson, LA	9 Jul 63
Barrow, Thaddeus P.	2LT	Co. I, 3rd NC Inf Regt	Spotsylvania C.H., VA	12 May 64
Bartholemy, John C.	1LT	Co. H, 20th LA Inf Regt	Port Hudson, LA	9 Jul 63
Barton, Andrew J.	2LT	Co. D, 55th GA Inf Regt	Cumberland Gap, TN	9 Sep 63
Barton, William L.	2LT	Co. H, 2nd MS Inf Regt	Tupelo, MS	4 May 63
Bass, Washington P.	2LT	Co. A, 15th AL Inf Regt	The Wilderness, VA	6 May 64
Batchelor, Charles J.	2LT	Co. E, 2nd LA Inf Regt	Spotsylvania C.H., VA	12 May 64
Bates, Dwight E.	1LT	Jeff Davis (AL) Art	Spotsylvania C.H., VA	12 May 64
Batte, Peter V.	MAJ	F&S, 44th VA Inf Bn	Petersburg, VA	15 Jun 64
Baughman, Francis M.	1LT	Co. C, 1st SC Inf Regt (McCreary's)	N Anna River Br, VA	24 May 64
Baxter, John B.	1LT	Co. F, 23rd AR Inf Regt	Port Hudson, LA	9 Jul 63
Bedell, William H.	2LT	Co. E, 1st AL Cav Regt	McMinnville, TN	23 Oct 63
Bedford, Alexander M.	1LT	Co. D, 3rd MO Cav Bn	Big Black River, MS	17 May 63
Bell, Erasmus L.	1LT	Co. K, 10th VA Inf Regt	Spotsylvania C.H., VA	12 May 64
Benson, Peru H.	1LT	Co. I, 23rd AR Inf Regt	Port Hudson, LA	9 Jul 63
Bentley, John B.	2LT	Co. F, 22nd GA Inf Regt	Gettysburg, PA	2 Jul 63
Benton, Peter G.	2LT	Co. C, 11th MO Inf Regt	Helena, AR	4 Jul 63
Bernard, William L.	1LT	Co. G, 37th VA Cav Bn	Leesburg, VA	16 Jul 64
Berry, Thornton J.	2LT	Co. C, 25th VA Inf Regt	The Wilderness, VA	5 May 64
Bessonett, Francis M.	2LT	Co. H, 12th MS Inf Regt	Chester Gap, VA	24 Jul 63
Birkhead, Burwell W.	1LT	Co. I, 22nd NC Inf Regt	Hanover Jct., VA	24 May 64
Bishop, William T.	1LT	Co. G, 16th AL Inf Regt	Baxter, AL	20 Jun 63
Bissell, William S.	2LT	Co. I, 2nd SC Inf Regt	Gettysburg, PA	4 Jul 63

Blaine, John A.	2LT	Co. H, 16th NC Inf Regt	Falling Waters, MD	14 Jul 63
Blair, John C.	CPT	Co. D, 1st NC Cav Regt	Yellow Tavern, VA	11 May 64
Bland, Stewart D.	2LT	Co. A, 18th VA Cav Regt	Pendleton Co, (W)VA	24 Jan 64
Bludworth, James H.	2LT	Co. C, 4th NC Cav Regt	Brandy Station, VA	11 Oct 63
Blue, Evander McN.	CPT	Co. C, 35th NC Inf Regt	Petersburg, VA	17 Jun 64
Board, Thomas H.	CPT	Co. I, 58th VA Inf Regt	Spotsylvania C.H., VA	12 May 64
Boddie, Elijah	1LT	Co. C, 7th TN Inf Regt	The Wilderness, VA	5 May 64
Boggs, William W.	1LT	Co. I, 20th VA Cav Regt	Loudoun Co, VA	16 Jul 64
Bohannon, Simon S.	CPT	Co. I, 28th NC Inf Regt	Spotsylvania C.H., VA	12 May 64
Bond, Julien D.	1LT	Co. G, 59th AL Inf Regt	Petersburg, VA	17 Jun 64
Booton, Daniel F.	MAJ	F&S, 3rd GA Cav Regt	Fair Gardens, TN	27 Jan 64
Boss, James J.	1LT	Co. G, 35th GA Inf Regt	The Wilderness, VA	6 May 64
Boswell, William J.	1LT	Co. B, 55th GA Inf Regt	Cumberland Gap, TN	9 Sep 63
Bowers, Michael E.	1LT	Co. K, 25th VA Inf Regt	The Wilderness, VA	5 May 64
Bowie, Robert S.	2LT	Co. B, 37th VA Inf Regt	Spotsylvania C.H., VA	12 May 64
Bowman, J. Dowling	1LT	Co. G, 15th LA Inf Regt	Spotsylvania C.H., VA	12 May 64
Boyd, James W.	CPT	Co. F, 6th TN Inf Regt	Corinth, MS	1 Jul 63
Boyd, Thomas	CPT	Co. B, 1st MS Inf Regt	Port Hudson, LA	9 Jul 63
Bradburn, Mark S.	CPT	Co. I, 16th AR Inf Regt	Port Hudson, LA	9 Jul 63
Bradford, Moses J.	CPT	Co. G, 10th MO Inf Regt	Helena, AR	4 Jul 63
Bradford, Nero G.	CPT	Co. I, 26th NC Inf Regt	Gettysburg, PA	5 Jul 63
Bradley, Thomas E.	2LT	Co. A, 23rd TN Inf Regt	Chickamauga, GA	19 Sep 63
Branch, Sanford W.	1LT	Co. B, 8th GA Inf Regt	Gettysburg, PA	4 Jul 63
Branch, Thomas P.	MAJ	Staff to GEN R. Ranson	Drury's Bluff, VA	18 May 64
Brand, George C.	2LT	Co. B, 2nd MO Cav Regt	Holly Springs, MS	3 May 63
Breedlove, John P.	1LT	Co. B, 4th AL Inf Regt	Gettysburg, PA	4 Jul 63
Brent, John L.	CPT	Co. F, 18th AR Inf Regt	Port Hudson, LA	9 Jul 63
Brinkley, Hugh G.	2LT	Co. I, 41st VA Inf Regt	Nansemond Co, VA	3 Sep 63
Bronaugh, David T.	1LT	Co. F, 16th AR Inf Regt	Port Hudson, LA	9 Jul 63
Brothers, Joseph W.	1LT	Co. C, 67th NC Inf Regt	Kinston, NC	22 Jun 64
Brown, Alexander H.	2LT	Co. H, 30th NC Inf Regt	Kelly's Ford, VA	7 Nov 63
Brown, Benjamin L.	1LT	Co. E, 59th GA Inf Regt	Gettysburg, PA	3 Jul 63
Brown, Bezaliel G.	CPT	Co. I, 7th VA Inf Regt	Gettysburg, PA	3 Jul 63
Brown, John G.	2LT	Co. D, 49th VA Inf Regt	Cold Harbor, VA	3 Jun 64
Brumley, Ozni R.	CPT	Co. B, 20th NC Inf Regt	Gettysburg, PA	1 Jul 63
Bryan, Robert C.	2LT	Co. A, 2nd TN Cav Regt (Ashby's)	Tippah Co, MS	25 Apr 63
Bryan, Robertson C.	2LT	Co. F, 48th VA Inf Regt	Spotsylvania C.H., VA	12 May 64
Buist, Henry	CPT	Co. G, 27th SC Inf Regt	Petersburg, VA	24 Jun 64
Bull, Alexander L.	2LT	Co. C, 5th FL Inf Regt	The Wilderness, VA	6 May 64
Bullard, David S.	2LT	Co. A, 18th NC Inf Regt	Spotsylvania C.H., VA	12 May 64
Bullock, John T.	1LT	Co. E, 23rd NC Inf Regt	Spotsylvania C.H., VA	12 May 64
Bullock, William M.	2LT	Co. H, 48th MS Inf Regt	Spotsylvania C.H., VA	12 May 64
Burgess, John M.	1LT	Co. H, 8th LA Inf Regt	Spotsylvania C.H., VA	12 May 64
Burgin, John M.	2LT	Co. K, 22nd NC Inf Regt	Gettysburg, PA	3 Jul 63
Burke, John H.	CPT	Co. B, 2nd TN Cav Regt (Ashby's)	Lancaster, KY	30 Jul 63
Burnett, John A.	2LT	Co. E, 50th VA Inf Regt	Spotsylvania C.H., VA	12 May 64
Burnett, W. B.	CPT	Co. G, 10th AR Inf Regt	Port Hudson, LA	9 Jul 63
Burney, Iverson L.	1LT	Co. A, 49th GA Inf Regt	Gettysburg, PA	4 Jul 63
Burt, Augustus W., Jr.	1LT	Co. A, 7th SC Inf Regt	Gettysburg, PA	3 Jul 63
Burton, John W.	CPT	Co. D, 6th AL Inf Regt	Gettysburg, PA	4 Jul 63
Busbee, Charles M.	SGTMAJ	F&S, 5th NC Inf Regt	Spotsylvania C.H., VA	12 May 64

Caldwell, Oliver H. P.	2LT	Co. K, 19th AR Inf Regt (Dockery's)	Big Black River, MS	17 May 63
Callahan, William P.	1LT	Co. B, 25th TN Inf Regt	Petersburg, VA	17 Jun 64
Camden, Edwin D.	CPT	Co. C, 25th VA Inf Regt	Spotsylvania C.H., VA	12 May 64
Cameron, William N.	2LT	Co. A, 25th TN Inf Regt	Drury's Bluff, VA	16 May 64
Campbell, Gilbert R.	CPT	— 21st TN Cav Regt (N.Carter's)	Shelbyville, TN	29 Oct 63
Campbell, Richard F.	CPT	Co. I, 49th AL Inf Regt	Port Hudson, LA	9 Jul 63
Campbell, Robert C.	2LT	Co. D, 53rd VA Inf Regt	Gettysburg, PA	3 Jul 63
Campbell, Watson C.	2LT	Co. E, 25th TN Inf Regt	Petersburg, VA	17 Jun 64
Campbell, William L.	CPT	Co. I, 11th SC Inf Regt	Petersburg, VA	9 May 64
Cannoy, Barney B.	2LT	Co. F, 4th VA Inf Regt	Spotsylvania C.H., VA	12 May 64
Cantwell, John L. P.	CPT	Co. F, 3rd NC Inf Regt	Spotsylvania C.H., VA	12 May 64
Carder, William B.	2LT	Co. D, 4th VA Inf Regt	Gettysburg, PA	3 Jul 63
Cargile, Christopher W.	1LT	Co. A, 10th AR Inf Regt	Port Hudson, LA	9 Jul 63
Carr, Robert B.	1LT	Co. A, 43rd NC Inf Regt	Gettysburg, PA	5 Jul 63
Carr, Thomas J.	1LT	Co. G, 43rd GA Inf Regt	Champion Hill, MS	16 May 63
Carrington, James McD.	CPT	Charlottesville (VA) Art	Spotsylvania C.H., VA	12 May 64
Carson, John C.	1LT	Co. A, Jeff Davis (MS) Legion (Cav)	Trevillian Sta., VA	12 Jun 64
Carson, Leroy P.	CPT	Co. D, 35th TN Inf Regt	Sequatchie Co, TN	19 Aug 63
Carson, Samuel F.	1LT	Co. D, 5th VA Inf Regt	Morton's Ford, VA	6 Feb 64
Carter, Edward	CPT	Co. K, 8th VA Inf Regt	Gettysburg, PA	3 Jul 63
Carter, George W.	1LT	Co. H, 23rd AR Inf Regt	Port Hudson, LA	9 Jul 63
Carter, Thomas M.	CPT	Co. I, 14th GA Inf Regt	The Wilderness, VA	6 May 64
Carter, William P.	CPT	King William (VA) Art	Spotsylvania C.H., VA	12 May 64
Carver, Elias A.	2LT	Co. I, 1st NC Inf Regt	Spotsylvania C.H., VA	12 May 64
Cash, James M.	1LT	Co. D, 4th TN Cav Regt (Murray's)	Lexington, KY	8 Feb 64
Cason, John R.	3LT	Co. I, 17th MS Inf Regt	Gettysburg, PA	2 Jul 63
Cathey, Alexander A.	1LT	Co. G, 34th NC Inf Regt	Gettysburg, PA	3 Jul 63
Cauthorn, Andrew B.	2LT	Co. C, 26th VA Inf Regt	Petersburg, VA	15 Jun 64
Cavanaugh, Patrick H.	1LT	Co. B, 1st LA Inf Regt (Nelligan's)	The Wilderness, VA	6 May 64
Chadbourne, Henry A.	1LT	Co. C, 10th AL Inf Regt	Gettysburg, PA	2 Jul 63
Chadduck, Charles T.	1LT	Co. H, 33rd VA Inf Regt	Spotsylvania C.H., VA	12 May 64
Chalkley, George B.	2LT	Co. D, 14th VA Inf Regt	Gettysburg, PA	3 Jul 63
Chambers, Charles E.	CPT	Co. B, 13th AL Inf Regt	Gettysburg, PA	3 Jul 63
Chandler, Thomas C.	CPT	Co. K, 47th VA Inf Regt	Spotsylvania C.H., VA	12 May 64
Chandler, William B.	2LT	Co. C, 13th NC Inf Regt	The Wilderness, VA	6 May 64
Cherry, William C.	2LT	Co. D, 4th GA Inf Regt	Spotsylvania C.H., VA	10 May 64
Chew, William H.	2LT	Co. A, 7th GA Cav Regt	Trevillian Sta., VA	11 Jun 64
Childs, James H.	1LT	Co. H, 4th VA Cav Regt	Markham Station, VA	6 Jan 64
Childs, Jesse	1LT	Co. A, 42nd VA Inf Regt	Spotsylvania C.H., VA	12 May 64
Childs, Robert	1LT	Co. G, 4th GA Inf Regt	Spotsylvania C.H., VA	10 May 64
Chinn, Addison B.	2LT	Co. A, 8th KY Cav Regt	Buffington Island, OH	19 Jul 63
Chisholm, Charles A.	2LT	Co. E, 10th LA Inf Regt	Spotsylvania C.H., VA	12 May 64
Chisholm, John N.	CPT	Co. I, 9th AL Inf Regt	Gettysburg, PA	2 Jul 63
Chitwood, Lewis S.	CPT	Co. A, 5th AL Inf Regt	Spotsylvania C.H., VA	12 May 64
Christian, Charles B.	LTC	F&S, 49th VA Inf Regt	Bethesda Church, VA	30 May 64
Christian, Jones R.	CPT	Co. F, 3rd VA Cav Regt	Spotsylvania C.H., VA	12 May 64
Clifton, Henry J.	1LT	Co. K, 21st SC Inf Regt	Petersburg, VA	18 Jun 64
Coalter, Henry T.	ADJ	F&S, 53rd VA Inf Regt	Gettysburg, PA	3 Jul 63

Cobb, James E.	1LT Co. F, 5th TX Inf Regt	Gettysburg, PA	2 Jul 63
Coble, George S. P.	2LT Co. G, 44th NC Inf Regt	South Anna Bridge, VA	26 Jun 63
Cockerham, David S.	CPT Co. H, 54th NC Inf Regt	Rappahannock Sta., VA	7 Nov 63
Coffee, Holland T.	CPT Co. A, 48th MS Inf Regt	Spotsylvania C.H., VA	12 May 64
Coffey, Hiram V.	2LT Co. I, 27th TX Cav Regt	Franklin, TN	27 Apr 63
Coffield, Joseph B.	3LT Co. H, 1st NC Inf Regt	Spotsylvania C.H., VA	12 May 64
Coffman, Daniel M.	2LT Co. A, 38th AR Inf Regt	Ripley Co, MO	25 Dec 63
Coggin, Jeremiah	3LT Co. C, 23rd NC Inf Regt	Gettysburg, PA	1 Jul 63
Cole, Alexander T.	CPT Co. D, 23rd NC Inf Regt	Spotsylvania C.H., VA	12 May 64
Coles, Isaac	1LT Co. E, 6th VA Cav Regt	Brandy Station, VA	9 Jun 63
Collier, William A.	1LT Co. K, 7th TX Inf Regt	Raymond, MS	12 May 63
Collins, James B.	2LT Co. A, 5th FL Inf Regt	The Wilderness, VA	6 May 64
Connally, James H.	CPT Co. E, 44th GA Inf Regt	Spotsylvania C.H., VA	10 May 64
Cook, Henry H.	2LT Co. I, 44th TN Inf Regt (Consolid.)	Drury's Bluff, VA	16 May 64
Cooke, Alexander B.	2LT Co. G, 23rd VA Inf Regt	Spotsylvania C.H., VA	12 May 64
Coon, David A.	1LT Co. I, 11th NC Inf Regt	Gettysburg, PA	3 Jul 63
Corbett, George W.	1LT Co. E, 18th NC Inf Regt	Spotsylvania C.H., VA	12 May 64
Cottingham, James R.	2LT Co. I, 3rd LA Inf Regt	Haynes Bluff, MS	30 Apr 63
Coulter, David B.	CPT Co. G, 12th AR Inf Regt	Port Hudson, LA	9 Jul 63
Councill, James C.	LTC F&S, 26th VA Inf Regt	Petersburg, VA	15 Jun 64
Covington, Cameron D.	2LT Co. B, 45th TN Inf Regt	Lebanon, TN	6 Feb 63
Covington, William W.	CPT Co. G, 23rd SC Inf Regt	Petersburg, VA	17 Jun 64
Cowan, John	CPT Co. D, 3rd NC Inf Regt	Spotsylvania C.H., VA	12 May 64
Cowan, Samuel N.	2LT Co. H, 6th KY Cav Regt	Cheshire, OH	20 Jul 63
Cowper, John C. C.	2LT Co. E, 33rd NC Inf Regt	Gettysburg, PA	3 Jul 63
Cracraft, George K.	CPT Co. G, 23rd AR Inf Regt	Port Hudson, LA	9 Jul 63
Craft, William H.	CPT Co. A, 15th TN Inf Regt	Knoxville, TN	29 Dec 63
Crapon, George M.	2LT Co. F, 3rd NC Inf Regt	Spotsylvania C.H., VA	12 May 64
Crawford, Thomas D.	2LT Co. B, 26th GA Inf Regt	Newberne, NC	27 Mch 64
Crisp, Charles F.	2LT Co. K, 10th VA Inf Regt	Spotsylvania C.H., VA	12 May 64
Critcher, Andrew J.	CPT Co. B, 37th NC Inf Regt	Jericho Mills, VA	24 May 64
Crocker, Jules O. B.	CPT Co. I, 9th VA Inf Regt	Gettysburg, PA	3 Jul 63
Crow, William P.	1LT Co. B, 6th KY Cav Regt	Cheshire, OH	20 Jul 63
Dalton, Peter W.	1LT Co. H, 42nd VA Inf Regt	Spotsylvania C.H., VA	12 May 64
Darden, Joseph H.	1LT Co. A, 3rd NC Inf Regt	Spotsylvania C.H., VA	12 May 64
Darracott, Charles R.	1LT Sturdivant's (VA) Art	Hanover C.H., VA	19 May 64
Daugherty, Ferdinand H.	LTC F&S, 13th TN Cav Regt (Dibrell's)	Livingston, TN	8 Feb 64
Davies, John F.	2LT Co. I, 14th GA Inf Regt	The Wilderness, VA	6 May 64
Davis, John W.	2LT Co. E, 20th VA Cav Regt	Frederick, MD	10 Jul 64
Davis, Joseph B.	2LT Co. H, 7th CS Cav Regt (Claiborne's)	Petersburg, VA	7 May 64
Davis, Seligman M.	2LT Co. A, 4th FL Inf Regt	Missionary Ridge, TN	23 Nov 63
Dawson, William A.	2LT Co. C, 27th VA Inf Regt	Spotsylvania C.H., VA	12 May 64
Day, William H.	CPT Co. K, 1st NC Inf Regt	Spotsylvania C.H., VA	12 May 64
Deadwyler, Henry R.	CPT Co. H, 38th GA Inf Regt	Spotsylvania C.H., VA	12 May 64
DeGournay, Paul F.	LTC F&S, 12th LA Hvy Art	Port Hudson, LA	9 Jul 63
DeLoach, Joseph D.	1LT Co. H, 61st GA Inf Regt	Spotsylvania C.H., VA	12 May 64
DeLoach, William H.	1LT Co. B, 7th GA Cav Regt	Trevillian Sta., VA	11 Jun 64
Dent, Simon M.	1LT Co. B, 5th VA Cav Regt	Yellow Tavern, VA	11 May 64
DePriest, Emmett E.	CPT Co. H, 23rd VA Inf Regt	Spotsylvania C.H., VA	12 May 64

Dewar, William A.	CPT Co. I, 31st NC Inf Regt	Cold Harbor, VA	1 Jun 64
Dickinson, Henry C.	CPT Co. A, 2nd VA Cav Regt	Meadow Br, Hanover Co, VA	12 May 64
Diggs, Eugene	CPT Co. B, 2nd MD Cav Bn	Martinsburg, (W)VA	15 Oct 63
Dillard, Robert Y.	2LT Co. H, 16th AR Inf Regt	Port Hudson, LA	9 Jul 63
Dixon, Hugh M.	CPT Co. H, 35th NC Inf Regt	Petersburg, VA	17 Jun 64
Dobson, William B.	2LT Co. C, 5th VA Cav Regt	Yellow Tavern, VA	11 May 64
Dobyns, Abner	CPT Co. B, 42nd VA Inf Regt	Spotsylvania C.H., VA	12 May 64
Doles, William F.	3LT Co. H, 32nd NC Inf Regt	Spotsylvania C.H., VA	10 May 64
Donaghe, John A.	2LT Co. C, 10th VA Inf Regt	Spotsylvania C.H., VA	12 May 64
Dorsey, Elisha W.	2LT Co. B, 11th NC Inf Regt	Gettysburg, PA	5 Jul 63
Douglass, Merry S.	1LT Co. H, 44th TN Inf Regt (Consolid.)	Petersburg, VA	17 Jun 64
Doyle, Little B.	1LT Co. G, 5th VA Inf Regt	Spotsylvania C.H., VA	12 May 64
Doyle, Thomas S.	1LT Co. C, 33rd VA Inf Regt	Spotsylvania C.H., VA	12 May 64
Drake, Benjamin S.	1LT Co. M, 2nd KY Cav Regt (Duke's)	Buffington Island, OH	19 Jul 63
Duff, Michael H.	2LT Co. F, 37th VA Inf Regt	Spotsylvania C.H., VA	12 May 64
Duff, William P.	CPT Co. G, 50th VA Inf Regt	Spotsylvania C.H., VA	12 May 64
Duley, Edmund G.	1LT Co. A, 1st MD Cav Regt	Gettysburg, PA	5 Jul 63
Dumas, William J.	CPT Co. K, 53rd GA Inf Regt	Knoxville, TN	29 Nov 63
Dunkle, John J.	CPT Co. K, 25th VA Inf Regt	Spotsylvania C.H., VA	12 May 64
Dunlap, Hugh P.	1LT Co. B, 10th KY Cav Regt (Johnson's)	Cheshire, OH	20 Jul 63
Dunlap, James	CPT Co. H, 26th VA Inf Bn	Cold Harbor, VA	3 Jun 64
Dunlap, William T.	1LT Co. F, 2nd KY Cav Regt (Duke's)	Farmer's Run, OH	22 Jul 63
Duralde, Alex V.	2LT Co. C, 9th LA Inf Regt	Port Hudson, LA	9 Jul 63
Durham, Napoleon B.	1LT Co. C, 44th GA Inf Regt	Spotsylvania C.H., VA	10 May 64
Duval, T. J.	1LT Co. F, 32nd TX Cav Regt	Deer Creek, MS	14 Jan 64
Eakins, Felix G.	1LT Co. G, 10th KY Cav Regt (Johnson's)	Cheshire, OH	20 Jul 63
Earl, Paul H.	1LT Co. G, 28th AL Inf Regt	Missionary Ridge, TN	23 Nov 63
Earp, Harris E.	1LT Co. C, 24th NC Inf Regt	Petersburg, VA	17 Jun 64
Easley, William B. W.	2LT Co. G, 48th TN Inf Regt (Voorhie's)	Hickman Co, TN	23 Jan 64
Easterling, Thomas W.	1LT Co. G, 5th SC Cav Regt (Ferguson's)	Trevillian Sta., VA	12 Jun 64
Eastham, Chapman B.	1LT Co. G, 10th VA Inf Regt	Spotsylvania C.H., VA	12 May 64
Eastin, Thomas E.	CPT Co. C, 8th KY Cav Regt	Buffington Island, OH	19 Jun 63
Edgar, Alfred M.	CPT Co. E, 27th VA Inf Regt	Spotsylvania C.H., VA	12 May 64
Edmondson, Joseph A.	CPT Co. G, 44th GA Inf Regt	Spotsylvania C.H., VA	10 May 64
Edwards, Alexander W.	1LT Co. C, 15th VA Cav Regt	Yellow Tavern, VA	11 May 64
Edwards, Bolivar	1LT Co. E, Miles' (LA) Legion	Port Hudson, LA	9 Jul 63
Elam, Robert S.	CPT Co. E, 22nd VA Inf Bn	Gettysburg, PA	3 Jul 63
Elkins, John Q.	2LT Co. H, 18th NC Inf Regt	Spotsylvania C.H., VA	12 May 64
Elliott, Galen R.	2LT Co. I, 8th TN Cav Regt (B.Smith's)	Sparta, TN	8 Jan 64
Elliott, John	CPT Co. G, 2nd LA Inf Regt	Spotsylvania C.H., VA	12 May 64
Ellison, George H.	CPT Co. E, 3rd AL Inf Regt	Spotsylvania C.H., VA	12 May 64
Elzey, Andrew J.	2LT Co. H, 17th TN Inf Regt	Petersburg, VA	17 Jun 64
Emanuel, William P.	MAJ F&S, 4th SC Cav Regt	Louisa C.H., VA	11 Jun 64

Embrey, Norman D.	2LT	Co. I, 11th VA Inf Regt	Milford Station, VA	21 May 64
Enos, William L.	2LT	Co. A, 26th VA Inf Regt	Petersburg, VA	15 Jun 64
Epps, William	2LT	Co. D, 4th SC Cav Regt	Trevillian Sta., VA	11 Jun 64
Evans, William C. D.	2LT	Co. E, 17th AR Inf Regt (Griffith's)	Natchez, MS	22 Dec 63
Ewing, Z. Whitefield	2LT	Co. H, 17th TN Inf Regt	Petersburg, VA	17 Jun 64
Ezell, Cullen R.	CPT	Co. G, 4th GA Inf Regt	Spotsylvania C.H., VA	10 May 64
Fannin, James W.	CPT	Co. A, 61st AL Inf Regt	Spotsylvania C.H., VA	12 May 64
Farrar, Absalom H.	2LT	Co. C, 13th MS Inf Regt	Gettysburg, PA	3 Jul 63
Fennell, Nicholas E.	3LT	Co. G, 61st NC Inf Regt	Bermuda Hundred, VA	16 Jun 64
Ferring, William A.	CPT	Co. C, 3rd CS Inf Regt	Mississippi Co, AR	18 Sep 63
Fickeissen, Jacob	1LT	Co. K, 14th LA Inf Regt	North Anna, VA	23 May 64
Finks, Alexander N.	CPT	Co. L, 10th VA Inf Regt	Spotsylvania C.H., VA	12 May 64
Finks, Simon H.	2LT	Co. L, 10th VA Inf Regt	Spotsylvania C.H., VA	12 May 64
Finley, Gaston	CPT	Co. K, 1st FL Cav Regt	Missionary Ridge, TN	23 Nov 63
Finley, George W.	1LT	Co. K, 56th VA Inf Regt	Gettysburg, PA	3 Jul 63
Fitzgerald, George B.	CPT	Co. A, 12th VA Cav Regt	Turin, VA	20 Aug 63
Fitzhugh, Claggett D.	PVT	Co. K, 1st VA Cav Regt	Hagerstown, MD	12 Sep 62
Fitzpatrick, John B.	1LT	Co. H, 14th LA Inf Regt	The Wilderness, VA	6 May 64
Fleming, Henry C.	1LT	Co. K, 25th TN Inf Regt	Drury's Bluff, VA	16 May 64
Fletcher, Richard M.	2LT	Co. F, 2nd LA Inf Regt	Spotsylvania C.H., VA	12 May 64
Floyd, Francis F.	3LT	Co. E, 51st NC Inf Regt	Bermuda Hundred, VA	16 Jun 64
Folk, George N.	COL	F&S, 6th NC Cav Regt	Kinston, NC	22 Jun 64
Foly, Timothy	2LT	Co. C, 19th MS Inf Regt	Spotsylvania C.H., VA	12 May 64
Fontaine, Lamar	MAJ	F&S, 4th AL Cav Regt (Roddey's)	Ringgold, GA	27 Nov 63
Ford, James W. A.	1LT	Co. G, 20th VA Cav Regt	near Washington, DC	14 Jul 64
Ford, William B.	2LT	Co. D, 8th KY Cav Regt	Buffington Island, OH	19 Jul 63
Fort, Gordon K.	2LT	Co. G, 7th GA Cav Regt	Trevillian Sta., VA	11 Jun 64
Foster, Anthony C.	2LT	Co. B, 4th AL Cav Bn	Florence, AL	30 Nov 63
Fousse, Frederick F.	2LT	Co. C, 25th VA Inf Regt	Spotsylvania C.H., VA	12 May 64
Fowler, Hardiman D.	CPT	Co. I, 1st NC Inf Regt	Spotsylvania C.H., VA	12 May 64
Fox, Isham A.	1LT	Co. B, 11th KY Cav Regt	Buffington Island, OH	19 Jul 63
Fraetas, Charles	2LT	Co. E, 3rd VA Inf Regt	Howlett's Farm, VA	18 Jun 64
Frasier, John W.	2LT	Co. H, 1st VA Cav Regt	Racoon Ford, VA	11 Oct 63
Frayser, Richard E.	CPT	CSA Signal Corps	Caroline Co, VA	20 May 64
Frink, John O.	1LT	Co. H, 18th NC Inf Regt	Spotsylvania C.H., VA	12 May 64
Frizell, William H.	1LT	Co. I, 12th MS Inf Regt	Spotsylvania C.H., VA	12 May 64
Fry, Henry	1LT	Co. C, 37th VA Inf Regt	Spotsylvania C.H., VA	12 May 64
Fulcher, James T.	2LT	Co. H, 37th VA Inf Regt	Spotsylvania C.H., VA	12 May 64
Fulkerson, Abram	COL	F&S, 63rd TN Inf Regt	Petersburg, VA	17 Jun 64
Funk, Jefferson W. O.	1LT	Co. A, 5th VA Inf Regt	Spotsylvania C.H., VA	12 May 64
Gallman, John J.	2LT	Co. H, 5th SC Inf Regt	The Wilderness, VA	6 May 64
Galloway, Moses P.	2LT	Co. G, 23rd SC Inf Regt	Petersburg, VA	17 Jun 64
Gamble, John F.	1LT	Co. D, 14th NC Inf Regt	Spotsylvania C.H., VA	12 May 64
Ganoway, John T.	2LT	Co. E, 50th VA Inf Regt	Spotsylvania C.H., VA	12 May 64
Garrett, Daniel W.	1LT	Co. E, 11th GA Inf Regt	The Wilderness, VA	6 May 64
Garrett, David W.	1LT	Co. C, 42nd VA Inf Regt	Spotsylvania C.H., VA	12 May 64
Gary, Samuel W.	2LT	Co. A, 3rd VA Inf Regt	Gettysburg, PA	3 Jul 63
Gash, Harvey Y.	2LT	Co. D, 6th NC Cav Regt	Kinston, NC	22 Jun 64
George, William W.	2LT	Co. H, 26th VA Inf Bn	Cold Harbor, VA	3 Jun 64

Gibson, Allen C.	CPT	Co. B, 4th GA Inf Regt	Spotsylvania C.H., VA	10 May 64
Gibson, Bruce	CPT	Co. A, 6th VA Cav Regt	Yellow Tavern, VA	11 May 64
Gilbert, Jacob H.	1LT	Co. E, 57th NC Inf Regt	nr Williamsport, MD	6 Jul 63
Gilkeson, John W.	1LT	Co. D, 25th VA Inf Regt	Spotsylvania C.H., VA	12 May 64
Gillespie, Rufus C.	PVT	Co. G, 45th VA Inf Regt	southwest VA	25 Oct 63
Gillock, James W.	1LT	Co. H, 27th VA Inf Regt	Gettysburg, PA	5 Jul 63
Gilmer, William S.	2LT	Co. C, 37th VA Inf Regt	Spotsylvania C.H., VA	12 May 64
Glenn, Robert A.	2LT	Co. I, 22nd NC Inf Regt	Hanover Jct., VA	23 May 64
Gobble, Thomas M.	CPT	Co. I, 48th VA Inf Regt	Spotsylvania C.H., VA	12 May 64
Goldsborough, William W.	MAJ	F&S, 2nd MD Inf Regt	Gettysburg, PA	4 Jul 63
Good, William C.	2LT	Co. H, 6th NC Cav Regt	Kinston, NC	22 Jun 64
Goodloe, Thomas J.	1LT	Co. K, 44th TN Inf Regt (Consolid.)	Petersburg, VA	17 Jun 64
Goodwin, David W., Jr.	3LT	Co. K, 44th GA Inf Regt	Spotsylvania C.H., VA	10 May 64
Gordon, David E.	2LT	Co. I, 4th SC Cav Regt	Trevillian Sta., VA	11 Jun 64
Gorham, Willis J.	CPT	Co. K, 35th GA Inf Regt	The Wilderness, VA	5 May 64
Gorman, John C.	CPT	Co. B, 2nd NC Inf Regt	Spotsylvania C.H., VA	12 May 64
Gowan, Benjamin A.	3LT	Co. G, 51st NC Inf Regt	Bermuda Hundred, VA	16 Jun 64
Grace, Christopher C.	1LT	Co. I, 12th GA Inf Regt	Spotsylvania C.H., VA	10 May 64
Grant, Benjamin S.	2LT	Co. F, 42nd MS Inf Regt	Falling Waters, MD	14 Jul 63
Gravely, Thomas M.	2LT	Co. F, 42nd VA Inf Regt	Spotsylvania C.H., VA	12 May 64
Graves, Frank N.	2LT	Co. F, 61st GA Inf Regt	Spotsylvania C.H., VA	12 May 64
Grayson, David C.	CPT	Co. K, 10th VA Inf Regt	Spotsylvania C.H., VA	12 May 64
Green, Augustus M.	2LT	Co. E, 12th GA Inf Regt	Spotsylvania C.H., VA	10 May 64
Green, Lucius	2LT	Co. K, 5th VA Cav Regt	Yellow Tavern, VA	11 May 64
Greer, James L.	1LT	Co. D, 4th GA Inf Regt	Spotsylvania C.H., VA	10 May 64
Greer, John W.	CPT	Co. B, 23rd AR Inf Regt	Port Hudson, LA	9 Jul 63
Greever, John D.	1LT	Co. C, 50th VA Inf Regt	Spotsylvania C.H., VA	12 May 64
Griffin, Wiley H.	CPT	Baltimore (MD) Lt Art	Yellow Tavern, VA	11 May 64
Groome, James W.	2LT	Co. D, 23rd VA Inf Regt	Spotsylvania C.H., VA	12 May 64
Gurganus, Andrew J.	2LT	Co. E, 3rd NC Inf Regt	Spotsylvania C.H., VA	12 May 64
Gurr, Thomas J.	2LT	Co. B, 51st GA Inf Regt	Cold Harbor, VA	1 Jun 64
Guthrie, William L.	CPT	Co. I, 23rd VA Inf Regt	Spotsylvania C.H., VA	12 May 64
Guyther, John M.	1LT	Co. H, 1st NC Inf Regt	Spotsylvania C.H., VA	12 May 64
Hall, Calvin D.	1LT	Co. G, 48th VA Inf Regt	Spotsylvania C.H., VA	12 May 64
Hall, Edward J.	CPT	Co. -, 1st LA Cav Regt	Natchez, MS	10 Dec 63
Hall, Reuben N.	2LT	Co. B, 4th FL Inf Regt	Missionary Ridge, TN	23 Nov 63
Hallford, Jesse G.	2LT	Co. E, 8th SC Inf Regt	Cold Harbor, VA	30 May 64
Halliburton, William	1LT	Co. B, Freeman's (MO) Cav Regt	Laurence Co, AR	7 Oct 63
Hammack, Thornton M.	CPT	Co. D, 10th KY Cav Regt (Johnson's)	Rutland, OH	20 Jul 63
Hancock, William A.	1LT	Co. F, 8th AR Inf Regt	Arkadelphia, AR	30 Oct 63
Handerson, Henry E.	CPT	Co. B, 9th LA Inf Regt	The Wilderness, VA	6 May 64
Hardin, Hopkins	2LT	Co. C, 19th VA Inf Regt	Gettysburg, PA	3 Jul 63
Harget, John M.	2LT	Co. G, 1st NC Inf Regt	Spotsylvania C.H., VA	12 May 64
Hargrove, Tazewell L.	LTC	F&S, 44th NC Inf Regt	South Anna Bridge, VA	26 Jun 63
Harman, Lewis	CPT	Co. I, 12th VA Cav Regt	Verdiersville, VA	5 May 64
Harper, Charles P.	1LT	Co. C, 21st VA Inf Regt	Spotsylvania C.H., VA	12 May 64
Harris, David T., Jr.	2LT	Co. E, 21st GA Inf Regt	Spotsylvania C.H., VA	10 May 64
Harris, John W.	2LT	Co. K, 58th VA Inf Regt	Spotsylvania C.H., VA	12 May 64
Harris, Thomas W.	CPT	Co. C, 12th GA Inf Regt	Spotsylvania C.H., VA	10 May 64
Harrison, Harris K.	CPT	Co. E, 7th GA Cav Regt	Trevillian Sta., VA	11 Jun 64

Hart, Edwin S.	CPL	Co. D, 23rd NC Inf Regt	Spotsylvania C.H., VA	12 May 64
Hart, Robert B.	2LT	Co. E, 5th VA Cav Regt	Yellow Tavern, VA	11 May 64
Hart, William E.	1LT	King William (VA) Art	Spotsylvania C.H., VA	12 May 64
Hartsfield, Lemuel H.	CPT	Co. E, 3rd NC Cav Regt	Hanover C.H., VA	27 May 64
Harvey, Richard	2LT	Co. H, 7th GA Cav Regt	Trevillian Sta., VA	11 Jun 64
Haskins, Noah A.	1LT	Co. B, 25th VA Inf Regt	The Wilderness, VA	5 May 64
Hastings, Joseph H.	2LT	Co. A, 17th TN Inf Regt	Petersburg, VA	17 Jun 64
Hatcher, William H.	2LT	Co. C, 42nd VA Inf Regt	Spotsylvania C.H., VA	12 May 64
Hawes, Samuel H.	2LT	Orange (VA) Art	Spotsylvania C.H., VA	12 May 64
Hawkins, John H.	1LT	Co. E, 10th VA Inf Regt	Spotsylvania C.H., VA	12 May 64
Haynes, Frank R.	2LT	Co. E, 24th VA Cav Regt	Cobb's Creek, VA	5 Oct 63
Haynes, John L.	1LT	Co. I, 14th AL Inf Regt	Spotsylvania C.H., VA	12 May 64
Haynes, Robert B.	2LT	Co. A, 3rd KY Cav Regt	Cheshire, OH	20 Jul 63
Heartsfield, Jacob A.	1LT	Co. I, 1st NC Inf Regt	Spotsylvania C.H., VA	12 May 64
Heath, James F.	2LT	Co. F, 67th NC Inf Regt	Swift Creek, NC	26 Apr 64
Helm, James W.	CPT	Co. K, 42nd VA Inf Regt	Spotsylvania C.H., VA	12 May 64
Hempstead, Junius L.	1LT	Co. F, 25th VA Inf Regt	The Wilderness, VA	5 May 64
Henderson, John H.	2LT	Co. K, 39th TN Inf Regt (Bradford's)	Monroe Co, TN	2 Feb 64
Henderson, John J.	CPT	Co. A, 61st GA Inf Regt	Spotsylvania C.H., VA	12 May 64
Henderson, Lewis J.	2LT	Co. G, 3rd NC Inf Regt	Spotsylvania C.H., VA	12 May 64
Henderson, Thomas B.	1LT	Co. H, 3rd NC Cav Regt	Greenville, NC	17 Dec 63
Hendricks, William N.	2LT	Co. A, 25th VA Inf Regt	The Wilderness, VA	5 May 64
Henritze, James J.	2LT	Co. C, 37th VA Inf Regt	Spotsylvania C.H., VA	12 May 64
Henry, John M.	2LT	Co. H, 44th TN Inf Regt (Consolid.)	Petersburg, VA	17 Jun 64
Herrington, William G.	2LT	Co. E, 25th VA Inf Bn	Cox's Farm, VA	12 Jul 64
Higley, Gilbert P.	2LT	Co. F, 51st NC Inf Regt	Cold Harbor, VA	1 Jun 64
Hillsman, James M. O.	CPT	Co. H, 44th VA Inf Regt	Spotsylvania C.H., VA	12 May 64
Hines, John C.	2LT	Co. C, 5th NC Cav Regt	Jack's Shop, VA	22 Sep 63
Hines, Samuel H.	CPT	Co. I, 45th NC Inf Regt	Spotsylvania C.H., VA	12 May 64
Hix, John S.	2LT	Co. B, 44th VA Inf Regt	Spotsylvania C.H., VA	12 May 64
Hixon, Madison	1LT	Co. B, 16th AR Inf Regt	Port Hudson, LA	9 Jul 63
Hobson, James M.	1LT	Co. E, 2nd NC Inf Regt	Spotsylvania C.H., VA	12 May 64
Hodges, James E.	CPT	Co. B, 32nd NC Inf Regt	Spotsylvania C.H., VA	12 May 64
Hogan, Patrick	2LT	Co. H, 4th VA Inf Regt	Spotsylvania C.H., VA	12 May 64
Hooberry, John W.	2LT	Co. I, 44th TN Inf Regt (Consolid.)	Petersburg, VA	17 Jun 64
Hood, William H.	MAJ	F&S, Hood's Bn. VA Reserves	Petersburg, VA	15 Jun 64
Hoover, Henry L.	1LT	Co. H, 25th VA Inf Regt	Spotsylvania C.H., VA	12 May 64
Hopkins, Francis W.	CPT	Co. G, 7th GA Cav Regt	Trevillian Sta., VA	11 Jun 64
Hopkins, George	CPT	Co. I, 10th VA Cav Regt	Henrico Co, VA	13 May 64
Horne, Henry W.	CPT	Co. C, 3rd NC Inf Regt	Spotsylvania C.H., VA	12 May 64
Horton, Thomas B.	CPT	Co. B, 11th VA Inf Regt	Milford Station, VA	21 May 64
Houser, Absalom J.	2LT	Co. D, 1st NC Inf Regt	Spotsylvania C.H., VA	12 May 64
Howard, George W.	CPT	Co. C, 1st MD Cav Regt	Hawes Shop, VA	27 May 64
Howard, Robert J.	2LT	Co. –, 1st MS Inf Regt	Port Hudson, LA	9 Jul 63
Howlett, Henry C.	1LT	Co. K, 5th VA Cav Regt	Chesterfield C.H., VA	10 May 64
Howlett, Robert B.	1LT	Co. A, 5th VA Cav Regt	Yellow Tavern, VA	11 May 64
Hudgins, Albert G.	LT	C.S. Navy	on CSS Bombshell	5 May 64
Hudson, Thomas J.	1LT	Co. B, 9th LA Inf Regt	Spotsylvania C.H., VA	12 May 64
Hughes, James M.	CPT	Co. K, 44th VA Inf Regt	Spotsylvania C.H., VA	12 May 64
Hughes, John S.	2LT	Co. A, 6th KY Cav Regt	Cheshire, OH	20 Jul 63

Hughes, John W.	2LT	Co. K, 44th VA Inf Regt	Spotsylvania C.H., VA	12 May 64
Hulbert, William W.	1LT	Co. D, 4th GA Inf Regt	Spotsylvania C.H., VA	10 May 64
Humes, Andrew R.	CPT	Co. K, 21st VA Cav Regt (Peter's)	Leetown, (W)VA	3 Jul 64
Humphreys, Alexander R.	2LT	Co. D, 26th VA Inf Bn	Cold Harbor, VA	3 Jun 63
Hunter, George W.	2LT	Co. G, 8th KY Cav Regt	Cheshire, OH	20 Jul 63
Hunter, Pilander D.	1LT	Staff to GEN Frazer, Artillery	Cumberland Gap, TN	9 Sep 63
Hunter, William L.	1LT	Co. A, 43rd VA Cav Bn	Aldie, VA	23 Apr 64
Hutcheson, C.L.	1LT	Co. H, 63rd TN Inf Regt	Petersburg, VA	17 Jun 64
Hutchison, Benjamin H.	2LT	Co. D, 8th VA Inf Regt	Gettysburg, PA	3 Jul 63
Hutton, Samuel J.	2LT	Co. F, 37th VA Inf Regt	Spotsylvania C.H., VA	12 May 64
Irvine, Joseph A.	2LT	Co. A, 9th TN Cav Bn (Gantt's)	Columbia, TN	8 Nov 63
Irwin, Thomas	2LT	Co. G, 11th TN Inf Regt	Missionary Ridge, TN	25 Nov 63
Israel, Abner B.	CPT	Co. E, 1st AR Inf Regt	Ripley Co, MO	25 Dec 63
Ivey, William D.	1LT	Co. D, 12th GA Inf Regt	Spotsylvania C.H., VA	10 May 64
Ivey, William H.	3LT	Co. H, 2nd NC Cav Regt	Spotsylvania C.H., VA	12 May 64
James, William N.	CPT	Co. C, 44th TN Inf Regt (Consolid.)	Petersburg, VA	17 Jun 64
Jarrett, James A.	2LT	Co. K, Holcombe's (SC) Inf Legion	Stony Creek Bridge, VA	7 May 64
Jastremski, Leon	CPT	Co. E, 10th LA Inf Regt	Spotsylvania C.H., VA	12 May 64
Jefferies, William T.	2LT	Co. E, Power's (CS) Cav Regt	Port Gibson, MS	14 Feb 64
Jeffers, Eugene	1LT	Co. I, 61st GA Inf Regt	Spotsylvania C.H., VA	12 May 64
Jenkins, Henry J.	1LT	Co. A, 15th NC Cav Bn (Wynn's)	Gatesville, NC	9 Jun 64
Jenkins, John D.	1LT	Co. K, 44th TN Inf Regt	The Wilderness, VA	6 May 64
Johnson, Charles P.	2LT	Co. B, 11th VA Cav Regt	Burlington, (W)VA	3 Dec 63
Johnson, H.L.W.	CPT	Co. C, 12th AR Inf Regt	Port Hudson, LA	9 Jul 63
Johnson, Jehu H.	CPT	Co. E, 25th VA Inf Regt	The Wilderness, VA	5 May 64
Johnson, Samuel J.	CPT	Co. K, 25th TN Inf Regt	Drury's Bluff, VA	16 May 64
Johnson, Seymour A.	2LT	Co. D, 23rd VA Inf Regt	Spotsylvania C.H., VA	12 May 64
Johnson, William E., Jr.	2LT	Co. K, 7th SC Cav Regt	Cold Harbor, VA	30 May 63
Johnson, William P.	PVT	Co. C, 1st NC Cav Regt	Bristoe Station, VA	25 Nov 63
Johnson, William T.	CPT	Co. H, 18th VA Inf Regt	Gettysburg, PA	3 Jul 63
Johnston, Thomas H.	MAJ	F&S, 1st MS Inf Regt	Port Hudson, LA	9 Jul 63
Johnston, Thomas L.	CPT	Co. A, 1st NC Inf Regt	Spotsylvania C.H., VA	12 May 64
Jones, David A.	MAJ	Staff to GEN JR Jones	Spotsylvania C.H., VA	12 May 64
Jones, Henry C.	2LT	Co. H, 50th VA Inf Regt	Spotsylvania C.H., VA	12 May 64
Jones, James McG.	CPT	Co. G, Cocke's (AR) Inf Regt	near Berryville, MO	4 Oct 63
Jones, Joel W.	2LT	Co. H, 1st MS Inf Regt	Port Hudson, LA	9 Jul 63
Jones, William T.	1LT	Co. C, 35th NC Inf Regt	Petersburg, VA	17 Jun 64
Keiser, George F.	2LT	Co. H, 5th VA Inf Regt	Spotsylvania C.H., VA	12 May 64
Kelley, Francis W.	CPT	Co. C, 50th VA Inf Regt	Spotsylvania C.H., VA	12 May 64
Kelley, James P.	2LT	Co. C, 4th VA Inf Regt	Spotsylvania C.H., VA	12 May 64
Kelly, John G.	CPT	Staff to GEN Hebert	Smithville, NC	29 Feb 64
Kelly, Thomas E.	1LT	Co. F, 5th LA Inf Regt	Spotsylvania C.H., VA	12 May 64
Kemp, William B.	CPT	Co. H, 3rd LA Cav Regt (Wingfield's)	Port Hudson, LA	9 Jul 63
Kendall, William A.	1LT	Co. A, 3rd KY Cav Regt	Cheshire, OH	20 Jul 63

Kent, Thomas N.	CPT	Co. F, 48th GA Inf Regt	Gettysburg, PA	5 Jul 63
Killian, George H.	1LT	Co. H, 5th VA Inf Regt	Spotsylvania C.H., VA	12 May 64
Killmartin, John	2LT	Co. -, 7th LA Inf Regt	Spotsylvania C.H., VA	12 May 64
King, Alexander McC.	CPT	Co. E, 50th VA Inf Regt	Spotsylvania C.H., VA	12 May 64
King, Festus	2LT	King William (VA) Art	Spotsylvania C.H., VA	12 May 64
King, John E.	2LT	Co. E, 3rd NC Inf Regt	Spotsylvania C.H., VA	12 May 64
King, John S.	2LT	Co. B, 37th VA Inf Regt	Spotsylvania C.H., VA	12 May 64
King, Thomas J.	2LT	Co. H, 24th VA Cav Regt	Charles City C.H., VA	13 Dec 63
Kirk, Thomas J.	1LT	Co. G, 4th VA Inf Regt	Spotsylvania C.H., VA	12 May 64
Kirkman, Alex J.	1LT	Co. D, 4th AL Cav Bn	Florence, AL	30 Oct 63
Kitchin, William H.	CPT	Co. I, 12th NC Inf Regt	Spotsylvania C.H., VA	12 May 64
Knox, John G.	CPT	Co. A, 7th NC Inf Regt	The Wilderness, VA	5 May 64
Knox, William C.	2LT	Co. D, 8th TN Cav Regt (B.Smith's)	Woodbury, TN	16 Nov 63
Kratzer, Joseph W.	2LT	Co. H, 12th VA Cav Regt	Bethany, VA	21 May 64
Kuykendall, Isaac	CPT	Co. F, 7th VA Cav Regt	Wire Bridge, (W)VA	19 Feb 64
Kyle, Jesse K.	CPT	Co. B, 52nd NC Inf Regt	Milford Station, VA	22 May 64
Lacy, Drury	2LT	Co. I, 23rd VA Inf Regt	Spotsylvania C.H., VA	12 May 64
Lambert, John M.	2LT	Co. I, 52nd VA Inf Regt	Bethesda Church, VA	30 May 64
Lane, Christopher C.	3LT	Co. A, 3rd NC Inf Regt	Spotsylvania C.H., VA	12 May 64
Lane, John W.	CPT	Co. I, 16th NC Inf Regt	The Wilderness, VA	6 May 64
Latham, Julian A.	1LT	Co. G, 1st NC Inf Regt	Spotsylvania C.H., VA	12 May 64
Lauderdale, John F.	1LT	Co. A, 2nd TN Cav Regt (Ashby's)	Spring Place, GA	28 Feb 64
Layton, David M.	1LT	Co. D, 25th VA Inf Regt	Spotsylvania C.H., VA	12 May 64
Leathers, William F.	2LT	Co. A, 2nd KY Cav Regt (Duke's)	Buffington Island, OH	19 Jul 63
Leatherwood, Albert N.	1LT	Co. E, 39th NC Inf Regt	Cherokee Co, NC	18 Feb 64
LeBreton, Emile St.M.	LTC	F&S, 4th LA Inf Militia	Port Hudson, LA	9 Jul 63
Ledford, Jesse A.	1LT	Co. H, 25th TN Inf Regt	Petersburg, VA	17 Jun 64
Ledyard, William N.	1LT	Co. A, 3rd AL Inf Regt	Gettysburg, PA	1 Jul 63
Leftwitch, Lincoln C.	LT	C.S. Navy	on CSS Minnie	7 May 64
Legg, Russell W.	2LT	Co. A, 50th VA Inf Regt	Spotsylvania C.H., VA	12 May 64
Leigh, William P.R.	2LT	Co. A, 5th VA Cav Regt	Lancaster Co, VA	13 Jun 64
Lemon, James L.	CPT	Co. A, 18th GA Inf Regt	Knoxville, TN	29 Nov 63
Lemon, John L.	CPT	Co. G, 14th LA Inf Regt	Spotsylvania C.H., VA	12 May 64
Leonard, James S.	2LT	Co. D, 7th CS Cav Regt	Swansboro, NC	30 Apr 64
Lewis, Andrew J.	CPT	Co. E, Power's (CS) Cav Regt	Port Gibson, MS	14 Feb 64
Lewis, Charles I.	CPT	Co. I, 8th VA Cav Regt	Leetown, (W)VA	3 Jul 64
Lewis, George W.	CPT	Co. I, 31st GA Inf Regt	Spotsylvania C.H., VA	12 May 64
Lewis, James B.	2LT	Co. F, 1st TN Cav Regt (Carter's)	Maynardsville, TN	3 Dec 63
Lewis, Oliver H.P.	1LT	Co. F, 31st VA Inf Regt	Highland Co, VA	10 Nov 63
Lewis, Thomas C.	CPT	Co. I, 18th NC Inf Regt	Spotsylvania C.H., VA	12 May 64
Lindsay, George H.	2LT	Co. K, 54th NC Inf Regt	Drury's Bluff, VA	16 May 64
Lindsey, James B.	3LT	Co. B, 31st NC Inf Regt	Cold Harbor, VA	1 Jun 64
Lipps, Jonas A.	CPT	Co. H, 50th VA Inf Regt	Spotsylvania C.H., VA	12 May 64
Logan, Matthew D.	CPT	Co. I, 3rd KY Cav Regt	Cheshire, OH	20 Jul 63
Logan, Robert D.	CPT	Co. A, 3rd KY Cav Regt	Cheshire, OH	20 Jul 63
Logsdon, Barnaby B.	1LT	Co. D, 1st KY Cav Regt	Charleston, TN	28 Dec 63
Long, Green B.	2LT	Co. F, 11th VA Inf Regt	Gettysburg, PA	3 Jul 63
Long, John	2LT	Co. D, 10th VA Inf Regt	Spotsylvania C.H., VA	12 May 64

Lovett, Joshua M.	CPT	Co. E, 23rd VA Cav Regt	Capon Bridge (W)VA	31 Jan 64
Lowdermilk, Zemeriah H.	2LT	Co. H, 3rd NC Inf Regt	Spotsylvania C.H., VA	12 May 64
Lowe, Schuyler	CPT	3rd Battery (MO) Lt Art	St.Joseph, LA	29 Jan 64
Lusk, Nathan B.	2LT	Co. G, 12th SC Inf Regt	The Wilderness, VA	6 May 64
Lyon, Robert H.	2LT	Co. H, 3rd NC Inf Regt	Spotsylvania C.H., VA	12 May 64
Lyons, Peter C.	1LT	Co. G, 18th GA Inf Regt	Cold Harbor, VA	1 Jun 64
Lytle, James K. Polk	CPT	Co. F, 23rd TN Inf Regt	Bean's Station, TN	14 Dec 63
Lytton, John F.	1LT	Co. C, 5th VA Inf Regt	Spotsylvania C.H., VA	12 May 64
MacRae, Walter G.	CPT	Co. C, 7th NC Inf Regt	The Wilderness, VA	6 May 64
Maddox, Joseph J.	1LT	Co. B, 38th GA Inf Regt	Locust Grove, VA	6 May 64
Mahoney, Daniel	1LT	Co. A, 10th LA Inf Regt	Spotsylvania C.H., VA	12 May 64
Malarcher, Lewis H.	CPT	Co. D, 7th LA Inf Regt	The Wilderness, VA	6 May 64
Mallett, Charles P.	1LT	Co. C, 3rd NC Inf Regt	Spotsylvania C.H., VA	12 May 64
Malloy, John D.	1LT	Co. D, 51st NC Inf Regt	Drury's Bluff, VA	16 May 64
Manning, Vannoy H.	COL	F&S, 3rd AR Inf Regt	The Wilderness, VA	6 May 64
Martin, Thomas B.	CPT	Co. I, Holcombe's (SC) Inf Legion	Stony Creek Bridge, VA	7 May 64
Martin, William A.	CPT	Co. B, 7th LA Inf Regt	Spotsylvania C.H., VA	12 May 64
Maskew, John	1LT	Co. E, 1st LA Inf Regt (Nelligan's)	Gettysburg, PA	5 Jul 63
Massie, D. Rodes	2LT	Charlottesville (VA) Art	Spotsylvania C.H., VA	12 May 64
Mastin, Edmund I.	1LT	Staff to GEN Kelly	Charleston, TN	28 Dec 63
Mathews, Jacob W.	CPT	Co. I, 25th VA Inf Regt	The Wilderness, VA	5 May 64
Mauck, Joseph W.	2LT	Co. H, 10th VA Inf Regt	Spotsylvania C.H., VA	12 May 64
Maxwell, Benjamin C.	1LT	Courtney (VA) Art	Spotsylvania C.H., VA	12 May 64
Maxwell, James W.	1LT	Co. F, 50th GA Inf Regt	Cold Harbor, VA	1 Jun 64
May, Samuel H.	1LT	Co. D, 10th LA Inf Regt	Gettysburg, PA	5 Jul 63
McCallum, James R.	CPT	Co. D, 63rd TN Inf Regt	Petersburg, VA	17 Jun 64
McCawley, William	1LT	Co. K, 9th VA Cav Regt	Ashland, VA	1 Jul 64
McConnell, William S.	CPT	Co. E, 48th VA Inf Regt	Spotsylvania C.H., VA	12 May 64
McCoy, Charles D.	CPT	Co. D, 25th VA Inf Regt	Spotsylvania C.H., VA	12 May 64
McCreary, James B.	MAJ	F&S, 11th KY Cav Regt	Cheshire, OH	20 Jul 63
McDonald, Daniel	CPT	Co. C, 61st GA Inf Regt	Spotsylvania C.H., VA	12 May 64
McDonald, James R.	MAJ	F&S, 51st NC Inf Regt	Cold Harbor, VA	1 Jun 64
McDowell, James W.	1LT	Co. D, 26th VA Inf Bn	Cold Harbor, VA	3 Jun 64
McIntosh, Franklin M.	1LT	Co. F, 18th NC Inf Regt	Spotsylvania C.H., VA	12 May 64
McLeod, Andrew J.	CPT	Co. C, 51st GA Inf Regt	Cold Harbor, VA	1 Jun 64
McLeod, Murdoch	1LT	Co. H, 26th NC Inf Regt	The Wilderness, VA	6 May 64
McMichael, James R.	CPT	Co. K, 12th GA Inf Regt	Spotsylvania C.H., VA	10 May 64
McMillan, John J.	1LT	Co. C, 1st NC Inf Regt	Spotsylvania C.H., VA	12 May 64
McNear, Benjamin F.	2LT	Co. I, 6th KY Cav Regt	Cheshire, OH	20 Jul 63
Meacham, Samuel B.	CPT	Co. E, 5th SC Inf Regt	The Wilderness, VA	6 May 64
Meadows, J. O.	2LT	Co. A, 3rd KY Cav Regt	Cheshire, OH	20 Jul 63
Meadows, James D.	CPT	Co. A, 1st AL Inf Regt	Port Hudson, LA	9 Jul 63
Merchant, Benjamin D.	1LT	Co. A, 4th VA Cav Regt	Bristoe Station, VA	29 Dec 63
Miller, Robert H.	CPT	Co. C, 44th VA Inf Regt	Spotsylvania C.H., VA	12 May 64
Miller, Robert L.	CPT	Co. B, 7th GA Cav Regt	Trevillian Sta., VA	11 Jun 64
Miner, Charles L.	CPT	Co. B, 1st MO Inf Regt	Saline Co, MO	13 Oct 63
Mitchell, Thomas S.	1LT	Co. G, 42nd VA Inf Regt	Spotsylvania C.H., VA	12 May 64
Mitchell, William T.	CPT	Co. E, 6th VA Cav Regt	Yellow Tavern, VA	11 May 64
Moles, Hanson	1LT	Co. F, 7th KY Cav Regt	Cheshire, OH	20 Jul 63
Moon, Thomas A.	CPT	Co. G, 6th VA Cav Regt	Yellow Tavern, VA	11 May 64
Moore, Docitheus C.	CPT	Co. F, Holcombe's (SC) Inf Legion	Jarrett's Sta., VA	8 May 64

Moore, Julius W.	CPT	Co. H, 3rd NC Cav Regt	Greenville, NC	17 Dec 63
Morgan, John G.	1LT	Co. F, 45th GA Inf Regt	The Wilderness, VA	6 May 64
Morgan, Sydney A.	1LT	Co. A, 25th TN Inf Regt	Petersburg, VA	17 Jun 64
Morgan, William H.	1LT	Co. C, 11th VA Inf Regt	Milford Station, VA	21 May 64
Morris, James D.	2LT	Co. D, 8th KY Cav Regt	Buffington Island, OH	19 Jul 63
Moseley, Milton M.	1LT	Co. B, 3rd GA Sharpshooter Bn	Spotsylvania C.H., VA	12 May 64
Moseley, Nathan S.	1LT	Co. F, 12th NC Inf Regt	Spotsylvania C.H., VA	12 May 64
Moses, Henry J.	1LT	Co. A, 51st GA Inf Regt	Cold Harbor, VA	1 Jun 64
Moss, Thomas O.	1LT	Co. G, 23rd VA Inf Regt	Spotsylvania C.H., VA	12 May 64
Mulvaney, James M.	CPT	Co. H, 27th SC Inf Regt	Petersburg, VA	24 Jun 64
Munce, Thomas Q.	CPT	Co. G, 12th MS Inf Regt	Petersburg, VA	24 Jun 64
Murphy, William F.	CPT	Co. K, 51st NC Inf Regt	Drury's Bluff, VA	16 May 64
Murray, John Ogden	CPT	Co. A, 11th VA Cav Regt	nr Martinsburg, (W)VA	18 Oct 63
Musser, George W.	CPT	Co. B, 29th VA Inf Regt	Cold Harbor, VA	6 Jun 64
Myers, Sanders	1LT	Co. B, 4th FL Inf Regt	Missionary Ridge, TN	23 Nov 63
Nash, George C.	1LT	Co. K, 6th KY Cav Regt	Cheshire, OH	20 Jul 63
Nelson, George W.	CPT	Hanover (VA) Art	Millwood, VA	26 Oct 63
Newton, Louis D.	2LT	Co. D, 3rd KY Cav Regt	Buffington Island, OH	19 Jul 63
Nicks, John	CPT	Nick's Indept Co. TN Cav	Hickman CO, TN	25 Dec 63
Norris, Almarine A.	CPT	Co. –, 14th KY Cav Regt	Cheshire, OH	20 Jul 63
Nunn, William C.	CPT	Co. E, 5th VA Cav Regt	Trevillian Sta., VA	11 Jun 64
Nutt, William C.	CPT	Co. A, 53rd GA Inf Regt	Knoxville, TN	29 Nov 63
O'Riley, William E.	CPT	Co. G, 9th LA Inf Regt	Rappahannock Sta, VA	7 Nov 63
Parham, Samuel J.	CPT	Co. K, 54th NC Inf Regt	Rappahannock Sta, VA	7 Nov 63
Patrick, Frederick F.	1LT	Co. A, 32nd NC Inf Regt	Spotsylvania C.H., VA	12 May 64
Patterson, John C.	CPT	Co. A, 14th AR Inf Regt (Power's)	Port Hudson, LA	9 Jul 63
Peake, Frank P.	2LT	Byrne's Co. KY Horse Art	Cheshire, OH	20 Jul 63
Perkins, Thomas F. Jr.	CPT	Co. I, 11th TN Cav Regt (Holman's)	Williamson Co, TN	8 Dec 63
Pinckney, Thomas	CPT	Co. D, 4th SC Cav Regt	Hawes' Shop, VA	28 May 64
Polk, James H.	CPT	Co. E, 6th TN Cav Regt (Wheeler's)	Hickman Co, TN	13 Jan 64
Prewitt, David N.	2LT	Co. A, 6th KY Cav Regt	Cheshire, OH	20 Jul 63
Pue, James A. V.	LT	Co. A, 1st MD Cav Regt	Hanover Jct, VA	24 May 64
Purgason, Joseph L.	CPT	Co. –, 32nd MS Inf Regt	Corinth, MS	4 May 63
Rice, Evan	LTC	F&S, 55th VA Inf Regt	Falling Waters, MD	14 Jul 63
Richards, Charles E.	2LT	Co. D, 5th KY Cav Regt	Cheshire, OH	20 Jul 63
Rosenbalm, Eli A.	2LT	Co. H, 37th VA Inf Regt	Spotsylvania C.H., VA	12 May 64
Roughton, George W.	1LT	Co. H, 49th GA Inf Regt	The Wilderness, VA	6 May 64
Stewart, William E.	MAJ	F&S, 15th AR Inf Regt (Johnson's)	Port Hudson, LA	9 Jul 63
Swindler, Aylette A.	MAJ	F&S, 7th VA Inf Regt	Rappahannock Co, VA	18 Mch 64
Tolbert, John H.	CPT	Co. B, 5th FL Inf Regt	The Wilderness, VA	6 May 64
Wilson, Micajah R.	MAJ	F&S, 8th AR Inf Bn	Port Hudson, LA	9 Jul 63
Woodram, Richard	MAJ	F&S, 26th VA Inf Bn	Cold Harbor, VA	3 Jun 64
Woolfolk, George W.	COL	unorganized KY Cav Regt	Germantown, KY	9 Dec 63
Zeigler, Martin G.	MAJ	F&S, Holcombe's (SC) Inf Legion	Stony Creek Bridge, VA	7 May 64

ENDNOTES

CHAPTER 1
"WHERE EVERY MAN IN UNIFORM CARRIED HIS LEAVE IN HIS POCKET AND HIS HEART ON HIS SLEEVE"

1. Hamilton Cochran, *Blockade Runners of the Confederacy* (New York, 1958), 21, 24, 50.

2. U.S. War Department. (comp.), *The War of the Rebellion: A Compilation of the Official Records of the Union and Confederate Armies* (Washington, 1880-1901), Ser. I, Vol. LIII, 104 (cited hereafter as *Official Records*).

3. John Johnson, *The Defense of Charleston Harbor, Including Fort Sumter and the Adjacent Island* (Charleston, S.C., 1890), passim.

4. Ibid., 208-14.

5. Cochran, *Blockade Runners*, 165. All of Fort Sumter's artillery had been dismounted by Federal fire after September 1863. None bearing on Morris Island were ever remounted. Whitworth telescopic sighted rifles were used for sniping at Union troops at Battery Gregg (E. Milby Burton, *The Siege of Charleston, 1861-65* [Columbia, S.C., 1970], 300).

6. Emma Holmes, *Diary of Emma Holmes*, 1861-65, edited by John F. Marszalek (Baton Rouge, 1979), 344, 374.

7. Cochran, *Blockade Runners*, 156-66.

8. Edward Manigault, *Siege Train: The Journal of a Confederate Artilleryman in the Defense of Charleston.* Edited by Warren Ripley (Columbia, S.C., 1986), 178. Locations in parentheses signify the modern address.

9. Ibid., 179.

10. Ben L. Bassham, "Conrad Chapman's Charleston," *Civil War Times Illustrated* XVI (April 1977): 35.

11. Wakelyn, Jon L., *Biographical Dictionary of The Confederacy* (Westport, Conn., 1977), 264.

12. Walter H. Powell, *Officers of the Army and Navy* (Philadelphia, 1894), 413.

13. Burton, *Siege of Charleston*, 296-300.

14. Johnson, *Defense of Charleston Harbor*, 224.

15. The Lehigh was a gunboat in the harbor, from which the observation was made (Johnson, *Defense of Charleston Harbor*, 228).

16. Ibid., 224.

17. At one point the Union forces started using incendiary shells, but they stopped when they realized that they were doing no harm in the rubble of the fort (Burton, *Siege of Charleston,* 297, and Johnson, *Defense of Charleston Harbor,* 224-25).

18. Burton, *Siege of Charleston,* 298; *Official Records,* Ser. I, Vol. XLVII, Pt. 2, 259-60.

CHAPTER 2

"IN NO CIRCUMSTANCES WILL HE BE ALLOWED TO MAKE EXCHANGES OF PRISONERS OF WAR"

1. Gen. Grant to Secretary of War Stanton, concerning Foster's possible plan to exchange the 600 officers (*Official Records,* Ser. I, Vol. XXXV, Pt. 2, 254).

2. M. H. Keen, *The Laws of War in the Late Middle Ages* (London, 1965), 156-85.

3. Francis T. Miller, ed., *Prisons and Hospitals,* vol. 7 of *Photographic History of the Civil War* (New York, 1911), 32. The Confederate Congress passed an act stating these same humane laws be adherred to on May 21, 1861 (*Official Records,* Ser. II, Vol. VIII, 345).

4. William B. Hesseltine, *Civil War Prisons, a Study in War Psychology* (New York, 1930), 98.

5. Miller, *Prisons and Hospitals,* 34-36.

6. Arch F. Blakey, *General John H. Winder C.S.A.* (Gainesville, Fla., 1990), 153-55.

7. Ibid., 159-61.

8. Miller, *Prisons and Hospitals,* 44, 54.

9. Wakelyn, *Biographical Dictionary,* 336.

10. Miller, *Prisons and Hospitals,* 106.

11. Ibid., 108; Blakey, Winder, 159-60.

12. Hesseltine, *Civil War Prisons,* 77.

13. Blakey, *Winder,* 159.

14. Frank Freidel, *Francis Lieber, Nineteenth-Century Liberal* (Baton Rouge, 1948), 307-16.

15. Ibid., 309.

16. Ibid., 309.

17. William E. S. Flory, *Prisoners of War, a Study in the Development of International Law* (Washington, 1942), 18-19.

18. Freidel, *Lieber,* 318.

19. Hesseltine, *Civil War Prisons,* 99; *Official Records,* Ser. II, Vol. VI, 185.

20. *Official Records,* Ser. II, Vol. VI, 147.

21. Benjamin Butler, *Butler's Book* (Boston, 1892), 584.

22. *Official Records,* Ser. I, Vol. XXXV, Pt. 2, 213, 254.

23. James Madison Page, *The True Story of Andersonville and Other Military Prisons of the South in 1864* (New York, 1908), 102.

24. Letter from agent Mulford about the Andersonville prisoners received, "Their physical condition is rather better than I expected" (Butler, *Butler's Book*, 609 and appendix).

25. Miller, *Prisons and Hospitals*, 160-63.

26. Luis F. Emilio, *History of the Fifty-Fourth Regiment of Massachusetts Volunteer Infantry, 1863-1865* (Boston, 1894), 218.

27. Manigault, *Siege Train*, 209.

28. *Official Records*, Ser. I, Vol. XXXV, Pt. 2, 132.

29. *Official Records*, Ser.II, Vol. VII, 185.

30. Ibid., 410.

31. *Official Records*, Ser. I, Vol. LIII, 104.

32. Ibid.

33. *Official Records*, Ser. I, Vol. XXXV, Pt. 2, 135.

34. *Official Records*, Ser. I, Vol. LIII, 105.

35. Ibid., 106.

36. *Official Records*, Ser. I, Vol. XXXV, Pt. 2, 151.

37. Miller, *Prisons and Hospitals*, 161.

38. Louis Fortescue, diary, Aug. 1, 1864, Southern Historical Collection, University of North Carolina.

39. Asa Isham, *Prisoners of War and Military Prisons* (Cincinnati, 1890), 69.

40. *Official Records*, Ser. II, Vol. VII, 410.

41. *Official Records*, Ser. I, Vol. XXXV, Pt. 2, 162.

42. Basil Duke, *Reminiscences* (Freeport, N.Y., 1911), 364-69.

43. Ibid.

CHAPTER 3

"FOR RETALIATION"

1. Miller, *Prisons and Hospitals*, 74.

2. Page, *True Story*, 61.

3. Ibid., 61-62.

4. Ibid., 155.

5. Ibid., 149.

6. Ibid., 76.

7. Miller, *Prisons and Hospitals*, 78.

8. Page, *True Story*, 76.

9. Edward W. Boate, "The True Story of Andersonville Told by a Federal Prisoner," *Southern Historical Society Papers* X (1882): 28.

10. Blakey, *Winder*, 172.

11. Miller, *Prisons and Hospitals*, 78-80.

12. *Southern Historical Society Papers* X (1882): 26.

13. Page, *True Story*, 82.

14. *Official Records*, Ser. II, Vol. VII, 624-25; Miller, *Prisons and Hospitals*, 80; letter from Wirz to Chandler, C.S. Quartermaster in Columbus, Ga., Aug. 1, 1864, *Official Records*, Ser. II, Vol. VII, 521-22.

15. *Southern Historical Society Papers* X (1882): 26-27.

16. *Official Records*, Ser. II, Vol. VIII, 599-600. Butler acknowledges that he never believed any ill-treatment of Federal prisoners was on purpose, and admits that the Confederate soldiers in the field in 1864 subsisted solely on corn bread. He also admits that the Confederate army could not supply its own soldiers with clothing or blankets; therefore, how could it possibly supply prisoners (Butler, *Butler's Book*, 610-11); also see letter from C.S. Asst. Surgeon J. Crews Pelot on medical conditions in *Official Records*, Ser. II, Vol. VII, 774.

17. Page, *True Story*, 148; Miller, *Prisons and Hospitals*, 76.

18. A new complication arose in the exchange game with the enlistment of negro troops in 1864. When the black soldiers were captured, any who were discovered to be runaway slaves were looked upon as property to be returned to their owners. Free negroes were treated as regular prisoners of war. As a hindrance to exchange, Grant demanded all negro soldiers be treated the same. The Confederate Congress debated the issue, agreed to conform to Union wishes, and gave Robert Ould the authority to remove any impediment to the exchange of soldiers. This was agreed upon early in 1864. The Union refusal to exchange any soldiers on the technicality of black troops not being exchanged was debated in Congress, and most agreed it was an inflexible and unnecessary impediment to exchange (Butler, *Butler's Book*, 606; *Congressional Globe*, Jan. 26, 1865, 428).

19. *Southern Historical Society Papers* X (1882): 31.

20. Jim Miles, *Fields of Glory—A History and Tour Guide of the Atlanta Campaign* (Nashville, 1989), 14-15.

21. *Southern Historical Society Papers* X (1882): 30.

22. Willis J. Keith, "Fort Johnson," *Civil War Times Illustrated* XIV (Nov. 1975): 35.

23. B. S. Calef, "Prison Life," *Harper's New Monthly Magazine* XXI (July 1865): 142.

24. *Official Records*, Ser. I, Vol. XXXV, Pt.2, 600; *Official Records*, Ser. II, Vol. VII, 502.

25. *Harper's New Monthly Magazine* XXI (July 1865): 143.

26. Fortescue, diary, Aug. 5, 1864, So. Hist. Coll., UNC. The reference to the officers on board ship pertains to the fifty who were sent from Fort Delaware and exchanged in August.

27. Ibid., Aug. 14, 1864.

28. Edward C. Anderson, *Confederate Foreign Agent: the European Diary of Major Edward C. Anderson*, edited by W. Stanley Hoole (University, Ala., 1976), 6-7.

29. Letter from Sickles to Lincoln dated Aug. 10, 1864. Sickles states 600 U.S. prisoners of war arrived in Charleston on Aug. 3. On Aug. 4, before he could have known this,

Foster notified Fort Delaware to send the Six Hundred to Hilton Head to be placed under fire (*Official Records*, Ser. II, Vol. VII, 575). Their names had already been chosen and plans made by the time Foster received the letter that they would be sent, dated Aug. 8, 1864 (*Official Records*, Ser. II, Vol. VII, 567). This suggests that Foster had intentions of bringing the 600 Confederate officers down before there was an excuse to retaliate for anything.

30. Page, *True Story*, 164.

31. Edward C. Anderson, diary, Vol. 7, Sept. 8, 1864, So. Hist. Coll., UNC.

32. Ibid., Oct. 5, 1864.

33. Page, *True Story*, 167.

34. John Fraser, *A Petition Regarding the Conditions in the C.S.M. Prison at Columbia, S.C.*, edited by George L. Anderson (Lawrence, Kans., 1962), 20.

35. Jefferson Davis, *Andersonville and Other War Prisons* (New York, 1890), [n.p.].

36. Butler, *Butler's Book*, 597.

37. *Official Records*, Ser. II, Vol. VII, 598.

38. When Butler was chosen as the agent of exchange, there was an outcry from Jefferson Davis, and most of the Confederate Congress. Butler had been declared an outlaw for the atrocities committed in New Orleans, when he occupied that city in 1862. His execution of William Mumford outraged everyone in the South. Therefore, any recognition of Butler in an official capacity was refused at first (Hesseltine, *Civil War Prisons*, 113-120).

39. Butler, *Butler's Book*, 605.

40. Davis, *Andersonville and Other War Prisons*.

41. Letter from Walt Whitman to *New York Times* reprinted in *Charleston Daily Courier*, Jan. 13, 1865.

42. Anderson, diary, Oct. 8, 1864, So. Hist. Coll., UNC.

43. *Official Records*, Ser. II, Vol. VIII, 348-49; *Official Records*, Ser. I, Vol. XXXV, Pt. 2, 231.

44. *Congressional Globe*, 38th Cong., 2d sess., Jan. 16, 1865, 267. Lincoln was notified by his own general, Dan Sickles, that retaliation was useless. Sickles wrote on Aug. 10, 1864, "Apart from the objections which exist to the policy of retaliation, it is at least doubtful whether it would inure to the benefit of our men, for the reason that the enemy are reported to be without the means to supply clothing, medicines, and other medical supplies even to their own troops" (*Official Records*, Ser. II, Vol. VII, 575).

45. *Congressional Globe*, 38th Cong., 2d sess., Jan. 16, 1865, 268.

46. Ibid.

47. Ibid.

48. Ibid., Jan. 24, 1865, 381.

49. Ibid., 389.

50. Herbert C. Fooks, *Prisoners of War* (Federalsburg, Md., 1924), 329.

51. Freidel, *Lieber*, 355-56.

52. *Congressional Globe*, Jan. 24, 1865, 381. Speech of Sen. Charles Sumner on Treatment of Prisoners of War. The legislation introduced for retaliation became known as the Lane Resolution, or Senate Resolution no. 97.

53. Ibid., 364, 390.

54. Ibid., 384.

55. Ibid., Jan. 25, 1865, 413. Quoted from *Woolsey's International Law*, 293; and Emmerick Vattal's Book II, Chpt. 18, 339.

56. Ibid., Jan. 23, 1865, 364.

57. *Official Records*, Ser. II, Vol. VII, 773.

58. *Official Records*, Ser. I, Vol. XXXV, Pt. 2, 213. In many secondary 20th century accounts it has been erroneously stated that Jones had the Union prisoners in Charleston to force an exchange similar to the exchange of the 50 officers in July. On the contrary, it is Foster who seems to have had initiating an exchange in mind, making it a Union motive to move the 600 Confederate officers down from Fort Delaware (Hitchcock to Stanton, Aug. 13, 1864, *Official Records*, Ser. II, Vol. VII, 575; Foster to Halleck, Aug. 17, 1864, *Official Records*, Ser. II, Vol. VII, 603).

59. *Official Records*, Ser. I, Vol. XXXV, Pt. 2, 247.

60. *Official Records*, Ser. II, Vol. VII, 763.

61. Ibid., 625.

62. *Official Records*, Ser. I, Vol. XXXV, Pt. 2, 247.

CHAPTER 4

"JOINED THE POST . . ."

1. Henry Clay Dickinson, *Diary of Captain Henry Dickinson* (Denver, 1913), 13.

2. J. William Jones, "Treatment of Prisoners During the War," *Southern Historical Society Papers* I (1876): 258.

3. Dickinson, *Diary*, 37.

4. Thomas Pinckney, "Reminiscences of War and Reconstruction Times", unpublished ms., Museum of the Confederacy, Richmond, Va., 24.

5. Nelson Family, Papers, VPI & SU.

6. Compiled Service Record, National Archives.

7. Edward Pinkowski, *Pills, Pen and Politics: The Story of General Leon Jastremski*, 1843-1907 (Wilmington, Del., 1974), 55, 58.

8. James Robert McMichael, diary (typewritten transcript), So. Hist. Coll., UNC, p. 1.

9. Dickinson, *Diary*, 38.

10. Ibid., 100.

11. W. Emerson Wilson, *Fort Delaware in the Civil War* (Fort Delaware Society, 1972).

12. Lt. Col. John Alexander Gibson, diary, entries for Nov. 1864, Virginia Historical Society, Richmond, Va.

13. Dickinson, *Diary*, 46-47.

14. J. Ogden Murray, *The Immortal Six-Hundred* (Winchester, Va., 1905), 27.

15. Dickinson, *Diary*, 58.

16. Ibid., 41.

17. William H. Morgan, *Personal Reminiscences of the War*, 1861-1865 (1911), 225.

18. Dickinson, *Diary*, 40-41.

19. Joseph Mauck, diary, Mus. of Confederacy, 12.

20. Dickinson, *Diary*, 49.

21. Pinckney, *Reminiscences*, 26.

22. Dickinson, *Diary*, 50-51.

23. House Committee on War Claims, *Claim of Certain Confederate Officers. Statement of Major J. Ogden Murray before the Committee on War Claims, in support of H.R. 14170, March 28, 1914*. 63rd Congress, 2d sess. (Washington, 1914), 23-24.

24. Several officers speak of two prayer meetings per day (see diaries of Handy, McMichael, Mauck).

25. McMichael, *diary*, So. Hist Coll., UNC, p. 2.

26. Rev. Isaac Handy, *United States Bonds; or Duress by Federal Authorities* (Baltimore, 1874), passim.

27. Leon Jastremski to John Jastremski, July 19, 1864, Jastremski Family papers, LSU.

28. Leon Jastremski to John Jastremski, Aug. 6, 1864, Jastremski Family papers, LSU.

29. M. Baker to Sanford Branch, Sept. 24, 1864, Margaret Sexton Branch papers, Univ. of Ga., Athens, Ga.

30. Moses J. Bradford to Melissa Jane Bradford, July 3, 1864, Bradford Family papers, Univ. Mo. - Columbia.

31. Handy, *United States Bonds*, 503.

32. Murray, *Immortal Six-Hundred*, 28.

33. Handy, *United States Bonds*, 504-5.

34. Murray, *Immortal Six-Hundred*, 29.

35. Pinckney, *Reminiscences*, 28-29.

36. McMichael, diary, So. Hist Coll., UNC, p. 4.

37. Sanford Branch to Charlotte Branch, Aug. 20, 1864, Branch family papers, UGA. Although the letter is dated the 20th, it must have been written on either the evening of the 19th or just after midnight.

38. Handy, *United States Bonds*, 507.

39. Leon Jastremski to John Jastremski, Aug. 20, 1864, Jastremski family papers, LSU.

40. Handy, *United States Bonds*, 514.

41. Murray, *Immortal Six-Hundred*, 31.

42. Pinckney, *Reminiscences*, 29.

43. Handy, *United States Bonds*, 515.

CHAPTER 5

"REBEL OFFICERS"

1. Dickinson, *Diary*, 31; The first colonel of the 54th Massachusetts, Robert G. Shaw, expressed similar sentiments. He stated he "would not exorcise fully his belief in inferiority until his men proved themselves in front of the Confederate Army." (Russell Duncan, ed., *Blue-Eyed Child of Fortune: The Civil War Letters of Colonel Robert Gould Shaw* [Athens, Ga: 1992], 21, 35, 40, 42.)

2. Pinkowski, *Pills, Pen and Politics*, 65; Murray, *Immortal Six-Hundred*, 33.

3. National Archives, War Records Division, Department of the Army, "Proceedings of a General Court Martial, U.S. Steamship *Delaware*, in the charges against Captain Daniel D. Latham and Second Mate William Baxter, Port Royal Harbor, S.C., August 25, 1864"; *Palmetto Herald*, Beaufort, S.C., Sept. 1, 1864.

4. McMichael, diary, So. Hist. Coll., UNC, p.4.

5. *Southern Historical Society Papers* I (1876): 249.

6. Morgan, *Reminiscences*, 235-36.

7. Walter G. McRae, "Confederate Prisoners at Morris Island," *Confederate Veteran* XXIX (1921): 178.

8. Morgan, *Reminiscences*, 233.

9. William A. Young, Jr., *Fifty-Sixth Virginia Infantry, of the Virginia Regimental History Series* (Lynchburg, Va., 1990), 105.

10. Dickinson, *Diary*, 64.

11. Fritz Fuzzlebug [John J. Dunkle], *Prison Life During the Rebellion* (Singer's Glen, Va., 1869), 20.

12. J. W. A. Ford, "Diary", *Journal of the Greenbrier Historical Society* II (1971): 37.

13. A. J. Hamilton, *A Fort Delaware Journal; The Diary of a Yankee Private* (Wilmington, Del., 1981), 58.

14. U.S. War Department (comp.), *The War of the Rebellion: A Compilation of the Official Records of the Union and Confederate Navies* (Washington, 1902), Ser. I, Vol. XV, 637 (cited hereafter as *Official Records, Navies*).

15. *General Court Martial Proceedings*, USS *Delaware*; *Palmetto Herald*, Beaufort, S.C., Sept. 1, 1864.

16. Hamilton, *Ft. Delaware Journal*, 59.

17. *General Court Martial Proceedings*, USS *Delaware*.

18. Pinckney, *Reminiscences*, 31.

19. Abram Fulkerson, "The Prison Experience of a Confederate Soldier," *Southern Historical Society Papers* XXII (1894): 136.

20. Letter of Richard H. Adams, *Confederate Veteran* II (1894): 90.

21. Murray, *Immortal Six-Hundred*, 35-36.

22. Dickinson, *Diary*, 66-67.

23. Dunkle, *Prison Life*, 20-21.

24. Murray, *Immortal Six-Hundred*, 36-37.

25. Dickinson, *Diary*, 68.

26. Ibid., 68-69.

27. *Jour. of the Greenbrier Hist. Soc. II* (1971): 38.

28. Hamilton, *Ft. Delaware Journal*, 59.

29. *General Court Martial Proceedings*, USS *Delaware*.

30. Sanford Branch to Charlotte Branch, Aug. 29, 1864, Branch Family papers, UGA.

31. Pinckney, *Reminiscences*, 32-33.

32. Compiled Service Record, National Archives.

33. Dickinson, *Diary*, 69-70.

34. *Jour. of the Greenbrier Hist. Soc. II* (1971): 38.

35. Dunkle, *Prison Life*, 23.

36. Alexander M. Bedford, diary, Aug. 26, 1864, Bedford Papers, Univ. of Mo. - Columbia.

37. John C. Gorman, diary, Oct. 3, 1864, Gorman Papers, Duke Univ.

38. *Southern Historical Society Papers* XXII (1894): 135.

39. *Confederate Veteran* XXIX (1921): 178.

40. Murray, *Immortal Six-Hundred*, 37.

41. Dunkle, *Prison Life*, 24-25.

42. Henry H. Cook, "The Story of the Six-Hundred," *Confederate Veteran* V (1897): 117.

43. Bedford, diary, Aug. 27, 1864, Univ. of Mo. — Columbia.

44. McMichael, diary, So. Hist Coll., UNC, p.9.

45. Dickinson, *Diary*, 70-71.

46. William Saxton, "War Reminiscences", The Courtland Standard, 1902. From clippings in scrapbook at Cortland Historical Society, Cortland, N.Y.

47. Dunkle, Prison Life, 18; *Official Records*, Ser. I, Vol. XXXV, Pt. 2, 1095.

48. Gorman diary, Aug. 24, 1864, Duke Univ.

49. *Official Records*, Ser. II, Vol. VII, 696.

50. *Official Records*, Ser. I, Vol. XXXV, Pt. 2, 261-62. Dahlgren states, "The whole world would cry out against the cowardly brutes who would expose unfortunate and defenseless prisoners to death from the cannon of their own friends" (*Official Records, Navies*, Ser. I, Vol. XV, 530).

51. *Palmetto Herald*, Beaufort, S.C., 1 Sept. 1864.

52. *Jour. of the Greenbrier Hist. Soc. II* (1971): 39-40.

53. Dickinson, *Diary*, 72.

54. *Official Records*, Ser. II, Vol. VII, 773; Ibid., 783, 625; *Official Records, Navies*, Ser. I, Vol. XV, 651.

55. *Jour. of the Greenbrier Hist. Soc. II* (1971): 41.

CHAPTER 6

MORRIS ISLAND

1. *Civil War Times Illustrated XII* (Nov. 1973): 33.

2. John Chipman Gray, *War Letters*, 1862-1865 (Boston, 1927), 281. Gray visited the magazine at Fort Gregg and commented,"it was with a curious feeling that I stood in the midst of cartridges and barrels filled with enough powder to blow the whole fort and almost the whole island into the air."

3. *Confederate Veteran* XXIX (1921): 178.

4. *Southern Historical Society Papers* I (1876): 249.

5. Emilio, *54th Massachusetts*, 222.

6. Dickinson, *Diary*, 73.

7. Emilio, *54th Massachusetts*, 222-23.

8. Junius L. Hempstead, "How Long Will This Misery Continue," *Civil War Times Illustrated* XIX (Feb. 1981): 21.

9. Dickinson, *Diary*, 73.

10. Bedford, diary, Sept. 7, 1864, Univ. of Mo. - Columbia.

11. Pinckney, *Reminiscences*, 33-34.

12. Dickinson, *Diary*, 77.

13. Emilio, *54th Massachusetts*, 224-25.

14. Murray, *Immortal Six-Hundred*, 44; Emilio, *54th Massachusetts*, 222, 224.

15. *Official Records*, Ser. I, Vol. XXXV, Pt. 2, 269.

16. *Civil War Times Illustrated* XIX (Feb. 1981): 21.

17. Dickinson, *Diary*, 73-74.

18. Bedford, diary, Univ. of Mo. - Columbia, passim; Mauck, diary, entries for Sept. 7-30, 1864, Mus. of Confederacy.

19. *Official Records*, Ser. I, Vol. XXXV, Pt. 2, 312.

20. Dickinson, *Diary*, 73.

21. Jastremski papers, obituary of Leon Jastremski, LSU.

22. Baltimore *Sun*, July 27, 1904, obituary of Col. DeGournay.

23. Tribute to Thomas Pinckney, *Confederate Veteran* XXIV (1916): 342-44.

24. May W. Mount, *Some Notables of New Orleans* (New Orleans, 1896), 168; Franklin Hildebrand, *As I Remember: Stories of Jefferson Davis Parish* (Jennings, LA, 1977), 42.

25. Biographical sketch, John Cantwell, *Confederate Military History* V (1897): 420-21.

26. *Official Records*, Ser. I, Vol. XXXV, Pt. 2, 276.

27. *Jour. of the Greenbrier Hist. Soc.* II (1971): 41-42.

28. Ibid., 42.

29. Leon to John Jastremski, Sept. 11, 1864, Jastremski Family papers, LSU.

30. Morgan, *Reminiscences*, 238-39.

31. Dickinson, *Diary*, 78.

32. Samuel Hawes, diary, Sept. 9, 1864, Katherine Hawes Papers, Va. Hist. Soc.

33. Dunkle, *Prison Life*, 36-37.

34. Dickinson, *Diary*, 78.

35. Young, *56th Virginia*, 105.

36. *Confederate Veteran* V (1897): 118.

37. *Official Records*, Ser. II, Vol. VII, 774-75.

38. Ibid., 625.

39. Ibid., 625; *Official Records*, Vol. XLIV, 625.

40. *Official Records*, Ser. I, Vol. XXXV, Pt. 2, 279.

41. Lewis Harman, Biographical File, VMI.

42. *Official Records*, Ser. I, Vol. XXXV, Pt. 2, 213, 247.

43. Ibid., 250-51, 295; Burton, *Siege of Charleston*, 300. The artillery mounted against Charleston excelled any ever brought on the field in a siege operation.

44. *Official Records*, Ser. II, Vol. VII, 976-77.

45. *Official Records*, Ser. I, Vol. XXXV, Pt. 2, 284-85.

46. Fortescue, diary, Aug. 18, 1864, So. Hist. Coll., UNC.

47. Page, *True Story*, 167.

48. *Harper's New Monthly Magazine* XXI (July 1865): 144.

49. Murray, *Immortal Six-Hundred*, 46-47.

50. *Official Records*, Ser. II, Vol. VII, 711.

51. W. W. George, *In a Federal Prison* (Bristol, Tenn., 1906), 6.

52. *Civil War Times Illustrated* XIX (Feb. 1981): 22.

53. *Confederate Veteran* XXIX (1921): 179.

54. *Southern Historical Society Papers* I (1876): 251.

55. Bedford, diary, Sept. 10-16, 1864, Univ. of Mo. - Columbia. The Federal officers referred to were Captains James Pike and Charles Gray, scouts for Sherman's army, who were captured as spies and put in close confinement (*Official Records*, Ser. II, Vol. VII, 769).

56. Dickinson, *Diary*, 74.

57. Pinckney, *Reminiscenses*, 43.

58. Murray, *Immortal Six-Hundred*, 49; Dunkle, *Prison Life*, 29, 30, 32.

59. *Official Records*, Ser. II, Vol. VII, 900.

60. Bedford, diary, Oct. 16, 1864, Univ. of Mo. - Columbia.

61. *Civil War Times Illustrated* XIX (Feb. 1981): 22.

62. Murray, *Immortal Six-Hundred*, 49.

63. Hawes, diary, Sept. 20, 1864, Va. Hist. Soc.

64. Dickinson, *Diary*, 84.

65. *Jour. of the Greenbrier Hist. Soc.* II (1971): 44.

66. House Committee on War Claims, *Claims of Certain Confederate Officers*, 34.

67. Emilio, *54th Massachusetts*, 225.

68. Dickinson, *Diary*, 79.

69. *Jour. of the Greenbrier Hist. Soc.* II (1971): 44.

70. *Civil War Times Illustrated* XIX (Feb. 1981): 21-22.

71. McMichael, diary, So. Hist. Coll., UNC, p. 8.

72. *Official Records*, Ser. I, Vol. XXXV, Pt. 2, 290-294.

73. Ibid., 213.

74. Ibid., 254.

75. *Official Records*, Ser. II, Vol. VII, 703-704. Gen. Ethan Allen Hitchcock was appointed Director of prisoner exchange in February 1862 after turning down Lincoln's offer as replacement for McClellan.

CHAPTER 7

LIFE UNDER FIRE

1. Adams, Richard H., Jr., diary, in possession of Mrs. Minnie Fitting, Radford, Va.

2. Dickinson, *Diary*, 94.

3. Pinckney, *Reminiscences*, 39.

4. McMichael, diary, So. Hist. Coll., UNC, p. 8.

5. Hawes, diary, Sept. 23, 1864, Va. Hist. Soc.

6. *Jour. of the Greenbrier Hist. Soc.* II (1971): 45.

7. *Official Records*, Ser. I, Vol. XXXV, Pt. 2, 309-10.

8. Murray, *Immortal Six-Hundred*, 52; *Official Records*, Ser. II, Vol. VII, 783.

9. *Harper's New Monthly Magazine* XXI (July 1865): 147.

10. Murray, *Immortal Six-Hundred*, 49. Robert G. Shaw to Sarah Shaw, June 13, 1863, Duncan, *Blue-Eyed Child of Fortune*, 348.

11. Dickinson, *Diary*, 88.

12. Pinckney, *Reminiscences*, 37.

13. Murray, *Immortal Six-Hundred*, 49.

14. *Civil War Times Illustrated* XIX (Feb. 1981): 22.

15. Dunkle, *Prison Life*, 29-30.

16. Dickinson, *Diary*, 92.

17. Pinckney, *Reminiscences*, 42-43.

18. Dickinson, *Diary*, 86.

19. Murray, *Immortal Six-Hundred*, 57.

20. *Southern Historical Society Papers* I (1876): 249-50.

21. Pinckney, *Reminiscences*, 37-38; Henry Handerson, *Yankee in Gray* (Cleveland, OH, 1962), 78.

22. "Imprisoned Under Fire," *Southern Historical Society Papers* XXV (1897): 371.

23. Emilio, *54th Massachusetts*, 226.

24. *Southern Historical Society Papers* I (1876): 250-51. The excessive disciplinary measures used by the officers of the 54th Massachusetts were controversial and abusive (Duncan, *Blue-Eyed Child*, 33-35).

25. Bedford, diary, Sept. 8, 1864, Univ. of Mo. - Columbia.

26. Walter Clark, ed., *Stories of the Several Regiments and Battalions from North Carolina in the Great War 1861-1865*, Vol. V (Goldsboro, N.C., 1901), 620-21.

27. Emilio, *54th Massachusetts*, 226.

28. Pinckney, *Reminiscences*, 41.

29. Ibid., 36.

30. House Committee on War Claims, *Claims of Certain Confederate Officers*, 36.

31. *Official Records*, Ser. II, Vol. VII, 827.

32. *Jour. of Greenbrier Hist. Soc.* II (1971): 43.

33. Ibid., 48.

34. *Civil War Times Illustrated* XIX (Feb. 1981): 21.

35. Bedford, diary, Sept. 21, 1864, Univ. of Mo. - Columbia.

36. "Two of the Six Hundred," *Confederate Veteran* VII (1899): 415.

37. Pinckney, *Reminiscences*, 35.

38. Dickinson, *Diary*, 76-77.

39. Handerson, *Yankee in Gray*, 78. The sergeant referred to is Sgt. Lennox of the 54th Mass.

40. David Gordon, diary, Sept. 22, 1864, Mus. of Confederacy.

41. Dickinson, *Diary*, 15.

42. William Ledyard to Sanford Branch, Sept. 21, 1864, Branch Family papers, UGA.

43. McMichael, Diary, So. Hist Coll., UNC, p. 9.

44. Dickinson, *Diary*, 52.

45. *Civil War Times Illustrated* XIX (Feb. 1981): 21.

46. House Committee on War Claims, *Claims of Certain Confederate Officers*, 25.

47. *Confederate Veteran* V (1897): 118.

48. Dunkle, *Prison Life*, 22.

49. *Civil War Times Illustrated* XIX (Feb. 1981): 22.

50. Compiled Service Record, National Archives.

51. Murray, *Immortal Six-Hundred*, 50-51.

52. Compiled Service Record, National Archives.

53. John W. Northrop, *Chronicles From the Diary of a War Prisoner in Andersonville and Other Military Prisons* (Wichita, Kans., 1904), 135, 159.

54. Ibid., 153.

55. *Official Records*, Ser. II, Vol. VII, 1047.

56. Fraser, *Petition*, 28-29.

57. *Official Records*, Ser. II, Vol. VII, 981-82.

58. *Jour. of Greenbrier Hist. Soc.* II (1971): 49.

59. John C. Allen, diary, Oct. 17, Va. Hist. Soc.

60. Dickinson, *Diary*, 88.

61. Bedford, diary, Oct. 7, 1864, Univ. of Mo. - Columbia.

62. Dickinson, *Diary*, 87. Chadfield was one of the new batteries constructed on Morris Island after the Six Hundred arrived.

63. Bedford, diary, Oct. 17, 1864, Univ. of Mo. - Columbia.

64. House Committee on War Claims, *Claims of Certain Confederate Officers*, 35.

65. Mauck, diary, Oct. 15, 1864, Mus. of Confederacy.

66. Murray, *Immortal Six-Hundred*, 53.

67. William Epps, Diary, in *History of Williamsburg*, edited by William Boddie (Columbia, S.C.: 1923), 420.

68. Dickinson, *Diary*, 76.

69. *Official Records*, Ser. I, Vol. XXXV, Pt. 2, 279.

70. House Committee on War Claims, *Claims of Certain Confederate Officers*, 36-37

71. *Civil War Times Illustrated* XIX (Feb. 1981): 22.

72. Dunkle, *Prison Life*, 37.

73. *Official Records*, Ser. I, Vol. XXXV, Pt. 2, 282.

74. Ibid., 260, 295.

75. Saxton, "War Reminiscenes," Courtland Standard.

76. Murray, *Immortal Six-Hundred*, 55.

77. *Confederate Veteran* V (1897): 118.

Chapter 8

"I WILL MAKE THIS THE MODEL MILITARY PRISON OF THE UNITED STATES"

1. Albert R. Barlow, *Company G: A Record of the Services of One Company of the 157th New York Volunteers in the War of the Rebellion* (Syracuse, N.Y., 1899), impassim.

2. Col. Brown to wife, Folder 130, Archives, Fort Pulaski National Monument. The furniture Brown speaks of was stolen from homes in Savannah.

3. Barlow, *Company G,* 196.

4. Dickinson, *Diary,* 93.

5. *Confederate Veteran* I (1893): 252.

6. Mauck, diary, Oct. 21, 1864, Mus. of Confederacy.

7. Murray, *Immortal Six-Hundred,* 57.

8. Dickinson, *Diary,* 95.

9. Adams, diary.

10. Dickinson, *Diary,* 96.

11. Barlow, *Company G,* 197-98.

12. Adams, diary.

13. Ralston B. Lattimore, *Fort Pulaski National Monument,* National Park Service Historical Handbook Series no. 18 (Washington, 1954).

14. Saxton, "War Reminiscences," Courtland *Standard.*

15. Pinckney, *Reminiscences,* 47.

16. Dickinson, *Diary,* 97.

17. Mauck, diary, Oct. 27, 1864, Mus. of Confederacy.

18. Pinckney, *Reminiscences,* 47.

19. Adams, diary.

20. Dickinson, *Diary,* 98.

21. Gordon, diary, 24 Oct. 1864, Mus. of Confederacy.

22. Pinckney, *Reminiscences,* 48.

23. Dickinson, *Diary,* 99-100.

24. Hawes, diary, Nov. 11, 1864, Va. Hist. Soc.

25. Murray, *Immortal Six-Hundred,* 58.

26. Dickinson, *Diary,* 100.

27. George Nelson to Molly Scollay, Oct. 31, 1864, Nelson Family papers, VPI & SU.

28. House Committee on War Claims, *Claims of Certain Confederate Officers,* 37.

29. *Official Records,* Ser. I, Vol. XLIV, 517.

30. Saxton, "War Reminiscences," Courtland *Standard*.

31. Gen. Foster to Col. Brown, Folder no. 30, Archives, Fort Pulaski National Monument.

32. Dickinson, *Diary*, 100.

33. Pinckney, *Reminiscences*, 48.

34. McMichael, Diary, So. Hist Coll., UNC, p. 15.

35. Dickinson, *Diary*, 100-101.

36. Bedford, diary, Oct. 29, 1864, Univ. of Mo. - Columbia.

37. Dickinson, *Diary*, 103.

38. Ibid., 105-106.

39. Fort Delaware roll used on Aug. 20, 1864, National Archives.

40. Dickinson, *Diary*, 106-107.

41. House Committee on War Claims, *Claims of Certain Confederate Officers*, 37-38.

42. Regulations for prisoners at Ft. Pulaski, Archives, Fort Pulaski National Monument.

43. Receipts for Letters Containing Money Addressed to Prisoners, Nov. 1864-Apr. 1865, Hilton Head, S.C., Prison Camp, Microcopy 598, Vol. 79, National Archives.

44. David Harris to wife, Nov. 2, 1864, David T. Harris, papers, Ga. State Archives, Atlanta, GA.

45. Dickinson, *Diary*, 118.

46. Saxton, "War Reminiscences," Courtland *Standard*.

47. McMichael, Diary, So. Hist. Coll., UNC, p. 16.

48. Dickinson, *Diary*, 107-108.

49. Gordon, diary, Nov. 25, 1864, Mus. of Confederacy.

50. Ibid., Nov. 1, 1864.

51. Dickinson, *Diary*, 107-108.

52. Pinckney, *Reminiscences*, 49.

53. Anderson, diary, Vol. 7, Nov. 9-11, 1864, So. Hist. Coll., UNC.

54. Dickinson, *Diary*, 109-110.

55. House Committee of War Claims, *Claims of Certain Confederate Officers*, 38.

56. Mauck, diary, Nov. 6-8, 1864, Mus. of Confederacy.

57. Dickinson, *Diary*, 115.

58. House Committee on War Claims, *Claims of Certain Confederate Officers*, 39.

59. Henry H. Cook, "The Story of the Six-Hundred," *Confederate Veteran* V (1897): 148.

60. Bedford, diary, Nov. 19, 1864, Univ. of Mo. - Columbia.

61. Hawes, diary, Nov. 19, 1864, Va. Hist. Soc.

62. Mauck, diary, Nov. 19, 1864, Mus. of Confederacy.

63. Dunkle, *Prison Life*, 38.

CHAPTER 9

"WHAT HAVE I OFFENDED AGAINST THEE, OR AGAINST THY SERVANT, OR AGAINST THIS PEOPLE, THAT YE HAVE PUT ME IN PRISON?"

1. Dickinson, *Diary*, 119, 122.

2. Sanford Branch to mother, Nov. 10, 1864, Margaret Branch Sexton Collection, UGA.

3. *Official Records*, Ser. I, Vol. XLIV, 517.

4. Dickinson, *Diary*, 123-24.

5. *Confederate Veteran* V (1897): 148.

6. Dickinson, *Diary*, 110, 124.

7. Pinckney, *Reminiscences*, 49-50.

8. Dickinson, *Diary*, 131.

9. John C. Allen, diary, Nov. 23 and 26, 1864, Va. Hist. Soc.

10. Clark, Regiments from *North Carolina* V: 621.

11. Dickinson, *Diary*, 133.

12. Ibid.

13. Ibid., 112.

14. Saxton, "War Reminiscences," Courtland *Standard.*

15. Dickinson, *Diary*, 116; Bedford, diary, Oct. 31, 1864, Univ. of Mo. - Columbia.

16. Dickinson, *Diary*, 129.

17. Pinckney, *Reminiscences*, 50.

18. Dickinson, *Diary*, 132.

19. House Committee on War Claims, *Claims of Certain Confederate Officers*, 39-40

20. McMichael, diary, So. Hist Coll., UNC, p. 16.

21. Gordon, diary, Dec. 2, 1864, Mus. of Confederacy.

22. George Crapon to John Cantwell, Nov. 24, 1864, John Lucas Cantwell papers, So. Hist Coll., UNC.

23. Dickinson, *Diary*, 134-35.

24. Clark, *Regiments from North Carolina* V: 622.

25. Pinckney, *Reminiscences*, 51-52.

26. Gordon, diary, Dec. 14, 1864, Mus. of Confederacy.

27. Dickinson, *Diary*, 140-41.

28. *Charleston Daily Courier*, Dec. 7, 1864.

29. Burger to Brown, Dec. 15, 1864, Folder no. 30, Archives, Fort Pulaski.

30. *Official Records*, Ser. I, Vol. XLIV, 725.

31. Allen, diary, Dec. 12, 1864, Va. Hist. Soc.

32. Dickinson, *Diary*, 145; *Official Records*, Ser. I, Vol. XXXV, Pt. 2, 1246.

33. Ibid., 112; *Southern Historical Society Papers* XXII (1894): 134.

34. Dickinson, *Diary*, 112.

35. John M. Guyther, Compiled Service Record, National Archives.

36. This action was also called Honey Hill (Jim Miles, *To The Sea* [Nashville, Tenn., 1989], 196-97).

37. Dickinson, *Diary*, 130, 142.

38. House Committee on War Claims, *Claims of Certain Confederate Officers*, 40.

39. Dickinson, *Diary*, 145-46.

40. Ibid., 125.

41. House Committee on War Claims, *Claims of Certain Confederate Officers*, 39.

42. *Confederate Veteran* V (1897): 148.

43. Gordon, diary, Nov. 25, 1864, Mus. of Confederacy.

44. House Committee on War Claims, *Claims of Certain Confederate Officers*, 39.

45. Dickinson, *Diary*, 128-29.

46. Murray, *Immortal Six-Hundred*, 71.

47. Dickinson, *Diary*, 139-40.

48. Murray, *Immortal Six-Hundred*, 60.

49. Dickinson, *Diary*, 148-49.

50. House Committee on War Claims, *Claims of Certain Confederate Officers*, 41.

51. *Official Records*, Ser. II, Vol. VIII, 160. States rations for Florence Prison camp as: 1 lb. meat, one-half lb. peas, 3 lbs. salt per 100 rations. Andersonville rations are one-half lb. beef everyday plus bread ration. Iverson is requesting an increase.

52. *Southern Historical Society Papers* XXII (1894): 140.

53. Dickinson, *Diary*, 151.

54. George, *In a Federal Prison*, 8.

55. Murray, *Immortal Six-Hundred*, 59.

56. *Confederate Veteran* V (1897): 149.

57. Dickinson, *Diary*, 152-53.

58. Hempstead file, Murray papers, Va. Hist. Soc.

59. Dickinson, *Diary*, 150.

CHAPTER 10

"IN PERILS BY MINE OWN COUNTRYMEN;
IN PERILS AMONG FALSE BRETHREN"

1. *A Standard of Georgia and Georgians* V (Chicago, 1917), 2300.

2. Daniel White, *Dear Wife, Letters of a Civil War Soldier*, edited by Jack C. Davis (Louisville, 1991), 76, 78- 79.

3. Hawes, diary, Nov. 20, 1864, Va. Hist. Soc.

4. White, *Dear Wife*, 79.

5. Mauck, diary, Nov. 20, 1864, Mus. of Confederacy.

6. Hawes, diary, Nov. 22, 1864, Va. Hist. Soc.

7. Bedford, diary, Nov. 22, 1864, Univ. of Mo. - Columbia.

8. White, *Dear Wife*, 81.

9. Hawes, diary, Nov. 23, 1864, Va. Hist. Soc.

10. Bedford, diary, Nov. 23, 1864, Univ. of Mo. - Columbia.

11. Dunkle, *Prison Life*, 39.

12. Hawes, diary, Nov. 26, 1864, Va. Hist. Soc.

13. Bedford, diary, Nov. 26, 1864, Univ. of Mo. - Columbia.

14. Mauck, diary, Nov. 26, 1864, Mus. of Confederacy.

15. White, *Dear Wife*, 86.

16. James H. McKee, *Back "In War Times"* (1903), 209.

17. *Civil War Times Illustrated* XII (Nov. 1973): 34.

18. White, *Dear Wife*, 87.

19. Morristown, Tenn., *Daily Gazette* Mail, Mar. 4, 1962.

20. Ibid.

21. Elizabeth Ware Pearson, ed., *Letters From Port Royal 1862-1868* (New York, 1969), passim. These letters were written by Harriet Ware, one of the women who came to Port Royal from Boston as a teacher; Gorman, diary, Oct. 3, 1864, Gorman Papers, Duke Univ.; Dunkle, *Prison Life*, 44, 45.

22. Dunkle, *Prison Life*, 39, 40.

23. Hawes, diary, Nov. 30, 1864, Va. Hist. Soc.

24. White, *Dear Wife*, 85.

25. Bedford, diary, Dec. 31, 1864 and Jan. 5, 1865, Univ. of Mo. - Columbia.

26. Young, *56th Virginia Infantry*, 106.

27. Mauck, diary, Dec. 15, 1864, Mus. of Confederacy.

28. Epps, diary, in *History of Williamsburg*, 421.

29. Morristown, Tenn., *Daily Gazette* Mail, Mar. 18, 1962; Murray, *Immortal Six-Hundred*, 92.

30. Dunkle, *Prison Life*, 41.

31. Bedford, diary, Dec. 10, 12, 21, 1864, Univ. of Mo. - Columbia.

32. James Cobb to Cora Williams, Dec. 11, 1864, Cobb-Hunter Letters, So. Hist. Coll., UNC.

33. Hawes, diary, Dec. 25, 1864, Va. Hist. Soc.

34. James Cobb to Cora Williams, Dec. 25, 1864, Cobb-Hunter Letters, So. Hist. Coll., UNC.

35. Mauck, diary, Dec. 25, 1864, Mus. of Confederacy.

36. Murray, *Immortal Six-Hundred*, 100.

37. Ibid., 102.

38. Dunkle, *Prison Life*, 43.

39. Epps, diary, in *History of Williamsburg*, 421.

40. Bedford, diary, Jan. 14, 1865, Univ. of Mo. - Columbia.

41. Mauck, diary, Jan. 4, 1865, Mus. of Confederacy. "25 of the late captured lot" refers to prisoners from Savannah confined with the 600.

42. Hawes, diary, Jan. 28, 1865, Va. Hist. Soc.

43. Dunkle, *Prison Life*, 43.

44. *Official Records*, Ser. II, Vol. VIII, 50.

45. Morristown, Tenn., *Daily Gazette* Mail, Mar. 25, 1962.

46. Ibid.

47. White, *Dear Wife*, 126-27.

48. Stewart Woodford to B. W. Thompson, Feb. 11, 1865. Letters received by the provost marshal, Dept. of the South. Pt. 1, E-4277, Box 2. National Archives.

49. Murray, *Immortal Six-Hundred*, 111.

50. White, *Dear Wife*, 126.

51. Mauck, diary, Jan. 3, 1865, Mus. of Confederacy.

52. Dunkle, *Prison Life*, 45.

53. *Southern Historical Society Papers* XXV (1897): 368-69.

54. Bailey, William, 5th Fla. Inf., Compiled Service Record, National Archives.

55. Ibid.

56. Ibid.

57. Bedford, diary, Jan. 27, 1865, Univ. of Mo. - Columbia.

58. *Official Records*, Ser. I, Vol. XLVII, Pt.2, 27. It had been over three months since the Union prisoners of war were removed from Charleston.

CHAPTER 11

"MURDER OF THE MOST TERRIBLE KIND"

1. Murray, *Immortal Six-Hundred*, 65.

2. *Southern Historical Society Papers* I (1876): 253-54.

3. David B. Coulter, "Personal account," *Genealogy of John M. Coulter of Southwest Arkansas*, by J. W. Coulter (publisher unknown, 195-), 174.

4. Murray, *Immortal Six-Hundred*, 70-71.

5. James Wyngarrden and Lloyd Smith, eds., *Textbook of Medicine* (Philadelphia, 1982), 1365-84.

6. Moses J. Bradford to Malissa Jane Bradford, Dec. 13, 1864, Bradford Family papers, Univ. of Mo. - Columbia.

7. Handerson, *Yankee in Gray*, 81.

8. *Confederate Veteran* V (1897): 149.

9. *Southern Historical Society Papers* I (1876): 253.

10. Morgan, *Reminiscences*, 246.

11. Thomas B. Martin, narrative, Archives, Fort Delaware Society.

12. Murray, *Immortal Six-Hundred*, 65.

13. Dickinson, *Diary*, 152.

14. Coulter, *Genealogy of John M. Coulter*, 172.

15. Dickinson, *Diary*, 155.

16. *Southern Historical Society Papers* I (1876): 254.

17. Murray, *Immortal Six-Hundred*, 65-66.

18. Handerson, *Yankee in Gray*, 82.

19. Dickinson, *Diary*, 156-57.

20. Murray, *Immortal Six-Hundred*, 61.

21. Dickinson, *Diary*, 151-52.

22. Allen, diary, Jan. 6, 1865, Va. Hist. Soc.

23. House Committee on War Claims, *Claims of Certain Confederate Officers*, 41.

24. Dickinson, *Diary*, 147.

25. McMichael, diary, So. Hist. Coll., UNC, p. 20.

26. Gordon, diary, Jan. 25, 1865, Mus. of Confederacy.

27. *Southern Historical Society Papers* I (1876): 254.

28. Dickinson, *Diary*, 158-59.

29. Murray, *Immortal Six-Hundred*, 67-68. Though in 1864 there was no specific law against Brown's claim that he was obligated to follow orders, the Nuremberg Trials in 1946 rejected the argument that following orders from superiors relieved soldiers from the moral duty of disobeying inhumane orders.

30. Dickinson, *Diary*, 149; Letter, Col. Brown to Gen. Foster, Dec. 16, 1864; telegram, Hdqtrs. Dept. South to Col. Brown, stating ration cut, Nov. 21, 1864, Folders No. 28 and 30, Fort Pulaski Archives.

31. Murray, *Immortal Six-Hundred*, 68-69.

32. Handerson, *Yankee in Gray*, 80-81.

33. Murray, *Immortal Six-Hundred*, 68.

34. Dickinson, *Diary*, 160-61.

35. *Congressional Globe*, Jan. 27, 1865, 460. Apparently Foster acted illegally. Sen. Henderson made his statement in response to Sen. James R. Doolittle, of Wisconsin, who stated: "I would prefer to resort to some other mode of retaliation, and to select, perhaps by lot, officers of the enemy, beginning with the highest in our hands, and give the enemy notice that on a given day . . . a certain number should be shot to death, and continue

that mode of retaliation until the object was effected." There is little doubt that the law of retaliation would have continued had not exchange been reinstated.

36. *Confederate Veteran* V (1897): 149-50.

37. Dickinson, *Diary*, 161.

38. Pinckney, *Reminiscences*, 56.

39. *Official Records*, Ser. II, Vol. VIII, 163.

40. Dickinson, *Diary*, 159.

41. Murray, *Immortal Six-Hundred*, 2nd ed. (1912), 236-37

42. Dickinson, *Diary*, 165.

43. Murray, *Immortal Six-Hundred*, 76-77.

44. Ibid., 77.

45. Ibid., 78-79.

46. Ibid., 81.

47. Ibid., 83.

48. Dickinson, *Diary*, 169.

49. Murray, *Immortal Six-Hundred*, 83.

50. Dickinson, *Diary*, 166-67.

51. Morgan, *Reminiscenses*, 248.

52. Dickinson, *Diary*, 170.

53. *Official Records*, Ser. I, Vol. XLVII, Pt. 2, 27-28; *Official Records*, Ser. II, Vol. VIII, 8.

54. *Official Records*, Ser. I, Vol. XLVII, Pt. 2, 452.

CHAPTER 12

"ALL THAT WAS LEFT OF THEM, LEFT OF SIX HUNDRED"

1. Edward Molineaux, diary, Feb. 21, 1865, Archives, Fort Pulaski National Monument.

2. *Confederate Veteran* V (1897): 150.

3. Dickinson, *Diary*, 163.

4. Morgan, *Reminiscences*, 244.

5. Dicksinson, *Diary*, 166. The escape referred to is that of Hatcher and Stewart from the hospital.

6. Ibid.

7. Molineaux, diary, Feb. 26, 1865, Fort Pulaski.

8. Dickinson, *Diary*, 169-70.

9. *Confederate Veteran* V (1897): 219.

10. Molineaux, diary, Feb. 21, 1865, Fort Pulaski.

11. *Confederate Veteran* V (1897): 219.

12. Dickinson, *Diary*, 171.

13. *Southern Historical Society Papers* I (1876): 254-55.

14. Pinkowski, *Pills, Pen & Politics*, 74.

15. *Southern Historical Society Papers* I (1876): 254-55.

16. Murray, *Immortal Six-Hundred*, 84.

17. *Confederate Veteran* V (1897): 219.

18. Mauck, diary, autographs from the end of book, Mus. of Confederacy.

19. Van Manning to Finley, Finley diary, UVA.

20. McMichael, diary, So. Hist. Coll., UNC, p. 45.

21. *Southern Historical Society Papers* I (1876): 255.

22. Mauck, diary, Mar. 4, 1865, Mus. of Confederacy.

23. Dickinson, *Diary*, 173.

24. *Confederate Veteran* V (1897): 219-20.

25. Mauck, diary, Mar. 5, 1865, Mus. of Confederacy.

26. J. E. Cobb to Cora Williams, Mar. 18, 1865, Cobb-Hunter Letters, So. Hist. Coll., UNC.

27. Dickinson, *Diary*, 172.

28. *Official Records*, Ser. II, Vol. VIII, 218.

29. *Southern Historical Society Papers* XXII (1894): 143.

30. Dickinson, *Diary*, 174. The Major Weymouth referred to was the U.S. provost marshal at Point Lookout Prison.

31. *Confederate Veteran* V (1897): 220.

32. *Southern Historical Society Papers* XXII (1894): 143.

33. Pinckney, *Reminiscences*, 57.

34. *Official Records*, Ser. II, Vol. VIII, 419.

35. Dickinson, *Diary*, 174-75.

36. Morgan, *Reminiscences*, 251-52.

37. Dickinson, *Diary*, 175.

38. Dunkle, *Prison Life*, 47.

CHAPTER 13

"OUR COMRADES SCARCELY KNEW US, SO CHANGED WERE OUR FEATURES"

1. Mauck, diary, Mar. 11, 1865, Mus. of Confederacy.

2. Dickinson, *Diary*, 175-77.

3. Murray, *Immortal Six-Hundred*, 107-8.

4. Mauck, diary, Mar. 12, 1865, Mus. of Confederacy.

5. Dickinson, *Diary*, 177.

6. *Southern Historical Society Papers* XXII (1894): 144.

7. "Diary of Capt. Robert E. Park, 12th Ala. Regt.," *Southern Historical Society Papers* III (1877): 124-25.

8. Mary L. Thornton, ed., "Diary of Francis A. Boyle," *North Carolina Historical Review* XXXIX (1962): 80.

9. *Southern Historical Society Papers* I (1876): 256.

10. *Confederate Veteran* I (1893): 78.

11. Thomas B. Martin, narrative, Archives, Fort Delaware Society.

12. Dunkle, *Prison Life*, 47.

13. *Official Records*, Ser. II, Vol. VIII, 419.

14. *Southern Historical Society Papers* III (1877): 183.

15. *Southern Historical Society Papers* XXII (1894): 145.

16. Murray, *Immortal Six-Hundred*, 86.

17. *Southern Historical Society Papers* XXII (1894), 145.

18. Dickinson, Diary, 179.

19. *Southern Historical Society Papers* I (1876): 256.

20. Nelson to Scollay, Mar. 13, 1865, Nelson family papers, VPI & SU.

21. Mauck, diary, Mar. 13, 1865, Mus. of Confederacy.

22. Dickinson, *Diary*, 178.

23. Mauck, diary, Mar. 22, 1865, Mus. of Confederacy.

24. Nelson to Scollay, Mar. 31, 1865, Nelson family papers, VPI & SU.

25. Carrington to Fitzhugh, Sept. 18, 1905, Chandler file, VMI Archives.

26. Dickinson, *Diary*, 180.

27. Morgan, *Reminiscences*, 266.

28. McMichael, diary, So. Hist. Coll., UNC, p. 23.

29. Bedford, diary, Apr. 11, 1865, Univ. of Mo. - Columbia.

30. Mauck, diary, Apr. 15, 1865, Mus. of Confederacy.

31. Murray, *Immortal Six-Hundred*, 314.

32. Morgan, *Reminiscences*, 267.

33. Dickinson, *Diary*, 180.

34. McMichael, diary, So. Hist Coll., UNC, pp. 23-24.

35. Mauck, diary, Apr. 26, 1865, Mus. of Confederacy.

36. Dickinson, *Diary*, 180-81.

37. Mauck, diary, Apr. 30, 1865, Mus. of Confederacy.

38. Dickinson, *Diary*, 182, 184.

39. Mauck, diary, May 2, 1865, Mus. of Confederacy.

40. J. E. Cobb to Cora Williams, May 2, 1865, Cobb-Hunter letters, So. Hist Coll., UNC.

41. Nelson to Scollay, May 3, 1865, Nelson family papers, VPI & SU.

42. Dickinson, *Diary*, 184.

43. McMichael, diary, So. Hist. Coll., UNC, p. 24.

44. Epps, diary, in *History of Williamsburg*, 424.

45. Bedford, diary, May 7, 1865, Univ. of Mo. - Columbia.

46. Dickinson, *Diary*, 185-186.

47. Nelson to Scollay, May 4, 1865, Nelson family papers, VPI & SU.

48. Ibid., May 10, 1865.

49. *Official Records*, Ser. II, Vol. VIII, 633.

50. Ibid., 432.

51. Finley to Hargrove, May 25, 1865, Granby papers, So. Hist. Coll., UNC.

52. Dickinson, *Diary*, 178.

CHAPTER 14

HOMECOMINGS

1. Savannah, MO, Reporter, Dec. 20, 1912, p. 1.

2. Dickinson, *Diary*, 13-14.

3. *Confederate Veteran* XXIV (1916): 343-44; *Men of Mark in South Carolina* I (1907): 302-304.

4. Personal communication, Mrs. Thomas Pinckney, Nov. 11, 1992.

5. Ibid.

6. House Committee on War Claims, *Claims of Certain Confederate Officers*, 30.

7. Martin, narrative, Fort Delaware Society.

8. Murray, *Immortal Six-Hundred*, 2nd ed. (1912), 248-49; *Biographical Cyclopedia of Representative Men of Maryland* (1879), 475.

9. Ibid., 108-109.

10. Pinkowski, *Pills, Pens, & Politics*, 80.

11. Baton Rouge *State-Times*, May 28, 1974, Jastremski papers, LSU.

12. "D'Gournay's Battalion of Artillery," *Confederate Veteran* XIII (1905): 32.

13. Obituary, *Baltimore Sun*, July 27, 1904.

14. Young, *56th Virginia*, 110.

82

15. "The Six Hundred to Meet in Louisville," *Confederate Veteran* VIII (1900): 116; XIII (1905): 211, 519.

16. Joseph R. Baker and Louis W. McKernan, *Selected Topics Connected with the Laws of Warfare* (Washington, 1919), 493.

17. Minneapolis *Evening Journal*, Feb. 20, 1912.

18. No evidence was found that the bill ever came out of committee.

19. Hempstead to Cantwell, letter, Nov. 22, 1865, Cantwell papers, So. Hist. Coll., UNC.

20. Ibid.

21. Junius Hempstead, *The Deschanos* (New York, 1909).

22. Hempstead to Murray, letter, Aug. 17, 1907, Murray Papers, Va. Hist. Soc.

23. *Confederate Veteran* XXIX (1921): 179.

24. Biographical sketch with transcript, McMichael, diary, So. Hist. Coll., UNC.

25. Thomas C. Chandler, file, Archives, VMI.

26. *1911 Minutes of the Immortal Six Hundred Society*, 9-10.

27. Robert Krick, *Lee's Colonels*, 3rd ed. (Dayton, 1992), 43.

28. Murray to Cantwell, letter, Dec. 12, 1901, Cantwell Papers, So. Hist Coll., UNC.

29. Houston *Post*, Oct. 7, 1920, 7.

30. Krick, *Lee's Colonels*, 16.

EPILOGUE

1. *Southern Historical Society Papers* X (1882): 32.

2. Charleston, S.C., *News and Courier*, Jan. 19, 1930.

BIBLIOGRAPHY

MANUSCRIPTS

Duke University. Durham, N.C. Special Collections.
  Gorman, John C. Papers.
  Van Noppen, Charles Leonard. Papers—Biographical Sketches.
Fitting, Mrs. Minnie. Radford, Va. Private Collection.
  Adams, Richard H., Jr. Diary.
Fort Del. Society. Delaware City, Del. Archives collection.
  Martin, Thomas B. narrative.
Fort Pulaski National Monument. Savannah, Ga. Archives collection.
  Mollineaux, Gen. Edward. Diary.
Georgia State Archives. Atlanta, Ga.
  Harris, David Terrell. Papers.
Louisiana State University. Baton Rouge, La.
  Jastremski, Leon. Family papers.
Maryland Historical Society. Baltimore, Md.
  Society of the Army and Navy of the Confederate States in Maryland.
  Applications and Minutes.
Museum of the Confederacy. Richmond, Va.
  Gordon, David. Diary.
  Mauck, Joseph. Diary.
  Pinckney, Thomas. "Reminiscences of the War and Reconstruction."
National Archives. Washington, D.C.
    Adjutant and Inspector General's Office, C.S.A. Inspection Reports
      and Related Records Received by the Inspection Branch in the Con-
      federate A & IGO Office.
    Hilton Head, S.C. Prison Camp. Receipts for Letters Containing Money
      Addressed to Prisoners. Nov. 1864-Apr. 1865. Microcopy 598. Roll
      79.
    Register of Prisoners compiled by the Office of the Commissary Gen-
      eral of Prisoners, 1863-65. Microcopy 598. Roll 3.
    Unclaimed Valuables of Dead; Clothing Permits. Microcopy 598. Roll 9.

War Department Collection of Confederate Records. Compiled Service Records of Confederate General and Staff Officers and Nonregimental Enlisted Men. Record Group No. 109.

War Department Collection of Confederate Records. Compiled Service Records of Confederate Soldiers. Record Group No. 109.

War Records Division, Department of the Army. "Proceedings of a General Court Martial, U.S. Steamship *Delaware*, in the charges against Captain Daniel D. Latham and Second Mate William Baxter, Port Royal Harbor, S.C., August 25, 1864."

North Carolina Department of Cultural Resources. Division of Archives and History. Raleigh, N.C.

Cantwell, John L. Papers.

Gorman, John C. Diary and letters, Gorman family papers.

South Carolina Historical Society. Charleston, S.C.

Buist, Henry. File.

University of Georgia. Athens, Ga.

Margaret Branch Sexton Collection.

University of Missouri-Columbia. Western Historical Manuscript Collection. Columbia, Miss.

Bedford Family. Papers.

Bradford, Moses J. Letters 1863-1865.

Missouri Confederate Home, Higginsville, Miss. Records.

United Daughters of the Confederacy, Missouri Division. Records.

University of North Carolina at Chapel Hill. Chapel Hill, N.C. Southern Historical Collection.

Anderson, Edward C., Sr. Diary, Vol. 7.

Cantwell, John L. Papers.

Fortescue, Louis R. Diary.

McMichael, James Robert. Diary.

Cobb-Hunter Letters.

Briggs-Granby Papers. Folder 13. Letters from Col. T. L. Hargrove.

University of Virginia. Charlottesville, Va.

Finley, George W., Collection.

Virginia Historical Society. Richmond, Va.

Gibson, John Alexander. Diary.

Allen, John C. Diary.

Hawes, Samuel Horace. Diary. Katherine Heath Hawes Papers.

Murray, J. Ogden. Papers.

Virginia Military Institute. Lexington, Va. Archives.

Carrington, James McDowell. File.

Councill, James. File.

Fulkerson, Abraham. File.

Harman, Lewis. File.

Hempstead, Junius Lackland. File.

Carter, Edward. File.
Chandler, Thomas C. File.
Hood, William Henry. File.
Virginia Polytechnic Institute and State University. Blacksburg, Va. Special
  Collections.
Nelson Family. Papers.
West Virginia University. Morgantown, W. Va. West Virginia Collection.
Murray, J. Ogden. Scrapbook 1901-1906.

THE SIX HUNDRED'S ACCOUNTS AND REMINISCENCES

Barnes, Francis C. and Frayser, Richard E. "Imprisoned Under Fire," *South-
  ern Historical Society Papers* XXV (1897): 365-77.
Cook, Henry H. "The Story of the Six-Hundred," *Confederate Veteran* V (1897):
  116-18, 148-50, 219-20.
Coulter, David B. "Personal account," in *Genealogy of John M. Coulter of
  Southwest Arkansas*, by J. W. Coulter. Publisher unknown, 195-.
Dickinson, Henry Clay. *Diary of Captain Henry C. Dickinson.* Denver: Will-
  iam Haffner Co., 1913.
Epps, William. "Diary," in *History of Williamsburg*, by William W. Boddie.
  Columbia, S.C.: The State Co., 1923.
Ford, James W. A., "Diary of J. W. A. Ford, 1864," *Journal of the Greenbrier
  Historical Society* II (1971): 29-53.
Fulkerson, Abram. "The Prison Experience of a Confederate Soldier," *South-
  ern Historical Society Papers* XXII (1894): 127-46.
Fuzzlebug, Fritz [John J. Dunkle]. *Prison Life During the Rebellion.* Singer's
  Glen, Va.: J. Funk's Sons, Printers, 1869.
George, William W. *In a Federal Prison.* Baltimore: King Printing Co., 1906.
Goldsborough, William W. *The Maryland Line in the Confederate Army, 1861-
  1865.* Port Washington, N.Y.: Kennikat Press, 1972.
Handerson, Henry E. *Yankee in Gray: The Civil War Memoirs of Henry E.
  Handerson with a selection of his wartime letters.* Edited by Clyde L.
  Cummer. Cleveland: Press of Western Reserve University, 1962.
Hempstead, Junius L. "How Long Will This Misery Continue," edited by
  Bess Beatty and Judy Caprio, *Civil War Times Illustrated* XIX (Feb. 1981):
  20-23.
McRae, Walter G., "Confederate Prisoners at Morris Island," *Confederate
  Veteran* XXIX (1921): 178-79.
Morgan, William H. *Personal Reminiscences of the War 1861-1865.* Lynchburg,
  Va.: J. P. Bell Co., 1911.
Murray, J. Ogden. *The Immortal Six-Hundred.* New York: The Neale Publish-
  ing Co., 1905; Winchester, Va.; Eddy Press Corp., 1911.

OTHER PRIMARY SOURCES

Anderson, Edward C. *Confederate Foreign Agent: the European Diary of Major Edward C. Anderson*. Edited by W. Stanley Hoole. University, Ala.: Confederate Publishing Co., 1976.

Barlow, Albert R. *Company G: A Record of the Services of One Company of the 157th N.Y. Volunteers in the War of the Rebellion*. Syracuse, N.Y.: A. W. Hall, 1899.

Biographical and Historical Memoirs of Louisiana. 2 vols. Chicago: The Goodspeed Publishing Co., 1892.

Biographical Cyclopedia of Representative Men of Maryland. Baltimore: National Biographical Publishing Co., 1879.

Boate, Edward W. "The True Story of Andersonville Told by a Federal Prisoner," *Southern Historical Society Papers* X (1882): 25-32.

Boyle, Francis A. "Diary of Adj. Francis A. Boyle, CSA," edited by Mary L. Thornton, *North Carolina Historical Review* XXXIX (1962): 58-84.

Butler, Benjamin. *Butler's Book*. Boston: A. M. Thayer & Co. Book Publishers, 1892.

Calef, B. S., "Prison Life in the Confederacy," *Harper's New Monthly Magazine* XXI (July 1865): 137-50.

Davis, Jefferson. *Andersonville and Other War Prisons*. New York: Belford Co. Publishers, 1890.

Duke, Basil. *Reminiscences of General Basil W. Duke, CSA*. 1911. Reprint. Freeport, N.Y.: Books for Libraries Press, 1969.

Dyer, Gustavus W. and John Trotwood Moore. *Tennessee Civil War Veterans Questionnaires*. 5 vols. Easley, S.C.: Southern Historical Press, 1985.

Emilio, Luis F. *History of the Fifty-fourth Regiment of Massachusetts Volunteer Infantry, 1863-1865*. Boston: The Boston Book Company, 1894.

Fraser, John, Col. *A Petition Regarding the Conditions in the C.S.M. Military Prison at Columbia, S.C.* Edited by George L. Anderson. Lawrence: University of Kansas Libraries, 1962.

Gray, John Chipman. *War Letters, 1862-1865*. Boston: Houghton Mifflin Company, 1927.

Hamilton, Alexander J. *A Fort Delaware Journal, The Diary of a Yankee Private*. Edited by W. Emerson Wilson. Wilmington, Del.: Fort Delaware Society, 1981.

Handy, Isaac W. K. *United States Bonds; or Duress by Federal Authorities*. Baltimore: Turnbull Brothers, 1874.

Holmes, Emma. *Diary of Miss Emma Holmes 1861-1866*. Edited by John F. Marszalek. Baton Rouge: Louisiana State University Press, 1979.

Isham, Asa B. *Prisoners of War and Military Prisons*. Cincinnati: Lyman and Cushing, 1890.

Johnson, John. *The Defense of Charleston Harbor, Including Fort Sumter and the Adjacent Islands*. Charleston, S.C.: Walker, Evans, & Cogswell Co., 1890.

Jones, J. William. "The Treatment of Prisoners During the War Between the States," *Southern Historical Society Papers* I (1876): 113-327.

Jordan, Weymouth T. (comp.) *North Carolina Troops, 1861- 1865: A Roster.* Raleigh: North Carolina Division of Archives and History, 1966-).

Manigault, Edward. *Siege Train—The Journal of a Confederate Artilleryman in the Defense of Charleston.* Edited by Warren Ripley. Columbia, S.C.: University of South Carolina Press, 1986.

McGrath, Franklin. *The History of the 127th New York Volunteers.* [n.p.], 1900.

McKee, James H. *Back "In War Times": The History of the 144th Regiment New York Volunteer Infantry.* New York: H. E. Bailey, 1903.

Men of Mark in South Carolina. Vol. 1. Washington, D.C.: Men of Mark Publishing Co., 1907.

Mount, May W. *Some Notables of New Orleans.* Published by the author. New Orleans, La., 1896.

Northrop, John Worrell. Chronicles *From the Diary of a War Prisoner in Andersonville and Other Military Prisons of the South in 1864.* Wichita, Kans., 1904.

Page, James Madison. *The True Story of Andersonville Prison, A Defense of Major Wirz.* New York: The Neale Publishing Co., 1908.

Park, Robert E. "Diary of Capt. Parks, 12th Alabama Regiment," *Southern Historical Society Papers* III (1877).

Pearson, Elizabeth Ware, ed. *Pearson: Letters From Port Royal 1862-1868.* New York: Arno Press and the *New York Times,* 1969.

Saxton, William. "War Reminiscences," The Courtland *Standard,* 1902. Clippings in scrapbook at Courtland Historical Society, Courtland, N.Y.

Shaw, Robert G. *Blue-Eyed Child of Fortune: The Civil War Letters of Colonel Robert Gould Shaw.* Edited by Russell Duncan. Athens, Ga.: University of Georgia Press, 1992.

A *Standard of Georgia and Georgians,* Vol. V. Chicago: Lewis Publishing Co., 1917.

Society of the Immortal Six-Hundred. *Minutes of Annual Meeting.* 1908-1911.

Thompson, Benjamin W. "Back to the South," *Civil War Times Illustrated* XII (Nov. 1973): 32-34.

United Daughters of the Confederacy. Georgia Division. *Ancestor Roster.* 5 vols. 1992-93.

United Daughters of the Confederacy. Tennessee Division. *Confederate Patriot Index 1924-1978.* 1978.

University of Virginia. *Students of the University of Virginia, A Semi-Centennial Catalogue with Biographical Sketches.* Baltimore: 1878.

Virginia Military Institute Alumni Association. *Register of Former Cadets, 1839-1989.* Lexington, Va.: 1989.

Washington and Lee University. *Catalogue of the Officers and Alumni of Washington and Lee University, 1749-1888.* Baltimore: 1888.

White, Daniel. *Dear Wife, Letters of a Civil War Soldier.* Edited by Jack C. Davis. Louisville, Ky.: Sulgrave Press, 1991.

PERIODICALS

Confederate Veteran. 40 vols. Nashville: S. A. Cunningham, 1892-1932.
Civil War Times Illustrated. 1966-86.
Harper's New Monthly Magazine. New York, 1865.
Journal of the Greenbrier Historical Society. Greenbrier, W.Va.
North Carolina Historical Review.
Southern Historical Society Papers. 52 vols. Richmond: Southern Historical Society, 1876-1952.

NEWSPAPERS

Baltimore *Sun.*
Baton Rouge *State-Times.*
Beaufort, S.C., *Palmetto Herald.*
Charleston *Daily Courier.*
Charleston *News and Courier.*
Cortland, N.Y., *Standard.*
Houston *Post.*
Minneapolis *Evening Journal.*
Morristown, Tenn., *Daily Gazette Mail.*
Savannah, Mo., *Reporter.*

FEDERAL GOVERNMENT PUBLICATIONS AND DOCUMENTS

Baker, Joseph R. and Louis W. McKernan, *Selected Topics Connected with the Laws of Warfare, as of August 1, 1914.* Washington: Government Printing Office. 1919.
Congressional Globe. 46 vols. Washington, D.C., 1834-73.
Lattimore, Ralston B. *Fort Pulaski National Monument.* National Park Service Historical Handbook Series no.18. Washington: GPO, 1954.
U.S. Congress. House. Committee on War Claims. *Claim of Certain Confederate Officers. Statement of Major J. Ogden Murray before the Committee on War Claims, in support of H.R. 14170, March 28, 1914.* 63rd Congress, 2d sess., Washington: GPO, 1914.
U.S. Department of War. *War of the Rebellion: A Compilation of the Official Records of the Union and Confederate Armies.* 128 vols. Washington: GPO, 1880-1901.
U.S. Department of War. *War of the Rebellion: A Compilation of the Official Records of the Union and Confederate Navies.* 30 vols. Washington: GPO, 1880-1927.
U.S. Department of War. Adjutant General's Office. *Official Army Register of the Volunteer Force of the U.S. Army for the Years 1861-65.* Washington, 1865.

SECONDARY SOURCES

Bassham, Ben L. "Conrad Chapman's Charleston." *Civil War Times Illustrated* XVI (Apr. 1977): 34-41.

Beers, Henry Putney. *The Confederacy: A Guide to the Archives of the Government of the Confederate States of America.* Washington: National Archives and Records, 1986.

Blakey, Arch Fredric. *General John H. Winder C.S.A.* Gainesville: University of Florida Press, 1990.

Burton, E. Milby. *The Siege of Charleston 1861-1865.* Columbia, S.C.: University of South Carolina Press, 1970.

Cochran, Hamilton. *Blockade Runners of the Confederacy.* New York: Bobbs-Merrill Co., 1958.

Collier, Calvin L. *They'll Do To Tie To! The Story of the Third Regiment, Arkansas Infantry, CSA.* Little Rock, Ark.: Pioneer Press, 1959.

Clark, Walter, ed. *Stories of the Several Regiments and Battalions from North Carolina in the Great War 1861-65.* 5 vols. Goldsboro, N.C.: 1901.

Cunningham, Edward. *The Port Hudson Campaign 1862-1863.* Baton Rouge: Louisiana State University Press, 1963.

Evans, Clement A., ed. *Confederate Military History.* 16 vols. 1899.

Flory, William E. S. *Prisoners of War, a Study in the Development of International Law.* Washington: American Council on Public Affairs, 1942.

Fooks, Herbert C. *Prisoners of War.* Federalsburg, Md.: J. W. Stowell Publishing Co., 1924.

Freidel, Frank. *Francis Lieber, Nineteenth-Century Liberal.* Baton Rouge: Louisiana State University Press, 1948.

Hesseltine, William Best. *Civil War Prisons, a Study in War Psychology.* New York: Frederick Ungar Publishing Co., 1930.

Hempstead, Junius. *The Deschanos.* New York: Ben Franklin Publishing Co, 1905.

Hildebrand, Franklin. *As I Remember: Stories of Jefferson Davis Parish.* Jennings, La.: 1977.

Keen, Maurice H. *The Laws of War in the Late Middle Ages.* London: Routledge and K. Paul, 1965.

Keen, Nancy T. "Confederate Prisoners of War at Fort Delaware." *Delaware History* XIII (April 1968): 1-27.

Krick, Robert. *Lee's Colonels.* 3rd ed. Dayton, Ohio: Morningside Press, 1992.

Lonn, Ella. *Foreigners in the Confederacy.* Chapel Hill, N.C.: University of North Carolina Press, 1940.

McConnell, Catherine S. *High on a Windy Hill.* Bristol, Tenn.: King Printing Company, 1968.

Miles, Jim. *Fields of Glory—A History and Tour Guide of the Atlanta Campaign.* Nashville, Tenn.: Rutledge Hill Press, 1989.

Miles, Jim. *To The Sea—A History and Tour Guide of the Atlanta Campaign.* Nashville, Tenn.: Rutledge Hill Press, 1989.

Miller, Frances T., ed. *Photographic History of the Civil War. Vol. 7, Prisons and Hospitals.* New York: Review of Reviews Co., 1911.

Pinkowski, Edward. *Pills, Pen and Politics: The Story of General Leon Jastremski, 1843-1907.* Wilmington, Del.: Capt. Stanislaus Mlothowski Memorial Brigade Society, 1974.

Powell, William H., ed. *Officers of the Army and Navy (Volunteers) Who Served in the Civil War.* Philadelphia: L. R. Hamersley, 1892.

Story of Fort Delaware. Pamphlet issued by Fort Delaware Society, Delaware City, Del.

Tennessee Civil War Centennial Commission. *Tennesseans in the Civil War.* 2 vols. Nashville, Tenn.: 1964.

Virginia Regimental History Series. Lynchburg, Va.: H. E. Howard, Inc.

Wakelyn, Jon L. *Biographical Dictionary of the Confederacy.* Westport, Conn.: Greenwood Publishing Co., 1977.

Wallace, Lee A., Jr. *A Guide to Virginia Military Organizations 1861-1865,* 2nd ed., of the *Virginia Regimental History Series.* Lynchburg, Va.: H. E. Howard, Inc., 1986.

Wilson, W. Emerson. *Fort Delaware in the Civil War.* Delaware City, Del.: Fort Delaware Society, 1972.

Wyngaarden, James B. and Lloyd H. Smith, eds. *Textbook of Medicine.* Philadelphia: W. B. Saunders Co., 1982.

Young, William A., Jr. *Fifty-Sixth Virginia Infantry,* of the *Virginia Regimental History Series.* Lynchburg, Va.: H. E. Howard, Inc., 1990.

INDEX

341

Carter, Lt. George W., 75, 208
Carter, Capt. William P., 144, 209, 253
Cason, Lt. John R., 188, 236
Chambers, Capt. Edward, 175, 208, 216, 222, 225, 251
Chandler, Capt. Thomas C., 140, 254, 276
Charleston, 240
    siege of, 1-8
    harbor defenses, 2, 5-7
    conditions of city in 1864, 3-4
    prisoners in, 16-21, 30, 40-41, 98-99
Chew, Lt. William H., 223, 224-25, 248
Chitwood, Capt. Lewis S., 248
Christian, Lt. Col. Charles B., 153, 156
Christian, Capt. Jones, 140
City Point, Va., 240
Coalter, Lt. Henry T., 170
Cobb, Lt. James E., 96, 193, 195, 239, 260
Coffee, Capt. Holland, 50-51, 90, 108-10, 138-39
Coffey, Lt. Hiram, 96
Columbia, S.C., 30, 36, 111, 126, 172, 192
Confederate Relief Association, 177
Cook, Lt. Henry C., 79, 97, 108, 124, 132, 156, 176,
    181, 210, 218, 231, 232, 233, 235, 239, 241
Coon, Lt. David, 253
Coulter, Maj. David B., 208, 211
Covington, Lt. Cameron D., 239
Covington, Capt. William W., 92
Cowan, Sen. Edgar, 39
Cowan, Capt. John, 168, 169
Cowper, Lt. John C., 53, 125
Craft, Lt. William H., 239
Crapon, Lt. George M., 167
Crescent City, 63-69, 94, 169
    conditions on board, 64-66, 79-81, 83
Crisp, Lt. Charles F., 271
Crow, Capt. William P., 125, 170

D

Dalton, Lt. Peter, 144, 156, 160
Daugherty, Lt. Col. James, 170
Davis, President Jefferson, 10, 11, 34, 260
Davis, Lt. John W., 199-200, 240
DeGournay, Lt. Col. Paul F., 42, 51, 69, 91, 96, 147,
    148, 149, 168, 171, 219, 270-71
DePriest, Lt. Emmett, 195, 245, 246, 270
Dickinson, Capt. Henry C., 42-46, 48, 49, 50, 65, 69,
    71, 73, 80, 83, 87, 88, 89, 90, 95, 96, 101, 103,
    109-10, 112, 114, 121, 122, 123, 128, 130, 136,
    138, 139, 142, 143, 144, 145, 146, 147, 149, 150,
    151, 152, 153, 154, 155, 160, 162, 163, 164, 165,
    168, 170, 172, 174, 175, 176, 177, 180, 181, 182,
    211, 213, 214, 216, 218, 219, 220, 221, 225, 228,
    231, 232, 234, 238, 239, 240, 242, 243, 247, 251,
    253, 255, 258, 259, 261, 262, 265, 268, 281
Dillard, Lt. Robert Y., 245-46
Dix, Maj. Gen. John, 10
Dix-Hill Cartel, 9, 11, 283
Dixon, Capt. Hugh M., 114
Dobyns, Capt. Abner, 149, 208

Donaghe, Lt. John A., 187
Douglass, Lt. Merry S., 239
Doyle, Lt. Little B., 240
Doyle, Lt. Thomas S., 207, 208
Duke, Brig. Gen. Basil, 21-22
Dunkle, Capt. John J., 66, 70, 75, 79, 96, 113, 124,
    131, 150, 157, 186, 192, 197, 202, 243, 250
Dunlap, Capt. Hugh, 125, 165, 223-25

E

Easterling, Lt. Thomas, 167
Eastham, Lt. Chapman B., 238
Edwards, Lt. Alexander W., 244
Edwards, Lt. Bolivar, 167
Ellison, Capt. George H., 72-73
Emanuel, Maj. William P., 51, 116, 122, 144, 156
Emilio, Capt. Luis F., 16, 87, 89, 116, 117
Epps, Lt. William, 51, 60, 112, 116, 122, 130, 144, 166,
    192, 197, 262, 269, 275, 282
escapes and escape attempts, 69-71, 72-73, 108-10,
    188-90, 222-25
Exchange agents, 167-68

F

Fannin, Lt. James W., 228, 248
Fickiessen, Lt. Jacob, 108-10
54th Massachusetts Colored Infantry, 88-89, 101-2,
    112, 115
    in 1863, 2, 85, 86-87, 117
Finks, Capt. Alexander N., 92
Finks, Lt. Simon H., 92
Finley, Capt. George W., 65, 96, 123, 153, 187, 191,
    237, 265, 271
Fitzgerald, Capt. George B., 152-53
Fitzhugh, Pvt. Claggett D., 162, 168, 171
Fitzpatrick, Lt. John B., 165
Frayser, Capt. Richard E., 116
Folk, Col. Nathaniel, 72, 149, 188
Foly, Pvt. Timothy, 239
Ford, Lt. James W. A., 66, 71, 73, 82-83, 93-94, 103,
    104, 111, 119, 127, 154
Fort, Lt. Gordon K., 161
Fort Delaware
    conditions, 48, 52, 252-53
    treatment of prisoners, 45-49
Fort McAllister, 174, 194
Fort Moultrie, 94, 95, 96-97, 104, 128
Fort Pulaski, Georgia
    description, 131, 132, 140-42, 197, 276, 277,
        280, 281
    conditions, 146, 154, 176-78, 209-12
Fort Sumter, 1-2, 6-7, 16-17, 97, 104, 128
Fortescue, Lt. Louis R., 20, 30, 98-99
Foster, Maj. Gen. John G., 3, 5-7, 17, 20, 39, 40-41,
    71-72, 80, 82, 83, 93, 97, 98, 100, 105, 111, 127,
    131, 155, 161, 173, 175, 178, 181, 187, 192, 206,
    218, 219, 229, 272
Fousse, Lt. Frederick, 163
Fraser, Col. John, 127

Freedman's Bureau, 190
Fry, Lt. Henry, 123, 162, 163, 228
Fulkerson, Col. Abram, 68-69, 75, 173, 177, 180, 240, 241, 247, 251
Funk, Lt. William O., 207, 212, 217

G

Galloway, Lt. Moses P., 92
Gardner, Gen. William M., 126
Garrett, Lt. David W., 90, 144, 253
General Orders No. 11, 172, 187
George, Lt. William W., 100, 180, 225
Gibson, Capt. Allen C., 248
Gibson, Capt. Bruce, 115, 276
Gillespie, Rufus C., 165, 223-25, 239
Gillmore, Maj. Gen. Quincy A., 2, 218, 219, 228, 241
Goldsborough, Maj. William W., 53, 69, 115, 149, 162, 172, 271
Gordon, Lt. David, 42, 51, 122, 143, 144, 153, 166, 167, 170, 176, 215, 219, 241, 269
Gorman, Capt. John C., 75, 81-82
Grant, Maj. Gen. U. S., 39, 82, 105, 131, 146, 218, 229, 233, 234, 240, 241, 250, 264
Graves, Lt. Frank N., 144
Gray, Maj. John C., 85
Grayson, Capt. David C., 103, 129, 131, 145, 150, 155, 156, 174, 175, 176, 179, 214, 279
Griffin, Capt. Wiley H., 51, 223, 224
Gurgannus, Lt. Andrew J., 168
Guyther, Lt. John M., 173

H

Hall, Capt. Edward J., 145
Halleck, Maj. Gen. Henry W., 14, 15, 39, 40, 98, 206, 218, 240
Halliburton, Lt. William, 239
Hallowell, Col. Edward N., 85-86, 87, 99-101, 102, 112-13, 115, 116-17, 125, 130, 142, 277
Hamilton, Pvt. Alexander J., 66-67, 71
Hammock, Capt. Thornton, 76, 137, 149, 163, 212
Handerson, Capt. Henry E., 121, 163, 209, 212, 216
Handy, Rev. Isaac W., 52, 54, 55, 59, 60, 61, 123
Hardee, Lt. Gen. William J., 127, 229, 240
Hargrove, Lt. Col. Tazwell L., 264-65
Harman, Capt. Lewis, 98, 108-10, 138-39, 208
Harris, Capt. David T., 151
Harris, Lt. John, 114, 144
Harris, Capt. Thomas W., 123, 147, 149, 151, 215, 216, 242, 244, 245, 248
Harrison, Gen. George P., 183, 198
Harrison, Capt. Harris K., 140, 198
Hatcher, Lt. William H., 220-22, 269, 280
Hawes, Lt. Samuel H., 95, 103, 111, 144, 156, 184, 185, 186, 190, 194, 197
Hempstead, Capt. Junius L., 88, 89, 92-93, 98, 100, 102, 104, 113, 119, 123, 124, 131, 182, 208, 272, 274, 275
Hendricks, Sen. Thomas A., 37-38, 39
Hill, Maj. Gen. Daniel H., 10
Hilton Head Island, S.C., 71, 72, 105, 150, 156, 183, 276, 281

conditions, 185, 187, 198, 274
rations, 190-93
Hitchcock, Maj. Gen. Ethan Allen, 13, 105
Hobson, Capt. James M., 120
Hodges, Capt. James E., 185
Hoffman, Brig. Gen. William, 12, 18, 228, 240
Holmes, Emma, 3
Hooberry, Lt. John W., 170
Hoover, Capt. Henry L., 163, 228
Horton, Capt. Thomas, 49, 51, 65
Howard, Capt. George, 168, 169, 170, 171, 175
Hughes, Lt. John S., 151
Humes, Capt. Andrew R., 236

I

Immortal Six Hundred
choosing on Aug. 20, 1864, 55, 58-59
aboard *Crescent City*, 63-84
description of appearance, 87
Society of, 272, 274, 275
Isham, Lt. Asa B., 20

J

James Island, S.C., 93
Jastremski, John, 52-53, 59, 94
Jastremski, Capt. Leon, 44, 52-53, 59, 90, 91, 94, 108-9, 245, 246, 270
Jones, Maj. David, 177
Jones, Dr. Joseph, 27
Jones, Maj. Gen. Samuel, 5, 17, 20, 29, 39-40, 83, 97, 111, 126, 127, 206

K

Kelly, Capt. John G., 239, 278
Kemp, Capt. William, 167
Kendall, Lt. William A., 225
Kent, Capt. Thomas N., 73, 223, 224-25
Killmartin, Lt. John, 188
King, Capt. Alexander, 216, 281
Kirkman, Lt. Alexander Jackson, 143
Kitchin, Capt. William H., 195

L

Ladies Aid Society of Charleston, 129
Lane, Sen. Henry Smith, 37
Latham, Daniel D., 64, 67, 71-72, 82
LeBreton, Lt. Col. Emile S. M., 208, 219
Ledyard, Lt. William N., 122
Legg, Lt. Russell W., 215
Lemon, Capt. James L., 140
Lewis, Capt. Andrew J., 145, 165
Lieber, Frances, 13-14
Lieber Code, 14, 38, 255
Lincoln, President Abraham, 10, 13
assassination, 256-57
Lindsey, Lt. James B., 117
Logan, Capt. Matthew D., 92
Logan, Capt. Robert D., 92
Lowe, Capt. Schuyler, 144, 149